Innovation and Change in Professional Education

Volume 12

Series Editor:

W.H. Gijselaers, School of Business and Economics, Maastricht University,
The Netherlands

Associate Editors:

L.A. Wilkerson, David Geffen School of Medicine, University of California,
Los Angeles, CA, USA
H.P.A. Boshuizen, Center for Learning Sciences and Technologies,
Open Universiteit Nederland, Heerlen, The Netherlands

Editorial Board:

T. Duffy, School of Education, Indiana University, Bloomington, IN, USA
H. Gruber, Institute of Educational Science, University of Regensburg,
Regensburg, Germany
R. Milter, Carey Business School, Johns Hopkins University, Baltimore, MD, USA
EunMi Park, JH Swami Institute for International Medical Education,
Johns Hopkins University School of Medicine, Baltimore, MD, USA
Eugene L. Anderson, American Dental Education Association, Washington, DC, USA

SCOPE OF THE SERIES

The primary aim of this book series is to provide a platform for exchanging experiences and knowledge about educational innovation and change in professional education and post-secondary education (engineering, law, medicine, management, health sciences, etc.). The series provides an opportunity to publish reviews, issues of general significance to theory development and research in professional education, and critical analysis of professional practice to the enhancement of educational innovation in the professions.

The series promotes publications that deal with pedagogical issues that arise in the context of innovation and change of professional education. It publishes work from leading practitioners in the field, and cutting edge researchers. Each volume is dedicated to a specific theme in professional education, providing a convenient resource of publications dedicated to further development of professional education.

More information about this series at http://www.springer.com/series/6087

Anders Siig Andersen • Simon B. Heilesen
Editors

The Roskilde Model: Problem-Oriented Learning and Project Work

Editors
Anders Siig Andersen
Simon B. Heilesen
Roskilde University
Roskilde, Denmark

ISBN 978-3-319-09715-2   ISBN 978-3-319-09716-9 (eBook)
DOI 10.1007/978-3-319-09716-9
Springer Cham Heidelberg New York Dordrecht London

Library of Congress Control Number: 2014954097

© Springer International Publishing Switzerland 2015
This work is subject to copyright. All rights are reserved by the Publisher, whether the whole or part of the material is concerned, specifically the rights of translation, reprinting, reuse of illustrations, recitation, broadcasting, reproduction on microfilms or in any other physical way, and transmission or information storage and retrieval, electronic adaptation, computer software, or by similar or dissimilar methodology now known or hereafter developed. Exempted from this legal reservation are brief excerpts in connection with reviews or scholarly analysis or material supplied specifically for the purpose of being entered and executed on a computer system, for exclusive use by the purchaser of the work. Duplication of this publication or parts thereof is permitted only under the provisions of the Copyright Law of the Publisher's location, in its current version, and permission for use must always be obtained from Springer. Permissions for use may be obtained through RightsLink at the Copyright Clearance Center. Violations are liable to prosecution under the respective Copyright Law.
The use of general descriptive names, registered names, trademarks, service marks, etc. in this publication does not imply, even in the absence of a specific statement, that such names are exempt from the relevant protective laws and regulations and therefore free for general use.
While the advice and information in this book are believed to be true and accurate at the date of publication, neither the authors nor the editors nor the publisher can accept any legal responsibility for any errors or omissions that may be made. The publisher makes no warranty, express or implied, with respect to the material contained herein.

Printed on acid-free paper

Springer is part of Springer Science+Business Media (www.springer.com)

Foreword

The Learning Dynamics at Roskilde University: A Student's Experiences

This is a short account of my experiences of studying at Roskilde University. I admit that going from high school to university is always an upheaval. You move to a higher level in the educational system, and the transition often involves changing where you live. For me it meant moving from peripheral rural Denmark to the capital Copenhagen.

Therefore, many of my experiences are quite normal for any young student enrolling at a university. However, some originate from the particular educational structure and learning dynamics at Roskilde University. These are what my story is about.

The Transition

Roskilde University is roughly 30 min by train from metropolitan Copenhagen. Travelling out there, you see how the scenery changes into open fields of maize and turnips, and small rural villages. In many respects, the trip gives me a feeling of leaving the urban sprawl of Copenhagen and travelling to the outskirts of rural Denmark. It is there that I have spent the last couple of years studying for a bachelor in Social Science and soon also a master degree in Welfare Studies and Geography.

The secluded rural location of the university might make me feel more at home, except for the striking transition from the way I was taught in high school. Back then, the days were structured around class teaching in different subjects. Here, at Roskilde University, my days are divided into lectures, reading and project work.

Since enrolling at the university, I have experienced a highly structured and open-ended progression in my education. I began by choosing one of the four basic bachelor programmes, and from there I went on to choose the two subjects of specialization for my bachelor and master degrees. Each semester I have decided on projects to write, and I have had to choose classes according to my interests. Having the option of postponing the choice of areas of specialization was important for my original choice of university. Not having a clear idea of my academic interests and future career, I chose the bachelor programme in social sciences at Roskilde University. One and a half years later, I was able to make a more qualified decision about the two subjects for my bachelor specialization.

Another unique Roskilde University feature is the house structure, where each body of new students is divided up into 'houses' of approximately 120 students. The house is a physical entity – each group of 120 students is located in a campus building where all the lectures and group work are organized. You spend the first 2 years of your bachelor programme in a house with some 120 fellow students. This contributes greatly to the social and academic environment at the university.

Learning the Academic Trade

Just as at any other university there are lectures at Roskilde University. But a lot of your time is spent outside the classroom, either reading in the library or doing project work together with your fellow students. Each semester you form project groups of two to six students. In the group, you have the freedom and obligation of choosing a thematic issue to which to apply the relevant knowledge from lectures, as well as additional knowledge acquired through reading and research. In my experience, the lectures serve as overall introductions to established knowledge. But it is through the project work that you practice the craft of academic research.

Training, Learning and Specializing

In the beginning, project work provided me with a training ground where I could break the code of academic conduct. It might sound silly, but nothing in my past – neither my years at high school nor coming from a family with a low level of education – has given me much experience in discussing and producing scientific meaning. My subjects in the early projects ranged from investigating the socio-economic impacts of industrial mining in the Democratic Republic of the Congo, to studying the functional implications of implementing restorative justice in the Danish system of justice. In many ways the lessons learnt in these first projects were not so much about the subjects of inquiry – which of course were interesting – but about the process of conducting problem-oriented and interdisciplinary research, as well as collaborating with other people.

Later, I became more confident and focused, and my latest projects have functioned as specializations both with regard to my choice of bachelor and master subjects and to my future career path. Here my focus has been on the use of quantitative data in the planning and assessment of welfare policies and regional development in the EU.

Thus, throughout my years of study I have been engaged in projects with different fellow students and different supervisors. The project work has given me a lot of personal feedback and academic experience with regard to my ability to produce research material and to collaborate with people with complementary competences. The appointed supervisors have given me an important form of academic apprenticeship, where my project group and I have been given qualified feedback that has enhanced our learning and project outcomes. Thus, project work has been and continues to be an important forum for me to make trials and errors, and to improve my competences.

What Then Are the Learning Dynamics of Roskilde University?

My experience at Roskilde University is that the pedagogical approach provides me with a combination of learning processes and academic progression, where I learn *from* academic texts and lectures, I learn *through* research collaboration with like-minded students and support from supervisors, and I learn *by* communicating and discussing research themes, theories and findings with fellow students and academic staff in presentations, examinations and written assignments. This combination has provided huge support for my orientation and specialization in and across the academic disciplines.

Roskilde University Thomas Aarup Larsen
Roskilde, Denmark

Preface

Corals can only live in very pure and salty water in constant movement. Therefore, corals on the lee side of reefs die, whereas corals on the windward side, where waves and currents are strongest, grow and develop into large, beautiful colonies. It is, however, the older parts of the reef that provide the strength and power to resist the beating of the waves throughout the centuries.

The logo of Roskilde University is a coral: http://www.ruc.dk/en/about-the-university/about-roskilde-university.

This book discusses how the 'Roskilde Model' is used in the organization of university studies and in the pedagogical planning of teaching. The Roskilde Model is a complex concept, referring to:

Firstly, problem-oriented interdisciplinary participant-directed project work as it is practised at Roskilde University in Denmark. Half of all study activities at the university are organized in accordance with the principles of this particular pedagogical approach. Whereas problem-oriented project work at other educational institutions comprises only a limited share of academic student activities, at Roskilde University it is the pivotal pedagogical principle. In fact, for four decades the hallmark of the university has been to develop the concept of problem-oriented, interdisciplinary and participant-directed project work into a unique model of education and educational design. The everyday term for this rather lengthy concept would be 'Problem-oriented Project Work' or 'Problem-oriented Project Learning' (PPL). Throughout the book, for the sake of brevity, we will refer to PPL.

Secondly, the concept of the Roskilde Model refers to a special way of organizing university education on the basis of four broad basic programmes in the humanities, social sciences, natural sciences, and the humanistic-technological sciences. The basic programmes are integrated with 3-year bachelor programmes, giving admission to a superstructure of 2-year master programmes in a broad range of disciplines.

Thirdly, the Roskilde Model refers to the special academic and professional profile of the university. Most studies at the bachelor and master levels are completed as double-major bachelor and master degree programmes. This means that the students are able to design their own professional profiles, and that they may combine subjects in a manner unique to Roskilde University. In addition, some master programmes are being offered as interdisciplinary single-major master degree programmes, often oriented towards the solution of socially-oriented problems, and based upon the interdisciplinary research environments at the university.

The Roskilde Model is characterized by combining the various learning concepts into a nexus, providing the foundation for a consistent pedagogical practice that is strongly supported by the educational structure and the academic profile of the university.

As an integrated part of the Roskilde Model, the PPL provides a concrete and historically rooted pedagogical framework for university studies, which has attracted the interest of universities around the world. PPL studies are characterized by an explicit orientation towards social relevance and high academic standards. In addition, PPL is meaningful and motivating in terms of student needs and interests and deliberately oriented towards the development of innovative and creative skills.

The PPL concept shares some key pedagogical ideas with the internationally more well-known concept of Problem Based Learning (PBL). The two, however, originate from quite different historical contexts. Both concepts advocate that the learners should be working with carefully selected problems that require them to apply domain-specific and domain-general knowledge, self-directed learning strategies, and team participation skills. In PPL, however, there is a stronger emphasis on the students defining problems of their own choice, as well as on aligning study work with research procedures.

The genesis of the Roskilde Model took place in a specific historical situation and was closely entwined with a national and broader European political context. As the years have passed, the Roskilde Model has proved to be unique as well as changeable. The logo of Roskilde University expresses this in a short and concise form: "In tranquillo mors – in fluctu vita" (in stillness death – in movement life). In this book, we describe, analyse and critically reflect on the political context and the internal organizational context of the Roskilde Model as well as the development of pedagogical concepts and educational practice. We are confident that the book will enable readers to understand and critically reflect on the Roskilde Model. Hopefully, some readers may even find inspiration in the experiences of Roskilde University.

The purpose of this volume is to enhance knowledge about all three aspects of the Roskilde Model. However, special emphasis is placed on communicating a deep and context-based understanding of how problem-oriented interdisciplinary and participant-directed project work may serve as a basis for planning and applying educational activities at institutions of higher learning. The book focuses on the strengths of consistently using these principles as the basis for an overall educational and pedagogical model. At the same time, the book points out the dilemmas, problems, and divergent assessments that have challenged the model. Under the motto of 'preservation through change', they have led to a number of reforms and experiments that have modified practice in many ways, without however compromising the basic principles.

Pedagogical Foundations

The pedagogy of the Roskilde Model is discussed in depth in the various chapters of this volume. However, for the sake of clarity, a brief introduction to the key concepts will be presented below.

Roskilde University rests on problem-oriented interdisciplinary participant-directed project work. In 1972 when the university first opened its doors, this was a notable innovation in Danish higher education pedagogy, and it also attracted attention among European universities. The PPL format constitutes an overall pedagogical and professional concept. Other key concepts connected with PPL are group work, the exemplary principle, and social relevance. The unique characteristics of PPL however, arise from the coherence and interrelations of the following concepts.

Project work: Project work has been practised for centuries as an approach to learning, emphasizing the transfer of knowledge and skills from education to working life, and also as a means of stimulating the motivation of learners. Generally speaking, a project represents extended work on a well-defined subject that must be completed within a given time frame. At Roskilde University it is carried out by students working in groups of two or more.

Problem-orientation: Project work at Roskilde University is characterized by being problem-oriented. Problem-oriented denotes that the work consists of dealing with real-world scientific and social problems rather than just submitting papers and assignments. It is not simply the acquisition of theories and methods that governs the curriculum.

Interdisciplinarity: The pedagogical basis at Roskilde University is to link interdisciplinarity to problem-orientation, i.e. to allow the problem of a project, rather than a traditional discipline, to determine the choice of theories and methods.

The Exemplary Principle: It is the strength of problem-oriented, interdisciplinary project work to study specific problems in depth, identifying and analysing them by drawing on theory and methods. However, the somewhat narrow focus of exploring a specific problem is a weakness in the problem-oriented approach.

This possibly weak point raises the question of how one can gain a broad insight into a field or subject using problem-oriented interdisciplinary project work as a point of departure. In terms of project work, the answer has been the exemplary principle. It is tied to the selection of materials and to the wider context that evolves from this.

Participant-directed learning: Participant-directed learning activities are a central element of the problem-oriented project work at Roskilde University, and are manifested in the students' free choice of problems and of their direction of the project, under supervision by a teacher. There are two reasons for referring to participant-directed rather than student-directed learning. Firstly, a teacher will be allocated to supervise the students. Secondly, participant-directed activities will always take place within the framework of a formal curriculum that to a greater or lesser extent will affect the substance of the students' work.

Group work: At Roskilde University group work is the general principle for organizing project work.

Target Groups

The book has two primary target groups:

- Faculty and students in higher education interested in how ideas about problem-oriented studies, interdisciplinarity, student-centred and student-directed learning, collaborative learning, research-based learning, and project work may be implemented in the pedagogical practice at their own institutions.
- Managers and planners in higher education tasked with designing models of education and organizing teaching on an institutional or departmental level.

It has also been written with two secondary target groups in mind:

- Educational managers and teachers at various types of institutions with a broad interest in pedagogical and educational issues.
- Educational planners, politicians, journalists, and members of the general public with both an interest in the interplay between concepts of education and educational planning, and also a social interest in qualifications, democratization, academic socialization, and personal development.

Structure and Content of the Book

In creating this book, our intention has been to offer an overall representation of a number of educational and pedagogical issues that are often dealt with separately in educational research. Our aim has been to establish a vertical coherence ranging from the development of the Danish system of higher education, via the development

Preface xiii

of Roskilde University as an institution, to the concrete pedagogical planning of teaching at the university. It has been an additional aim to establish an understanding of the horizontal coherence between pedagogical tenets, matters of educational structure, and the academic and professional standards of the academic programmes.

The approach in this volume has been to ask various domain experts to share their insights in the many aspects that add up to the Roskilde Model. The 20 authors of the book form a team representing all the main academic areas at the university as well as the points of view of faculty, students, and academic managers. The resulting mosaic of texts may be read as isolated chapters by those interested in particular aspects of education, or it may be read in its entirety as an exposition of the concepts and principles of the Roskilde Model approach to education, followed by an account of the framework in which this education is offered, and the actual way in which it is organized. These general chapters are followed by an in-depth examination of the most important aspects of PPL in practice as experienced by faculty as well as students, some experiments in rejuvenating the educational format, and, finally, a discussion of future directions as seen in perspective of the many issues dealt with in the previous chapters. To help the reader keep his or her bearings, we have arranged the chapters into six parts, the contents of which will be outlined below.

Part I: Roskilde University as a Pedagogical Alternative

In the first part of the book, we clarify the pedagogical concepts of problem-oriented, interdisciplinary and participant-directed project work (PPL). We compare PPL with the neighbouring concept of Problem-based Learning (PBL), and discuss the key PPL concepts in order to elicit the need for further theoretical clarification and development. We conclude the first part of the book by presenting an exemplary case study of how PPL works in practice.

Chapter 1 introduces the pedagogical foundations of the Roskilde Model, i.e. the concept of problem-oriented, interdisciplinary and participant-directed project work (PPL). This pedagogical concept is meant to support the social relevance of studies, to guarantee high academic standards, to make studies meaningful for students, to facilitate motivation, and to develop innovative and creative skills. The authors, Anders Siig Andersen and Tinne Hoff Kjeldsen, focus on the political and theoretical reasons for introducing the concept, and on a comparison with the related educational concept of 'Problem-based Learning'. This is done by first presenting the political background for introducing the pedagogical concept. The didactic and pedagogical ideas developed to underpin the concept are then discussed. This is followed by an explanation of the concepts of 'Problem-based Learning' and 'Project Work', and rounded off with a discussion of the shared and divergent features of the concepts of problem-based learning (PBL) and the Roskilde Model (PPL).

In Chap. 2, Anders Siig Andersen and Tinne Hoff Kjeldsen expand on the concepts introduced in Chap. 1 by discussing the various factors that have challenged the key concepts of PPL and the practises connected with these concepts. The chapter is based on the idea that a continued development of the conceptual understanding of the learning potentials of the Roskilde Model requires that critical factors for development as well as erosive trends are recognized as constituting the point of departure for further theoretical and practical refinement. The concepts underpinning the Roskilde Model have been interpreted in different ways and have been subject to controversy even at the university itself. Changes and adjustments have been made in the pedagogical practice due to changes in the student population, government requirements, and the work situation of the faculty members. The changes have resulted in shifts and transformations in the understanding of the pedagogical principles. The chapter concludes by identifying a number of areas where further conceptual development is required.

In Chap. 3, concluding Part I of the book, Tinne Hoff Kjeldsen and Anders Siig Andersen illustrate the various concepts and principles of the Roskilde Model by providing a concrete example of their application in practice. The chapter is both a narrative and an analysis of the course of an exemplary case of project work in the natural sciences.

Part II: Roskilde University as an Educational Alternative

In the second part of the book, we change perspective by attempting to elucidate the broader societal and political background for the Roskilde Model as an educational alternative, and to account for the historical development of Roskilde University. We also describe how the university's bachelor and master programmes are designed to actively support the PPL, and how they offer students unique opportunities to design their studies.

In Chaps. 4 and 5, Anders Siig Andersen provides the political, educational and historical background for the teaching and learning practices at Roskilde University. Chapter 4 discusses the development of the Danish higher education system from three perspectives: the historical development of the educational structure, followed by the management structure of the sector with particular emphasis on university management, and finally, the development of the management of education.

Chapter 5 explains the background for establishing Roskilde University, and traces its history over the first four decades from being an innovative creation in the higher education system to becoming a recognized and important educational alternative in the university world. Focal points are both the interaction between the university and broader society and the internal developments at the university, including the pedagogical ideas underlying the study programmes. The chapter concludes by describing the current situation where the university is setting new goals for organizing teaching and programme structure.

Next, the organization and actual workings of the Roskilde University study programmes are explained. In Chap. 6, the four bachelor-level directors of study outline the programmes in humanities, social sciences, natural sciences, and the humanities-technology combination. The authors discuss how the programmes have been developed, most recently in the reform of 2012, how the pedagogical principles of student-directed project work, problem orientation, exemplarity and interdisciplinarity have been implemented differently in the structures of each of the four bachelor programmes, and how they are realized in the pedagogical practices. Notable among these practices, and indeed unique in university education, is the possibility for students gradually to specialize in two subjects – possibly even from two different branches of science. The chapter concludes with reflections on the relations between the bachelor programmes, other parts of the university, and society at large.

In Chap. 7, Hanne Leth Andersen discusses the structure of the Roskilde University master programmes before and after the adaptation of the Bologna Model. The outcome has been a double structure where students can choose between either a new integrated master programme or the traditional one of combining two subjects. In either case, the specific feature is the problem-oriented approach by means of project work, which may lead to various forms of interdisciplinarity. It is, however, a challenge to strike a balance between students' designing their own education and the university's responsibility for the quality and the employability of the candidates. Employability is also the concern in ongoing efforts to state clearly the goals for competences both for specific programmes and for graduates in general, and also to develop relevant types of exams.

Part III: PPL in Practice

Part III focuses on the practical implementation of the PPL concept in teaching and supervision at Roskilde University. The chapters deal with supervision and the specific challenges related to the supervision of students in regard to theoretical and methodological issues. The chapters also analyse the students' project writing, and the particular challenges that international students are faced with at Roskilde University in the process of developing skills and competencies in PPL.

In Chap. 8, Anders Siig Andersen and Søren Dupont discuss in depth the important role of faculty members as project supervisors. Supervision is a skill to be learned, and the university devotes considerable resources to the training of faculty members. The chapter introduces first the different concepts regarding the role of faculty members as supervisors of project work. Next, the authors focus on the core framework for project work and supervision, i.e. the time and activity frame and the learning outcome that students must realize. On the basis of this framework, the various aspects of supervision are discussed, and they are summarized in a model showing: (a) the basic framework of project work, (b) the key supervisory tasks, and (c) other important support functions offered for student project work by the university. The authors conclude their chapter by relating the framework of project work and project supervision to the general educational strategy of Roskilde University.

In PPL, instead of reproducing insights from the curriculum and applying pre-selected theories or models to given case materials, students are expected independently to generate new knowledge relevant to their study subject. Thus, the study process is rather like a research process, and this entails that one of the supervisor's primary roles is to support the students' development of academic knowledge and competences. In Chap. 9, Inger Jensen argues that facilitating processes of acquiring academic competences by means of project work depend on the supervisor being keenly aware of a complexity of epistemological principles and research methods and paradigms. Moreover, it requires a willingness to let the students' curiosity and motivation continue to be the driver of the projects, while also acquainting the students with methodological and epistemological reflections. In the discussion of these requirements, the author addresses important methodological challenges that she has experienced as a supervisor of social science projects at various educational levels.

Although video and multimedia formats have been experimented with, most commonly the outcome of project work is a written report. In Chap. 10 on academic writing, Sanne Knudsen argues that the problem-oriented learning approach embraces and emphasizes particular aspects of the learning process such as critical thinking and self-directed learning. As a result, a particular genre has developed to scaffold and shape written problem-oriented knowledge and knowledge production. She briefly presents the history of the problem-oriented project report and goes on to discuss a key aspect of the genre, namely the inclusion of an active student voice, and she also analyses the three dominant variations of the genre. The chapter concludes by arguing that deliberate focus on genre and writing practices during supervision may further problem-oriented critical thinking, self-directed learning and academic enculturation.

Describing how complete outsiders learn to adapt to the Roskilde Model, Chap. 11 ends the part about practice by illustrating some of the challenges involved in applying the Roskilde educational approach. Using as an example international students enrolling in the Communication Studies master programme, Karsten Pedersen, from the point of view of an educational planner, demonstrates how to organize a programme for international students unaccustomed to the Roskilde brand of PPL.

Part IV: Students' Experiences and External Relations

In the fourth part of the book, we highlight some of the strengths of the Roskilde Model, viewed from the perspective of the students. We also describe students' engagement in external collaboration, the university's efforts to support their engagement, and different types of dialogue between the university and external partners concerning the study programmes.

As should be apparent from other chapters in this volume, at Roskilde University students play a key role not only in planning their own education, but also in shaping both social and academic life at the university. Representing students' views of studies at Roskilde University, Kasper Bjerring Petersen and Morten Brandrup in Chap. 12 provide an account of Roskilde University education as seen from a student perspective. Their main point is that student activities are based on the principles of volunteering, independence and learning in the activity itself. These principles provide a basis for making educated choices in the process of acquiring a bachelor and a master degree.

Roskilde University defines itself as an engaged university, critically collaborating with external partners. With the university priding itself on taking an interdisciplinary problem-oriented approach, it is natural for both researchers and students frequently to collaborate with external partners in defining problems and creating new ideas and innovative solutions. In the light of global competition in all areas of life, this characteristic has developed into a more general requirement, as politicians and political organizations have begun to show an increasing interest in strategic, administrative and financial planning at the universities. In her chapter on external relations (Chap. 13), Hanne Leth Andersen argues that no university can ignore the obligation to collaborate with external partners in new types of relations, in terms of research, education and funding. At the same time, in parallel with the massification of higher education, the quality is questioned and continuously evaluated by external bodies.

Part V: Pedagogical Experiments in PPL

PPL is continuously being developed and adapted to the needs of the various academic cultures at Roskilde University. In this part of the book, we describe two experiments that have changed the format of project work. The first experiment aims at a closer cooperation between researchers and students. The second experiment involves a new development in project organization as well as the written products of project work. Both experiments seek to establish learning communities across the individual project groups. In this part of the book, we also expand on some of the challenges caused by the rapid development of information and communication technology (ICT), and we exemplify how ICT can be used in supporting students' project work.

In Chap. 14 on students as co-researchers, Trine Wulf-Andersen, Peder Hjort-Madsen and Kevin Holger Mogensen report on an important experiment in renewing the project work form by means of realizing research-based learning in a literal way. In the experiment, groups of undergraduate students have been working on various tasks within the framework of an actual research project. Thus, the students have been at the centre of a research process and have organized their learning through interaction with 'real' research problems, empirical and theoretical fields, informants, and researcher colleagues. The chapter discusses two main perspectives of having students act as research learners and researchers act as project managers as well as supervisors: the contribution to the production of research knowledge, and the contribution to the learning processes of the students as research learners. The authors also discuss the potentials and challenges of intertwined and complex research.

The Anthology Experiment that Søren Dupont reports on in Chap. 15 was meant to develop and expand the framework for project work through the production of anthologies compiled collectively by a number of project groups. In the course developed for the experiment, some 50 students working in clusters and project groups were seen as 'research units' contributing articles rather than 'reports' to an anthology, which also required some coordination across the student groups. The complexity of the experiment offered challenges for students as well as supervisors, one of which was to develop a new exam format. However, the outcome of the experiment was so successful that the anthology format subsequently has been adopted in other courses.

Information and communication technology is reshaping the manner in which academic work in general is carried out. In terms of project work at Roskilde University, ICT tools have proven to be helpful in supporting and developing the work forms. However, in implementing and integrating the new technologies in academic practices, a number of challenges have had to be addressed. In Chap. 16, Simon Heilesen discusses four of these challenges: providing a physical and virtual framework for learning activities, directing student use of ICT in terms of making systems available and teaching academic computing, supervising and conducting project work online and in blended learning environments, and exploiting the potentials of ICT in problem-oriented group work by choosing helpful tools while maintaining a balance between advanced uses and a need to impose a measure of uniformity.

Part VI: Outlook

In the final part of the book, we argue that the Roskilde Model is highly relevant for meeting a number of contemporary challenges to university education. We highlight some of the key trends in the development of globalization, higher education and student identity, and consider their impact on future developments of the Roskilde Model.

In Chap. 17 of the book, Henning Salling Olesen and Anders Siig Andersen elaborate on some of the potentials of the Roskilde Model's three dimensions – the educational structure, the academic profile of the university's study programmes and the PPL model. Their intention is to discuss the ways in which the Roskilde Model may still be a valid proposal for a radical university reform – recognizing the learning processes and revisions that have occurred over more than four decades. The chapter also highlights some of the challenges that the European harmonization of education represents to the Roskilde Model as it takes place in a political climate that increasingly prioritizes narrow vocational considerations in organizing university study programmes.

Roskilde, Denmark
June 2014

Anders Siig Andersen
Simon B. Heilesen

Acknowledgements

The editors would like to thank the Roskilde University Library for its assistance in providing bibliographies, Paul Farmer and Prof. Henning Ørum for linguistic editing, Vibeke Lihn for layout of text and figures, our patient editor at Springer, and last but not least the contributors to this volume as well as numerous other colleagues who have participated in discussions about the Roskilde Model.

Contents

Part I Roskilde University as a Pedagogical Alternative

1 Theoretical Foundations of PPL at Roskilde University 3
  Anders Siig Andersen and Tinne Hoff Kjeldsen

2 A Critical Review of the Key Concepts in PPL 17
  Anders Siig Andersen and Tinne Hoff Kjeldsen

3 Case Analysis of Some Critical Factors in Relation to Learning
  Outcomes of PPL – The Formation of Flint 37
  Tinne Hoff Kjeldsen and Anders Siig Andersen

Part II Roskilde University as an Educational Alternative

4 Historical Transformations Within Danish Higher Education 49
  Anders Siig Andersen

5 The History of Roskilde University 63
  Anders Siig Andersen

6 The Bachelor Programmes and the Roskilde Model 79
  Morten Blomhøj, Thyge Enevoldsen, Michael Haldrup,
  and Niels Møller Nielsen

7 The Master Programmes and the Roskilde Model 107
  Hanne Leth Andersen

Part III PPL in Practice

8 Supervising Projects 121
  Anders Siig Andersen and Søren Dupont

9	Methodological Challenges – From a Supervisor's Experiences......... Inger Jensen	141
10	Genre and Voice in Problem-Oriented Reports .... Sanne Knudsen	155
11	PPL in Intercultural Settings .... Karsten Pedersen	177

Part IV Students' Experiences and External Relations

12	Experiencing PPL: The Student View .... Kasper Bjerring Petersen and Morten Brandrup	189
13	External Relations: Bridging Academia and Practice .... Hanne Leth Andersen	199

Part V Pedagogical Experiments in PPL

14	Research Learning – How Students and Researchers Learn from Collaborative Research .... Trine Wulf-Andersen, Peder Hjort-Madsen, and Kevin Holger Mogensen	211
15	Restructuring the Project Work Format: The Anthology Experiment .... Søren Dupont	233
16	Supporting Project Work with Information Technology..................... Simon B. Heilesen	245

Part VI Outlook

17	The Roskilde Model and the Challenges for Universities in the Future .... Henning Salling Olesen and Anders Siig Andersen	263

Appendix: Roskilde University at a Glance 281

Editors and Contributors

About the Editors

Anders Siig Andersen is Head of the Department of Psychology and Educational Studies, Roskilde University. His main research interests are: educational planning, social intervention, learning in working life, adult and vocational education, higher education, learning theories, qualitative methodology, and participatory research. He is the author and editor of a number of books and articles in these areas. He has had experience in conducting large projects in Denmark and Greenland. In 2010 and 2011 he was in charge of the development of a new bachelor model structure at Roskilde University. For publications and contact information, see: http://forskning.ruc.dk/site/person/siig.

Simon B. Heilesen is an Associate Professor of Net Media and ICT in Education at the Department of Psychology and Educational Studies, Roskilde University. Currently, he is managing the Academic IT Unit, which carries out research, development and training in effective uses of new media for teaching, researching, and communicating professionally. His main research focus is on the intersection of human-computer interaction, communication studies, and educational studies. He is the author and editor of a dozen books and numerous articles on the uses of new media for communicating, collaborating and learning. Current research projects include: (a) developing real-time platforms and online open platforms both for teaching in higher education and for professional communication targeted at general audiences, (b) planning and implementing ICT-based welfare technologies for senior citizens and (c) evaluating how awareness and use of welfare technologies are being integrated in professional training programmes. For publications and contact information, see: http://forskning.ruc.dk/site/person/simonhei.

Contributors

Hanne Leth Andersen is Rector and a Professor of University Pedagogy at Roskilde University. Her personal professional experience is in language education and university pedagogy, with specific focus on communication, supervision, evaluation, and examination forms. She has been a member of a large number of councils, boards and committees and currently works as an expert for the Norwegian NOKUT and EUA International Evaluation Programme. She has published more than a 100 scientific articles in Danish and international reviewed journals as well as several monographs. Current research and development projects include: developing open-end exams for entrepreneurial and innovative work forms and investigating models for new partnerships in education. For publications and contact information, see: http://forskning.ruc.dk/site/person/hanne-leth-andersen.

Morten Blomhøj is an Associate Professor of Mathematics at the Department of Science, Systems and Models, Roskilde University. He is the Head of Studies of the bachelor study programme in Natural Science (NATBACH). He was responsible for developing the study programme for NATBACH in the 2012 reform. He was Editor-in-Chief for the journal *Nordic Studies in Mathematics Education* 2006–2011. His research interests are in mathematical modelling, project work in mathematics, the use of ICT in the teaching and learning of mathematics, and systematic collaboration between the development of teaching practices and research in mathematics education. For publications and contact information, see: http://rucforsk.ruc.dk/site/person/blomhoej.

Morten Brandrup holds an M.Sc. and is currently a teaching assistant in the Computer Science and Informatics programme at the Department of Communication, Business and Information Technologies, Roskilde University. He is currently teaching the courses 'Introduction to Programming', 'Introduction to Web Applications', 'Design of Interactive Experiences', and he is also a project supervisor. One of his personal interests is the practical supervision of project groups and how to optimize the communication between group and supervisor by means of ICT. Contact information: http://www.linkedin.com/pub/morten-brandrup/31/5b1/b96.

Søren Dupont is an Associate Professor at the Department of Psychology and Educational Studies, Roskilde University. 2008–14 he was Head of the university's Pedagogical Training Unit (UniPed). He holds a Ph.D. in the 'history of ideas' and an M.A. in 'cultural work and communication', and he has worked at various universities for more than 30 years, and for the last 15 years at Roskilde University. For publications and contact information, see: http://forskning.ruc.dk/site/person/dupont.

Thyge Enevoldsen, Ph.D., is an Associate Professor at the Institute of Society and Globalization, Roskilde University. Since 2001, he has been Director of the bachelor programme in Social Science. Prior to that, he was Head of African Studies at Copenhagen University. His main areas of research and teaching are in international development studies, and the theories and praxis of interdisciplinarity. For publications and contact information, see: http://rucforsk.ruc.dk/site/person/thygee.

Michael Haldrup, Ph.D., is an Associate Professor of Cultural Geography, Department of Environmental, Social and Spatial Change, Roskilde University. He is Director of the bachelor programme in Humanities and Technology. His research interests include: tourist studies, design of experiences, consumer studies, identity and everyday life, science technology studies, methodology, and participatory design. He has published extensively within these fields including *Performing Tourist Places* with Bærenholdt, Larsen and Urry (2003), *Tourism, Performance and the Everyday* (with Larsen in 2010), and methodological chapters on design, technology and everyday life (with Svabo, in 2012). For publications and contact information, see: http://rucforsk.ruc.dk/site/person/mhp.

Peder Hjort-Madsen, Ph.D., is a Post Doc at the Danish Centre for Youth Research, Aalborg University, Copenhagen. His research focuses on young people's participation in education, school cultures, and young people's educational pathways and motivation for learning. Contact information; dk.linkedin.com/pub/peder-hjort-madsen/33/731/234.

Inger Jensen is M.Sc. in Psychology and an Associate Professor Emeritus in Social Psychology/Sociology at the Department of Communication, Business and Information Technologies, Roskilde University. Her research focus is on the societal processes that define legitimacy of organizational activities. She has had experience in educational management through positions as a member of the Senate, as Head of the Study Board, and as Vice-rector at Roskilde University. She has also acted as member/head of the board of directors at various university colleges and in upper secondary schools. She has cooperated with the Royal Institute of Management in Bhutan in a Danida project on developing faculty members' research competencies. Since 2007 she has been organizer of the EUPRERA annual international Ph.D. seminars in collaboration with European Universities. For publications and contact information, see: http://rucforsk.ruc.dk/site/person/inger.

Tinne Hoff Kjeldsen is an Associate Professor of Mathematics, Roskilde University. She is the Danish regional coordinator for European Women in Mathematics, member of the interdisciplinary group for the Danish Bibliometric Project, member of the Danish Commission for Mathematics Education, and a fellow of the American Mathematical Society. Her research interests are: history of twentieth century mathematics, the dynamics between internal and external (WWII) driving forces, history and epistemology of mathematical modelling, didactics of mathematics, the development of students' modelling competency, the function of mathematical modelling for learning mathematics, the function of history in mathematics education, and interdisciplinarity in university education. She has written and edited books and published extensively in international peer-reviewed journals and books. She has been an invited lecturer at numerous international conferences in Europe, North and South America and Asia. For publications and contact information: http://forskning.ruc.dk/site/person/thk.

Sanne Knudsen is an Associate Professor in Academic Writing and Communication at the Department of Communication, Business and Information Technologies,

Roskilde University. At present she is a member of the research environment Power, Media and Communication. Her research interests centre on academic communication and texts within a variety of contexts including specialist discourses, student writings and the framing of science and academic work in modern day media. A particular perspective has been on the strategic and heuristic use of metaphor in specialist as well as popular science communication within scientific discourse and writing (in particular in biology, economics and business communication). Her current work focuses on the framing of the humanities and human sciences as is expressed either in the scholarly texts themselves or in the public media. For publications and contact information, see: http://rucforsk.ruc.dk/site/person/sannekn.

Thomas Aarup Larsen is a graduate student of Geography and Welfare Studies at the Department of Environmental, Social and Spatial Change, and the Department of Society and Globalization at Roskilde University. He is currently writing a combined master thesis in his two master subjects on "the Demographic Aging and Mobility of the Elderly in Denmark". He works as a student assistant at Roskilde University Pedagogical Training Unit (UniPed) and as a project assistant at the Copenhagen Innovation and Entrepreneurship Collaboration (CIEL). Contact information: http://www.linkedin.com/pub/thomas-aarup-larsen/25/620/400.

Kevin Holger Mogensen, Ph.D., is a Post Doc at the Department of Psychology and Educational Studies, Roskilde University. His research is on young people's gendered educational practices, and the processes that make certain gender practices problematic among peers and in relation to the teachers in vocational college and high school. He is currently teaching at the master programme in Educational Studies. For publications and contact information, see: http://forskning.ruc.dk/site/person/kevin.

Niels Møller Nielsen is an Associate Professor of Danish Language and Communication at the Department of Culture and Identity, Roskilde University. He is currently the Director of Studies at the bachelor study programme in the Humanities. His main research focus is on argumentation studies, the philosophy of language, pragmatics and rhetoric. He has published papers and books on argumentation theory and analysis, and on corporate communication in rhetorical and pragmatic perspectives. For publications and contact information, see: http://forskning.ruc.dk/site/person/nmn.

Henning Salling Olesen is a Professor at the Department of Psychology and Educational Studies, Roskilde University. He is former Rector and Vice-rector of Roskilde University. He was a member of the founding bodies of the university (1970–1972) as a student representative. He is Chair of the European Society for Research in the Education of Adults (ESREA). He is Co-editor of the European online journal RELA, advisory professor at East China Normal University, Shanghai, and is on the Board of Ilisimatusarfik/University of Greenland (deputy chair). His research interests include learning theory, life history methodology and experience-based learning. His present tasks include supervision of doctoral students in the Graduate School of Lifelong Learning. He is currently doing research on psycho-societal methodology for the study of learning in everyday life, particularly workplace and professions, and critical studies of policies of lifelong learning. For publications and contact information, see: http://forskning.ruc.dk/site/person/hso.

Karsten Pedersen, Ph.D., is an Associate Professor of Communication Studies at the Department of Communication, Business and Information Technologies, Roskilde University. He specializes on public communication and has published extensively on the subject. Currently he is working on several projects, including information planning in local and regional elections, a historical view of public campaigns, hospital hygiene, letters from authorities, and a book on communication theory. He has been Head of Studies in Communication Studies for 3 years, International Coordinator for 4 years, and he has held various coordinating posts at his department. For the last few years he has been involved in internationalization of Roskilde University and is currently chairman of the University's subcommittee on internationalization. For publications and contact information, see http://forskning.ruc.dk/site/person/kape.

Kasper Bjerring Petersen is a graduate student of Global Studies at the Department of Society and Globalization at Roskilde University. He is currently working as student counsellor at the same department where he studies. Previously he has been a member of the Board of Directors of Roskilde University, appointed to represent the students on behalf of the Student Union. Before that he was a member of the Academic Council, the Research Committee, and of the working group on the new structure and substance of the remaking of the bachelor education. He takes interest in international policy and diplomacy, and also in quality in education and student interests. Contact information: dk.linkedin.com/pub/kasper-bjerring-petersen/26/737/643.

Trine Wulf-Andersen, Ph.D., is an Associate Professor at the Department of Psychology and Educational Studies, Roskilde University. Her research focus is on young people's everyday lives and meetings with welfare institutions and professionals – in educational, social work, community work and mental health contexts. She is currently teaching on the master programme in Educational Studies and the bachelor study programme in Social Sciences. For publications and contact information, see: http://forskning.ruc.dk/site/person/wulf.

Part I
Roskilde University as a Pedagogical Alternative

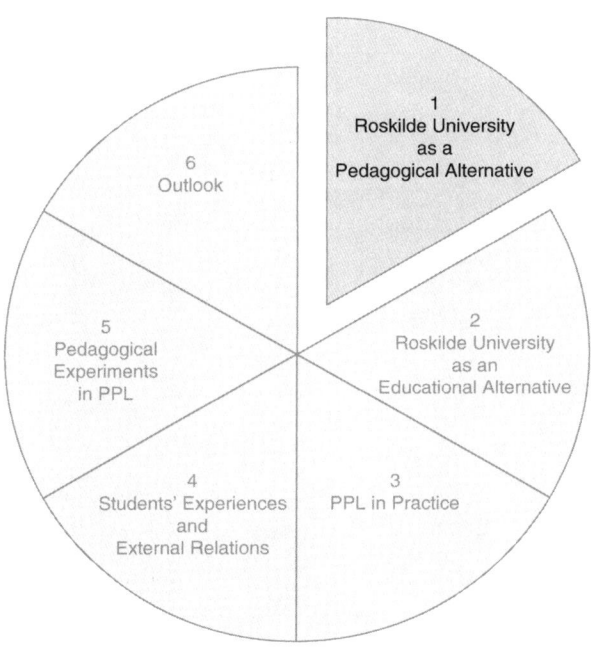

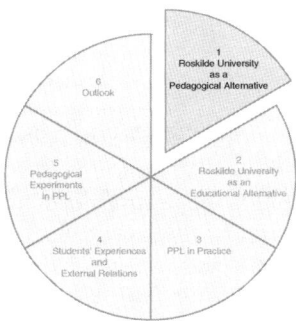

Chapter 1
Theoretical Foundations of PPL at Roskilde University

Anders Siig Andersen and Tinne Hoff Kjeldsen

1.1 Introduction

This chapter introduces the pedagogical foundation of the Roskilde Model (PPL). The aims of this pedagogical concept are to support the social relevance of studies, to guarantee high academic standards, to make studies meaningful for students, to facilitate motivation, and to develop innovative and creative skills. The focus will be on the practical and theoretical reasons for introducing the concept, and on a comparison with the related educational concepts of 'Project Work' and 'Problem-based Learning'. First, we present a brief exposition of the political background for introducing the pedagogical concept. Secondly, we present the didactic and pedagogical ideas that were developed to underpin the concept, drawing inspiration from German qualifications theory and constructivist learning theory. We then explain the concepts of 'Problem-based Learning' and 'Project Work'. Finally we offer a discussion of the common and divergent features of the concept of problem-based learning (PBL) and the Roskilde Model (PPL).

A.S. Andersen (✉) • T.H. Kjeldsen
Roskilde University, Roskilde, Denmark
e-mail: siig@ruc.dk; thk@ruc.dk

© Springer International Publishing Switzerland 2015
A.S. Andersen, S.B. Heilesen (eds.), *The Roskilde Model: Problem-Oriented Learning and Project Work*, Innovation and Change in Professional Education 12,
DOI 10.1007/978-3-319-09716-9_1

1.2 Problem-Based Project Work and the New University Centres in Denmark

The introduction of project work in Danish higher education has been described as 'a lucky punch' (Olesen 1999). Roskilde University was founded in 1972 at a time when universities were experiencing an increase in the number of students, transforming them from elite institutions into institutions of mass education. The labour market required graduates with new general and specialized skills, and the universities were faced with challenges related to more extensive curricula and academic specialization.

In the 1960s, politicians from different parties in Denmark expressed a wish to combine medium and long-term higher education in educational centres. They coupled this idea with considerations on the establishment of broad basic study programmes to qualify the students for various types of education. In the late 1960s, a broad spectrum of the political parties agreed on criticizing the existing universities for their rigid disciplinary boundaries (Hansen 1997, p. 47). Many politicians shared the view that modern society – through differentiation and functional specialization – had developed a need for new groups of employees that would support the development of the welfare state and the modernization of the private sector. They argued that this development had created a need for new types of higher education institutions, new broad initial study programmes and new interdisciplinary studies. This paved the way for experiments and reforms in higher education, most notably with the establishment in 1972 in Roskilde and in 1974 in Aalborg of such new university centres (see also Chaps. 4 and 5).

There were, however, distinct differences between, on the one hand, the ideas of politicians and educational administrators, and, on the other hand, the ideas formulated by the Danish student movement. Until 1969, The Danish Students Federation (DSF) had already been supporting a reform-based modernization of the educational system, but as the youth rebellion evolved in the late 1960s, the DSF became radicalized. In 1970, DSF published a leaflet called 'Who's in charge?' that outlined a new framework for the continued planning of university centres. In the leaflet, the students argued that new programmes should be based on the principles of problem-oriented, interdisciplinary and participant-directed project work. The role of the faculty members was to provide assistance in problem solving, there should be no examinations, and studies should be socially relevant (Hansen 1997, p. 43).

During the first decade after the founding of Roskilde University, the student movement seized the power of defining the pedagogical discourse. From the mid-1980s, however, the political-administrative rationale for the reform of higher education gained much more influence. Olesen describes the two conflicting rationales as follows: "In the historical process they took the shape of a synthesis – far from free of conflicts – between a welfare modernization of higher education and an anti-authoritarian and critical renewal of teaching and academic content mediated by the student movement" (Olesen 1999, p. 123).

1.3 The Critical Pedagogical Ideas of the Student Movement

Taking a critical pedagogical point of view, the representatives of the Danish Students Federation argued that problem-oriented, interdisciplinary and participant-directed project work would empower students and enhance their ability to critically analyse the division of labour in society and the social function of science. They emphasized that this would remove academic studies from their 'ivory tower'. They further argued that the new pedagogical model would enable university students to acquire new understandings of science that surpassed the usual approaches to and organization of subject matter at universities. They justified project work as a form of study that would offer students the opportunity to work with totalities, to investigate practice, and to achieve a different understanding of theory and methodology. Furthermore, they held the opinion that project work would include and motivate students from non-academic family backgrounds (Olesen 1972, pp. 120ff.).

The interest of the student movement was linked to the idea that the dynamics and forces that govern the development of various aspects of society should be the orientation framework for the students' project work. Issues would be analysed and reflected on in their unique character, and also in the perspective of society as a whole. The proponents of the student movement argued that participatory learning would facilitate discussion of the students' experiences, which would be subject to systematic investigation. This would enable students to gain an understanding of the established social orders, and it would allow them to develop different forms of academic and social critique. The students emphasized that the method of group work would transform the processes of acquiring knowledge and skills into collaborative processes that would counteract tendencies towards individualization in society.

According to the student movement, the purpose of higher education should be 'dual qualification'. Firstly, it should provide suitable academic and professional qualifications for today's society, including those of an innovative and creative nature. Secondly, higher education should help students to develop critical judgement, enhance their societal involvement, and increase social equality and justice. The goal of the students was emancipation on a social as well as an individual level. The inspiration for the educational model had many origins: constructivist learning theory, humanistic psychology, reform pedagogy, critical theory, Marxist theory of qualifications, etc. The inspiration also originated from the students' own experiences in developing criticism of the subjects and their content (internal subject criticism) and new cooperation established between students, researchers, and disadvantaged groups in society in order to change the social function of the subjects (external subject criticism).

1.4 Pedagogical Generalization of the Concept

In 1974, in his book "Problem Orientation and Participatory Learning – A Proposal for Alternative Didactics", educational researcher Knud Illeris further developed the theoretical foundation for the pedagogical principles of problem-oriented, interdisciplinary and participant-directed project work. Illeris explained his motives by the need for providing a systematic introduction to the theoretical ideas underlying the pedagogical principles as well as the need for gathering and organizing ideas on the planning and implementation of study programmes that were based on these principles. Illeris pointed out that there was scant experience of this form of pedagogy to date (Illeris 1974, p. 7f.). The key concepts of Illeris' book were 'problem formulation' and 'participant-directed learning'. He believed that these principles would be realized through a variety of teaching methods, including project work. However, in his practical application of these concepts, he attached great importance to problem-oriented, interdisciplinary, and participant directed project work. Some of Illeris' considerations were anticipated in a discussion paper from the Planning Council for Higher Education in a report from 1972 called 'The Internal Structure of Higher Education' (Planlægningsrådet 1972). The report was, however, planning-oriented and did not have the same level of theoretical ambition.

Illeris used a didactic concept adopted from a German critical didactic tradition. According to Illeris, critical didactics analyses

> study programmes in their social context, pursuing an emancipatory interest of knowledge. In order to pursue and protect the participants' social and class specific interests, the aims of the alternative didactics are to increase their understanding of the social functions of the educational system and of the objective conditions of their own lives. (Illeris 1974, p. 18 [authors' translation])

Illeris defined the primary goal of his endeavour as establishing and justifying certain fundamental didactic principles and pedagogical ideas to serve as a viable basis for the new forms of studying. A further goal was to go beyond the theoretical foundation of the German critical didactic tradition, which basically refers to sociotheoretical concepts, by also including psychological aspects concerning how development and learning take place in the 'human organism' (Illeris 1974, p. 9).

The German tradition of qualifications research, predominant in the 1960s and 1970s, identified tensions between (1) the qualifications required in specific jobs, (2) the skills generally required to submit to regular paid work and its organizational forms, and (3) the creative and innovative skills that society requires. According to Illeris, these tensions made it possible to organize study programmes that reflect an emancipatory interest, taking into account the fact that the programmes must produce the skills demanded by society (Illeris 1974, p. 52). He pointed out that societal demands for creative and innovative competencies include qualities such as independence, interpersonal skills and critical thinking, and that these qualities are essential not only to provide the labour market with the required skills, but also to provide the individual with skills to move beyond the status quo. Illeris used the concept of 'dual qualification' to characterize his educational goals:

> Changes in study programmes that will pursue an emancipatory agenda must necessarily take into account the requirements of the existing educational system (…). If graduates from alternative study programmes are not performing at least as well as those from traditional study programmes, the changes will lose their credibility. (Illeris 1974, p. 5 [authors' translation])

Illeris included psychological theory in his didactical considerations, primarily by referring to Piaget's constructivist theory of how development and learning take place in the individual as he or she interacts with the environment. Illeris argued that he chose Piaget's theory because it provides the most direct link between learning theory and applied pedagogy (Illeris 1974, p. 61). According to Illeris, the basis of Piaget's theory is that the psychological organization of the individual consists of cognitive, emotional, and physical capabilities that are actively adapting to the environment. The adaptation process takes place through the establishment of more or less stable states of equilibrium. Two complementary processes are involved in this adaptation: (1) Assimilation processes where what takes place in the external world is adapted to the individual's internal world, and (2) accommodation processes, where the individual's internal world adapts to the external world (Illeris 1974, p. 62).

Illeris' theorizing comprises a relatively abstract social theory and a predominantly individualistic theory of human development and learning. On this basis, he reflected on the fundamental principles that should be established with regard to the design of study programmes. His main answer was: problem orientation and participant-directed learning. He argued that the traditional division of academic subjects promotes an assimilative process that leads to the establishment of isolated and skill-related cognitive structures – and at the attitudinal level, the perception that issues are not related. For Illeris, the key feature of problem-oriented learning is that the starting point should not be the academic subjects, but rather problems that exist here and now. His argument was that in dealing with these problems, one needs contributions from the different theories and methods that are chosen and applied, depending on how relevant they are to the problems at hand. He thus introduced the concept of interdisciplinarity.

Illeris supported his argument for the principles of problem orientation by drawing on a number of other theorists. He referred to Dewey's principle that learning processes should be based on the learners' experience, and Roger's principle of student-centred teaching. Illeris also introduced the concept of the exemplary principle by pointing to the classical understanding of Wagenschein, who argued that the principle of exemplarity would establish coherent scientific understanding by being based on a single case or instance. In this context, he also referred to Negt, who linked the concept of exemplarity to concepts of experience and sociological imagination (see also Chap. 2).

The question of who decides what the problem is and how to work with it is crucial to Illeris. He argued that a problem is not a problem in the psychological sense, unless it is chosen by the person who has to work with it:

> If the solution, or at least the elucidation of the problem, does not appear as a personal challenge, the conditions for accommodative learning are not present and thus neither the conditions for the development of creativity and flexibility. (…) Accommodative learning is a

demanding process that requires commitment. You accommodate only in situations that are relevant to yourself and what you are doing. (Illeris 1974, pp. 82f. [authors' translation])

He also emphasized that the principle of participant-directed learning is not to be understood as student-directed learning. Faculty members must formulate broad problem areas that are of relevance to a given study programme, and students must follow curriculum requirements for particular qualifications.

Illeris formulated three criteria for the issues to be addressed in study programmes. The criteria, summarized below, are based on problem orientation and participant-directed learning:

1. They must be perceived as immediately relevant for the individual participants in a group of learners and of common interest to all learners in the group,
2. They must be of such a nature that they can elicit broader social structures and the basis for these structures,
3. They must cover the curricula of the relevant study programme in conjunction with other educational activities.
(Illeris 1974, p. 187 [authors' translation]).

Using as a point of departure his own theoretical considerations as well as his and others' experiences in the planning of problem-oriented and participant-directed study programmes, Illeris proposed the following steps in project work:

1. Introduction and definition of the framework for the project work,
2. Introduction of methods and the general subject area,
3. Social introduction and group formation,
4. Choice of topic and problem to be worked on,
5. Formulation of the project idea,
6. Writing, evaluation and corrections of the project.
(Illeris 1974, p. 151ff. [authors' translation]).

In 1981, Illeris published a book entitled: 'The Pedagogy of Counter-qualifications – Problem Orientation, Participant-directed Learning and Exemplary Learning'. Here, he radicalized his concepts in a political direction, and elaborated on the possible societal and individual potentials of criticism of academic subjects and society (Illeris 1981).

The learning-theoretical basis for problem-oriented project work has been gradually challenged by other learning theories. Illeris himself has been one of the challengers, as he now draws inspiration from a broad range of learning theories, not least from theory on transformative learning (Illeris 2013). Taking into account the collaborative characteristics of PPL and PBL, other educational theorists have turned to social learning theory. Recently, Hanney and Savin-Baden (2013) have provided a summary of social learning theory. They argue that learning occurs through:

- Problem encounters that offer the opportunity for the application of skills and knowledge that are required for decision-making, devising solutions, creativity and problem solving,

1 Theoretical Foundations of PPL at Roskilde University

- Boundary encounters that require negotiations with exterior communities and unfamiliar discourses,
- Access to a shared repertoire of language, terminology, technologies, tools, and techniques with which to engage, experiment and play,
- Negotiation of a joint enterprise, shared values, mutual evaluations of that enterprise, and moments of reflection,
- Access to reificative and participative memory; old timers, champions, mentors, sponsors and storytellers, as well as to traditional repositories such as libraries (Hanney and Savin-Baden 2013, p. 10).

Their summary covers essential parts of social learning theory. They downplay, however, the theory's emphasis on conflictual aspects of learning processes. Etienne Wenger, one of the originators of social learning theory, has outlined such aspects of learning processes in his book 'Communities of Practice', by defining the concepts of 'institutionalization', 'economies of meaning', 'peripheral location' and 'exclusion' (Wenger 1998; see also Andersen et al. 2007, p. 16 ff.). A number of learning theories hold in common that they argue for a learner-centred and group-based pedagogy, emphasizing that subject matter should be immediately meaningful for learners. In addition to constructivist theories (e.g. Gijselaers 1996) and social learning theories, this is also true of theories that apply psychoanalytical, critical cultural, and enactivist perspectives to the phenomenon of learning (Fenwick 2000).

1.5 Problem-Based Learning

At the time when the concept of problem-oriented, interdisciplinary, and student-directed project work was being developed, other similar pedagogical models for university teaching were also being constructed.

The concept most similar to the Roskilde Model is the concept of 'Problem-based Learning'. In the international debate, the concepts of 'Problem-based Learning' (PBL) and 'Problem-oriented, Interdisciplinary and Participant-directed Project Work' (PPL) sometimes seem to be confused, although there are some quite distinct differences. In the following, we briefly characterize the PBL concept, outline the history of the concept, and mention some of the problems the concept has run into at Maastricht University where it was implemented in the 1980s. At the end of the chapter, we will then use this characterization of the PBL concept as a background for outlining the main differences between the concepts.

Problem-based learning is a method in which students learn through facilitated problem solving. In PBL, student learning centres on complex real-world problems that resonate with the experiences of the students. The problems do not have one single correct solution, but are typically complex, open-ended, and ill-structured. Savin-Baden, who has studied the concept and the practice of PBL for many years, puts it this way:

> The focus here is in organizing the curricular content around specific problem scenarios rather than subjects or disciplines. (…) They [the students] are not expected to acquire a

predetermined series of 'right answers'. Instead they are expected to engage with the complex situation presented to them and decide what information they need to learn and what skills they need to gain in order to manage the situation effectively. (Savin-Baden 2000, p. 3)

The PBL tradition emphasizes that good problems often require multidisciplinary solutions. Students actively construct knowledge in collaborative groups. They engage in self-directed (SDL) and self-regulated learning (SRL) (see English and Kitsantas 2013), and they apply their new knowledge to the problem and reflect on what they learned and the effectiveness of the learning strategies employed. Rather than as an expert on the content itself, the teacher acts as an expert learner, able to model good strategies for learning and thinking (see also Chap. 8). The facilitator scaffolds student learning through modelling and coaching primarily through the use of questioning strategies (Hmelo-Silver 2004, pp. 235ff.).

Savin-Baden has described different models of problem-based learning that range from narrow disciplinary problem solving that requires predetermined solutions, to open-ended interdisciplinary problem solving that deals with messy or ill-structured problems. Common to these models is the use of a problem "that in some way reflects professional practice or configures a real-world encounter in relation to disciplinary knowledge" (Hanney and Savin-Baden 2013, p. 11).

Savin-Baden quotes David Boud for the following eight characteristics of many problem-based learning courses:

1. An acknowledgement of the base of experience of learners,
2. An emphasis on students taking responsibility for their own learning,
3. A crossing of boundaries between disciplines,
4. An intertwining of theory and practice,
5. A focus on the processes of knowledge acquisition rather than the products of such processes,
6. A change in staff role from that of instructor to that of facilitator,
7. A change in focus from staff assessment of outcomes of learning to student self- and peer assessment,
8. A focus on communication and interpersonal skills,
   (Savin-Baden 2000, pp. 17f.).

Savin-Baden has traced the origins of PBL to Socrates, who presented students with problems through questioning, and to Dewey who argued that knowledge was bound to activity. Socrates opposed theories that consider knowledge to be independent of its role in problem-solving inquiry (Savin-Baden 2000, p. 3f.). Savin-Baden points out that ideas of problem-based learning were popularized during the 1960s as a result of research by Barrows into the reasoning abilities of medical students. Barrows wanted to develop the students' ability to relate their theoretical knowledge to the problems which the patients presented (Savin-Baden 2000, p. 4).

According to Savin-Baden, problem-based learning was first implemented at McMaster University in Canada, where Barrows designed a medical school curriculum based on student-centred learning in small groups. The learning design was based on two assumptions:

The first was that learning through problem situations was much more effective than memory-based learning for creating a usable body of knowledge. The second was that the medical skills, that were most important for treating patients, were problem-solving skills, rather than memorization. (Savin-Baden 2000, p. 14)

Against this background, problem-based learning was adopted in the 1970s and 1980s in Canada, Australia, the Netherlands and the United States, and during the late 1980s also in the UK (Savin-Baden 2000 p. 4). In the 1990s and 2000s, the concept spread to Asia, and lately it has also inspired universities in Africa and Russia. Savin-Baden emphasizes that problem-based learning is an approach that can embrace liberal education, where students are encouraged to have virtually unrestricted access to knowledge and where knowledge is to be valued for its own sake, and operational curricula, where the focus is more narrowly on what the students are able to do in the context of accountability and market-related values (Savin-Baden 2000, pp. 4f.). She expresses some concerns as to how the concept may not always be supported in the growth areas by the organization into which it is placed, and thus she says: "Although there is growth, to some extent much of this is at the marginalized end of the system." (Savin-Baden 2000, p. 22).

Maastricht University in the Netherlands implemented the concept of PBL some 30 years ago. The University was founded as a small medical school. Since then, new schools in Health Sciences, Law, Economics, Psychology, and Liberal Arts have adopted the PBL concept. Many other universities have been inspired by the PBL model practised at Maastricht.

In the PBL curricula at Maastricht University, students are taught in consecutive courses or units of 6–8 weeks in which subject matter and skills are integrated around a central theme. Most units are multidisciplinary in nature (Moust et al. 2005, p. 666). At the start of each unit, students are offered a unit guide that provides them with information about scheduled activities, an introduction to the theme of the unit, a set of problems, and a list of references and other learning resources. The tutorial group is the main educational vehicle, consisting of about eight students (Moust et al. 2005, p. 666). The 'Seven Jump' strategy is regarded as the general learning procedure:

1. Clarify unclear phrases and concepts in the description of the problem,
2. Define the problem; which means: Describe exactly which phenomena have to be explained or understood,
3. Brainstorm: Using your prior knowledge and common sense, try to produce as many different explanations as possible,
4. Elaborate on the proposed explanations: Try to construct a detailed coherent personal 'theory' of the processes underlying the phenomena,
5. Formulate learning issues for self-directed learning,
6. Try to fill gaps in your knowledge through self-study,
7. Share your findings in the group and try to integrate the acquired knowledge in a suitable explanation for the phenomena. Check whether you know enough. Evaluate the process of knowledge acquisition,
(Moust et al. 2005, p. 668; see also Gijselaers 1995, p. 46).

However, according to the authors working at Maastricht University, in some ways the model has been watered down: self-study time has decreased, preparation in tutorial groups is minimal, time spent on literature searches has dropped, the brainstorming and elaboration phase has been skipped, most students have a tendency to read the same resources, the students are given specific references for each problem instead of a long list of references, students are offered more and more lectures that are used to convey information, students rely more and more heavily on this information, student groups have grown from 6–8 to 12–14 students, and students are used as tutors to such an extent that students hardly meet faculty members as tutors (Moust et al. 2005, p. 670). Moust et al. explain this development by referring to several intertwined factors: (a) students are uncertain about the usefulness of activating their prior knowledge, and they have developed a more instrumental stance towards learning, (b) faculty members have become uncertain about whether students are learning enough and meeting the demands of the curricula, (c) both faculty members and students have a poor understanding of the underlying principles, and (d) resources for teaching have dropped significantly (Moust et al. 2005, p. 668).

As solutions to the problems, Moust et al. suggest the following:

1. Building learning communities by splitting the whole batch of 300 or more students into groups of 80 that are to remain closely together for a year. Each learning community should be guided by a permanent group of faculty members.
2. Offering students more variety in educational formats within the context of a PBL environment. Project-oriented learning is suggested as a format that could easily be built into a PBL environment. In this arrangement, it is proposed that students work in teams to solve real-life problems set by faculty or organizations outside the institution.
3. Developing computer-supported PBL environments.
4. Adopting new forms of assessment, e.g. portfolios and peer assessment, (Moust et al. 2005, p. 678).

1.6 Project Work

According to Hanney and Savin-Baden, for many years there has been a sharp division in the UK between project-based learning and problem-based learning, with the former adopting a more technical rationalist perspective than the latter, which adopts a more Socratic and dialogical approach (Hanney and Savin-Baden 2013, p. 7). However, project work has a long tradition within different parts of the educational system, ranging from (a) an early period, where it was used in technical and design-oriented education in order to increase the potential for transferring students' learning to their professional practice, to (b) a reformulation of the concept in the early twentieth century within the tradition of reform pedagogy and the extension of project pedagogy to include elementary school, and to (c) a development of the concept within a critical pedagogical tradition as it was introduced at the reform universities in the 1970s. Today, the three different varieties of project work are still in use, exerting varying influence in different parts of the educational system.

According to Apel and Knoll (2001), the pedagogical tradition of project work goes back to the schools of architecture in France and Italy in the sixteenth century. In the eighteenth century, project work spread to the area of engineering. Project work was then considered a pedagogical answer to the demand for functional harmony between educational programmes and the qualification requirements of working life. Project work offered the opportunity to establish close interaction between theory and practice in the learning of design and construction. The ideas of project work were transferred from Europe to the United States at the end of the nineteenth century by e.g. Woodward, dean of the Polytechnic Institute in St. Louis. Woodward was also inspired by a similar teaching approach developed in Russia. Once the Russian students had been through a series of technical exercises, they were allowed to develop technical projects individually or in groups (Apel and Knoll 2001, p. 24).

At the beginning of the twentieth century, proponents of reform pedagogy took inspiration from the pedagogical tradition of project work in their efforts to change existing pedagogical practices towards more child-centred modes of teaching. The life and experiences of the child would be the criteria for choosing learning content and teaching methods, and the formation of the child's personality would be at centre stage in the classroom as well as defining the goals of teaching. Within this tradition, learning was perceived as an active process based on the child's own experiences, interests and initiatives. Educational programmes should be characterized by democratic ideas about participation.

The impetus of reform pedagogy mainly emanated from the philosopher John Dewey's educational writings. Kilpatrick, his colleague at Teachers College, Columbia University, published a treatise on project method in 1918. His concept of project work focused on giving pupils the possibility of 'working heartily with deliberate intentions' rather than on the manufacturing of concrete products as part of a functional qualification process (Apel and Knoll 2001, p. 31). Kilpatrick envisioned different types of project goals: to produce something, to solve problems, to learn by heart, and to listen to music. According to Kilpatrick, project work would consist of four phases: formulation of the idea, planning, implementation and evaluation. All phases should be carried out by the pupils. He emphasized radical pupil-centred approaches more than didactical ways of thinking (Apel and Knoll 2001, p. 33).

Dewey mainly concentrated on the concept of 'inquiry-based learning', and did not present a comprehensive theory of project work. However, he set out four requirements for project work that emphasize the overall programme of the reform-pedagogical tradition:

- Projects should relate to students' needs and experiences,
- Projects should represent something valuable in life,
- Projects should not only involve manual skills, they should convey spiritual knowledge as well,

- Projects should possess continuity, i.e. projects should have a certain duration and the learning of the pupils should be continued in their next projects, with the aim of continuously expanding their horizon of experience (Apel and Knoll 2001, p. 38).

The method of project work also inspired proponents of reform pedagogy in Germany, France, and Russia, but often in a version that was more explicitly oriented toward action as in the concept of 'work pedagogy' (Kerchensteiner, Makarenko, etc.) (Tippelt and Amorós 2003, p. 12).

The intention of project work within the tradition of reform pedagogy primarily was to bring classroom activities closer to the experiences of the children on the basis of their natural development, aiming at personal growth and education for democracy. As project work was transferred to the universities in the 1970s, faculty members and students transformed the concept in a critical pedagogical direction. Now project work would aim at equality and social justice in society.

1.7 Comparison of the Concepts of PPL and PBL

It becomes evident when we compare the concept of 'Problem-based Learning' (PBL) with the concept of 'Problem-oriented, Interdisciplinary and Participant-directed Project Work' (PPL) that they have basic pedagogical ideas in common. Boud's characterization of the central features of problem-based learning applies to both concepts.

The development of the two concepts, however, arises from different social and political contexts and has a completely different history as they were originally developed from very different pedagogical-didactical and learning-theoretical assumptions. The crucial differences between the two concepts concern the questions of who formulates the problem for the participants to work with, and how their study work is progressing. In problem-based learning, the teachers formulate the problem or the problem scenario, and draw up a list of references. The students identify their knowledge and skills with regard to the problem, they work out tentative answers and solutions, and they set their own learning goals in terms of the knowledge and skills that they lack to find answers and solutions. The students also gather and synthesize their knowledge and provide answers or solutions to the problems. In the tradition of problem-based learning, it is the teachers and not the students who discuss what requirements must be formulated with regard to a good problem or problem scenario.

In the tradition of problem-oriented, interdisciplinary and participant-directed project work, it is viewed as crucial that the students formulate the problems of their project work, and that they themselves find literature of precise relevance to the study. This pedagogical model is inspired by models of research work. This means that students study in ways that are very similar to the ways researchers conduct their research projects, although they are supervised by a skilled researcher. This makes the students' problem formulation a very important part of their project work. The students choose a theme and a problem to study, they define and elicit the context of the chosen problem, and they argue for the relevance of the problem with regard to the formal requirements of their study programme and to similar scientific studies in a chosen field. Furthermore, the university requires that the students argue for the social relevance of their projects, and that the students choose and explain the epistemological, theoretical and methodological basis for their selected analytical models and literature (see also Chap. 8).

As emphasized above, academic requirements and quality standards derived from research projects have a high priority in project work at Roskilde University. Such requirements are also present in the PBL tradition. In many subjects, however, such as medicine, economics, and engineering, emphasis has been placed on establishing teaching methods which both support the motivation of the students and also facilitate a possible transfer from the study context to the professional work context (for a further presentation of differences between PBL, Project Work and Inquiry Based Learning, see Savery 2006).

Roskilde University easily recognizes some of the problems that Moust et al. disclose in relation to the problem-based learning at Maastricht University. The problem-oriented, interdisciplinary and participant-directed project work is also challenged in terms of the students' instrumental orientations, faculty members' preoccupation with their own academic disciplines and decreasing resources for education and teaching. We shall elaborate more on these challenges in the next chapter.

References

Andersen, A. S., Andersen, V., & Gleerup, J. (2007). *Modernisering og læring i staten* [Modernization and learning in the state]. Frederiksberg: Roskilde University Press.
Apel, H. J., & Knoll, M. (2001). *Aus Projekten Lernen* [Learning through projects]. Munich: Oldenburg Schulbuchverlag.
English, M. C., & Kitsantas, A. (2013). Supporting student self-regulated learning in problem- and project-based learning. *Interdisciplinary Journal of Problem-Based Learning, 7*(2), 128–158. Retrieved May 20, 2014, from http://ds.doi.org/10.7771/1541-5015.1339
Fenwick, T. J. (2000). Expanding conceptions of experiential learning: A review of the five contemporary perspectives on cognition. *Adult Education Quarterly, 50*(4), 243–272.
Gijselaers, W. H. (1995). Perspectives on problem-based learning. In W. H. Gijselaers, D. T. Tempelaar, P. K. Keizer, J. M. Blommaert, E. M. Bernard, & H. Kasper (Eds.), *Educational innovation in economics and business administration – the case of problem-based learning* (pp. 39–52). Dordrecht/Boston/London: Kluwer.
Gijselaers, W. H. (1996). Connecting problem-based practices with educational theory. In L. Wilkerson & W. H. Gijselaers (Eds.), *New directions for teaching and learning, no. 68* (pp. 13–21). San Francisco: Jossey-Bass.
Hanney, R., & Savin-Baden, M. (2013). The problem of projects: Understanding the theoretical underpinnings of project-led PBL. *London Review of Education, 11*(1), 7–19. Retrieved November 1, 2013, from http://dx.doi.org/10.1080/14748460.2012.761816.
Hansen, E. (1997). *En koral i tidens strøm. RUC 1972–1997* [A coral in the flow of time. RUC 1972–1997]. Frederiksberg: Roskilde University Press.
Hmelo-Silver, C. E. (2004). Problem-based learning: What and how do students learn? *Educational Psychology Review, 16*(3), 235–266.
Illeris, K. (1974). *Problemorientering og deltagerstyring. Oplæg til en alternativ didaktik. Arbejdstekster til Psykologi og Pædagogik* [Problem orientation and participatory learning. A

proposal for alternative didactics. Working texts for psychology and pedagogics]. Copenhagen: Munksgaard.

Illeris, K. (1981). *Modkvalificeringens pædagogik* [The pedagogy of counter-qualifications]. Unge Pædagogers skriftserie nr. B 28 [Young Educators' Publications No. B 28]. Copenhagen: Unge Pædagoger.

Illeris, K. (2013). *Transformativ læring og identitet* [Transformative learning and identity]. Copenhagen: Samfundslitteratur.

Moust, J. H. C., van Berkel, H. J. M., & Schmidt, H. G. (2005). Signs of erosion: Reflections on three decades of problem-based learning at Maastricht University. *Higher Education, 50*(4), 665–683.

Olesen, H. S. (1972). Politisering eller strømlinet modernisering – Om basisuddannelse og Humaniora [Politicization or streamlined modernization – basic education and the humanities]. In H. S. Olesen (Ed.), *Humaniora pensioneret af kapitalen* [Humanities pensioned off by capital]. Copenhagen: Danish Students Federation.

Olesen, H. S. (1999). RUC – a lucky punch. In J. H. Jensen & H. S. Olesen (Eds.), *Project studies – a late modern university reform?* Frederiksberg: Roskilde University Press.

Planlægningsrådet (Planning Council for Higher Education). (1972). *De højere uddannelsers indre struktur – Et Debatoplæg* [The internal structure of higher education – a discussion paper]. Report of 4 July 1972 by a working group under the Planning Council for Higher Education.

Savery, J. R. (2006). Overview of problem-based learning: Definitions and distinctions interdisciplinary. *Journal of Problem-Based Learning, 1*(1), 9–20. Retrieved May 20, 2014, from http://ds.doi.org/10.7771/1541-5015.1002.

Savin-Baden, M. (2000). *Problem-based learning in higher education: Untold stories.* Buckingham: SRHE and Open University Press.

Tippelt, R., & Amorós, M. A. (2003). Training and work – Tradition and activity focused teaching. In *Beiträge aus der Praxis der beruflichen Bildung* [Practice reports on vocational training], No. 6. Mannheim: InWEnt – Capacity Building International.

Wenger, E. (1998). *Communities of practice – learning, meaning and identity.* Cambridge: Cambridge University Press.

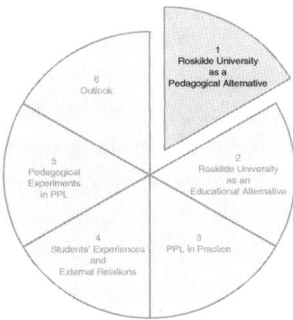

Chapter 2
A Critical Review of the Key Concepts in PPL

Anders Siig Andersen and Tinne Hoff Kjeldsen

2.1 Introduction

The educational philosophy of the Roskilde Model is based on the core concepts of problem-oriented, interdisciplinary, and participant-directed project work (PPL). Associated concepts are 'group work', 'the principle of exemplarity', and 'social relevance'. The concepts function in a social and historical reality and as such change over time. The university has adhered to the key concepts, but they have been adjusted and clarified in response to internal and external challenges. This chapter discusses the different factors that have challenged the conception of the principles and the pedagogical practices connected with the concepts. Here the international theoretical pedagogical debate will be taken into account. The chapter is based on the idea that a continued development of the conceptual understanding of the learning potentials of the Roskilde Model requires that critical factors for development as well as erosion trends are recognized as constituting the point of departure for further theoretical and practical refinement. In a strategic context, the educational philosophy and practices of the Roskilde Model are viewed as key competitive advantages in terms of attracting new students and faculty members. At the same time, they are expressions of an important aspect of the overarching pedagogical and academic identity of faculty members

A.S. Andersen (✉) • T.H. Kjeldsen
Roskilde University, Roskilde, Denmark
e-mail: siig@ruc.dk; thk@ruc.dk

and students. The concepts have been interpreted in different ways, and have been subject to some controversy at the university. Changes and adjustments have been made in the pedagogical practice due to changes in the student population, government requirements, and the faculty members' work situation. The changes have resulted in shifts and transformations in the understanding of the pedagogical principles. In this chapter, we will outline some of the conceptual discussions that have taken place by treating each of the concepts separately. At the same time, we will identify a number of areas where further conceptual development is required.

2.2 Interdisciplinarity

According to Szostak (2007, p. 6), scientific disciplines are characterized by: (a) a set of phenomena that are the focus of study, (b) one or a few key theories, (c) one or a few key methods, and (d) the 'rules of the game' governing hiring, promotion and publication. Various disciplines are organized within academic departments, and university degrees are often aligned with the disciplines. The departments and the degrees are examples of boundaries used to organize academic behaviour that always involve issues of coordination, power, and control (Holley 2009, p. 333). In Denmark in the early 1970s there was a desire to adopt an interdisciplinary approach at the new universities, and it was consequently implemented at the universities in Roskilde and Aalborg. This may be understood in the light of criticism that since the 1960s had been directed at the development of specialized disciplines at the older universities (see also Chap. 4). Politicians formulated their criticism on the basis of social criteria, researchers formulated their criticism referring to internal scientific criteria, educational planners and administrators put forward arguments concerning the effectiveness of the study programmes, and critical educators pointed out problems associated with the disciplines regarding the role of science and academics in society. In the following, we shall consider in more detail the different forms of criticism.

Politicians argued that interdisciplinary education and research was a necessary solution to pressing social, economic and cultural requirements. They believed that the structure of society and social issues are complex, and that they must be matched with interdisciplinary approaches that will shed light on the issues, and with academic staff qualified to solve the complex problems. The politicians demanded a higher proportion of applied research, which in many instances would require interdisciplinary approaches. Scientists argued that adhering to the disciplines might impede scientific progress. They emphasized that continued research in the traditional disciplines would only lead to the refinement of established theoretical and methodological knowledge, and that complex knowledge problems would be overlooked (Enevoldsen 2012, p. 34). Educational planners and administrators argued that interdisciplinary studies would allow students to change subjects without extending study time, that a deferred choice of study programmes would enable students to make more informed choices of programmes, and that interdisciplinary studies would qualify students to be more flexible with regard to changes in the job market situation (Enevoldsen 2012, p. 34). From the point of view of critical pedagogy, the main arguments against the disciplines were that they favoured certain types of knowledge, that they cemented power interests, that they created asymmetrical power relations between teachers and students, and that they avoided critical discussions of science in public spaces. Such characteristics contrast with the overall ideas of critical pedagogy, including "the intention to foster public spaces, in which learning within schools and higher education is not artificially separated from society, but rather engages with the broader society in a creative and transformative dialectic" (McArthur 2010, p. 302). Within critical pedagogy, this is seen as part of a broader project of democratic transformation in society and of providing students with the knowledge and skills necessary to think and act in critical ways.

In recent years the concept of interdisciplinarity has continued to evolve. Today, distinctions are often made between three and five forms of interdisciplinarity. In the following, three of them are described, i.e. 'multidisciplinarity', 'crossdisciplinarity' and 'transdisciplinarity'. Together, they cover the full range of the conceptual spectrum. The authors of this book use the concept of crossdisciplinarity in a very similar way to other researchers' use of the concept of interdisciplinarity (Enevoldsen 2012). Interdisciplinarity, however, in the present context will be used as an overarching concept, covering multidisciplinarity, crossdisciplinarity, and transdisciplinarity. Hence, we cannot use it as a sub-concept.

Multidisciplinarity features an additive approach to the disciplines (Holley 2009, p. 333). In a multidisciplinary approach, the collaborating researchers draw on knowledge, theories and methods from different disciplines, without altering the approach of their individual disciplines. The researchers each contribute with their own disciplinary traditions. The goal of multidisciplinarity is to facilitate a multi-perspective view on research projects. This may be a crucial point for scientific collaboration, as the researchers are trained in the mutual understanding of their different academic 'homelands' (Jensen 2012, p. 65f.). Furthermore, the goal is to raise awareness and insights across disciplines in order to counteract the negative effects of specialization (Jensen 2012, p. 61).

Crossdisciplinarity develops research on the same issues in real collaboration and mutual influence across the disciplines (Enevoldsen 2012, p. 32). To create holistic knowledge, issues and problems are addressed from many disciplinary perspectives, as theories developed within one discipline affect theories in other disciplines, or as methods developed within one discipline affect the methods of other disciplines. The purpose of crossdisciplinarity is "to integrate knowledge or modes of thinking in two or more disciplines or established areas of expertise to produce a cognitive advancement" (Holley 2009, p. 333). Through crossdisciplinarity, researchers from different disciplines create a common academic undertaking, and adopt relevant theories and methods from each other, while still retaining their disciplinary independence within the collaboration.

The concept of *transdisciplinarity* has many features in common with the definition formulated by Illeris regarding the relationship between problem-oriented and interdisciplinary approaches, i.e. that the disciplines needed to explain a problem should work together, subordinating their scientific axioms, theories and methods to the common research enterprise (see Chap. 1). Efforts have been made to differentiate the content and meaning of the concept of transdisciplinarity:

1. Transdisciplinary approaches may *supplement the disciplinary approaches* to the study of a research field, or they may be gradually converted into mono-disciplinary fields, as for instance in disciplines and subjects such as Biochemistry, Mathematical Economics, Cultural Studies, and Health Sciences. These examples represent successful efforts to integrate disciplines in order to create new specialized disciplines in the intersection of two existing disciplines (Jensen 2012, p. 61).
2. Transdisciplinary approaches may prove useful in *the study of social problems* as the contributions from single disciplines could be viewed as insufficient to grasp the social complexity. In this instance, the integration of disciplines is determined by the practical research problem, and transdisciplinarity is seen as the adequate answer to the need for scientific problem solving (Jensen 2012, p. 61).
3. Transdisciplinary approaches may be practice-oriented and involve external participants, stakeholders and people who are affected by the issues being investigated. This kind of research is defined as *Mode 2*. Mode 2 research is characterized by focusing on problems as they arise outside an academic context, by including external parties as producers of knowledge, and by knowledge being produced in the context of use. Mode 2 research exceeds the disciplinary boundaries as well as the academic standards (Enevoldsen 2012, pp. 39ff.). The ideal of Mode 2 research is to produce knowledge that is socially robust (Holm et al. 2012, p. 110). Problems are formulated in dialogue with the stakeholders, researchers and stakeholders use a range of heterogeneous skills and expertise to produce knowledge, and they develop research projects in the interaction between science and application.
4. Transdisciplinary approaches may aim at helping non-scientific local participants to change their situation, and give them the power to control their own lives (Enevoldsen 2012, p. 41). This type of research is termed *action research*. Within the tradition of action research, it is sometimes the local participants – citizens or workers – who formulate the problems to be solved and who include researchers in their problem solving. Researchers may support the local participants in formulating their needs for research and by providing expert assistance for developing solutions, keeping in mind that the local actors 'own their projects' (Enevoldsen 2012, p. 43).

The question of what kind of interdisciplinarity is implemented in a given academic context depends on the history and the development of the research traditions and academic cultures. Jensen (2012, pp. 66f.) distinguishes between five academic cultures at Roskilde University. In the following, we shall introduce the five academic cultures as a starting point for describing their relation to the various types of interdisciplinarity:

1. The *mathematical modelling academic culture* is primarily found in Mathematics and Physics. It may, however, also be present in the academic culture within disciplines such as Chemistry, Computer Science, and Economics. Within this academic culture, it is a prerequisite for interdisciplinarity that researchers have comprehensive knowledge and skills in their academic discipline. Disciplines may be included as support for other disciplines, but they have their own knowledge base which must be acquired. The disciplines may be included in multi- and crossdisciplinary collaboration with other disciplines or in transdisciplinary collaborations to form new subjects by adding specialized disciplines as for example in Mathematical Economics.
2. The *empirical experimental academic culture* is primarily dominant in Chemistry and different academic subjects within the field of Biology, and is also influential in subjects such as Geography and Technological-Societal Planning. This academic culture depends on its scientific theoretical basis, which offers specific criteria for the establishment of hypotheses, the conducting of experiments, and for the verification or falsification of hypotheses. The positivistic paradigm of the natural sciences must be adopted as the basis for collaboration with other disciplines, and researchers must possess basic knowledge and skills for experimental research. The empirical experimental disciplines may be included in multi-disciplinary and cross-disciplinary collaboration. Historically, this academic culture has also made significant contributions to action research, especially in relation to types of action research where experimental scientific knowledge has been crucial to the understanding of environmental and health and safety issues.
3. The *analytical and reflective academic culture* characterizes disciplines in the humanities such as History, Philosophy and Languages. This academic culture is characterized by analytical efforts to focus on cultural products in the form of signs and texts that may be of historical or contemporary nature. The texts are studied in order to increase academic understanding, to provide historical, cultural and philosophical information, and to develop theories and methods. The disciplines may be included in multi- and crossdisciplinary collaboration, and may also contribute to the establishment of new transdisciplinary subjects. At Roskilde University, this has happened through the establishment of academic subjects such as Linguistics & Cultural Encounters, and Public Relations Studies. The disciplines may also serve as elements in Mode 2 and action research projects dealing with the eliciting of cultural phenomena in organizations, or projects that contribute actively to the development of culture. This implies, however, a departure from the original analytical and reflective academic culture.
4. The *analytical academic culture oriented towards social problems* dominates research at Roskilde University, because of the university's ambitions to engage in society and to produce socially relevant research. This academic culture is

dominant in a range of subjects in the social sciences and the humanities. In many instances, these subjects have an interdisciplinary approach, such as in Educational Studies, Health Promotion & Health Strategies Studies, Technological-Societal Planning Studies, and International Development Studies. These subjects aim at analysing contemporary issues in society. Often, the subjects are involved in direct collaboration with interest groups outside the university. The subjects belonging to the problem-oriented analytical academic culture may be engaged in multi-, cross- and transdisciplinary collaboration.
5. The *creative constructive academic culture* is encountered especially in the areas of Communication Studies and Computer Science, and also in the university's new Humanistic-Technological Bachelor Programme (see Chap. 6). However, it is also present in subjects involving constructive work in social intervention and educational design. It is a common feature of the subjects belonging to this academic culture that they put strong emphasis on construction and design while still observing high academic standards. The subjects belonging to the creative constructive academic culture maintain their creative and constructive character when involved in different types of interdisciplinary cooperation.

The presence of different academic cultures means that there are academically legitimate differences in regard to how interdisciplinary approaches are practiced at Roskilde University.

The educational structure at Roskilde University provides another important example of how interdisciplinarity is practiced (see also Chap. 6). The first three semesters of the 3-year bachelor programmes, the so-called basic studies, are designed as broad programmes within the academic fields of the Humanities, the Social Sciences, the Natural Sciences, and the Humanistic-Technological Sciences. The basic studies are characterized by the students' problem-oriented projects in which they make use of different disciplines. The disciplines used in a particular project are determined by the problems the students in the project group have decided to work on. The bachelor and master programmes are designed as double or single degree programmes. In the double degree programmes, studies are organized in a combination of two parallel subjects. Here students are assigned the responsibility of constructing the interdisciplinary understanding between their two fields. In the single degree programmes, studies have an interdisciplinary design. The interdisciplinary organization of the teaching at Roskilde University makes it difficult for researchers to specialize in narrow fields, because their teaching forces them to possess broader knowledge.

At Roskilde University, the idea of interdisciplinarity is challenged by a set of dilemmas that are also visible in Danish research communities and research policy. On the one hand, it is emphasized by a broad political spectrum that real-life problems cannot be limited to a single academic discipline. These problems call for interdisciplinary research and require graduates that are able to draw on knowledge, methods and ways of thinking from different disciplines. In Denmark and in the EU, research funding increasingly is allocated to interdisciplinary strategic research on social, cultural, and environmental challenges, the so-called 'Grand Challenges', and to strategic research concerned with the social conditions of participation in global competition. On the other hand, academic specialization seems to be an embedded norm that persists throughout higher education with respect to research as well as the career opportunities of researchers. The reason is that the assurance of academic quality is connected to formal as well as unwritten rules stating (a) that good science at the universities is produced within the academic disciplines, (b) that high quality research is disseminated in scientific journals, which are aligned with the academic disciplines, and (c) that many academic positions continue to be filled in accordance with the research criteria of the disciplines (Enevoldsen 2012, p. 45). If researchers try to develop new research areas using interdisciplinary approaches they might encounter obstacles in the academic community.

Proponents of critical pedagogy have also developed arguments against interdisciplinary research and education. McArthur, who belongs to a critical pedagogical tradition, has this to say about the positive contributions of the academic disciplines:

> In the face of threats to define the purposes of higher education in very narrow, economic terms, they (the disciplines) offer a higher education that is: authentic (based upon complex and contested knowledge) and inclusive (where the boundaries are permeable and foster public spaces). As such, this higher education offers some chance to minimize the distortions of power and to allow teachers and students to engage in emancipatory pedagogy. (McArthur 2010, p. 312)

McArthur points out that the commercialization of higher education threatens to destroy the academic disciplines by reducing them to subjects that are exclusively offering training for employment-oriented skills. He criticizes the fact that "many reforms in higher education, and particularly the rise of the 'audit' and 'quality' culture, have attacked the integrity of disciplines, and regarded them as troublesome barriers to the desired change" (McArthur 2010, p. 312). In his perspective, the defence of preserving and developing the academic disciplines would be regarded as a defence against neo-liberal tendencies to undermine university autonomy.

Generally speaking, academic disciplines and academic traditions play an increasingly important role in discussions at Roskilde University, although different notions of interdisciplinarity continue to have a prominent position within the academic discourse (Enevoldsen 2012, p. 33 f.). The definition of interdisciplinarity varies with the different academic cultures, and with the constitution of subjects as either mono-disciplinary or interdisciplinary. The composition of the educational profile, however, reveals that interdisciplinary studies are still highly valued at Roskilde University. The interdisciplinary programmes include studies in Education, Environmental Biology, Environmental Risk Management, Technological & Societal Planning, Working Life, Social Science, Psychology, Communication Studies, Linguistics & Cultural Encounters, International Development, Social Entrepreneurship & Management, Social Intervention and Health Promotion & Health Strategies. Traditionally, some of these programmes have been based on disciplines, but have developed in interdisciplinary directions, whereas other programmes from the outset were constituted as transdisciplinary. New interdisciplinary programmes have often been established on the basis of collaboration between researchers from different disciplines, who have come in contact because of the interdisciplinary organization of studies. This explains why the interdisciplinary collaboration within and between the main academic areas has acted as a major driving force for continued educational innovation.

2.3 Problem Orientation

As outlined in Sect. 1.4, Illeris – in his exposition of the theoretical basis for the principle of problem-orientation – took his point of departure in the trinity of personal, study-related, and societal relevance. The criterion of personal relevance should ensure motivation and commitment, the criterion of study-related relevance should ensure that the studies corresponded to the curricula requirements, and the criterion of social relevance should ensure that the studies were oriented towards existing social problems.

The criterion of *study-related relevance* is closely linked to the curricula of the educational programmes (see also Sect. 8.3). The curricula for the elementary parts of the four bachelor programmes at Roskilde University require interdisciplinary studies of selected problems organized as project work (see also Chap. 6). In the subjects that are combined at the bachelor and master levels, the degree of interdisciplinarity typically shows greater variation. This means that the curriculum requirements with respect to the students' choice of problems are differentiated in terms of study level, and that they are heavily dependent on the different academic cultures that provide the research base of the programmes. The criterion of *social relevance* – one of the original main arguments in favour of problem orientation – has been reinterpreted, because it has been difficult to relate subjects in some academic cultures directly to this criterion. The social relevance criterion, in particular in the natural sciences and the humanities, has gradually moved towards an interpretation where the connection between the problems and the outside world passes through the problems of the academic disciplines rather than the other way round. It is characteristic that none of the various interpretations of the original concept of problem orientation have led to a common understanding of how the criterion can be attributed an unambiguous meaning. In spite of this, many of the projects that students carry out still reveal a great interest in social issues (see also Chap. 10). Nowadays, however, the social interest is seldom formulated on the basis of a profound critique of social justice, but rather on the basis of technical, social or human interests in reforms. The criterion of *personal relevance* has been challenged as well. Originally, personal relevance was tied to the students' common critical interest. But that is no longer decisive for the students' choice of problems for their projects. The criterion of personal relevance has shifted towards a concept of personal interests, where it is argued that projects must deal with problems where all participants in the project group share a common interest.

There have been a number of attempts to operationalize how the students should work with their problem formulations. First and foremost, emphasis has moved towards meeting the quality criteria within science itself. To make it possible to document the reality of the problems and to explain why they are important in scientific terms, however, it is still recommended that the students should situate their chosen problems within broader social areas as well as within the relevant scientific areas. These recommendations are viewed as important for helping the readers of project reports to gain an accurate understanding of the students' project ideas and the content of the projects, and also to support the students in keeping the 'main thread' during their project work (Pedersen 2009, p. 33). Furthermore, recommendations emphasize that the problem formulation should not be finalized until the project has been completed, and that there should be an ongoing iterative process between the problem formulation and the students' work on their project (see also Chap. 8). The recommendations highlight the fact that the directional character of the problem formulation only becomes operational through the students' deep understanding of their chosen theory of science, scientific theory and methodology (Pedersen 2009, pp. 37f.). This particular recommendation builds on arguments inspired from professional research practice.

2.4 The Principle of 'Exemplary Learning'

The principle of 'Exemplary Learning' was already at play in the early formulation of the theoretical basis for problem-oriented project work (see Chap. 1). It was acknowledged that project work involves a strong selectivity in the choice of problems, theories and methods, and that there was a need to secure the students' more general learning outcomes.

Illeris pointed out that the principle of exemplary learning is understood differently within different learning paradigms (see Sect. 1.4). He emphasized that the focus of the principle should be on the academic knowledge that students acquire through their participant-directed project work, and that it should be put to use by relating the content of the project work to broader social, political and cultural issues. His concept of exemplary learning was largely inspired by the German sociologist Oskar Negt, who in 1971 published his book 'Sociological Imagination and Exemplary Learning' (Negt 1971), which became very influential in the Danish context. In his book, Negt argues that the examples that the learners choose to study must be related to their experience as well as to the social conditions that influence their experience in decisive ways (Andersen 1996).

In Negt's theory, the educational content has an exemplary value if it both includes and transgresses the immediate interests of the learners. His concept is inspired by Wagenschein (1956), who saw the 'exemplary principle' as a method of reducing curricula without missing important learning outcomes, and who stressed how the principle would support the learners' comprehension of broader contexts. Negt, however, points out that Wagenshein's comprehension of the learning opportunities in the exemplary principle is blocked by two factors:

> Firstly, by a concept of history that is 'limited by the dimension of the past', i.e. a historicist concept primarily viewing history as continuity (without discontinuity, breakage and unrealized opportunities). Secondly, by the traditional division of labour between the sciences. (Nielsen 1997, pp. 285f. [authors' translation])

Furthermore, Negt's theoretical didactical considerations are inspired by Wright Mills' concept of 'sociological imagination'. For Mills, the role of social science is to clarify the public dialogue and to support the spread of democracy, understood as the strengthening of peoples' influence on the decisions that affect them in their everyday life (Mills 2002, p. 192). According to Mills, this implies that social sciences should be characterized by throwing light on the interplay between social conditions, the everyday environments of peoples' lives, and the circumstances of their lives as perceived from their life historical perspectives (Mills 2002, p. 42).

As holistic theories of the dynamics and structures of society have been declining, the ideas about exemplary learning have gradually taken more inspiration from Wagenschein's discipline-oriented understanding of the exemplary principle. To some extent, Roskilde University has returned to Wagenschein's concept, i.e. that exemplary learning is primarily acknowledged as a means of implementing reductions in curricula, without compromising the idea of students gaining insight into important aspects of their chosen subject. Two interpretations of the concept of exemplarity have emerged. One is that problem-oriented project work is considered a solution to the problem of excessive curricula. Here, project work must exemplify the academic discipline. Another interpretation is that exemplary learning should focus on analytical and empirical methods. Thus, it is emphasized that the students – through their project work – acquire methods and academic ways of working that provide them with generally applicable skills.

The principle of exemplary learning may be realized by different pedagogical strategies. Some examples would be to impose demands on the students' project reports to reflect on social, theoretical or methodological issues, to require that the students discuss their projects among themselves taking into consideration a broader scientific or societal framework, or to commit the students to reflection on the relationship between course content and their own project work. Experience shows that exemplary learning is not always realized if the responsibility is left to the students. Research indicates that some projects do not transgress the examination of relatively narrow issues. The reason may be that the principle of exemplary learning is not formulated clearly as a formal requirement for project work, or that the students only reach the point of completing the targeted study of relatively narrow problems (Ulriksen 1997, pp. 82ff.). This suggests that the exemplary principle must be formally ensured, including the curriculum level, and that the university should decide whether the principle of exemplary learning should involve social issues (Illeris), the link between everyday life, life history and society (Wright Mills and Negt), and/or scientific theories and methods (Wagenschein).

In this context, a renewed discussion of the principle of exemplary learning is called for. This discussion may draw inspiration from the theoretical work of Wolfgang Klafki. Klafki indicates that the principle of exemplary learning was discussed and sought promoted at German schools in the 1950s and 1960s, but faded into oblivion in the early 1970s (Klafki 2001, p. 173). He points out that the principle of exemplary learning was already mentioned as a curricular selection criterion in antiquity. He also shows that Comenius, Kant and Husserl presented theories on the function of examples with respect to the formation of recognition, moral consciousness, and aesthetic judgment (Klafki 2001, p. 175) Furthermore, Klafki states that Negt's theory of sociological imagination and exemplary learning is of great importance for critical education in school-based curricula.

Klafki argues that the principle of exemplary learning should aim at self-formation (Bildung) as well as at the development of scientific and work-related knowledge. He formulates the formative aspect of the principle of exemplary learning thus: "Formative learning (…) is not achieved through the learners' reproductive acquisition of the largest possible amount of individual knowledge, abilities and skills, but rather by the learners taking their departure in a number of selected examples progressing to (…) more or less far-reaching universal knowledge, skills and attitudes, or in other words, essential, structural, conceptual, typical and extensive statutory contexts" (Klafki 2001, p. 176, [authors' translation]). Klafki points out that learners should gain insight into dimensions of their social, cultural and political reality, and the possibility of understanding and acting on this reality by progressing from specific to general matters (Klafki 2001, pp. 176f.). Klafki argues that exemplary teaching with a formative perspective should clarify the historical roots of the issues under study, and that it should emphasize a focus on underlying interest and points of view (Klafki 2001, p. 188).

As a key question Klafki raises the issue: What criteria should define the structures, laws, principles and contexts if the goal is to support learners' understanding through their exemplary learning? He defines the criteria as follows: "In the end, one can only define these criteria by continuously arriving at a new consensus regarding the insights, skills and attitudes that may contribute in developing the abilities of young people to self-determination and solidarity" (Klafki 2001, p. 186 [authors' translation]). Klafki suggests that one should search for 'key issues' which link peoples' individual and social existence to contexts that are important for their present and future opportunities (Klafki 2001, p. 187). In particular, he points to issues such as peace, the environment, the interaction between generations, the opportunities and dangers of economic and technological development, the social, political and cultural opportunities of individuals and small social groups, the system of organizations and bureaucracies, working life and unemployment, social inequality, economic and social power relations, the relations between majorities and minorities, gender roles, women's rights in developed and developing countries, competition between different faiths and communities of faith, health and disease, as well as the mass media and their effects (Klafki 2001, pp. 187f.).

Klafki, however, points out that the principle of exemplary learning has relevance not only with respect to the social, political and cultural formation of human beings. He stresses that the principle is also highly relevant in regard to the acquisition of specific content, taking into account that different areas of knowledge and action possess different criteria for the construction of relations between exemplars and general knowledge. All in all, Klafki's considerations point towards a balanced view of the principle of exemplary learning, referring to different academic traditions and cultures, and at the same time balancing the purposes of scientific learning, self-formation and peoples' ability to think and act critically (for a discussion of the generalization and contextualization of knowledge with regard to PBL see Gijselaers 1996, p. 19).

2.5 Participant-Directed Learning

Participant-directed learning is a key constituent of the student-centred educational philosophy at Roskilde University, and it implies meeting demands for more democratic forms of studying. Originally, Roskilde University justified the concept by anchoring it in the need for a shared orientation and a mutual responsibility among students and faculty members. When the university was established in 1972, there were no examinations, only internal evaluations. Faculty members and students would formulate constructive criticisms in the evaluations with respect to the product of the project work as well as the work process. The students would make sure that their projects dealt with something that mattered to them; thus they safeguarded the personal aspect. The faculty members safeguarded the social aspect, making sure that the projects were anchored in deep insights as to the relevance of the projects for society.

Because the students and teachers no longer share interests and justifications to the same extent as before, the concept of participant-directed learning has changed. According to Ulriksen (1997, p. 74) the concept of participant-directed learning has changed meaning from being a shared issue to being a two-sided construction, where the students choose projects according to their own interests, while the teachers make sure that the projects satisfy the institutional requirements. The main justification for participant-directed learning gradually has been changed in the direction of motivating a new type of student, who is driven by the desire to learn and is striving for subjective meaning and self-realization through his or her studies (Ulriksen 1997, p. 74).

Participant-directed learning is still an ideal in regard to problem-oriented project work, but developments at the university have created a number of contradictions:

- Contradictions between the needs and interests of supervisors and students: the supervisors want to feel competent in supervising the students to completion of their projects. This may be in contrast to the students' perceptions of participant-directed learning.
- Contradictions between the supervisory function and the obligation of the supervisors to control the result of the students' project work: the function of the supervisor requires that he or she acts in solidarity with the students' project work. However, for examinations the supervisors assume a different role. Representing the educational system, they have to assess the performance of the individual student measured in terms of the formal learning outcome that is prescribed for each study programme. This creates dilemmas in relation to the principle of participant-directed learning, for both students and supervisors. The students may feel doubtful about whether or not the supervisors primarily are engaged in measuring how projects meet the set of outcomes, i.e. uncertain about the supervisors acting in solidarity with the students' project goals. The supervisors might feel caught in the dilemma of whether to focus on students' learning processes or to assume responsibility for ensuring that students are doing well in examinations by concentrating on the outcome of the project work.

- Contradictions between the students' needs and interests and the curriculum requirements: the curriculum-related provisions concerning learning outcomes can be experienced as constricting frameworks in regard to students' personal study interests.

These contradictions are discussed only to a limited degree among supervisors and students at Roskilde University. This creates a risk that students' influence on their project work becomes less prominent.

Regarding course work, the student-centred pedagogical philosophy at Roskilde University is not implemented to the same extent as in project work. Especially in the basic part of the bachelor programmes, many courses provide academic overviews, and faculty members lecture to large audiences. The University has chosen this pedagogical form as a means of giving greater priority to resources for project supervision.

There would seem to be a need for revitalizing the arguments for participatory pedagogy. Cath Lambert tries to do exactly that in an article from 2009. Lambert is a sociology lecturer and researcher working at the Retention Centre for Undergraduate Research, a collaborative 'Centre for Excellence in Teaching and Learning' in the UK. I 2009, 74 centres of excellence were funded by the Higher Education Funding Council in England. The purpose of these centres was to promote 'Excellence' across all subjects and aspects of teaching and learning in higher education (Lambert 2009, p. 306). In an attempt to redress the historical bias towards research, the centres are illustrative of a shift in higher educational policy making towards improving and gaining more recognition for teaching and learning (Lambert 2009, p. 296).

Lambert's point of departure is a critique of the neo-liberal discourse of education. The neo-liberal discourse claims that there is a demand for life-long learners, who are flexible problem solvers, and who can select, organize and use information appropriately in new situations (see also Chap. 4). The goal is to produce self-sufficient, independent and creative thinkers. In Lambert's words: "Not only do contemporary universities have a significant role to play in the production of a skilled workforce, but they are also a key site for the production of the 'ideal' neo-liberal subject: a self-regulating, motivated, flexible worker who participates in the (educational, social and economic) opportunities provided" (Lambert 2009, p. 297). In a broader sense the neo-liberal goal of the educational system is to build a dynamic knowledge-based economy (Lambert 2009, p. 297).

Lambert views the practice of participatory pedagogies as a form of critique that may challenge the hegemony of key tenets of the neo-liberal discourse, especially "the logic of education as a commodity of service" (Lambert 2009, p. 303). She sets out to explore the possibility that a focus on the resources offered by students' intellectual participation in higher education, combined with a necessary reconfiguration of the teaching relationship provides a more hopeful basis from which to critically and productively intervene in the question of what the university is and does, and what we want it to be and do (Lambert 2009, p. 296). Lambert's idea is to "reinvigorate the idea of participation in such a way that it makes sense of the everyday, embodied activities of student researchers, and captures the social and political importance of both intellectual and participatory practice" (Lambert 2009, p. 296). She stresses, however, that this should be done without succumbing to a narrative of emancipation. She supports her argument by quoting Bill Readings: "Being smart in the present situation requires another kind of thinking altogether, one that does not seek to lend work in the University a unified ideological function." (Lambert 2009, p. 305). Lambert argues that this kind of thinking involves resisting grand narratives and instead working with/in the multiple and often contradictory discourses and circumstances which characterize the university landscape. She mentions different approaches to participatory pedagogics that are applied in higher education: 'research-', 'enquiry-' and 'problem-based' learning, and argues that it is common to these approaches that they accentuate an explicit commitment to the idea that students should be producers of knowledge and not only consumers.

Lambert's deliberations call for a renewal of the arguments for student-directed projects and student-centred learning that aligns with the critical pedagogical arguments, but also formulates the need for student-orientation in the light of the contemporary situation in higher education. In a way, her arguments revive Humboldt's ideas of what a university should be (see Sect. 4.2), but against a very modern background and with a pointed critique, on the one hand, of the kind of consumerism that is supported by neo-liberalism, and, on the other hand, of the instrumental consequences of aligning university studies with short-sighted demands for qualifications and competences. From day one, now as before, students at Roskilde University are working in student-centred and research-like ways. Accepting Lambert's view, one could argue that this is still an idea worth fighting for.

2.6 Project Work

Problem-oriented, interdisciplinary and participant-directed project work was introduced in Denmark at the new university centres, in 1972 at Roskilde and in 1974 at Aalborg. The educational planners put emphasis on the particular innovative potential that project work holds in relation to the development of both science and academic qualification (see also Chap. 5). Through the dissemination and use of project work in various educational institutions and settings, the concept now covers a wide variety of educational approaches. Yet at Roskilde University project work is not only considered as one way of teaching among many. Instead, both the entire educational planning and the educational structure of the university are based on project work.

As mentioned above, a project at Roskilde University is a fixed-term activity lasting one semester. The project work is carried out in groups of two to eight students who decide on the course of the project and its final output, and it is guided by a supervisor who is a faculty member. In the course of the project, participants draw on various disciplines and methods in order to achieve their goals. Over time, student activity revolves around a complex series of interactions among the team members, just as it draws on a range of transferable skills such as communication and planning. By engaging in the projects, students work with theory and scientific methods. This means that theory and method are employed as means of working towards one objective. At the same time, theory and method are placed in a context where they have a purpose beyond mechanical acquisition (Simonsen and Ulriksen 1998, p. 137, see also Hanney and Savin-Baden 2013, p. 8).

At Roskilde University, all parties agree that project work should be carried out primarily in project groups. One important reason is that group work supports collaborative learning processes appropriate for creating more advanced knowledge than most individuals are able to create by themselves. Furthermore, participants in group processes learn from each other, and by extension also learn how to work in group settings. The group organization of project work has been challenged by the fact that an increasing number of projects have been conducted by individuals, especially at graduate level. However, as of 2012, the university requires all project work to be carried out in groups. If students do not have the opportunity to work in a group, they are asked to produce arguments strong enough to convince the members of the study boards to make exemptions from the rule. The logic of this not entirely uncontroversial decision is that the learning outcome of the educational programmes can be realized only on the basis of extensive experience of group project work.

Over the years, different types of projects have developed at the University that meet the requirements of different academic cultures. Most of the projects are modelled on the format of the academic dissertation (see also Chap. 10). Other projects focus on the dissemination, planning and design of products. Special needs for more design- and product-oriented studies have made it necessary for project work in some subjects and some semesters to be toned down in favour of pedagogical models with course work and workshops that include relatively long and intensive periods of designing and producing.

During their bachelor and master studies, students complete a total of nine projects and a master thesis. Some students have called for a reduction in the number of projects, because of what they call 'project fatigue'. This wish has led to the upcoming introduction of a so-called project-free semester at the graduate level. In the graduate study programmes, however, project work will continue to constitute half of the students' study time, because the master thesis covers a full semester's work.

Recently, the question has been raised as to whether students at Roskilde University succeed in acquiring a sufficient range of project-related skills that are also applicable in the labour market. This is an important question, because labour market demands for project skills are significant for justifying the use of project work at the university. Research indicates that employers are looking for the following work-related project competencies:

- Knowledge of how projects are dependent on internal and external contexts, rationales, resources, structures, systems, and cultures of companies and organizations,
- Knowledge of the various forms of project management that are used within companies and organizations, i.e. project management as linear, complex, circular, chaotic, etc., and the ability to critically reflect on strengths and weaknesses of different forms of project management,

- Knowledge of various tools that are designed to optimize project work as part of professional working practices, and which are included in the common language of business and organizational contexts and in the expectations for project skills,
- Knowledge of the expectations in companies and organizations with regard to personal skills of communication, collaboration, conflict resolution, creativity and innovation, balancing the relation between context and self, and management of the self,

(Andersen 2013; see also Saynish 2010, and Kapsali 2011).

It would probably be useful for university graduates in transferring their experiences from project work in their studies to project work in the labour market to be aware of such requirements and to be able to 'translate' and 'transform' their explicit and tacit knowledge from project work in a university context to the application of project work in other contexts. At the same time, some of the tools that have been developed in a professional context in order to optimize the different aspects of project work would probably help to enhance the quality of project work at the university. However, there is reason for cautioning against uncritically importing business perceptions of project management into university studies. Hanney and Savin-Baden express it in the following way:

> The common 'techno-rationalist' conception of project management such as: 'a purely technical process of implementing a time-limited undertaking that seeks to minimize uncertainty and maximize predictability' may lead to a reification of the abstract object of project management (tools, processes and strategies) (…). This then results in the project being subsumed by an ideology of control dampening the possibilities of creativity. (Hanney and Savin-Baden 2013, p. 9)

2.7 Key Challenges

Faculty members at Roskilde University are currently challenging the conceptual understanding and practice of problem-oriented, interdisciplinary and participant-directed project work. Also broader social trends challenge the Roskilde approach. We may point out the following fields of tension:

- Conservatism regarding single academic subjects – 'I only want to teach my own academic subject based on my own research' – this may be seen as a critical voice against politically defined strategic research and the adaptation of academic educational programmes to specialized labour market demands. Furthermore, it may be seen as a means to meet academic publishing requirements that many believe can be best achieved through publishing in journals that align with the academic disciplines. The conservatism of the academic subjects is easy to comprehend, but it represents a challenge to the concept of problem-oriented and interdisciplinary project work.
- Politicians and business managers are clearly in favour of interdisciplinary project work at the universities. However, by emphasizing that study programmes

should be directed towards the immediate needs of society and the labour market, they provide little space for the students' sometimes critical search processes.
- The national accreditation institution of Denmark often draws on representatives from the single academic subjects, when panels are composed to assess interdisciplinary study programmes at the universities (see also Chap. 4). This puts pressure on the universities that may be tempted to develop standardized solutions for all universities, which will counteract interdisciplinarity, especially in those programmes that bridge the main academic fields.
- Students have different needs and requirements. Some students embrace problem-oriented, interdisciplinary and student-directed project work. Other students have chosen studies at Roskilde University but discover that they prefer teacher-directed single-subject programmes with more instrumental descriptions of the learning outcome.

These tension fields emphasize the necessity of an ongoing reflection of the rationales and conceptual understandings of problem-oriented, interdisciplinary and participant-directed project work. There is a need to reflect, refine, and explicate the following relationships: (1) between disciplinarity and interdisciplinarity, (2) between the understandings and practices of interdisciplinarity within different academic cultures at the university, (3) between the employment-related and the academic skills, which in many ways are interdependent, but which none the less represent a dual demand that challenges project work, and (4) between academic skills, employability and academic freedom, as there is a need to maintain an 'arm's length principle' in relation to external stakeholders, both with regard to studies and to research activities.

The latter tension points to a need for Roskilde University to reformulate 'social relevance' as an important aspect of the concept of problem-oriented, interdisciplinary and participant-directed project work. The concept was originally born with visions of social relevance and skills to analyse scientific as well as social development in critical and constructive ways. Such skills cover ideals of polytechnical knowledge, knowledge of social dynamics, interests and power relations and personal skills to participate in democratic processes. Presently, these types of skills are often associated with efforts to maintain and develop democracy and active citizenship as well as the many facets of sustainability, i.e. economic, technological, ecological, political, cultural, and identity-oriented sustainability.

As mentioned, interdisciplinary project work increasingly has become subject to multilateral pressures from proponents of the single disciplines, the governance mechanisms of power and economy and groups of students and faculty members who support disciplinary and teacher-directed forms of learning. The challenge is how the university can preserve and revitalize the problem-oriented, interdisciplinary and participant-directed project work by organizing the studies at the crossroads of high academic standards, dynamic vocational qualifications, issues regarding personal formation, and the need to develop sustainable social solutions.

References

Andersen, A. S. (1996). *Tolkning og erfaring* [Interpretation and experience] (Publication No. 40 from the Adult Education Research Group). Roskilde: Roskilde University.

Andersen, A. S. (2013). Projektarbejdets kompetenceprofil mellem videnskab og profession [The competence profile of project work – between science and profession]. *Spor – et tidsskrift om Universitetspædagogik [Tracks – a Journal on University Teaching], 1*. Retrieved November 3, 2013, from http://ojs.ruc.dk/index.php/spor/article/view/2531.

Enevoldsen, T. (2012). Tværfaglighed – rødder og typer [Interdisciplinarity – its roots and types]. In T. Enevoldsen & E. Jelsøe (Eds.), *Tværvidenskab i teori og praksis* [Crossdisciplinarity in theory and practice] (pp. 19–49). Copenhagen: Hans Reitzels Forlag.

Gijselaers, W. H. (1996). Connecting problem-based practices with educational theory. In L. Wilkerson & W. H. Gijselaers (Eds.), *New directions for teaching and learning, no. 68* (pp. 13–21). San Francisco: Jossey-Bass.

Hanney, R., & Savin-Baden, M. (2013). The problem of projects: Understanding the theoretical underpinnings of project-led PBL. *London Review of Education, 11*(1), 7–19. Retrieved November 3, 2013, from http://dx.doi.org/10.1080/14748460.2012.761816.

Holley, K. A. (2009). Interdisciplinary strategies as transformative change in higher education. *Innovative Higher Education, 34*(5), 331–344. Retrieved May 20, 2014, from http://10.1007s10755-009-9121-4.

Holm, J., Søndergård, B., & Hansen, O. E. (2012). Omstilling af komplekse teknologisystemer [Adaptation of complex technological systems]. In T. Enevoldsen & E. Jelsøe (Eds.), *Tværvidenskab i teori og praksis* [Crossdisciplinarity in theory and practice] (pp. 91–112). Copenhagen: Hans Reitzels Forlag.

Jensen, J. H. (2012). På tværs af videnskaberne [Across sciences]. In T. Enevoldsen & E. Jelsøe (Eds.), *Tværvidenskab i teori og praksis* [Crossdisciplinarity in theory and practice] (pp. 50–72) Copenhagen: Hans Reitzels Forlag.

Kapsali, M. (2011). Systems thinking in innovation project management: A match that works. *International Journal of Project Management, 29*, 396–407.

Klafki, W. (2001). *Dannelsesteori og didaktik – nye studier* [Formation theory and didactics – new studies]. Århus: Forlaget Klim.

Lambert, C. (2009). Pedagogies of participation in higher education: A case for research based learning. *Pedagogy, Culture & Society, 17*(3), 295–309.

McArthur, J. (2010). Time to look anew: Critical pedagogy and disciplines within higher education. *Studies in Higher Education, 35*(3), 301–315.

Mills, C. W. (2002). *Den sociologiske fantasi* [The sociological imagination]. Copenhagen: Hans Reitzels Forlag.

Negt, O. (1971). *Sociologisk fantasi og eksemplarisk indlæring* [Sociological imagination and exemplary learning]. Copenhagen: RUC Forlag og Boghandel [RUC Publishers and Bookshop].

Nielsen, B. S. (1997). Det eksemplariske princip – inspirationen fra Oskar Negt [The exemplary principle – inspiration from Oskar Negt]. In K. Weber, B. S. Nielsen, & H. S. Olesen (Eds.), *Modet til fremtiden* [Courage for the future] (pp. 269–316). Copenhagen: Roskilde University Press.

Pedersen, P. B. (2009). Problemstilling og problemformulering [Problems and problem formulation]. In P. B. Olsen & K. Pedersen (Eds.), *Problemorienteret projektarbejde – en værktøjsbog* [Problem-oriented project work – a book of tools] (pp. 25–44). Copenhagen: Roskilde University Press.

Saynisch, M. (2010). Mastering complexity and changes in projects, economy, and society via project management second order (PM-2). *Project Management Journal, 41*(5), 4–20.

Simonsen, B., & Ulriksen, L. (1998). *Universitetsstudier i krise – fag, projekter og moderne studier* [University studies in a crisis – subjects, projects and modern studies]. Copenhagen: Roskilde University Press.

Szostak, R. (2007). How and why to teach interdisciplinary research practice. *Journal of Research Practice, 3*(2). Retrieved November 3, 2013, from http://jrp.icaap.ord/index.php/jrp/article/view/92/89.

Ulriksen, L. (1997). *Projektpædagogik – hvorfor det?* [Project pedagogics – why?] (Publication No. 57 from the Adult Education Research Group). Roskilde: Roskilde University.

Wagenschein, M. (1956). Zum Begriff des Exemplarischen Lehrens [On the concept of the exemplary in teaching]. *Zeitschrift für Pädagogik, 2*, 129–156.

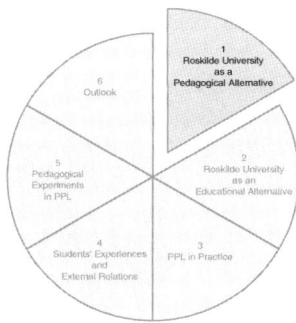

Chapter 3
Case Analysis of Some Critical Factors in Relation to Learning Outcomes of PPL – The Formation of Flint

Tinne Hoff Kjeldsen and Anders Siig Andersen

3.1 Introduction

The analysis of concepts in the preceding chapters identifies a number of ideals and challenges with regard to the conceptual foundation of the Roskilde University model. We will conclude this part of the book by exploring how the key concepts function in practice. The key concepts will be exemplified through the analysis of a project carried out in 2010 by a group of second semester students in the basic study programme in natural science. This project may be characterized as an interdisciplinary project that belongs to the empirical experimental academic culture (see also Chap. 2).

The main point will be that under certain conditions, project work can generate a very substantial learning outcome, but that the learning outcome depends on a number of assumptions that are closely linked to the understanding of the key concepts and the practical framework for teaching. At worst, project work will be subject-oriented, eclectic, bigoted, unguided, and atomistic and thus lack all the characteristics that ought to characterize projects at a university.

T.H. Kjeldsen (✉) • A.S. Andersen
Roskilde University, Roskilde, Denmark
e-mail: thk@ruc.dk; siig@ruc.dk

© Springer International Publishing Switzerland 2015
A.S. Andersen, S.B. Heilesen (eds.), *The Roskilde Model: Problem-Oriented Learning and Project Work*, Innovation and Change in Professional Education 12,
DOI 10.1007/978-3-319-09716-9_3

The second semester students of 2010 in the natural science programme who conducted the project work that is discussed below belonged to House 13.1, which is the ground floor of a two-storey building on campus. This "house" consists of a large classroom for teaching, a small kitchen, a secretary's office and 10 group rooms of different sizes (see Fig. 12.1 for a similar design). When the project groups have been formed, each group is assigned a group room for the semester. This particular semester, House 13.1 consisted of 45 students, 9 professors who were assigned to supervise the project work, a house coordinating teacher, and a secretary who handled the administration of the project work and dealt with the students' minor and major problems on a day to day basis (see also Chap. 6 for the organizational structure around the project work).

The students work on their project throughout the entire semester in parallel with course work. Half of their study time is devoted to the project, and the other half is devoted to more traditional courses. In general, the project work is completed with a written project report that documents the work of the students. The entire project is a collective enterprise. The students may divide responsibilities among themselves during the project work. But in the end each student is responsible for the entire project and everything that is documented in the project report. Typically, a project report in the science programme is about 50–100 pages long, depending on the problem and the number of students in the project group. The report must live up to academic writing standards with a clear problem formulation that is argued for with respect to how the students contribute to knowledge production, and how it is related to current research in the field of inquiry. The students formulate hypotheses that they justify scientifically, they choose and present their methodology and reflect upon its strengths and weaknesses, and how their solutions to their project problem depend on the chosen methodology. They design and perform experiments based on scientific theories and the construction of models. They analyse their results and write a conclusion describing how far they managed to solve their problem. Finally, they discuss further perspectives and how to proceed from the knowledge produced and documented in their project report. During the project work, the students consult textbooks and research publications. Besides their supervisors, they also often consult with other scientists outside the university (and often also abroad) who are doing research in their area. All statements in the groups' project report must be documented with references to national and/or international research literature, university textbooks, or by the students' own experimental work and analyses.

3.2 Welcome to House 13.1: February 1st 2010

Monday morning, February 1st 2010, is an exciting and important day for the 45 students in House 13.1. They are about to be introduced to the second semester of the 2-year (now 1½-year) interdisciplinary Bachelor of Science programme. The first week of the semester is devoted to students choosing problems to work on and forming groups. This is an interactive process that moves back and forth. Groups of students meet to see if they can agree on a problem, groups dissolve again when the differences between the students' wishes and interests are too great. At the end, each student must be in a group and each group must have an outline of a problem for the group's project. Even though some of the groups might end up working on problems within the same areas of inquiry, the groups almost always work on different problems. It is important to be present at this session, because half of a student's study programme for the semester, i.e. the half consisting of the second semester project, will be decided on during this week.

The programme begins at 9:30 with breakfast. The house coordinating teacher greets the students and sets the scene for the upcoming week, explains the rules, the requirements, the procedures and the deadlines for the formation of project groups. It is not new to these students, as they have tried it once before. They know that there is no fixed curriculum attached to the project work. They know that they can work with a problem they propose themselves as long as it fulfils firstly the constraints for second semester projects at the natural science programme, thematically and academically, and secondly if they can interest enough of their fellow students to form a project group that is big enough to be assigned a supervisor who does not need to divide the time allotted for supervising one project group between two or more smaller groups. This might happen in cases where the students form more groups than the allocated supervising resources allow for (see below). So, what the students are most eager to hear about is the constraints on second semester projects and the amount of allocated supervising resources.

The theme for the second semester is "models, theories and experiments in natural sciences". The purpose of the second semester project is for the students to gain experience in how scientific knowledge is produced. The students will have to go backstage in research laboratories, or the 'research workshop' of mathematicians and computer scientists, and act as scientists themselves, using the tools available for scientists to solve scientific problems. Through a representative problem, the students must acquire insights into how models, theories and experiments interact and function in the production of scientific knowledge (see also Chap. 2).

The second semester theme of the natural science programme does not vary from year to year, unlike the students, the supervising professors and the problems the students choose to work on. The projects carried out under the second semester theme by the natural science students over the years are exemplary in the sense of Wagenschein (1956) (see also Chap. 2). The students' projects are oriented towards problems within the sciences – the students perform basic science. In their first semester, the students worked on problems that were oriented more towards problems in society or nature to gain experience of the application of science to solve problems that lie outside the sciences themselves, and in the third semester, they have to choose problems through which they can acquire knowledge about science, scientific knowledge, as a cultural and societal phenomenon. In the other three bachelor programmes at Roskilde University, the projects in the various semesters are structured in other ways (see also Chap. 6), and many of these projects are oriented towards societal and cultural problems in the world outside the university and the academic disciplines.

After the presentation of the second semester theme, the project market opens officially. Each of the nine professors in the house this semester is allocated to supervise one project group (see also Chap. 8 for more information about the role of supervisors). This means that in order to be sure to have a supervisor to themselves, the students must form groups that average five participants. The professors come from various academic fields: environmental biology, molecular biology, geology, chemistry, physics, mathematics, computer science and geography. Hence, the job is also to choose problems and form groups that utilize the professors' scientific competences, knowledge and skills in the best possible way. This is not an easy task, but it is an important factor for the success of the project. Both professors and students are responsible for working towards as optimal a match as possible, while upholding the students' rights to choose to work with problems based on their own interests.

The project market is indeed like a market place. The students who have ideas for second semester projects present their ideas. These are then discussed in the whole body of students. The student who proposes the problem or the project idea explains why he or she thinks this is interesting. The other students ask questions like: "How is the problem related to the semester theme?" "Will any of the supervisors be willing to supervise such a project?" "Which of the sciences will they need to draw on to solve the problem?" The professors also present broad themes for projects either within their own field of research or in related areas where they know of problems that are suitable for second semester projects. The students move around during the project market. They meet in smaller groups and discuss possible ideas for projects. They meet with the professors either alone or in small groups to discuss ideas or get new ideas for projects.

The 2010 formation of groups went very smoothly, and on Wednesday evening when the house coordinating teacher met with the students to get an overview of how the process had progressed so far, it looked as if nine groups were about to materialize – nine groups that almost matched the supervisors' competences one to one. So the coordinator went home, very happy and relieved. The next morning, when she met with the students again, it had all collapsed overnight and they were back to square one – almost. During Thursday and Friday seven new groups began to materialize. However, as the weekend approached, a group of seven students had still not committed themselves to a project or a group. Originally they had been grouped with other students, investigating other possible subjects for their project. But during the re-grouping process they all ended up not joining any of the groups that were gradually being established and consolidated towards the end of the week – and they began to panic. On Friday afternoon, however, they overheard a discussion between two of the project supervisors, the chemist and the geologist, about how flint is formed. The students were surprised to hear that this was an open question and that the two scientists apparently did not agree on essential questions concerning the formation of flint. This surprise triggered them into forming a new group with the project of investigating how flint is formed and why scientists disagree about it. The project market closed on Monday February 8th with eight groups having been formed. The matching with the supervisors was almost one to one and the 'flint' group was assigned both the chemist and the geologist as supervisors.

3.3 How Is Flint Formed? A Second Semester Project in the Natural Sciences

Illustrative of the idea of free choice of project, here we have an example of a project group getting the inspiration for their project from a scientific discussion between two teachers allocated as project supervisors. The students probably would not have come by the problem themselves, but through interaction with their teachers they were made aware of the existence of a scientific problem that aroused their curiosity. In the project report the students put it like this:

> There are already many geological and physical/chemical hypotheses that attempt to describe the formation of flint. The geological hypotheses often lack a chemical foundation, while the chemical hypotheses do not take the geological perspective into account. The question of the formation of flint interests us because it is still an open question. The geological explanation of the precipitation of flint does not answer our problem fully, but often leads to further wondering. Nonetheless, several of these hypotheses are treated as theory, and they are taught at Danish universities. We have been surprised that such hypotheses are taught when they are in conflict with chemical knowledge. It is interesting that within the same faculty there are great differences between the methods of the different subjects and that theories/hypotheses exist that exclude the use of another subject. We are interested in bridging this interdisciplinary gap, and wonder to what extent the gap exists in other areas than the formation of flint. (Witt et al. 2010, p. 9 [authors' translation])

As was explained above, in the second semester the study regulations for the basic study programme in natural sciences require the students to work on a problem internal to science. The idea is that through such project work the students should experience how scientific knowledge is produced. Their problem of the formation of flint is an internal scientific question. It is an open question and, as the students clarified in their report, the problem (and their project work with the problem) is exemplary for how scientific knowledge is produced in interaction between theories, models and experiments.

The project is clearly problem-oriented. Actually, both a scientific problem and a meta-problem are represented above in the students' description of their motivation for choosing this project: the formation of flint is an open scientific problem, and the meta-problem regards the phenomenon that theories and hypotheses in one scientific field are in disagreement with knowledge from another scientific field. The meta-problem brought the students to reflect upon differences in scientific cultures and practices – an insight most science students in more traditionally organized curricula do not experience until they graduate and start working.

The project illustrates the change in the conception of problem orientation in the Roskilde University model with respect to the social relevance of the problem. As mentioned in Chap. 2, there has been a move towards an interpretation where the connection between the problem and the outside world passes through the problems of the academic discipline or, as in this case, disciplines. Flint is visible in the outside world, but the problem of how flint is formed is a problem within the scientific disciplines of geology and chemistry. However, even though this is the case, the students' motivation originally was triggered by the strong and fundamental disagreement among the two professors. The students justified their choice of problem not only through its status as an unsolved problem in the academic disciplines, but also qua a critique of *the* scientific method and of natural science's self-image as the provider of true, objective and necessary knowledge. It is characteristic of the students' choice of project in the science studies, especially in the basic study programme in natural science, that it is oriented towards either social relevance and significance, a critique of the natural sciences, or problems internal to the scientific disciplines – and the third type of projects are often related to either the first or the second type in one way or another, as illustrated by the Flint project. Regarding the students' free choice of problem, we have here an example where the students did not define the problem themselves. The problem arose as a consequence of a scientific discussion/dispute between two professors. In the process of forming project groups and choosing problems to work on, the students' free choice is often discussed in plenum. In principle, the students' choice of problem for their project work is constrained only by the study regulations mentioned above. However, the supervisors, i.e. the professors who are assigned to supervise the project groups throughout the semester, will present ideas and examples for project work that fulfil the semester requirements. Some supervisors will present ideas that are, if not identical, then at least very closely related to their own research, while others will present a broader range of examples. In the first case, students who choose to follow a supervisor's research agenda will often end up working on a project where they are 'water skiing' after their supervisor. In such cases, the students' project report is often very impressive compared to project reports from groups that have worked more independently, either because they came up with a problem themselves or because the problem was presented by a supervisor, but not directly related to the supervisor's own research. However, if we evaluate project work from the perspective of student learning, the groups who are 'water skiing' after a supervisor often assume the role of research assistants who do what the supervisor tells them to do. This means that they do not delimit the problem themselves, and they do not investigate, consider, discuss and choose the methods, the experiments and hypotheses themselves. So, in terms of the definition of problem-oriented project work given in Chap. 1, it may be questioned whether students in this kind of project actually participate in problem-oriented project work. In the last decade, the number of 'water skiing' projects has increased, and we see fewer student-proposed projects in the first year of the basic natural sciences programme. This is one of the challenges that the Roskilde model of problem-oriented project work faces, due partly to the massive focus on and prioritizing of professors' research in universities at the expense of teaching, and partly to the steadily increasing teaching workloads.

In the flint project, as we have seen, the students did not come up with the problem themselves. However, neither of the professor-supervisors was doing research on the formation of flint. Hence, there were no researchers that the students could 'just' follow around in their labs. The students were 'forced' into the research position themselves. They had to choose methods, experiments and hypotheses themselves, and they had to produce solutions themselves – all of this based on discussions with and guidance from their two supervisors. As the students wrote in their report on the methodology:

> In our project we deal with a problem that is unsolved. Therefore, we cannot proceed only by way of a literature search. We need to form our own hypotheses about the formation of flint. We test these hypotheses through experiments, observations and analyses. We form our hypotheses on the basis of our study of the literature on flint and the chemistry of silica, which flint consists of, and on observations of flint in nature.
>
> To solve our problem, we need to draw on geology, chemistry and physics. That is, we work in an interdisciplinary setting with subjects that use different methods and have different ways to proceed in order to gain knowledge. Hence, we need to describe how we use the methods of the different subjects. (Witt et al. 2010, p. 9 [authors' translation])

This project is exemplary for the ideal version of the problem-oriented project work in the basic science programme in natural sciences at Roskilde University and for the Roskilde model of participant-directed, interdisciplinary and problem-oriented project work as it has developed in the natural sciences where not all projects originate in problems in society related to the students' life-world, but are exemplary for the sciences in the sense of Wagenschein (see also Chap. 2). However, as indicated above, sometimes the project work is reduced to students 'simply' doing what they are told by their supervisor. Or worse, they choose to work on a problem that is not really a problem, in the sense that the students can solve the problem without being forced into learning processes of assimilation and accommodation using the terms of Piaget (see also Chap. 1). In such cases, the project loses all the features that ought to characterize project work at the university level.

The students' project report provides some insights into the learning outcomes of the project work. In the report, the students reflect upon how their project work fulfils the requirements of the study regulations in the following words:

> The purpose of the second semester project is to gain experience of basic research in the natural sciences and thereby work with models, experiments and theory in science. The idea is that by using the tools of science, we experience how these are used to 'get closer' to scientific knowledge. The interesting thing is that different science disciplines make use of these tools in different ways, as we have experienced in our project.
>
> The key point in our project work is that it does not originate in one discipline. It is a problem-oriented project in which we work with the inner core of science. We use the tools of science in our attempt to solve a problem. The problem of the project comes from scientific curiosity concerning a well-known material with an unknown formation process. We are interested in the reasons why this process has not been explained, since it can be attributed to several parameters. Maybe the process has not been investigated thoroughly, maybe it is controlled by as yet unknown phenomena, or maybe the boundaries between chemistry and geology 'block the way'. Flint is a material observed in nature by geologists. Flint consists mainly of silica, a well-known substance in chemistry. In this sense we can say that the formation of flint is investigated at the molecular level in the laboratory and at the level of a stone in nature. How silica is transformed into flint is a problem that cannot be answered within one discipline. Hence, it is the project that defines what disciplines we are dealing with. The project uses theory and empirical findings from chemistry and geology. In an attempt to answer our problem, we have tried to break down the boundaries between the disciplines. […]. The process of our project work has been central for our understanding of the boundaries of science and differences between scientific disciplines. Our work has had the character of basic research and we

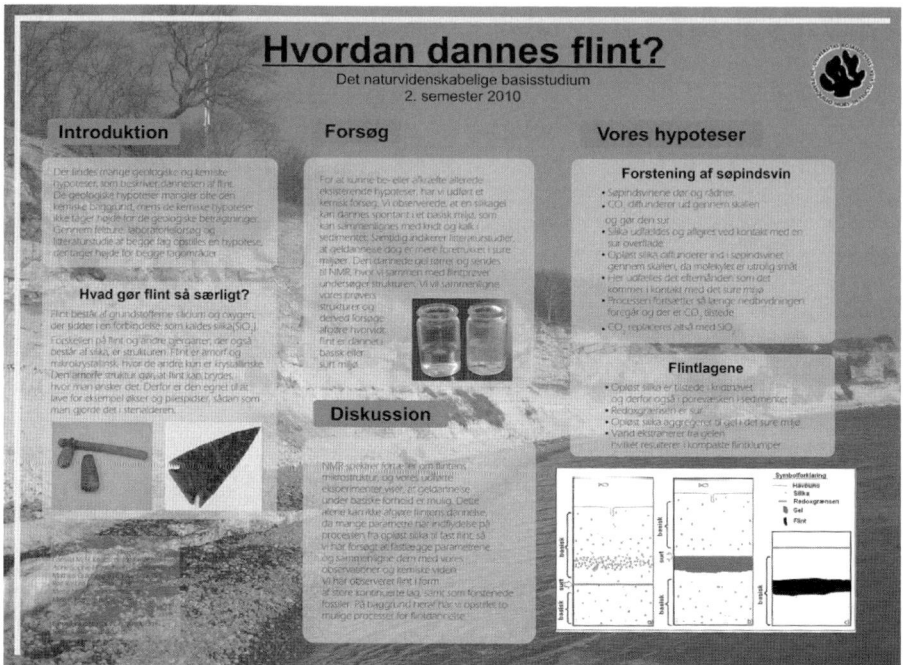

Fig. 3.1 The Flint Project poster

have had many considerations and discussions. The missing knowledge about the subject has forced us to acquire knowledge from many different areas […]. There has been a rapid development during the process from an open question to a well-defined 'area of study' from which we can use the knowledge we have acquired to deduce various plausible hypotheses. (Witt et al. 2010, pp. 11–12 [authors' translation])

The problem formulation that the students ended up with was the following:

How and under what circumstances is flint formed? We want to pose a plausible hypothesis about the formation of flint that is in accordance with geological observations and chemical realities. (Witt et al. 2010, p. 12 [authors' translation])

The students did not manage to formulate such a hypothesis, but they did manage to derive and discuss new possibilities and related problems which could be of interest for further investigations in the pursuit of formulating a single plausible hypothesis for the formation of flint. The students list six areas for further investigations, observations and experiments, and explain how these can contribute towards a final hypothesis.

As was seen above, the students emphasized the process of their project work as very important for their learning process and hence, the learning outcome of the project. During the semester, the students consulted 51 written sources, many of which are research papers published in international scientific journals. They had many discussions with their supervisors during the semester. The discussions changed character in the course of the project work from the supervisors giving input and mini-lectures confronting and challenging the two supervisors' different ideas and explanations, comparing them and holding them up against the knowledge and open questions the students had acquired through their study of the literature.

The students worked in the way scientists work when they do research. They read the latest literature, they did geological field studies and observations of flint, and they designed experiments to test chemical hypotheses.

At the end of the semester, in addition to submitting a report, all groups created posters explaining the outcome of their project work. The flint group's poster also contained a plan for the next step in the pursuit to form a plausible hypothesis for the formation of flint (see Fig. 3.1).

References

Wagenschein, M. (1956). Zum Begriff des Exemplarischen Lehrens [On the concept of the exemplary in teaching]. *Zeitschrift für Pädagogik, 2*, 129–156.

Witt, M. N., Guldberg, M., Rasbro, R., Heinrichsen, A. S., Jensen, A. S. C., Hansen, M. P., & Knudsen, C. H. (2010). Dannelse af Flint [The formation of flint]. Roskilde University, Basic Study Programme in Natural Science, 2nd semester, Spring 2010, House 13.1, Group 2.

Part II
Roskilde University as an Educational Alternative

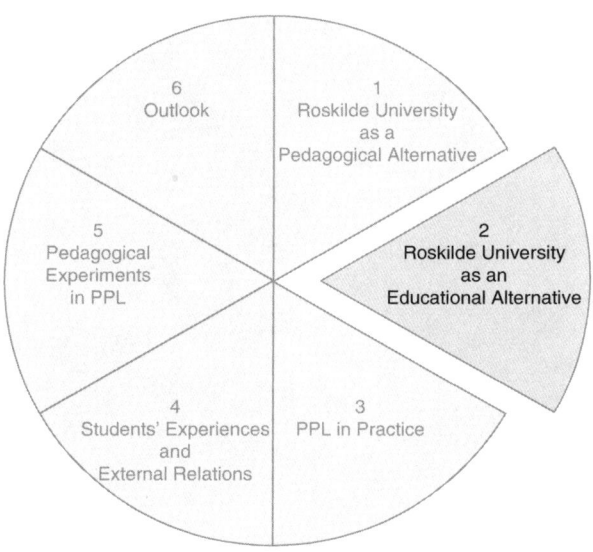

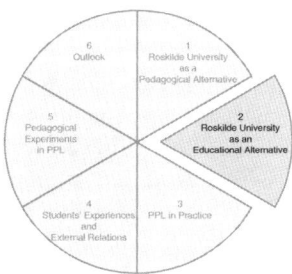

Chapter 4
Historical Transformations Within Danish Higher Education

Anders Siig Andersen

4.1 Introduction

A brief account of the Danish higher education scene is required to provide a context for understanding not only the framework within which Roskilde University has been evolving pedagogically, educationally and institutionally, but also the potentials for future change.

This chapter discusses the development of the Danish higher education system from three perspectives. Firstly, we outline the historical development of the educational structure from consisting of a number of loosely connected institutions, each with its own historical background, to a public educational system with clearly defined types of institutions and distribution of responsibilities. Secondly, we describe the management structure of the sector with particular emphasis on the management of the universities. The management structure has evolved from institutional autonomy to supranational governance and democratization and to the introduction of one-tier management and New Public Management. Thirdly, we describe the development of the management of education. Over the past 15 years, educational management has been characterized by increasing output control, and

---

A.S. Andersen (✉)
Roskilde University, Roskilde, Denmark
e-mail: siig@ruc.dk

© Springer International Publishing Switzerland 2015
A.S. Andersen, S.B. Heilesen (eds.), *The Roskilde Model: Problem-Oriented Learning and Project Work*, Innovation and Change in Professional Education 12,
DOI 10.1007/978-3-319-09716-9_4

by the implementation of the recommendations of the Bologna Process and EU requirements with respect to educational structure and quality assurance.

As a point of departure, we will briefly discuss the following two questions: Why is it important to understand the political and social framework of higher education in order to understand the development of the universities? How can one understand the relationship between context and institution? We try to answer these questions by looking at universities in the same way as we would look at organizations in general. This understanding provides the necessary background for the next chapter which focuses on the historical development of Roskilde University.

As organizations, universities can be considered as being based on the following characteristics: (a) membership, (b) limits, (c) roles and qualifications, (d) distribution of authority, (e) establishment of predictable relationships through contracts and measuring systems and (f) a repertoire of procedures and policies (Wenger 1998). To ensure survival, universities are faced with the challenge of constantly having to interpret changes in the society and to determine how to adapt to these (Andersen et al. 2007, p. 18). The relationship between universities and society is mediated by the organizational configuration of communities, interests, and power constellations. This means that essentially universities are involved in social learning and social reconfiguration. The environment may affect universities in many ways: through wider economic, technological, social and cultural change, or through changes in resource supply, legislation, contracts and agreements. Some external influences may have direct consequences, whereas others affect the life of universities more indirectly. In most cases, the external influences are mediated through negotiations in which the negotiating parties attempt to use these influences in different ways to promote their own views and interests. Thus, the organizational development of universities is not linear, but a result of the interaction between changes in the organization and changes in broader society.

Sometimes, universities manage to resist influences from the outside world, while at other times these influences more or less determine the internal development of the universities. This means that it is not possible to understand changes at the universities by focusing only on their internal conditions and dynamics, or by focusing only on the changes in society around them. In order to understand the development of the universities, one must apply a dialectical view, considering the interplay between external and internal factors in a historical perspective.

4.2 The Historical Development of Higher Education in Denmark

Below we focus on the external factors, starting with a historical overview of the development of the field of higher education in Denmark. The story goes back more than 500 years, beginning with the founding of Copenhagen University in 1479 by the Danish king with the permission of the Pope. The University of Copenhagen thus forms part of the long history of European universities dating back to the 1200s. During the entire period from 1200 until the early 1900s, the main tasks of the universities were to maintain and communicate existing knowledge. The universities were organized into lower arts faculties (grammar, rhetoric, logic, arithmetic, geometry, astronomy, and music) and three upper profession-oriented faculties (theology, law and medicine). Subjects were taught according to a scholastic science concept originating from the Middle Ages, which excluded research in a modern scientific sense (Kristensen 2007, p. 33).

Formally the medieval universities were governed by a secular or ecclesiastical authority, but were otherwise largely self-governing. Until the Reformation in 1536, the University of Copenhagen was part of the Roman Catholic Church and was under the supervision of a bishop. Like other European universities, Copenhagen University possessed a high degree of autonomy with its own laws, courts and prison services. In connection with the Reformation, the State took over the supervision of the University of Copenhagen. In 1563, the State decided that the rector, the deans and the teaching staff should form the University Senate, a body that for nearly 400 years was to have ultimate responsibility for the university. Right until the twentieth century, it was the general rule that a professor at the university would cover a whole field of study or a major independent part of it. One might say that 'the professor was the subject'. The first degree at the University of Copenhagen was introduced in 1675, and in 1788 examinations were introduced in all faculties.

Towards the end of the eighteenth century the European universities were threatened (Kristensen 2007, p. 33). They were subjected to harsh criticism because their teaching and learning management stood in stark contrast to the more vibrant forms of intellectual environments that had emerged in the public sphere during the Enlightenment. In Germany and England, there were attempts to renew the classical medieval university, while in France the medieval university was abolished as a result of the French Revolution in 1789. In France, this led to a separation of professional education and research in different types of autonomous institutions. In England, a distinction was introduced between the undergraduate college, where teaching was not research-based, and specialization at the graduate level at research universities.

Inspired by Humboldt (1767–1835), the former German kingdom of Prussia developed a university model, which was based on (a) the universities' internal self-government and autonomy without the direct influence of church and state, (b) the unity of research and education, and (c) the principle of freedom of research and education (Kristensen 2007, pp. 42ff.). Humboldt's legitimization of the model was founded on ideals about the shaping of the human being with respect to his or her 'humanity' and intellectual skills ('Bildung' in German). According to Humboldt, the principle of the unity of research and teaching would lead to the individual's self-formation through the promotion by science of the moral culture and spiritual life of the nation. In contrast to professional and vocational education where the students were taught limited skills, the new university should be a place where science would always be treated as consisting of ongoing problems and where teaching staff and students should be continuously involved in cooperation on research. The seminar should be the forum where faculty members and students could jointly explore scientific problems (Kristensen 2007, pp. 4f.). In practice, the new university became based on Humboldt's ideals regarding its organization, but the ideal of 'Bildung' faded into the background in favour of an ideal of science as methodologically controlled and increasingly specialized research (Kristensen 2007, p. 57). At the University of Copenhagen, the scientific specialization began in the mid-nineteenth century, particularly in medicine, science, law and political science (University of Copenhagen 2008).

The second university in Denmark was founded in 1928 as 'University Teaching in Jutland'. In 1933 the university changed its name to Aarhus University, which refers to the location of the university in Denmark's second largest city. In the early years, the university taught humanities and medicine, but in the 1940s, 1950s and 1960s the educational field of the university was expanded to include economics, law, political science, psychology, theology and science. In 1962, a third University with a medical school was founded in Denmark's third largest city, Odense. Two years later, this university expanded with three new faculties: humanities, social sciences and natural sciences. Like the university in Copenhagen and the universities in Germany, these two new universities were founded on the idea of a university as an autonomous community of scholars. According to this idea, the university's legitimacy functions independently of broader society, and the scientific criteria are internally defined. The legitimacy of the autonomy is derived positively from the principle of authority belonging to those best qualified (Degn and Sørensen 2012, p. 70), and negatively from the principle that pure science cannot thrive if it is affected by economic interests or political power. By 1970 there were thus three universities in Denmark, all based on the German model, i.e. universities as public institutions with several faculties and specialized research and education, where research formed the basis of academic teaching.

The breakthrough of the empirical and experimental sciences in the sixteenth and seventeenth centuries passed the European universities by. Instead, these sciences found their forms of organization in the Royal Societies and Academies of Science. The same trend occurred within art and architecture. The growing need for practical, artistic and utilitarian higher education gave rise to new types of academies and schools in the eighteenth and nineteenth centuries (Kristensen 2007, p. 31). In Denmark, these institutions were responsible particularly for higher education in fine arts and architecture (1754), agronomy (1859), engineering (1829), educational science (1904) and business studies (1912). Also, professional teacher training (1791) and nursing (1863) were established outside the universities. The same applied to education in childcare (1885) and social work (1937). People with a technical or commercial educational background were offered opportunities for further training in a system of post-secondary education.

Until 1970, the Danish system of higher education could be described as a fourfold system consisting of higher academic education at the universities, higher specialized education at academies and other institutions, intermediate higher education at e.g. teacher training colleges, and post-secondary education at institutions of 'further training of short duration' (short cycle). Outside the universities, a number of research institutes were established, serving central and local government by producing scientific knowledge in areas such as transport, building, fisheries, agriculture, space science, occupational health and safety, school and kindergarten, welfare and social issues, geology and public health.

4.2.1 From Elite to Mass University

In the late 1950s, education in the Western world generally expanded to become considered a necessary condition for economic growth. Education therefore became subject to systematic planning. In Denmark, the demand for upper secondary and tertiary education grew explosively in the 1960s and 1970s. This was also recognized as a challenge in many other parts of the world. At the OECD, this challenge was discussed under the heading "the transition from elite universities to mass universities" (Hansen 1997, p. 34). As the access to further education was not regulated in Denmark, pressures arose regarding the capacity of universities. Against this background, the Danish government established the 'Planning Council for Higher Education' with representatives from the universities, the academies, the student organizations and the central administration. The objective of the Council was to ensure wider gender and socio-economic access to higher education (Nielsen et al. 1997, p. 6). In 1965–1967 the Council prepared an 'Outline for the Development of Higher Education in the Period up to 1980', which was known as the 'Outline'. According to the Outline, it was expected that higher education would expand significantly and that there would be a need to establish new institutions in the form of educational centres.

The idea of educational centres had been anticipated in the early 1960s. Politicians had held discussions on whether Denmark should introduce the bachelor model known from the Anglo-Saxon world, or should keep to the model of complete 5–6-year graduate study programmes Opponents of the bachelor model argued that Denmark already had a wide range of practice-oriented intermediate higher education programmes, which trained teachers, nurses, social workers, engineers and employees in business and commerce. They argued that one should not undermine the standard of long-term higher education at the universities. Against this background, the Government chose not to implement the bachelor model, and instead proposed to modernize and streamline the educational system through the establishment of educational centres for both professional and higher education (Hansen 1997, p. 34).

The formulation of the concept of educational centres may be viewed as a consequence of the fact that the three existing universities in Denmark had not achieved a modernization that enabled them to meet society's challenges. Some of these challenges were that universities should admit a greater number of new students, that they should make better use of resources, that the period of study should be shortened, that drop-out rates should be reduced, that the social relevance of studies should be enhanced, that graduates should be better prepared for employment, that the overcrowded curricula should be reduced, and that the students should be offered greater opportunity to acquire general competences such as interpersonal skills, communication skills, etc. The educational centres were to bring together different types of higher education under the same roof, by placing the German university model in the same physical frame as professional education (Nielsen et al. 1997, p. 11). The educational centres would be based on broad basic study programmes, followed by specialization. Thus students would first take a basic programme and only after 1 or 2 years decide for example whether to study primary school teaching for 4 years or to study Danish literature for 5 years. The aim of the Outline was to realize this model, and the key word was flexibility.

The Executive Committee of the Planning Council established a subcommittee, the so-called Centre Committee, which proposed the creation of a new educational centre in the town of Roskilde, approximately 30 km west of Copenhagen. One of the purposes of The Roskilde Centre was to relieve the University of Copenhagen in the fields of humanities, social sciences and natural sciences. In 1970, The Danish Parliament passed a law on the establishment of this new university centre, which was to admit its first students in 1972. The same year Parliament passed a law to establish a similar university centre in the town of Aalborg in northern Jutland, which would admit students from 1974.

4.2.2 Concentrations Within the Higher Education System

Until 2000, vocational higher education in Denmark consisted of a large number of institutions offering separate programmes in child care, social work, health care, office work, technical work, communications and media. In 2000, the Danish Parliament decided that these programmes should lead to the title of 'Professional Bachelor'. The programmes were thus equated with university undergraduate programmes, but without being directly research-based. The title implied that they should include knowledge about key trends in the development of the professions (knowledge about the professions), be based on the teachers' developmental activities in professional work (knowledge about how to develop professional work) and include knowledge of research in the field provided by collaboration with universities (research-based knowledge). It was also decided that the different educational institutions should be concentrated in Centres for Higher Education (Andersen and Sommer 2003, p. 50). In the same year the Government decided to merge 75 institutions which offered courses for people with a technical or commercial training background into 15 new educational institutions (Andersen and Sommer 2003, p. 49).

In 2006 a university reform widened the ambition of concentrating educational institutions by including the university area. The consequence of the reform was that

12 universities and 13 research institutes were gradually merged into 8 universities. Roskilde University and four research institutes did not join the merging process (Hansen 2012, p. 195). The goal of the Government was to achieve stronger and more internationally competitive universities that could provide a research basis for new programmes, utilize research facilities better, be more successful in accessing EU funding, and ensure closer cooperation between university research and industry. There were clear expectations that the integration of commissioned research into sector-based research institutions in the universities would increase direct socio-economic orientation both in academic teaching and research at universities.

In 2008, through a series of mergers, the Centres for Higher Education were converted into seven University Colleges. The Council of Rectors declared that the new University Colleges should be recognized nationally and internationally as institutions engaged in applied research and education at bachelor, master and PhD level. The Rector Assembly of the university colleges announced the following aims to be achieved by 2015:

- To provide educational programmes based on applied research and development,
- To provide training at bachelor, master and PhD level,
- To aim for 20 % of university college faculty to have a PhD degree,
- To achieve recognition as institutions carrying out applied research,
- To obtain the right to recruit staff responsible for carrying out research,
- To offer PhDs in collaboration with universities,
- To obtain government funding to support applied research.

Most of these aims were reached in 2013. However, university colleges still may not offer courses at master level and award PhD degrees.

These developments mean that higher education is currently offered by four types of higher education institutions:

1. Academies of Professional Higher Education offering professionally oriented short degree courses (academy profession degree),
2. University Colleges offering professionally oriented degree courses (professional bachelor degree),
3. University level institutions offering bachelor, master and PhD degree courses in subject fields such as architecture, design, music and fine and performing arts (bachelor, master and PhD degree),
4. Research universities offering bachelor, master and PhD degree courses in all academic disciplines.

Overall, the merging process has resulted in high concentration and centralization in the higher education area. The universities and university colleges have become competitors for research funding from Government. However, these developments also point towards an increasing degree of research-based teaching in higher education as a whole.

4.3 Developments in Management of Higher Education Institutions in Denmark

In 1971, a Government Act for universities and university colleges was adopted in Denmark. Until that time, the government of universities had been the concern of the professors on the university senates, faculty boards and study boards, since the universities had managed to maintain their tradition of faculty-based management and autonomy from the state. With the Government Act, universities became subject to public control. Professors now had to give up their exclusive right to decide on how to run universities, and students and junior staff achieved significantly greater influence than before.

Through a revision of the Government Act in 1973, students gained 50 % representation on the study boards. In senates and on faculty boards, students gained 25 %, technical and administrative staff also gained 25 %, while faculty had 50 % representation. The Government Act meant that all faculty members and teachers now had equal rights to participate in decision-making processes regardless of their job category (Hansen 1997, p. 40). The introduction of the Government Act can be understood partly in the light of the Danish student rebellion in 1968 and student demands for the abolition of professorial control, and partly in the light of public interest in the modernization of the universities. Such modernization, it was assumed, required that junior staff and students gained more influence, and that the state developed an instrument that could be used to regulate the universities (Hansen 1997, p. 40).

The introduction of the Government Act meant that the universities abandoned management based on the principle of 'primus inter pares'. The new act determined that university management was in the hands of potentially conflicting interests (academic staff, students and administrative staff). The assumption was that an internal coalition formation and representation of specific group interests would improve academic functioning and performance (Degn and Sørensen 2012, p. 79).

4.3.1 From Democratic Governance to One-Tier Management and New Public Management

By the late 1970s, management of the public sector in Denmark was being accused of being expensive, bureaucratic and inefficient. Under the heading 'modernization' a restructuring process was initiated with a gradual implementation of a new system of financial operations and the introduction of new forms of management. At this point, objectives and resources in the public policy of modernization were ambiguous and complex. The modernization efforts of the 1980s were aimed primarily at streamlining and rationalizing public institutions in order to reduce the level of spending in the public sector. In the 1990s, the goal of public modernization became 'negative growth'. Restructuring of management and organizational structures was implemented in order to improve efficiency of public services. The aim was also to improve people's experience of public services and to guarantee the flexibility of the organizations and their ability to evolve (Andersen et al. 2007, pp. 10f.). The inspiration for modernization in the 1990s increasingly was derived from the principles of New Public Management. This concept is characterized by the attempt to implement organizational, managerial and human resource policies inspired by the private sector. Emphasis is placed on output management, performance metrics and a reorganization of the relationship between local and central government.

A new University Act in 1993 introduced a one-tier management structure and external representation in the senates and faculty councils. However, the government of the universities was not changed decisively until the Danish Parliament adopted new University Acts in 2003 and again in 2011. Universities were now established as independent institutions with boards that should have an external majority, with one-tier management and with rectors, vice-rectors, deans and heads of departments who should be employed under contract. The former rights of collegiate bodies to make decisions were abolished, but it was required that the university boards should seek to develop internal procedures to ensure that leaders would involve faculty members, staff, and students as advisers in the decision-making processes.

The changes in organization and management reflect a new view on the role of universities in society. Increasingly, their role is presented as an important element in Denmark's attempt to compete in a globalized market, where the country's competitiveness must be based on a highly educated workforce with clear links between science, higher education and business. One can identify a double discourse that challenges the traditional discourse on research and education. The new discourse finds its political legitimacy in the discourse of globalization and in the derived discourse of growth and innovation. It finds its organizational expression in the models approved by the New Public Management wave (Aagaard and Mejlgaard 2012, p. 7). In this context, one may refer to a denunciation of the social contract between politics and science. This contract was based on the assumption that the internal quality assurances by science itself would ensure optimal social benefits of public research and education. In place of this, a new social contract has been introduced. Increased funding for public research should be matched by knowledge that will directly contribute to economic growth and social development. Furthermore, increased funding for education should target community and business needs more efficiently. The production of knowledge and education must be documented to both the political system and the taxpayers who finance the operation. There is an increased emphasis on value for money, accountability, transparency, efficiency and effectiveness (Aagard and Mejlgaard 2012, p. 16). Kristensen (2007) makes the point that there has been a transition from collegiate autonomy to independent but economically controlled and tightly managed service universities:

> In short, the idea of a (more or less) publicly regulated university that is designed to accommodate and meet societal needs (…), and a university that for this purpose must submit its operation to a thorough business logic and transform itself into a management university that is able to compete in an increasingly globalized market. (Kristensen 2007, p. 16 [my translation])

4.4 Developments in Management of Higher Education in Denmark

Over a relatively long period, some of the basic rationales in Danish educational planning have been expressed as follows:

- To educate as many as possible as quickly as possible with as low drop-out rates as possible,
- To make the education system flexible by modularization of study programmes and built-in opportunities to study across the different parts of the education system,
- To strengthen the individual's effective use of the system,
- To enhance stakeholder influence and cooperation with employers,
- To match output with labour market needs,
- To enhance the efficiency of institutions,
- To develop the quality of educational programmes,
- To internationalize education.
  (Andersen and Sommer 2003, pp. 52f.).

The educational initiatives of successive Danish governments have been strongly influenced by cooperation at a European level and not least by cooperation within the EU. This collaboration points towards increased harmonization among educational systems. Within the higher education area, The Bologna Declaration has been the basis for a comprehensive harmonization of higher education. The Bologna Process is a cooperative effort initiated by a number of European Ministers of Education in 1999 on a voluntary basis. The goal was to develop Europe as a common area of higher education, where scholars and students should be able to move freely across borders. The Bologna Process has been developed continuously and a series of communiqués have been published, spelling out the following objectives: comparable qualifications, a degree structure with bachelor, master and PhD degrees, a common credit system based on the European Credit Transfer System (ECTS), removing obstacles to mobility for faculty members and students, the development of quality assurance, and strengthening of the European dimension in higher education (Christiansen et al. 2013, pp. 35f.).

4.4.1 From Qualifications to Competence and Lifelong Learning

Under the influence of changes in the global educational discourse, the Danish educational discourse has also changed significantly. From the 1960s to the early 1990s, the discourse was dominated by a concept of qualifications. On the one hand, this qualification concept referred to types of knowledge and skills linked to those required in the labour market. This kind of qualification can be assessed through qualification analysis. On the other hand, the concept referred to the knowledge and skills produced by the educational system, which can be documented by examinations (Andersen and Iversen 1995, pp. 16ff).

According to Hermann (2003), the concept of competences replaced the concept of qualifications in the early 1990s. It began with Human Resource Management thinking, but in the 1990s it also played a significant role in the various modernization programmes of the Danish government. In contrast to the concept of 'qualification', the concept of 'competence' refers to the translation of internal, personal dynamics (attitudes, will, emotions, values) as well as knowledge and insight into specific situations where specific problems or specific challenges are to be dealt with (Hermann 2003). Both the concept of qualifications and the concept of competence are linked to the development of society's wealth by matching supply and demand for skills and knowledge. However, with the introduction of the concept of competence, the focus shifts to personality as something that must evolve and change throughout life.

In Denmark, the conceptual development started with a simple concept of skills (skilled and unskilled work). The concept of qualifications was introduced at a time when the relationship between the individual and work requirements had become challenging on a societal scale. The concept of competence was then introduced when a narrow focus on the development of knowledge and skills was felt to be an insufficient basis to support the development of production and services, i.e. when a demand had evolved for the use of all human capacities in the service of work (Andersen 2013, p. 10). At that time lifelong learning replaced the discourse about education and training as something to finish rather early in life that would provide the individual with skills to last a lifetime. In order to use all human capabilities, all structures contributing to the facilitation of learning processes in society must be activated. This applies to educational institutions in that they should offer courses that can be used by participants at different times in their career. It also applies to work and recreational organizations in that they may be transformed into learning organizations. Finally, it applies to individuals, who are assigned the responsibility of transforming not only knowledge and skills but also themselves in a lifelong change project (Andersen 2013, p. 11).

Currently both the concepts of qualifications (knowledge and skills) and of competence are in use. The European Qualifications Framework for Lifelong Learning is both output- and level-oriented (European Parliament and Council 2008). The framework characterizes the qualification and competence levels through a taxonomic description of learning outcome. This contrasts with the past, when graduation requirements were described in terms of various curricula that the student should be able to master in an examination situation. The output orientation in the Danish Qualifications Framework for Higher Education is expressed by the fact that it focuses on the qualifications and competencies that a student must be able to demonstrate after completion of a learning process at a given level. The key elements in the course descriptions such as admission requirements, academic progression, teaching and learning methods, and test and examination requirements are all formulated to ensure the realization of the learning outcome.

In the Danish Qualifications Framework, the concept of 'competency profile' is the overarching concept for qualifications and competences, and the concept of qualifications is divided into knowledge and skills. This means that the competency profile for a specific programme establishes a comprehensive framework for the description of knowledge, skills and competences for all elements of the programme and for the learning outcome. In the Framework, the concept of 'knowledge' refers both to knowledge about a topic and to an understanding of the topic expressed by the ability to contextualize the knowledge. The concept of 'skill' refers to the practical, cognitive, creative or communicative performance of a person. The notion of 'competence' refers to the person's ability to apply knowledge and skills in a study or work situation (Andersen 2013, pp. 10f.). One might say that the Qualifications Framework builds on the idea that the scientific disciplines are transformed into subjects and that the theories and methods of the subjects form the basis of the knowledge and skills that students should acquire. In order to use the knowledge and skills in a study and business context, there is a need for competences, i.e. personal, social and communicative qualities that can be used to realize the knowledge and skills in concrete situations – including the ability to manage processes, collaborate, and take responsibility for personal learning.

4.4.2 Accreditation and Quality Assurance

In 2007, the Danish Government stipulated by law that the earlier ministerial approvals of higher education should be replaced by accreditation. This decision was inspired by guidelines from the EU. The basis for the accreditation included the Danish Qualifications Framework. Moreover, the accreditation is based on guidelines drawn up by the European Association for Quality Assurance in Higher Education (ENQA), which has received European support to develop a common paradigm based on explicit standards and guidelines for quality assurance in higher education (Thorslund and Andersen 2012, p. 62). Initially, two separate institutions were established to accredit, respectively, professional educational programmes (The Danish Evaluation Institute) and university education (ACE Denmark). Both institutions considered accreditation applications and made recommendations to the Accreditation Council. Work on the accreditation of university programmes was organized with self-assessment reports and review panels that made visits to the universities and prepared accreditation reports. Accreditation was made on the basis of predetermined criteria, called criteria pillars. They include: (1) Need for the programmes, (2) Research-based teaching, (3) Competency profile and educational objectives, (4) Structure and organization, and (5) Ongoing quality assurance. Accreditation is granted both for existing programmes and in terms of the approval of new ones.

In 2013 it was decided to phase in a new model for institutional accreditation instead of the model for accrediting courses of study. For existing study programmes, this implies that the higher education area must develop quality assurance policies, systems and procedures, and that these must be accredited. On the other hand, new programmes will continue to be accredited centrally with particular focus on assessing employment opportunities. As the responsibility for the professional colleges and universities was united in one government department in 2013, it was decided to introduce the same accreditation system for both types of institutions.

4.5 New Management Regimes and the Quality of Higher Education

The Bologna process has resulted in a much stronger focus on the educational activities of the universities. The pressure on public finances and the introduction of new management ideologies such as New Public Management has sharpened the political focus on accountability (registration and monitoring systems), value for money (production-based funding and focus on completion times and dropout rates), as well as quality assurance and employability (accreditation of existing and new study programmes, documentation of graduates' employment opportunities, and strong relationships between universities and employers). The motto is 'more for less' with a significantly increased focus on employability in relation to the existing labour market. This may conflict with the development of academic quality and long-term skills development. Some argue that Denmark has gone to great lengths in the adaptation of university education to business requirements compared to other European countries.

The division into bachelor, master and PhD courses is a direct consequence of the adaptation to the Bologna process. In Denmark, the number of graduates at the PhD level has increased significantly. This means that the required level of research in graduate programmes has been lowered. At the same time Government has put pressure on faster completion rates in the master courses, and imposed strict formal requirements for theses, including reducing the number of pages of a thesis. This goes hand in hand with the introduction of a new grading scale, which no longer operates with a highest score to honour independent studies measured on a scientific scale. Instead, the quality of student work is measured in relation to the extent to which it corresponds to the pre-formulated output requirements in the competency profile of the study programmes.

Generally, the Bologna process has led to a homogenization of educational structures and to a standardization and harmonization of educational models and quality work at the European universities. From a Danish point of view this may be understood as a somewhat contradictory process, that has helped to raise the average quality of university education, but that also implies a tendency to lower the academic level of ambition in the bachelor and master programmes.

References

Aagaard, K., & Mejlgaard, N. (2012). På vej mod en ny forskningspolitik [Towards a New Research Policy]. In K. Aagaard & N. Mejlgaard (Eds.), *Dansk forskningspolitik efter årtusindskiftet* [Danish research policy in the new millennium] (pp. 11–36). Aarhus: Aarhus University Press.

Andersen, A. S. (2013). Projektarbejdets kompetenceprofil mellem videnskab og profession [The competence profile of project work – between academic and professional standards]. *Spor – et tidsskrift om Universitetspædagogik [Tracks – A Journal on University Teaching], 1*. Retrieved November 26, 2013, from http://rossy.ruc.dk/ojs/index.php/spor/index.

Andersen, A. S., & Iversen, K. S. (1995). *Kvalifikationsudvikling og praktikoplæring på kontorområdet* [Skills development and apprenticeship in the office] (Publication No. 36 by the Adult Education Research Group). Roskilde: Roskilde University.

Andersen, A. S., & Sommer, F. M. (2003). Reform på reform. Voksen-, erhvervsrettet og professionsrettet uddannelse [Continuing reforms. Adult, vocational and professional education]. In A. S. Andersen & F. M. Sommer (Eds.), *Uddannelsesreformer og levende mennesker. Uddannelsernes erhvervsretning i livshistorisk perspektiv* [Educational reforms and living people. The vocational direction of educational programmes in a life-historical perspective] (pp. 29–78). Frederiksberg: Roskilde University Press.

Andersen, A. S., Andersen, V., & Gleerup, J. (2007). *Modernisering og læring i staten* [Modernisation and learning in the state]. Frederiksberg: Roskilde University Press.

Christiansen, F. V., Harboe, T., Horst, S., Krogh, L., & Sarauw, L. L. (2013). Udviklingstendenser i universitetets rolle [Developmental trends in the role of the university]. In L. Rienecker, P. S. Jørgensen, J. Dolin, & G. H. Ingerslev (Eds.), *Universitetspædagogik* [University teaching] (pp. 17–40). Frederiksberg: Samfundslitteratur.

Degn, L., & Sørensen, M. P. (2012). Universitetsloven fra 2003. På vej mod konkurrenceuniversitetet? [The University Act of 2003. Towards the competitive university?] In K. Aagaard & N. Mejlgaard (Eds.), *Dansk forskningspolitik efter årtusindskiftet* [Danish research policy in the new millennium] (pp. 59–94). Aarhus: Aarhus University Press.

European Parliament and Council. (2008). Recommendation of the European Parliament and of the Counsil of 23 April 2008 on the establishment of the European Qualifications Framework for lifelong learning. *Official Journal of the European Union, C 111/01*. Retrieved May 20, 2014, from http://eurlex.europa.eu/LexUriServ/LexUriServ.do?uri=OJ:C:2008:111:0001:0007:EN:PDF.

Hansen, E. (1997). *En koral i tidens strøm* [A coral in the flow of time]. Frederiksberg: Roskilde University Press.

Hansen, H. F. (2012). Fusionsprocesserne – Frivillighed under tvang. In K. Aagaard & N. Mejlgaard (Eds.), *Dansk forskningspolitik efter årtusindskiftet* [Danish research policy in the new millennium] (pp. 195–228). Aarhus: Aarhus University Press.

Hermann, S. (2003). Fra styring til ledelse – om kompetencebegrebets udvikling [From steering to leadership – the development of the concept of competence]. *Undervisningsministeriets tidsskrift Uddannelse* [The Ministry of Education Journal 'Education'], No. 1, January 2003. Retrieved November 26, 2013, from http://udd.uvm.dk/200301/udd200301-01.htm.

Kristensen, J. E. (2007). Gamle og nye idéer med et universitet – universitetsloven 2003 som anledning [Old and new ideas about a university – in the context of the University Act of 2003]. In J. E. Kristensen, K. Elstrøm, J. V. Nielsen, & H. Sørensen (Eds.), *Ideer om et universitet – Det moderne universitets idehistorie fra 1800 til i dag* [Ideas of a university – the intellectual history of the modern university from 1800 to the present] (pp. 9–22). Aarhus: Aarhus University Press.

Nielsen, J. C., Jensenius, N. H., & Olesen, H. S. (1997). *Utopien der slog rod. RUC – radikalitet og realisme* [The Utopia that took root. RUC – radicalism and realism]. Roskilde: The RUC Student Council.

Thorslund, J., & Andersen, U. S. (2012). Kvalitetssystemer og kvalitetssikring af uddannelse [Quality systems and quality assurance in education]. In H. L. Andersen & J. C. Jacobsen (Eds.), *Uddannelseskvalitet i en globaliseret verden. Vidensøkonomiens indtog i de videregående uddannelser* [The quality of education in a globalised world. The entry of the knowledge economy into higher education] (pp. 59–80). Frederiksberg: Samfundslitteratur.

University of Copenhagen. (2008). History of the university. Retrieved November 26, 2013, from http://introduction.ku.dk/presentation/history.

Wenger, E. (1998). *Communities of practice – learning, meaning and identity*. Cambridge: Cambridge University Press.

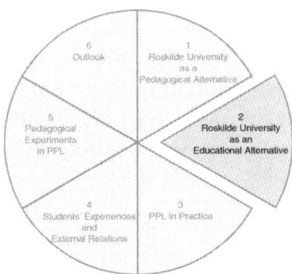

Chapter 5
The History of Roskilde University

Anders Siig Andersen

> The spirit of the times was crucial. In the early '70s, everything could be done, things had to change, now was the time. (Hansen 1997, p. 29, cited conversation with Børge Klemmensen [my translation])

5.1 Introduction

This chapter describes the background for the establishment of Roskilde University, and traces its history over the first four decades. The focus will be partly on the interaction between the university and broader society and partly on the internal developments at the university. Since its inception in 1972, Roskilde University has evolved from being a key innovative creation in the higher education system, in many ways ahead of its time, to become a university that today is recognized as an important educational alternative in the university world. We highlight the historical background of the founding of the university, with a particular focus on the interplay between its institutional and structural framework, and the development of the pedagogical ideas underlying the study programmes. The basic view is that the change process can best be understood through a presentation of the historical development of the interplay between, on the one hand, the university and the outside world, and on the other hand, various interests and points of view within the

---

A.S. Andersen (✉)
Roskilde University, Roskilde, Denmark
e-mail: siig@ruc.dk

university (see also Chap. 4). Furthermore, the basic tenet is that pedagogical and didactic ideas do not exist in a vacuum as they are heavily dependent on the organization of the studies, the character of the research, and the quality of the study environments at the university. We conclude the chapter by describing the background to the current situation, as the university sets new goals for organizing teaching, as well as for programme structure and content.

5.2 The Background

The original name of Roskilde University was Roskilde University Centre. The University Centre was established in 1972 on the basis of the 'Outline for the Development of Higher Education in the Period up to 1980', prepared by the Planning Council for Higher Education, and drawing on the work of the so-called Centre Committee (see also Chap. 4). The new university centre was conceived as an initial realization of political and ministerial visions for new educational centres in Denmark which were to include middle-range professional and higher academic education. Furthermore, the new university centre was meant to relieve the University of Copenhagen, which had insufficient capacity for accommodating the number of students that the Government wanted to give access to higher education (Fig. 5.1).

A former professor at the University of Copenhagen and Member of Parliament was appointed Rector of Roskilde University Centre. His personal experiences from the U.S. made him strongly in favour of broad basic entry programmes at the universities, and of problem-oriented, interdisciplinary and participant-directed project work. Following the appointment of the new Rector, The Ministry of Education set up an interim steering committee that was made up of the Rector, three academics each

Fig. 5.1 Aerial view of Roskilde University showing the original layout with some later additions

responsible for one of the three main study areas (humanities, social sciences and natural sciences), a chief librarian, an administration manager, and a representative of the Danish Student Federation. The steering committee had 22 months to plan for the new university: buildings, courses, recruitment of faculty members and other staff, and student enrolment (Hansen 1997, p. 53). Based on the preparatory work the Ministry set up three interim study boards to prepare reports providing guidelines for designing the three basic types of study programme at Roskilde University Centre.

At the time, the educational and pedagogical foundations for the new educational centre were controversial. A ministry committee published a report in 1970 proposing new basic study programmes in social sciences. The report proposed that the study programmes should be based on the established disciplines and subject divisions in a model that deferred the choice of certain subjects (Hansen 1997, p. 42). In response, the Danish Student Federation drafted an alternative model based on problem-oriented, interdisciplinary and participant-directed project work, a new role for the faculty members in providing students with assistance in problem solving, and a principle of no examinations, i.e. that the students' work should be assessed by internal evaluations. The students' ideas were inspired by the German student movement. At the end of the day, the student proposals were implemented in the establishment of Roskilde University Centre. The general principles involved 2-year 'basic study programmes' that would be continued for 3 years in 'superstructure study programmes'. Studies would primarily be organized as problem-oriented, interdisciplinary and participant-directed project work in accordance with the ideals of research projects.

The studies were basically organized as nine project groups with seven participants in each group, i.e. a total of 63 students in each physical unit which was called a 'house' (for a detailed description see Chap. 6). Each group would have its own group room in the house, there would be a larger room for all groups, a kitchen with cooking facilities, and a printing room with printing machines for reproducing project reports (see Fig. 12.1). Each of the six faculty members who were allocated to the house would have his or her own office, the house would have a secretary, and the house was to form the physical and organizational framework for the ongoing joint planning and coordination of study and social activities. Faculty members would primarily act as project supervisors and study counsellors. The students' project work would partly be assessed by internal evaluations, where faculty members and students would engage in ongoing dialogue, and partly through a final presentation seminar where students were required to present their project reports to their fellow students in the house, allowing each project group to provide answers to constructive criticism from the other students (Nielsen et al. 1997, p. 60) (Fig. 5.2).

The Planning Council endorsed the principles of problem-oriented, interdisciplinary and participant-directed project work, and accepted that there should be a strong emphasis on continuous internal assessment of student work. The Planning Council expressed concern regarding the rejection of externally assessed exams and the absence of a common evaluation system. Nonetheless, the Council decided that the planning was to proceed, but with the allocation of experimental status to the new university centre, meaning that it would be closely monitored, and that adjustments could be expected if developments proved problematic.

Fig. 5.2 Project work in the 1970s

5.3 Implementation of the Basic and Superstructure Study Programmes

The realization of the new basic study programmes revealed some of the strengths and challenges of implementing a new educational model and new pedagogical ideals for university education. In practice, the implementation of the Roskilde Model became a challenging learning experience for all participants. Various evaluation reports identified the following general issues:

- A contrast between the students' former learning experiences and the demands made at Roskilde University Centre for autonomy and interpersonal skills,
- A contradiction between the faculty members' background in the academic disciplines and the demands placed on them when asked to supervise interdisciplinary project work,
- A contrast between, on the one hand, the relatively vague ideas about study organization that were formulated in the reports from the interim study boards, and, on the other hand, the requirements of project work in practice and the organization into houses as physical and social environments for the study activities,
- Difficulties for the students in giving and receiving constructive criticism in group work and in plenary sessions (Nielsen et al. 1997, p. 74ff.).

However, the general impression of the new basic study programmes was that Roskilde University Centre had succeeded in making studying more democratic. The house and group organization were seen as crucial factors for this success. The new University Centre had also succeeded in implementing new pedagogical principles that were markedly different from the pedagogical ideas of the other Danish universities. Furthermore, there was much greater emphasis on social equity in student enrolment than ever seen before at other Danish universities (Nielsen et al. 1997, p. 80f.).

The governance principles of Roskilde University Centre were formalized in 1972. In 1973, with the adoption of the new Government Act for all universities in Denmark, a few minor corrections were made (see also Chap. 4). The University Centre had a Senate as its highest authority, and councils for the three main academic areas, which would decide on the distribution of economic resources. The University Centre also established study boards responsible for each of the three basic study programmes, and a central study board responsible for the new superstructure programmes (Hansen 1997, p. 73).

In 1973, the Ministry published a report describing the common academic and pedagogical principles for the three basic study programmes at Roskilde University Centre: students should be able to analyse the societal functions for which the study programmes qualified them, they should be able to combine theory and practice, and they should be able to communicate their academic knowledge to non-professionals. The report confirmed the principles of interdisciplinary, problem-oriented and participant-directed project work (Nielsen et al. 1997, p. 82).

In the spring of 1974, plans for the superstructure courses were completed and approved by the Ministry. The curricula were developed jointly by the faculty members and representatives of the (prospective) employers. The same year, the first students started on the superstructure programmes. These were (a) a one and a half year programme that qualified students for social work, (b) two 3-year interdisciplinary postgraduate programmes in Technological and Societal Planning and Public Management respectively, and (c) a number of programmes where the students had to combine 2 subjects of 18 months each (three semesters) to obtain a graduate degree that qualified them for teaching in high schools. It was possible to combine the following subjects: Danish, English, German, French, History, Social Sciences, Mathematics, Physics, Biology, Geography, and Computer Science. To become a high school teacher, the student also had to complete a 6-month practice period (Hansen 1997, p. 116). The original plan was to integrate general teacher training into the new university centre, but this plan was rejected by the Ministry. The reason was probably a combination of reports claiming that the university centre had become too left-wing politically, and the fact that existing teacher training institutions were lobbying to prevent the introduction of teacher training at the universities.

The superstructure programmes were organized on the basis of socially relevant themes where students from different subjects completed projects within a common thematic framework, under the guidance of faculty members with different disciplinary backgrounds. The idea underlying the themes was that they should constitute the basic framework for the students' interdisciplinary project work as well as for the faculty members' interdisciplinary research. It was also envisaged that study and research should be in direct and reciprocal interaction. The first themes were: (1) The Social Development of Science and Technology in the Industrial Society, (2) Economy, State and Planning, (3) Working Class History and Consciousness, and (4) Socialization, Education and Society (Fig. 5.3).

The organization into 'houses' was continued in the superstructure. Many of the students' projects were interdisciplinary, involving two chosen subjects and

Fig. 5.3 A mixture of collaborative studies and social activities in one of the programmes (1970s)

implying that they would work on their projects for two and sometimes three semesters instead of the one semester scheduled. The syllabus was limited and mostly optional. Whereas the students in the basic programmes had an internal evaluation on completion of their projects, the students in the superstructure had to pass an examination assessed by both internal and external examiners (see Sect. 13.1 for the institution of external examiners). The experiences of evaluative problem formulation seminars and midterm seminars from the basic programmes led to these features being introduced in the superstructure programmes.

5.4 The External Rectors: The Reorganization of Roskilde University Centre

In 1974, Roskilde University Centre ran into a political storm, as the then former rector criticized the basic study programme in social sciences. He alleged that the academic level of the university was too low, and that some of the influential faculty members were agitating for leftist views. Against this background, the Minister of Education demanded that the basic study programmes should be reorganized. The requirements for reorganization resulted in major internal conflicts within Roskilde University Centre as well as between the University Centre and the Ministry of Education. In 1976, these conflicts led to the decision that the University Centre should be placed under the administration of an external body of rectors that was empowered to amend all decisions in the governing bodies and the decisions taken by the internal rector.

5 The History of Roskilde University

Fig. 5.4 Student demonstration in the 1970s

In Parliament, the right-wing parties demanded that Roskilde University Centre should be closed. This proposal, however, was rejected by a one-vote margin.

The following years were turbulent. Two hundred students from the basic humanities programme boycotted the examination. The reason was that the external rectors had decreed the introduction of new forms of examination that did not follow the examination regulations. First the students were expelled from the university centre, but as a result of nationwide student actions they were then re-admitted. The external rectors demanded that as of autumn 1977 no further students should be admitted to the basic study programme in social sciences until the reorganization of Roskilde University Centre had been completed (Fig. 5.4).

After many internal discussions and student actions that same year, a group of faculty members started negotiations with the body of external rectors on the normalization of the governance of the University Centre. The faculty members reached a joint proposal for a comprehensive reorganization. The proposal contained four elements:

1. The establishment of financially independent departments for each main subject,
2. The admission of students to the basic social science programme,
3. The creation of new superstructure programmes,
4. The downgrading of the capacity of the body of external rectors to intervene in Roskilde University Centre's internal decisions (Hansen 1997, p. 187).

The external rectors accepted the proposals, except for the proposal to admit students into the basic social science study programme. In response, the rector of Roskilde University Centre proposed that students should be admitted 6 months later, i.e. in the spring semester of 1978. The entire proposal came to a vote among faculty members, and was adopted by a very close margin (Hansen 1997, p. 190).

In October 1977, the body of external rectors proposed new regulations for Roskilde University Centre, and these were approved by the Ministry of Education 2 months later. Nine departments were established and the councils of the main academic areas were abolished, a decision that was based on assessments by external experts who stated that this organizational structure would discourage the interdisciplinary nature of the University Centre (Hansen 1997, p. 198).

Many faculty members and students perceived the establishment of departments based on single disciplinary fields as a move towards a more traditional organization of the fields of study, as it would mean that faculty members' research would be rooted in relatively narrow academic disciplines. The formation of departments meant that teaching on the superstructure programmes became tied to specialized academic fields. These programmes would no longer be linked to the house themes as their primary setting. Simultaneously with the introduction of the new regulations, it was decided to develop new programmes. A programme in Media (later Communication Studies) was thus established in 1978, and in 1979 a psychology teacher training programme was established (Hansen 1997, p. 210).

In 1977, the external rectors decided that all students from the basic humanities programme had to choose at least one language course at the superstructure level. They also decided that students from the basic humanities programme could no longer choose to study social work. They pointed out that the humanities study programme had evolved in a direction that came too close to social science, which was at the expense of core skills in the humanities (Hansen 1997, p. 211). This decision turned out to have quite serious consequences. The number of student applications to the basic humanities programme dropped drastically because of the restrictions on the choice of subjects. In the light of this, the body of external rectors withdrew its decision (Fig. 5.5).

Fig. 5.5 The body of external rectors. From *left*: Social science professor Jørn Henrik Petersen, historian and archivist Erik Stig Jørgensen, and veterinarian Jørgen Baltzer

5.5 The 'Broad Outline': State Management of the Educational Profile of Roskilde University Centre

In November 1981, the Ministry issued the so-called 'Broad Outline' as a proposal for the future academic profile of Roskilde University Centre. The 'Broad Outline' was grounded in poor employment prospects for high school teachers and social workers. It was proposed to discontinue a number of study programmes, and even to reduce the teaching at the University Centre to two main areas (Natural Sciences and Social Sciences) or to just one main area (Social Sciences). Roskilde University Centre protested against the 'Broad Outline', and received support from the other universities because they regarded this initiative as a general threat to the autonomy of universities (Hansen 1997, p. 232). These reactions led to the Ministry withdrawing the 'Broad Outline'. Instead, the Ministry established a contact committee with representatives of the Ministry and the University Centre to coordinate future planning. Concurrently, the Minister of Education decided that the governing bodies of Roskilde University Centre should be given back control (Hansen 1997, p. 237).

Before the contact committee had completed its work, however, there was a change of government. The new Minister of Education formulated a comprehensive proposal which included the abandonment of the basic humanities programme, the discontinuation of a number of subjects oriented towards teaching in high schools, as well as the closure of the social work programme. The fate of Roskilde University Centre was now once again on the parliamentary agenda. This time the opposition voted down the proposal.

The contact committee completed its work in 1984, and recommended that the teacher training programmes in Social Science, Biology and Psychology should be abolished as well as the programme in Social Work. The committee also recommended setting up new programmes in Business, Business Data Processing and Environmental Biology (Hansen 1997, p. 245). According to the recommendations, it should still be possible to combine the remaining programmes to enable a student to qualify for high school teaching. It should also be possible to combine programmes not directed at high school teaching. In this way Roskilde University Centre introduced a general 'combination model' as the cornerstone of the educational structure. As a consequence, the students now had the opportunity to compose their academic study programme from a wide range of options (Hansen 1997, p. 250). However, the generalized combination model also involved the problem that faculty members would only be responsible for teaching their own subject, which accounted for only half of each combination in the superstructure, i.e. the organizational framework for the last 3 years of study.

From its humble beginning in 1972 to the mid-1980s, Roskilde University Centre had undergone a development from threats of closure and conflicts to a general acceptance as a university equal to others. It had also been able to maintain its educational model with (a) 2-year basic courses and 3-year courses in the superstructure,

(b) a deferred choice of subjects, (c) three main academic fields, (d) options for students to compose their own combinations of programmes across the main academic fields, and (e) problem-oriented, interdisciplinary and participant-directed project work. At the same time, the University Centre had been subject to fundamental changes with respect to its academic profile, faculty-student cooperation, and the link between research and study programmes.

To widen access for people at work, Roskilde University Centre established an Open University in the late 1980s. It also established PhD courses and an international version of the basic humanities study programme with the enrolment of both Danish and foreign students. This initial international programme was later supplemented with international basic programmes in the social and natural sciences. The University Centre also established a so-called Science Shop which would facilitate contact between student groups and groups outside the university, by inviting the external groups to advertise for project groups to conduct studies or developmental work in companies, organizations, or civil society.

In 1988, one of Denmark's major newspapers conducted a survey of how business rated universities, and Roskilde University Centre came in first place. In spite of all its internal conflicts, this rating was generally perceived by faculty members and students as an endorsement of the University Centre's educational, academic and pedagogical model for producing qualified graduates.

5.6 Roskilde University Centre as a Recognized Alternative University

I 1993, the Danish Parliament passed a new University Act that established a one-tier governance structure (see also Chap. 4). The Rector was given responsibility for all activities at the university, whereas the influence of the Senate was limited. The Act also gave the heads of department enhanced powers to assign faculty members specific tasks (Degn and Sørensen 2012, p. 62). However, the University Act did not negate the principle that university leaders should be elected. Roskilde University Centre implemented the regulations of the new Act, but did not, however, implement the organizational model with faculties headed by deans.

In the 1990s, Danish educational policy focused strongly on the educational structures in higher education. It was decided that the universities should adopt the Anglo-Saxon model with a distinction between 3-year bachelor courses, 2-year master courses and 3-year PhD courses. This was a challenge for the educational model of Roskilde University Centre which consisted of 2-year basic programmes and 3-year superstructure programmes. The University Centre chose to retain the original structure, but adjusted the basic programmes to align 'formally' with the national academic requirements for the bachelor level by introducing a new distinction between bachelor and master programmes. The educational model now consisted of three levels: the basic study programmes (2 years), the bachelor modules (1 year) and the master modules (2 years). This meant that the students had to complete a basic programme as well as a required bachelor module (3 years of study in total) to obtain a bachelor degree. However, it was decided that the bachelor modules should not be orientated narrowly towards vocational skills and the labour market. Instead, the emphasis should be on methodological and generic skills (Hansen 1997, p. 280).

As late as in 1995, Roskilde University Centre received its first Ministerial Order. This confirmed its pedagogical and educational profile, but also laid down stricter requirements for the academic coherence and progression of the courses and their pedagogical organization. At least half of study work in the basic programmes should consist of courses and related activities. Previously, the rule had been that at least half of the study activities should be project work (Hansen 1997, p. 315).

Until the adoption of the Ministerial Order, the discussions at the University Centre pointed to a number of internal disagreements on its educational and organizational structure. Some faculty members and students preferred 1-year basic study programmes, while others preferred to maintain the 2-year basic programmes. Some wanted students to be allowed to study a single subject in their bachelor courses, while others preferred that the students should be obliged to study two subjects. Finally, some thought that Roskilde University Centre should implement a faculty structure similar to that of other universities, whereas others preferred to maintain the existing structure without faculties. The discussions did not result in immediate change, but pointed to some latent contradictions which also came to influence developments at the University Centre in the years to come.

At the same time, the pedagogical basis for the university was discussed, not with arguments to abolish the problem-oriented, interdisciplinary, and participant-directed project work, but as an attempt to develop and clarify the model in the light of experience. It was pointed out that (a) the students were unsure as to how much supervision time they would be assigned, (b) the role of the supervisor was practised in a variety of ways, which were not always equally effective, (c) there was a lack of knowledge of how to deal with group processes among both students and faculty, (d) some supervisors were not sufficiently committed to the task of supervision, and (e) the study guidance was not always adequate. Furthermore, a survey showed that quite a large number of students worked individually on their projects, rather than in groups (Hansen 1997, p. 301f.). As a result of this critical discussion, Roskilde University Centre launched a pedagogical investigation and a development project, and created a 'University Pedagogical Training Unit' (UniPed), which would mainly deal with the pedagogical training of faculty members (see also Sect. 8.7).

From the late 1990s and until 2006, developments at Roskilde University Centre were quite orderly. The educational model was retained, and the University Centre expanded its educational activities to new subject areas. The majority of the new programmes were integrated into the combination structure. New programmes were established in Journalism, Social Sciences, Performance Design, Health Promotion & Health Strategies, Philosophy & the Theory of Science, Culture & Language

Studies, Psychology, Pedagogy & Educational Studies, Medical Biology and Molecular Biology. The planning of a fourth basic course in the area of Humanistic Technology was also initiated.

In the anniversary publication on the occasion of Roskilde University Centre's 25th anniversary in 1997, the Rector took the opportunity to describe Roskilde University Centre as an alternative university which had been through many changes, but which had retained its pedagogical and educational core values (Jensen 1997, p. 15).

5.7 Reform of the Studies at Roskilde University Centre

In 2006, the Danish parliament passed a new 'University Act'. It established universities as independent institutions within the realm of public administration. It also introduced new University Boards with external majority as the supreme authority of the universities, and it specified that heads of universities, faculties and departments should no longer be elected by faculty members, staff and students. Instead, they should be hired on contract (see also Chap. 4). This meant that the former elected councils were stripped of their decision-making powers and transformed into purely advisory bodies (Degn and Sørensen 2012, p. 67). The reform led to some conflicts at Roskilde University Centre, not least because the institution also faced budget cutbacks and a risk of job losses. The atmosphere of conflict, however, was relatively quickly replaced by a more stable situation.

In 2008, Roskilde University Centre changed its name to Roskilde University, accepting that the idea of university centres would never be realized. In the same year, it was decided that the University would align fully with the divisions in the Bologna Model between bachelor, master and PhD courses. Already in 2006, the university introduced rules which formally adapted the educational structure to the Bologna model. This involved a redefinition of the basic study programmes as basic units which were then included as part of the bachelor programmes. However, the governance structure was not changed as the University kept the separate study boards for the basic and superstructure elements. Now, the goal was to align the governance structure by implementing separate study boards for the bachelor and the master programmes. At the bachelor level, the University might have chosen just to implement study boards for each of the four main bachelor areas. However, both faculty members and students articulated an interest in more comprehensive changes. One proposal for change was to reduce the basic units to 1 year as an initial part of the 3-year bachelor courses, while another was to establish more specialized bachelor programmes, which in turn would be placed within the 3-year continuous bachelor academic environments to prevent students from changing academic environments several times during their studies.

The new bachelor model was designed through a process that took place in 2009 and 2010, and all faculty members and students were involved. The process opened for constructive discussion of the numerous internal disputes among various groups about the educational structure. The result was a model that was viewed by a large majority as the best possible compromise.

The reform process was based on conditions significantly different from those originally stipulated for Roskilde University Centre:

- In each house for the basic programmes, there were now twice as many students (120) as when the University was established, but the same number of faculty members to handle project supervision and teaching.
- In 2006, the government had decided that group examinations would no longer be allowed at Danish educational institutions. Until then, group examinations had been used with great success at Roskilde University because this form of examination supported the key learning objectives of project work.
- The original Roskilde Model of continuous assessment of project work included problem formulation seminars and intermediate evaluation seminars, as well as final internal assessments of project work in semesters without examinations. The seminars were attended by the project group and the group supervisor, and also by an opponent group with their supervisor. However, in all the basic programmes this model was now changed and reduced because of a lack of resources.
- In all basic programmes, distinctions were made between broader interdisciplinary basic courses and subject-oriented courses. However, there was no common practice with regard to whether such courses primarily should present an overview of an academic area or whether they should mainly support project work.
- With the establishment of departments, the faculty members were assigned offices on the department premises. Here, most of their research was conducted, and here they taught and supervised students during the last 3 years of their studies. Teaching in the basic programmes was undertaken by faculty members from several departments, and was not conducted in the premises of the departments. The result was that it seemed less attractive for faculty members to teach in the basic programmes, which were now no longer the setting for a particularly strong learning community of faculty members and students. Extensive use was made of non-permanent teachers, especially in the basic programme in Social Sciences.

In addition there were some challenges that had been highlighted by different groups at the University throughout the reform process:

- Some suggested that the strengths of the problem-oriented, interdisciplinary and participant-directed project work were not communicated and developed sufficiently to emerge as significant competences in the view of students and employers,
- Some criticized the fact that the educational structure meant that the students achieved only short-term identification with the academic environments in the departments,
- Some expressed concerns that the academic and social environment in the bachelor programmes was too weak,
- Some formulated a need to increase students' academic and professional methodological skills.

On the other hand, there was widespread agreement on the strengths of the 'Roskilde Model':

- The broad academic nature of the basic studies and the possibility to defer subject choices,
- The interdisciplinary character of the studies,
- The great freedom for the students to combine subjects in the double degree programmes,
- The problem-oriented, interdisciplinary and participant-directed project work,
- The relatively close relationship between students and supervisors during project work,
- The study environment in the basic programmes where the students were assigned to the physical and social environment of a house for an extended period of time.

Further positive emphasis was placed on the fact that the bachelor programmes readily attracted new students, and that they had a low drop-out rate and a fast completion rate.

Roskilde University adopted a new comprehensive strategy in 2010, which also came to influence the reform process. According to the new strategy, the University needed to be further developed as a critical, socially committed, experimental university with an international orientation within key areas. The university should have a solid foundation in interdisciplinary, problem-oriented and participant-directed project work. The university should be characterized by a strong research base linked to the study programmes and a strong relationship between students and researchers. The university should also continually develop educational traditions, including project work, alternative teaching methods, and the relationship between these and project work. Furthermore, the evaluation culture and the examination methods should be developed to support the learning objectives in the best possible ways, and to enhance the students' learning opportunities (Rektorsekretariatet 2010).

The organization of the new bachelor programmes took place from the autumn of 2010 to the summer of 2012. The organization of these programmes involved work in a wide variety of areas, including the regulatory framework, governance models, resource allocation, administrative organization, study guidance, course logistics, types of courses, course content, social and academic study environment, and methods of assessment and examination. The efforts resulted in the creation of four new bachelor programmes which enrolled their first students in autumn 2012 (see Chap. 6).

References

Degn, L. & Sørensen, M. P. (2012). Universitetsloven fra 2003. På vej mod konkurrenceuniversitetet? [The University Act of 2003. Towards the Competitive University?] In K. Aagaard & N. Mejlgaard (Eds.), *Dansk forskningspolitik efter årtusindskiftet* [Danish research policy in the new millennium] (pp. 59–94). Aarhus: Aarhus University Press.

Hansen, E. (1997). *En koral i tidens strøm* [A coral in the flow of time]. Frederiksberg: Roskilde University Press.
Jensen, H. T. (1997). RUC – Nu og i morgen. Sammenhænge og perspektiver [RUC – now and tomorrow. Contexts and perspectives]. In H. T. Jensen, K. S. Jakobsen, E. Ebbe, & N. S. Clausen (Eds.), *RUC i 25 år* [RUC - 25 years] (pp. 15–29). Frederiksberg: Roskilde University Press.
Nielsen, J. C., Jensenius, N. H., & Olesen, H. S. (1997). *Utopien der slog rod. RUC – radikalitet og realisme* [The Utopia that took root. RUC – radicalism and realism]. Roskilde: The RUC Student Council.
Rektorsekretariatet. (2010). *Strategi RUC 2015* [RUC strategy to 2015]. Roskilde: Roskilde University. Retrieved November 29, 2013, from http://www.ruc.dk/fileadmin/assets/adm/rektoratet/strategi2015/RUC_strategi_2015.pdf

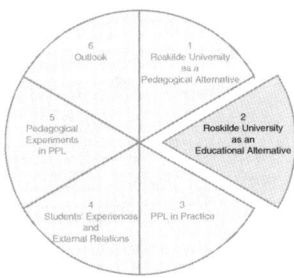

Chapter 6
The Bachelor Programmes and the Roskilde Model

Morten Blomhøj, Thyge Enevoldsen, Michael Haldrup, and Niels Møller Nielsen

6.1 Introduction

The entrance level at Roskilde University consists of the four bachelor programmes: SAMBACH (the social sciences programme), HUMBACH (the humanities programme), NATBACH (the natural sciences programme), and HUMTEK (the humanities and technology programme). The first three programmes are also offered in English as international bachelor programmes. All four programmes are 3-year programmes each with a common basic *interdisciplinary* one and a half year basic programme with built-in support for the students' gradual specialization in two subjects. All four programmes are based on the four central pedagogical principles of *problem-orientation, interdisciplinarity, participant-directed project work* and *exemplarity* as these principles are defined and discussed in Chap. 2 (see also Olesen and Jensen 1999, pp. 16–17).

In this chapter we look specifically at how these principles are prominent in both the substance of the programmes and in the ways in which they are organized. We do so by giving a range of examples of how these principles come to the fore in the specific forms of teaching, supervising and in managing studies in the programmes.

M. Blomhøj (✉) • T. Enevoldsen • M. Haldrup • N.M. Nielsen
Roskilde University, Roskilde, Denmark
e-mail: blomhoej@ruc.dk; thygee@ruc.dk; mhp@ruc.dk; nmn@ruc.dk

© Springer International Publishing Switzerland 2015
A.S. Andersen, S.B. Heilesen (eds.), *The Roskilde Model: Problem-Oriented Learning and Project Work*, Innovation and Change in Professional Education 12,
DOI 10.1007/978-3-319-09716-9_6

As a basis for the discussions we give brief descriptions in Sect. 6.3 of each of the four programmes, underscoring their structural differences. Next, we organize the discussion thematically in Sect. 6.4 with regard to the principles of problem-orientation, exemplarity and interdisciplinarity, highlighting particular instances and examples of how these principles come into force in the four bachelor programmes as they are planned, carried out, evaluated and further developed. In Sect. 6.5 we discuss the practical organization of the bachelor programmes and in particular how this organization supports participant-directed project work. The chapter ends with a section on the relation of the bachelor programmes to society at large.

However, before proceeding to the application of the above mentioned principles, we compare the old bachelor programme model at Roskilde University (adaptations of the original 1972 model) with the recently implemented, new model of 2012. Following that, we discuss some of the differences in the ways in which the new model is being implemented across the four bachelor programmes at Roskilde University.

From early on in the university's history, the study programmes at Roskilde University were devised with the deliberate intention of attracting students from a broader segment of society than that of the traditional universities. Within each of the main academic areas of natural sciences, humanities and social sciences, a 2-year interdisciplinary basic study programme was designed to provide the students with a broad interdisciplinary background before they moved on to studying more specialized subjects (see also Chap. 5). These broad entry-level study programmes, as well as the more specialized master programmes, were all based on the four overarching pedagogical principles mentioned above. The general idea, no less relevant today than it was at the outset in the 1970s, is that these principles not only cater for a broader segment of students that may not have the benefit of a suitable cultural background for traditional, elite academics, but in fact also yield learning results that prove to be superior to more classical approaches based on traditional conceptions of learning (Illeris 1999).

In 2008, a fourth basic programme was established in Humanities and Technology (HUMTEK), and from 2012 the four basic study programmes have been adjusted to comply with the Bologna standards transforming them into full 3-year bachelor programmes. In Sect. 6.2 we look more closely at the development of the new bachelor model at Roskilde University.

As we shall see, the four principles are still very much in force in the bachelor programmes. In general, they imply that students themselves decide which problems they want to work with in their projects, and these problems guide the project work, including the decisions of which academic, scholarly or scientific disciplines, theories and methods to include in their projects. The principle of exemplarity balances the three other principles with general insights and the educational goals that the project work is meant to develop among the students. These principles were seen – and still are – as the general pedagogical answer to the challenge of forming a critical university that can produce university education of societal relevance (Christiansen 1999, pp. 57–58).

The introduction of different forms of project work is a common element in modern reforms of university studies. A frequent argument used for the introduction of project work is the expected positive effects on students' motivation for working with the scientific and academic disciplines. An equally common argument against project work, on the other hand, holds that the coverage of curricula through project work is highly inefficient.

In our opinion, both these arguments miss the point. Problem-oriented project work can and should serve other educational purposes than traditional forms of teaching and should, therefore, not be seen as just a motivating but ineffective form of teaching scientific and academic disciplines to students. The educational value of project work goes beyond motivating students – even though project work may also have that effect. Instead, project work should be justified and evaluated on the basis of clarified educational goals. In general, if it is an educational goal that students should be able to formulate and investigate complex problems in collaboration with others, it follows that some form of problem-oriented project work seems appropriate as a constituent of the study programme. Moreover, as we shall see, problem-oriented project work can serve high-level educational goals related to interdisciplinarity and to reflection and criticism in general.

However, in academic university studies, project work cannot do the job alone. Course work where the students are introduced to and systematically trained in using concepts, theories and methods of the different scientific disciplines is an indispensable element of university studies. Project work and course work can be seen as complementary elements in our bachelor programmes. They play different educational roles and they are organized very differently. Although courses can take many different forms, in general the courses are directed by the teacher and organized according to the logic and tradition of the particular discipline. The activities for the students are planned by the teacher to support the students' construction of a particular body of knowledge in the best way possible.

The 50-50 balance between project work and course work has been an important dogma for Roskilde University for many years. Of course one could argue that the ideal balance between project work and course work depends on the subjects under consideration. However, in the history of Roskilde University the dogma has proven to be very important for maintaining problem-oriented, interdisciplinary and participant-directed project work as the most important characteristic of Roskilde University education. In particular this has been the case in the 2012 reform. The balance between projects and courses were not part of the discussions even in this reform context where everything else was discussed. In the bachelor programmes the 50-50 dogma is applied even at semester level. In each semester, half of the students' study work is devoted to student-directed and problem-oriented project work, while the other half consists of different forms of course work.

6.2 Towards a New, Integrated Bachelor Model

As an early reform university, Roskilde University introduced a revolutionary entrance level study programme from the outset in 1972, i.e. the 2-year basic studies programme. The programmes were interdisciplinary, aimed at student participation, problem-oriented project work and exemplarity (see also Chap. 5). After 2 years of studies, students would then move on to more specialized studies in the university's superstructure programmes for 3 years in order to obtain master degrees in two subjects of equal weight or in some cases in one subject with double weight (see also Chap. 5). The bachelor degree did not exist in Denmark until the late 1980s, and the original model at the university was conceived as a 2+3 structure for all study programmes. For the sake of comparison, Fig. 6.1 shows the first 3 years of the full master programme in the original model, i.e. what would later be transformed into the Roskilde University bachelor programme model when the 3 year bachelor structure was superimposed on the basic studies. The new bachelor structure is shown in Fig. 6.2.

	Project work 15 ECTS	Courses work 15 ECTS
	The Basic Studies/ Specialisation Model Roskilde University 1972 - 2012	
6. sem.	Project subject 2	Course work subject 2
5. sem.	Project subject 1	Course work subject 1
4. sem.	Basic Project 4	Course work for specialisation
3. sem.	Basic Project 3	Course work for specialisation
2. sem.	Basic Project 2	Basic studies course work
1. sem.	Basic Project 1	Basic studies course work

Fig. 6.1 The original model with programmes of four-semesters of basic studies followed by studies in two specific subjects under separate study regulations. For the sake of comparison the figure shows only the 1st year of the specialized programmes, i.e. in total the three 1st years of the programme that would later be transformed into the bachelor programme model shown in Fig. 6.2. In the original model, after two more years with the same structure as in the 3d year, the students completed their master education in the two chosen subjects

6.2.1 The 2012 Reform

The 2012 reform of the bachelor programmes was initiated with the main purposes of (1) implementing the Bologna model, (2) supporting the students' earlier and gradual specialization and (3) making it easier for the students to specialize in two subjects from different branches of science.

The bachelor reform was organized as a bottom-up process where committees from each of the university's four main academic areas provided ideas and suggestions to a central steering committee assigned the task of arriving at a common model for the bachelor programmes.

The general structure arrived at for the bachelor study programmes at Roskilde University in the 2012 reform is depicted in Fig. 6.2. The model is interpreted in various ways in the four bachelor study programmes, but for the sake of simplicity we provide a general model as an overview.

The bachelor programmes have retained an initial broad, interdisciplinary part, worth 85 ECTS credits, which serves as the foundation for subsequently choosing two specialized subject modules of 35 ECTS each. The subject modules include one project (15 ECTS) and four subject courses (each of 5 ECTS) with the exception of SAMBACH where one of the subject courses is replaced by a course on methods, see Fig. 6.3. In addition, all the bachelor programmes include two 5 ECTS optional courses, which can be used to make the choice of subject modules more flexible. If the student changes his or her choice of subject module after having taken one or two

	The Bachelor Study Programme Model Roskilde University 2012			
	Project work 15 ECTS	Courses 5 ECTS	Courses 5 ECTS	Courses 5 ECTS
6. sem.	Bachelor Project Subject 1 and / or subject 2	Optional	Optional	Basic Studies
5. sem.	Project subject 2	Subject 2	Subject 2	Subject 2
4. sem.	Project subject 1	Subject 1	Subject 1	Subject 1
3. sem.	Basic project 3	Subject 1	Subject 2	Basic Studies
2.sem.	Basic project 2	Basic Studies	Basic Studies	Basic Studies
1. sem.	Basic project 1	Basic Studies	Basic Studies	Basic Studies

Fig. 6.2 A generalized representation of the new bachelor programmes at Roskilde University, the 3 + 2 year model. (The area-specific variation is omitted here; see Figs. 6.3, 6.4, 6.5 and 6.6 for details). The individual study activities do not necessarily have to be taken in the order depicted in the model

subject courses in, say, the 3rd semester, the optional courses can be used as subject courses in the new subject module, thus preventing a prolongation of the bachelor studies for the student. The bachelor programmes are rounded off by a bachelor project (15 ECTS), which could be an interdisciplinary project within a main academic area or in the intersection of the two chosen subjects, or it could be a project within one of the chosen subjects. While one of the subject modules must be within the main academic area of the bachelor programme in question, the other subject module is likely to be chosen across the boundaries of the main areas. The content of the subject modules is regulated by the study board of the subject. All other elements for the study programmes are regulated by the Bachelor Study Board.

As is evident from Figs. 6.1 and 6.2, a range of changes have been introduced. Where the original model had a sharp distinction between the basic studies and the specialization studies, regulated by separate sets of study regulations under separate boards of study, the new model is designed to integrate all elements of the bachelor programme. Hence each of the new bachelor study programmes is regulated by an integrated set of study regulations, and managed by one study board only.

Another major change is that whereas the old model offered the students a range of choices (e.g. in the specialization courses), the new model incorporates many more optional study activities that can be taken at various stages in the programme. One such choice applies to the optional courses, which could serve different purposes, e.g. flexibility in the choice of subject modules as already mentioned, the possibility to take extra subject courses in other subject modules as auxiliary courses, the option of taking more 'exotic' courses in the pursuit of the students' personal interests, and the possibility of getting full credit for a semester as an exchange student.

The bachelor project in the 6th semester is also an important new common feature in the bachelor programmes. The bachelor project can be an interdisciplinary study of a problem within the domain of the branch of science, or it can be based explicitly on one or both of the subjects already covered during semesters 4 and 5.

While the reform has fundamentally changed the bachelor programme at the organizational level, the new model also carries over a number of ideas from the old model. The transition from covering the broad spectrum of the subject area of the branch of science in question at the outset, and then zooming in on chosen specialized subjects is retained in the new model. The substance covered in the basic studies part is also in most cases rooted in the old model. These common features will be treated in detail in Sects. 6.4 and 6.5 of the present chapter.

6.3 Implementing the Reform: Common Features and Differences

The general model represented in Fig. 6.2 has been implemented with some variation across the four bachelor study programmes. In this section we briefly comment on how differences in academic and disciplinary tradition as well as political views on education and learning in the academic areas of Roskilde University are mirrored in how the general model is realized in the four bachelor programmes.

6.3.1 The SAMBACH Programme Structure

The model that was finally accepted by the central steering committee was originally one of two models proposed by the committee for the social sciences. The model was later revised in order to accommodate the other branches of science (see the generalized model in Fig. 6.2), but SAMBACH has retained a version of the model which adheres closely to the original model proposed by the social sciences committee. This model is shown in Fig. 6.3 and exemplified here with a combination of *Politics and Administration* and *Communication* as the two subject modules.

In SAMBACH the general idea is that students in the programme stay attached to the same bachelor house for the entire duration of the bachelor programme. (See Figs. 6.7 and 6.8 for images of a bachelor house and Fig. 12.1 for a ground plan of a bachelor house). Within the integrated framework, students study their two subject

	The Bachelor Study Programme In Social Science Roskilde University 2012			
	Project work 15 ECTS	Courses 5 ECTS	Courses 5 ECTS	Courses 5 ECTS
6. sem.	Bachelor Project Subject 1 and / or subject 2	Administrative Law (Subject 1)	Political Communication (Optional)	Analysis Strategies (Method course)
5. sem.	Project subject 2 Communication Studies	Communication: Participants, Processes and Contexts (Subject 2)	Planned Communication with Print Media Production	Workshop in Planned Subject Specific Communication (Subject 2)
4. sem.	Project subject 1 Politics and Administration	Management in Public Organizations (Subject 1)	Theoretical Perspectives in Communication Studies (Subject 2)	Quantitative Methods (Method course)
3. sem.	Basic project 3	Political Institutions and their Interactions (Subject 1)	Political Thinkers, Old and Modern (Optional)	Philosophy of Social Science
2. sem.	Basic project 2	Economics and Planning (Basic course)		Qualitative Methods
1. sem.	Basic project 1	Political Science and Sociology (Basic course)		Project Work Methodology (Method course)

Fig. 6.3 The programme structure for SAMBACH illustrated with a study programme for a student who chooses *Politics and Administration* and *Communication* as the two subject modules in his or her bachelor education. As in the following diagrams (Figs. 6.4, 6.5 and 6.6), the sequence of the subject projects in semesters 4 and 5 and of the subject courses can be chosen differently. Likewise, the optional courses are just examples of courses, which make sense in this particular combination

modules simultaneously, in what is referred to as the 'vertical study scheme'. This structure was chosen to address a problem in the horizontal model, where the student in the combination structure alternates between academic environments and can be absent for up to a year, which of course hampers the possibility of continuous progression in the chosen subject. In a vertical structure, the students will be present in the academic environment of the chosen subjects, and can participate in both the academic and the social life.

Another central idea in the SAMBACH model (Fig. 6.3) is the column of common methodology courses in the right-hand side. The methodology course structure implies that all students in the house have common activities each semester, regardless of their choice of specialization modules. The rationale for this structure is that the social sciences are characterized by certain general methods and methodologies, which may be applied to different types of societal problem areas. Thus, the methodology courses represent a form of *crossdisciplinarity* in the study programme (see Sect. 2.1). Sharing and developing common methods and methodologies are therefore seen as an important constituent of the SAMBACH programme. Another constituent is the common approach in a problem-oriented analytical academic culture, which gives the SAMBACH programme some possibilities not shared by the other programmes. The methodology courses are linked to the projects in four of the six semesters (e.g. in semesters 1, 2, 3, and 6), emphasizing the problem orientation of the learning process and its exemplary qualities in relation to the use and criticism of the methodologies.

As explained, the general study structure at Roskilde University gives the student the possibility of combining subjects from the different branches of science. In SAMBACH, students can choose between more than 60 combinations, in theory at least. However, in reality most students choose from the smaller number of more profiled combinations. More than 40 % of the students combine a subject module in Social Sciences with one from the Humanities, and here the most popular combinations are Business Studies with Journalism or Communication, or Politics and Administration with Journalism or Communication, as shown in Fig. 6.3.

Combinations like these demand and develop high competences in interdisciplinary studies. Students' interdisciplinary competences are supported through optional courses, e.g. in political communication, which could be an optional course taken in the 6th semester.

The possibility of combining subjects between the different bachelor programmes, and continuing to do so in the graduate programme, allows students to specialize in unusual combinations of qualifications and competences, which can be directed towards specific areas of employment. Students may also use this possibility to focus on expanding markets, as in the given example, where the growing media focus on the function of spin doctors in public relations has made this combination popular.

6.3.2 The HUMTEK Programme Structure

The interpretation of the model in HUMTEK is somewhat similar to the SAMBACH version. In the 1st year, students are introduced to basic concepts and methodologies in Technical Science, Design and the Humanities, by participating in compulsory course work and workshop modules. In the 2nd and 3rd year, the study of two subjects is integrated with course work within a range of specialized areas ('profile courses') meant to provide students with skills and competences from particular design domains. For the time being, the students can choose between the following profile courses: Urban Design, Interaction Design, Health and Welfare Design, and Organization and Management of Design Processes. These profile courses each support particular combinations of subject modules and help to orient the bachelor studies towards particular labour markets. For instance, the course in Urban Design taken in combination with subjects such as Planning/Geography and Communication can profile the study for students aiming at a future career as an urban planner or designer, community worker or related professions. Figure 6.4 shows how a student might combine Computer Science and Performance Design and take optional courses in urban design. Such a study programme will enable the student to work with e.g. installation art, the management of cultural events or other areas in the culture/tourism/experience sector.

	Project work 15 ECTS	Courses 5 ECTS	Courses 5 ECTS	Courses 5 ECTS
The Bachelor Study Programme In Humanities and Technology Roskilde University 2012				
6. sem.	Bachelor Project Subject 1 and / or subject 2	Project Management and Design Practice (Subject 2)	Situation, Place and Space (Subject 2)	Urban Design II (Optional)
5. sem.	Project subject 2 Performance Design	Performance Design (Subject 2)	Performance Design and Design Methods (Subject 2)	Urban Design I (Optional)
4. sem.	Project subject 1 Computer science	Essential Computing II (Subject 1)	Interactive Digital Systems (Subject 1)	Interaction Design II (Profile course)
3. sem.	Basic project 3 Subjectivity, Technology and Society	Essential Computing I (Subject 1)	Modelling & Knowledge Management (Subject 1)	Interaction Design I (Profile course)
2. sem.	Basic project 2 Technological Systems and Artefacts	Media and technology (TSA II) (Dimension)	Subjectivity, Technology and Society (Dimension)	Design course
				Rapid prototyping / 3D print
1. sem.	Basic project 1 Design and Construction	Technological Systems and Artefacts I (Dimension)	Subjectivity, Technology and Society (Dimension)	Design course
				Creative computing

Fig. 6.4 The HUMTEK structure illustrated with a possible programme for a student combining *Computer Science* and *Performance Design*. The programme utilizes all the possibilities for choosing between optional workshops and profile courses to gradually specialize in the chosen directions

6.3.3 The HUMBACH Programme Structure

The range of disciplinary traditions in the humanities at Roskilde University is more heterogeneous than in the social sciences. Some disciplines across the field can be perceived as 'new humanities' oriented towards practice and intervention, to some degree involving a mixture of methodologies from the humanities and social sciences. On the other hand, the humanities include more classical 'arts' approaches which are rooted in a hermeneutic tradition of more interpretative methodology. These differences run across the three departments contributing to the programme, and within these general groups there are yet other deeply rooted differences in terms of the use of theory, method, concepts and practice. In consequence, the HUMBACH model is rather more oriented towards focusing on the specialization modules where students concentrate for one semester at a time on their chosen subject, and on the theory, method, and concepts particular to that field. What was a methodological column in SAMBACH is conceptualized in HUMBACH as a portfolio of courses supporting a formal progression in the project work done in each semester. This progression runs from introducing students to the practical and methodological elements involved in doing project work (semester 1), to giving the students a sense of the heterogeneity of methodology in the humanities (semester 2), through helping students to gain competence in reflecting on the humanistic knowledge they produce in their project work (semester 3) to finally introducing key elements involved in communicating their project work to specified target groups (semester 6) (Fig. 6.5).

Whereas the specialization modules in semesters 4 and 5 focus on the particular subjects chosen within the broad field of the humanities, the 1st year and a half of the programme, on the other hand, is clearly interdisciplinary in its focus. As we shall discuss further below, the four dimensions covered in this introductory phase of the programme, Culture and History, Subjectivity and Learning, Text and Sign, and Science and Philosophy, are emphatically not conceptualized as collections of mono-disciplinary fields. On the contrary, they aim to make students look at problems unconstrained by disciplinary boundaries and explore the humanities as a complex academic totality in order to develop their understanding of the problems. Indeed, the four dimensions taken together are conceived as a *formative education* that enables students in the humanities to enter disciplinary fields with a set of broad, humanistic competences, encouraging them to have a greater contextual understanding of the types of knowledge in their chosen field.

As mentioned earlier, the humanities at Roskilde University offer a wide scope of choices between subject modules. In the above representation, the two subject modules of Philosophy and Cultural Encounters are given as examples of a meaningful combination. The combination represents a meeting between the above-mentioned classic conception of the humanities as the locus of interpretation, hermeneutics and argumentation and the more recent conception of considering the humanities as a field in which interpretive insights may be converted into action or intervention.

	Project work 15 ECTS	Courses 5 ECTS	Courses 5 ECTS	Courses 5 ECTS
	The Bachelor Study Programme In Humanities **Roskilde University 2012**			
6. sem.	Bachelor Project Subject 1 and / or subject 2	Globalisation and Psychology (Optional)	Critical Thinking (Optional)	Communication (Progression)
5. sem.	Project subject 2 Philosophy and Science Studies	History of Philosophy 1600-1900 (Subject 2)	Ethics and Political Philosophy (Subject 2)	Metaphysics and Epistemology (Subject 2)
4. sem.	Project subject 1 Cultural Encounters	Categorisation and Power (Subject 1)	Cultural Analysis (Subject 1)	Globalisation and the Transnational (Subject 1)
3. sem.	Basic project 3	Cultural Theory (Subject 1)	History of Philosophy and Science until 1600 (Subject 2)	Theory for the Humanities (Progression)
2. sem.	Basic project 2	Culture and History (Dimension)	Subjectivity and Learning (Dimension)	Method (Progression)
1. sem.	Basic project 1	Text and Sign (Dimension)	Science and Philosophy (Dimension)	Project Technique (Progression)

Fig. 6.5 The programme structure for HUMBACH illustrated with a possible programme for a student combining *Cultural Encounters* and *Philosophy and Science Studies*. It should be noted that the subject modules are recommended to be studied 'horizontally' in semesters 4 and 5 respectively

Where, at the outset, the former represents the classic humanities and the latter the new conception, both chosen subjects are open to the whole methodological range of humanistic inquiry and action. The combination offers competences highly relevant to several job markets, such as the ability to reflect on ideology, identity and ethics in contexts of cross-cultural and transnational diversity.

The combination can involve a range of optional courses that will all be highly relevant. Here the optional courses are represented by a course dealing with social psychological effects of globalization offered by the psychology department, and an optional course in critical thinking offered by the philosophy department.

6.3.4 The NATBACH Programme Structure

The NATBACH programme differs from the other programmes in the structure and discipline orientation of the course programme. In each semester the student takes a so-called intensive course for the first 5 weeks, followed by two other courses in parallel over a period of 8 weeks. In general, the courses worth 5 ECTS in NATBACH require between 40 and 65 h of class sessions or experimental work in labs. To enable students to work on their projects along with the courses throughout the semester, it was decided that the students should take no more than two courses in parallel. The common courses in the three 1st semesters and some courses with a substantial experimental element are offered as intensive courses (Fig. 6.6).

The common courses in the three 1st semesters establish foundations which can be utilized in the project work and built upon in the discipline-oriented courses. In the two first courses in Empirical Data and Experimental Methods the students are provided with concepts, methods, computer tools and practical experimental experiences relevant across all the natural science disciplines. In the third

	The Bachelor Study Programme In Natural Science Roskilde University 2012			
	Project work 15 ECTS	Courses 5 ECTS	Courses 5 ECTS	Courses 5 ECTS
6. sem.	Bachelor Project Subject 1 and / or subject 2	EssentialComputing 1 (Optional)	Genetics (Subject 2)	Mixtures and Separation (Subject 1)
5. sem.	Project subject 2 Molecular Biology	Methods in Molecular Biology (Subject 2)	Biochemistry (Subject 2)	The Analytical Chemistry of Ions (Subject 1)
4. sem.	Project subject 1 Chemistry	Biophysics (Optional)	Chemical Thermodynamics and Kinetics (Subject 1)	Quantum Chemistry and Spectroscopy (Subject 1)
3. sem.	Basic project 3 Natural Sciences and Theory of Science	Theory of Natural Science (Common course)	Molecules of life (Subject 2)	Statistical Models (Basic course)
2.sem.	Basic project 2 Interaction between Model, Theory, Experiment, and Simulation	Experimental Methods (Common course)	The Chemical Reaction (Basic course)	Biological Chemistry (Basic course)
1. sem.	Basic project 1 Applications of Science in Technology and Society	Empirical Data (Common course)	Organic Chemistry (Basic course)	Cell Biology (Basic course)

Fig. 6.6 The programme structure for NATBACH illustrated with a possible programme for a student choosing Chemistry and Molecular Biology as the two subject modules in his or her bachelor studies

common course the students are introduced to theory of the natural sciences as a basis for meta-reflections on and criticism of the practices of natural sciences and their epistemological foundations. Together the three common courses represent elements of a *transdisciplinary* common core in the natural sciences, which can come into play and be further developed in the problem-oriented thematic projects of semesters 1 to 3.

However, in the main academic area of the natural sciences the subjects are also characterized by hierarchical knowledge and discipline structures. During the first three semesters the programme allows students to prepare for specialization in two natural science subjects by giving them the option to choose between General Biology, Environmental Biology, Chemistry, Computer Science, Geography, Mathematics, Microbiology, Medical Biology, and Technological and Socio-Economic Planning. In order to accommodate this need for flexibility, five courses can be chosen by the students from a 'course buffet' offered each semester. These courses are discipline-oriented and each subject module can specify up to two of these courses as recommended foundations for studying the subject module. In this way the programme supports discipline-structured progression. Most of the courses offered on the buffet serve as auxiliary disciplines for more than one subject module. This is particularly true for some mathematical and elementary computer science courses, which are relevant across all the subjects, as well as for crossdisciplinary courses in different branches of biology, in biology and chemistry, chemistry and mathematics, chemistry and physics, mathematics and computer science, and mathematics and physics.

In general the NATBACH programme is the most complex of the bachelor programmes due to the difficult balance between the demands for educational coherence, flexibility and subject matter progression. The challenges of maintaining this balance are reinforced by the fact that NATBACH is also the smallest programme measured in number of students and therefore the required large variation in courses is rather expensive.

6.4 Substantial Features of the Bachelor Model

6.4.1 Problem Orientation

Probably the most important aspect of having project work as the principal method of learning is the fact that project work deals with *problems,* not with *topics, subjects,* or *assignments* (see also Sect. 2.3). Topics and subjects are accounts of some aspect of reality, either narrow or broad, but inherently not invested with the students' personal interest. They comply with a scientific ideal of the researcher being disinterested and withdrawn from any normative stake in the process of investigating the object before him. When assignments are given to students to account for their learning of topics and subjects it might be remote from any real sense of motivation other than the instrumental rationale of passing the exam. In this situation the person who is supposed to fulfil the assignment (the student), is by definition not the same person as the one giving the assignment (the teacher); and with regard to learning, this role distribution is not optimal.

In project work, on the other hand, students formulate a problem that will form the basis of and point of departure for their project. Since the formulation of the problem rests on the project group members themselves, it is possible to design a project in which the members of the group can have a genuine interest in understanding the problem better or even providing a solution to it. The intricate connection between knowledge and interest is not only reflected in Habermas' well-known observation that, in general, the differing interests of the sciences, i.e. theoretical interest (the natural sciences), practical knowledge (the humanities), and emancipatory interest (the social sciences) (Habermas 2005) render any notion of value-free research not only impossible, but indeed undesirable. It is also a central point that on the smaller scale of the individual researcher's view of reality, knowledge *presupposes* human interest. Knowledge is here taken in a very broad sense to include also practical knowledge obtained through direct hands-on 'situated' experience (cf. Lave and Wenger 1991) and even knowledge-in-action (cf. Schön 1983). As a way of obtaining knowledge in this broad conception, project work emphatically has human interest at its core.

Working in groups is essential for problem-oriented, interdisciplinary and participant-directed project work. It is the prerequisite for the students to acquire the special competencies offered by Roskilde University. Good group work develops both the academic competence and the social abilities of the individual. The fact is that project work is not a predictable linear process, proceeding from start to end. It is a process demanding constant reflection on the chosen problem, considering the ever-present choice between what theoretical angles and methodical approaches may be relevant in dealing with the problem.

Thus, in a group the students practise their ability to expound their own thoughts and viewpoints, and those of others, through written and oral presentations, which are then discussed. They practise summarizing texts and theories, and communicating them to others. They learn to evaluate the work of others and to give feedback. They train giving and receiving criticism, both academically and personally. They are forced into the art of collaboration. It encourages the ability to solve academic and personal conflicts. Each student's ambitions and wishes for a good learning process lead him or her to make demands and set limits. Listening to others and making way for the viewpoints of others are abilities which may be difficult to master.

In the following, we look at three aspects of utilizing the problem orientation towards achieving the learning goals connected to the project work in the bachelor programmes. We look at how project work can be organized around house-specific themes (NATBACH), how progression can be built into the sequence of projects (SAMBACH), and how academic dimensions serve to structure project work (HUMBACH and HUMTEK).

6.4.2 Thematic Organization of Project Work in NATBACH

The project work in first three semesters of the NATBACH programme is organized around so-called semester themes. The students are expected to formulate and conduct projects within the following thematic frameworks: 1st semester: *Application of the natural sciences in technology and society;* 2nd semester: *Interaction between model, theory, experiment, and simulation in natural sciences;* and 3rd semester: *Natural sciences and theory of science.*

The function of the themes is to ensure that the students acquire insights into, knowledge about, and experiences with different kinds of issues regarding (1) the role of science and mathematics in society, (2) the methods of science; the significance of models, theories, simulations, and experiments and their mutual relationships, and (3) science and mathematics as a cultural and social phenomenon with a history. A more detailed description of the project work in NATBACH including analyses of project examples representing the themes for each of the three 1st semesters can be found in Blomhøj and Kjeldsen (2009).

The underlying idea is that students, through problem-oriented project work, become acquainted with mathematics and the sciences observed from different perspectives. Seen as a whole the three themes constitute an ambition of versatility of perspective, and students are supposed to gain exemplary experiences with these three themes through their project work.

The themes do not give any guidance as to what should, or could, be the scientific content of projects. This is not decided beforehand; in fact it is solely defined by the problems with which the students choose to work. Basically, the project problem is only subject to three requirements: it should be clearly related to natural sciences including mathematics, it has to fulfil the semester theme requirements, and it should be exemplary, in the sense that it represents a larger range of problems (see also Chap. 3).

6.4.3 Project Work Progression in SAMBACH

In SAMBACH, there is a built-in progression in the requirements for the projects, so that the requirements for e.g. the 1st semester project are also expected to be met in the 2nd semester project. Thus, the 4th semester project must include not only an independent discussion of empirical material, but also the use of one or more methods of social science, and a substantiated choice of theory and empirical material based on the philosophy of social science.

In the 1st semester the project must draw up, substantiate and investigate a problem formulation chosen by the group.

In the 2nd semester, the project (based on a problem formulation chosen by the group) must be analysed in an interdisciplinary manner involving perspectives from at least two of the four subject areas included in the basic part of the bachelor programme. The analysis must be substantiated theoretically. Furthermore, the project must involve methodological reflections involving different methods in social science.

In the 3rd semester, the problem field of the project must be analysed in an interdisciplinary perspective. The analysis must be theoretically substantiated. Choice of problem, theory and empirical material must be substantiated, based on the philosophy of social science.

Originally in the 2-year study programme, the 4th semester projects had to include an independent discussion of empirical material. After the adjustment following the adoption of the Bologna structure this has been changed, so that the project in the 6th semester is supported by a course in Analysis Strategies.

During the project work phase, the group has a supervisor allocated, who is responsible for the academic supervision of the group and assists in suggesting literature, interpreting the material, including academic problems and concepts (see also Chap. 8). In addition, the project work is supported by workshops intended to enhance the quality of the projects.

6.4.4 *Organizing Project Work by Dimensions in HUMBACH and HUMTEK*

In HUMBACH, all projects done during the first three semesters must be anchored academically in at least one of the four interdisciplinary dimensions, and by the end of the 3rd semester, all students should have covered all four dimensions in their projects combined:

- Science and Philosophy,
- Text and Sign,
- Culture and History,
- Subjectivity and Learning.

These dimensions of the humanities are not based on an ad-hoc registration of which subjects are currently available to study at Roskilde University. Rather the dimensioning of the programme is based on perspectives on human experience that are transcendent and have been known since antiquity, such as the distinctions between past and future and between thought and action. The broader framework of the four dimensions is laid out in Larsen (2013).

The dimensions set the stage for problem formulation and eventually ensure that students obtain a comprehensive insight into the field of the humanities without constraining the choice of project more than necessary. Clearly, it is possible for any one student to put much more emphasis on studies within one dimension and treat other dimensions more superficially, and this is by no means a drawback. The dimension system merely ensures that all students have a broad, general understanding of the field, while there is no intention to make all students equally insightful into all dimensions.

During the course work in the first two semesters, students are introduced to all four dimensions; this is a process intended to support the academic level of the project work, where problems can be dealt with in the form of examples representing specific aspects of the dimensions. It is a key point that project work is not supposed to 'cover' dimensions, but rather that projects should be 'anchored' in at least one dimension. Furthermore, a project may be anchored in two dimensions at the same time, but in different ways, and with different weight. To give an example, a project may deal with the social construction of collective memory in ex-Yugoslavia. The angle may be on analyses of cultural identity processes, such as the way history is produced in order to substantiate identity work in a group of expatriate Serbs. Here the *main dimension* will be the 'Culture and History' dimension, as the theoretical and conceptual focus is central to the dimension. However, methodologically, the project may well focus on how the respondents provide their contributions through narratives, i.e. data that is most reliably understood through close, linguistic and narrative analyses of the interaction. This will mean that the 'Text and Sign' dimension is at work as a *supporting dimension*, since narrative analysis methods belong here. The project in question will become anchored in both dimensions, and in the project exam the students should be prepared to discuss questions arising from both dimensions.

In HUMTEK, a central element in the curriculum is to enable students to identify, analyse and suggest relevant solutions to real-life problems. For a more detailed discussion of this, see Haldrup and Svabo (2012).

All student work – whether projects, workshops or courses – is focusing on the three key dimensions in the bachelor programme:

- Design and Construction,
- Technological Systems and Artefacts,
- Subjectivity, Technology and Society.

The three 'basic projects' are each related to one of these dimensions and the 1st year includes parallel dimension courses in the three (see Fig. 6.4). The role of the courses can be seen both as a means to build disciplinary knowledge pointing towards the students' choice of disciplines in the 2nd year of their bachelor study (see below), but also as a way of enabling them to select and analyse problems of their own choosing. For example, the course Technological Systems and Artefacts (1st semester) gives a broad overview of how professionals work in engineering and technical science. In semester 2, students may choose to focus on a particular technological area, e.g. Health Technology or Media Technology. In this way the course work enables students to recognize and identify what a 'technological problem' is and what it is not (project theme in semester 2).

6.4.5 Gradual Enablement for Subject Choice

Apart from being the logical approach to doing project work that defies disciplinary isolation, by definition interdisciplinarity also entails a more practical, but very fruitful educational benefit. Through basic interdisciplinary studies, students get a good chance of getting acquainted with various disciplines, including their interdisciplinary potential, which turns out to become an asset in the students' later choices of specialized subject modules (cf. Fig. 6.2). It is a central point in the structure of the bachelor programmes that students' choices of specialization are *gradually enabled* in the course of the programmes. On the economic side, this should reduce drop-out rates, and more importantly, in terms of academic learning outcome, it means that graduates have gained an academic identity that is a reflection of rational, academic choice as well as of motivation and personal interest.

To take an example, in HUMBACH, choices occur in four different locations in the model depicted in Fig. 6.5. *Firstly*, the choice of project work in the first three semesters is free, albeit constrained by the dimension requirements discussed above. The free choice of project is enhanced by the support of supervisors in an interdisciplinary academic environment as well as by dialogue with fellow students. *Secondly*, the programme requires that the student chooses to study two subject modules. This choice may be enhanced by having gained insight into the four humanistic dimensions in course and project work in the first three semesters, and it may also be informed by optional courses taken in the 3rd semester. *Thirdly*, free choice is present in the 10 ECTS worth of optional courses (typically taken in the 6th semester, but may also be taken earlier). *Fourthly*, there is a choice of basing the bachelor project on one or the other of the two previously selected subject modules, as well as a choice of integrating the two disciplinary fields in a more or less interdisciplinary context. This final choice is enabled by the sum of experiences gained in the course of studying in HUMBACH.

6.4.6 Interdisciplinarity

When the interplay of disciplinary concepts, theories and methods is drawn together to shed light on a comprehensive problem formulation, the results in the forms of knowledge and normative potential ideally transcend what insights could have been generated by the involved disciplines in isolation, see Jantsch (1970) and Chap. 2. Below, we look at how the concept of interdisciplinarity is brought to bear in the bachelor programmes at Roskilde University.

In HUMTEK, interdisciplinarity appears in three different forms:

1. The fundamental curriculum based on the three dimensions mentioned above. Course work within each dimension during the 1st year introduces how disciplines (e.g. urban planning, computer science and philosophy) work with these three dimensions.
2. In the 2nd year, students choose two disciplines to be combined. One of these is a technical discipline (at Roskilde University: computer science, informatics, geography, urban planning, environmental planning, and health promotion).
3. In their 2nd and 3rd year, students can choose between specialized 'profile courses' that combine two of the three dimensions. For example the profile

courses in 'Interaction Design' combine the dimensions 'Design and Construction' and 'Technological Systems and Artefacts'. The bachelor project should also comprise two dimensions.

The logic behind this is that students should specialize gradually within the three key dimensions dominating studies the 1st year, use cross- or multidisciplinarity (working in the intersection between two disciplines or applying two or more disciplines to a problem) in the 2nd year, and transdisciplinarity in the final bachelor year (see also Chap. 2).

An important part of the curriculum consists of various practical exercises both in project work and in course work, especially in Design. This is done to provide students with practical knowledge of craftsmanship and competences within a variety of design domains. As discussed in Chap. 1, the tradition of project work in education has its historical roots in schools of architecture and engineering (from the seventeenth century onwards). Drawing from these fields as well as the more recent and widespread use of project methodologies in the social sciences and the humanities, the HUMTEK curriculum uses project work both in the sense of one-semester projects, and also shorter courses where students acquire (some) knowledge about practical design domains, e.g. IT design or architecture/urban design. By doing this, the curriculum stimulates reflection in action as a way of educating 'reflective practitioners' (Schön 1987) within a variety of fields relevant for further studies.

The history of the bachelor programme in Social Science at Roskilde University consists of a long continued discussion about the combination of disciplines and interdisciplinary project work: How to introduce students to the different disciplines within social science without biasing the students and thereby limiting their ability critically to reflect on societal problems in an interdisciplinary way? Such problems do not align with different subject areas, often crossing the boundaries. The problem orientation of the project work therefore demands various forms for interdisciplinarity, be it cross-, multi- or even transdisciplinarity.

On the other hand, to analyse societal problems the students need tools in terms of theory and methods. Therefore, SAMBACH studies are designed as an interaction between courses and project work. The aim of the different courses is to give the students a general and broad introduction to the central theory and methods of social science, while the project provides the possibility of a more in-depth study of a specific societal problem and academic issues concerning this problem. In this way the students learn to use theory and methods in practice.

6.4.7 *Exemplarity*

As we saw under the heading of 'problem orientation' (Sect. 6.4.1), *problems* are important, because they are representative of social reality, and their possible solutions are driven by the engagement and motivation with which we normally relate to our concrete surroundings, whereas *subjects* often will fail to engage students because they are not representative of reality, but of academia. At the heart of this lies the notion of *exemplarity*. While exemplarity is a central concept in all four bachelor programmes, in the following, we look at the concept from the viewpoint of NATBACH.

The pedagogical principles of exemplarity, problem-orientation, and interdisciplinarity are closely interrelated (see also Chap. 2). As explained by Christiansen (2001, pp. 8–12), the interpretation of exemplarity influences the way in which problem orientation, participant-directed studies, and interdisciplinarity are understood and implemented in study programmes. From the semester themes for the NATBACH programme, it is clear that exemplarity is interpreted in the tradition of Wagenschein (1956). The problems that guide the students' work have to be problems that are related to science, since the entities that the students' project work must reflect are related to perceptions of science. In the 1st semester, the entity is the application of science, i.e. its role in technology and society. In the 2nd semester, it is the inner parts of science, its methods and structures, and in the 3rd semester, it is the perception of science as a cultural phenomenon. In the course of their work with the projects, under the different themes, the students perceive science from different angles. This is seen as a form of interdisciplinarity, not the form where boundaries between individual disciplines are erased (*transdisciplinarity*), but rather a kind where the discipline is in focus but studied and viewed from different perspectives in order to avoid narrow-mindedness in relation to the object of study. The NATBACH project on the formation of flint discussed in Chap. 3 is exemplary for this form of interdisciplinarity.

6.5 Organization of the Bachelor Model

6.5.1 *Participant-Directed Project Work*

Whereas 'problem-based learning' is often taken to mean simply that learning is focused on problem solving, but that the problem may very well have been *assigned* by the teacher, the form of PPL practiced at Roskilde University has the students' active participation in and management of all aspects of academic problem posing and solving at its heart. Closely connected to the following subsection about problem orientation, the goal of having projects being directed by the students themselves has a fundamental pedagogical backdrop. As much as being a vehicle for insight and knowledge, learning is aimed at practice, and practices need to be rooted in interest on the part of the students.

Central to ensuring that project work is controlled by the students is the group formation process. The group formation process is carried out with some variation across the four bachelor study programmes. In HUMBACH, the process quite closely echoes the detailed description given by Westerling (2013); the main distinction lies between academic interest (the project formulation) and the social process of forming a group around that interest. Students need to indulge in a highly complex social dynamics while formulating a common idea and a strategy for pursuing it. The process is normally organized by the students themselves with the assistance of the experienced house coordinator, one of the house supervisors who has taken on the task of organizing in collaboration with the students all learning activities in the house. In most instances, the supervisors allocated to the house will have formulated a variety of project proposals that they present to the students as inspirational examples on the basis of which the students can advance their own problem formulations. Here the supervisors face a delicate balance between inspiring the students to formulate and investigate interesting problems with great learning potential on the one hand and on the other hand inviting the students just to follow a 'safe proposal' from a supervisor (see also Chap. 3). Therefore, it is crucial that the proposals from the supervisor are very brief so that the students need to personalize the idea and make their own investigations and reflections in order to formulate a genuine problem for a project. Normally, more than half of the projects in a house are based on proposals from individual students – in fact, some houses opt to have the group formation process oriented entirely to the students' own original project proposals. After presentations, the process develops over 2–4 days that alternate between local meetings organized around specific project interests, and common plenary sessions, where the progress of the process is monitored and evaluated, and possible joint decisions made. While the process may be experienced as inspiring, it can certainly be mentally trying as well. One rule is normally applied in order to diminish stress: *No group is finalized until every student has joined a group.*

In HUMBACH, the process has been integrated in a new portfolio of courses, called 'progression courses' since they focus on progressively acquiring general academic competencies. There are four progression courses taken in the bachelor study programme in the humanities: Project Technique (1st semester), Method (2nd semester), The Theory of Science (3rd semester), and Communication (6th semester).

The first progression course, Project Technique, is a sequence of seminars in semester 1. The first of these seminars is held by the house coordinator during the 1st semester introduction period and features practical exercises in group formation.

In all four programmes as mentioned earlier, the core of the curriculum (half of the work load) is based on student-directed project work. In HUMTEK, the project work is oriented towards design processes. Generally, in other design study programmes (e.g. architecture, industrial design), students focus on creating practical solutions to design problems. In contrast to this, HUMTEK students work on a self-elected problem in a problem-based setting throughout a whole semester (see Jørgensen 2013). Traditional design study programmes would emphasize the professional skill of one particular domain (e.g. architecture, music composition). In HUMTEK, students are encouraged to choose, explore and solve design problems with the ambition that this process will enable them to build competencies and knowledge regarding how design processes are conducted. A main source of inspiration for this has been the work of the learning theorist Donald Schön (1983, 1987) and his insistence on uncovering how professionals "think in action". As Schön argues, the integration of the practice (or design) perspective in a university programme calls for a rethinking of the role of the teacher (not unfamiliar to the role of the 'supervisor' in problem-oriented project work). In what Schön calls a 'reflective practicum' (such as HUMTEK), "the role and status of the coach takes precedence over those of a teacher" (Schön 1987 p. 311), and he continues: "[a] reflective practicum must establish its own traditions, not only those associated with project types, formats, media, tools and materials, but also those embodying expectations for the interaction of coach and student" (ibid.). In HUMTEK this 'coaching' approach is incorporated into the study programme in several ways:

1. During the 1st year, students combine their self-elected project work with participation in 2-week workshops each within a particular design domain (e.g. urban design, interaction design). In these workshops the purpose is *not* to become a competent 'designer' but to acquire an understanding of the design processes involved in the particular domain.
2. This is also the case with the self-elected project. Here students choose a design problem that they find important and relevant. The design problem is analysed, discussed and reformulated in dialogue with a supervisor. While the supervisor in this process assumes the role of an 'expert', the aim of the process is to facilitate the project work of the student group (this does not differ from the role of the supervisor more generally in PPL, see Nielsen and Danielsen 2012 and Chap. 8). In their project work, students have access to prototyping workshops as well as additional supervision in media, programming and prototyping.
3. As part of the final exams in their 1st year, students are expected to explain their project work through a concrete design proposal (1st semester) and a visual representation (2nd semester).

The students' rights and obligations to exercise influence on their education has been one of the hallmarks at Roskilde University since its establishment. In NATBACH too this is fully implemented in the project work, where the students choose and formulate the problems they want to work with, decide on methods, and find and read literature both in the form of textbooks and research papers published in scientific journals. They design experiments, perform empirical and/or theoretical analyses, and structure the entire process. In short, they do research on a mini-scale, and it often leads to new results and insights. All this takes place under the guidance of the supervisor. During the semester, several events take place where the students present their work in progress to the other groups and the supervisors in the house. Both at midterm and 2 weeks before the final deadline each group will present their project and have it evaluated by an opponent group and their supervisor. In these sessions the groups receive serious and constructive feedback on their work in both oral and written form (see also Chap. 8).

6.5.2 *The Processes of Assessing and Evaluating Project Work*

All four bachelor study programmes use continuous assessment and evaluation of project work and project supervision. In the following, we look specifically at the practice in NATBACH.

Before the semester begins, the supervisors allocated to the house for the coming semester take part in a 1-day seminar where they discuss pedagogical issues related to the project work, the semester theme and the exemplary qualities of the supervisors' proposed problems for projects within their field. During the semester, the group of supervisors meets regularly to discuss the projects of the house with regard to the semester theme, problems in particular project groups and issues related to the organization of the project work. In this way, the participant-directed project work is supported by all the supervisors in the house as well as by the requirements during the semester of participation in presentations to the house, the midterm evaluation, and the pre-deadline evaluations. In most cases, the group functions as a supporting unit for the individual student and creates a fruitful interplay between the common challenge of making a good project and the social aspect of the project work. If necessary, the groups work day and night to get their project ready, and it is quite rare that a group misses the deadline for submitting the project report.

At the end of each semester, the project work is subject to an oral group examination, during which each individual student answers a question related to the project and given to the student 3 days in advance. This takes 10 min per student. Besides answering the question, the students in the group should be able to give an account of what is written in the project report and to discuss the project in general in an academic way with the examiners.

In the process of grading the students, a general assessment of the written project report determines the point of departure for the examination in the form of the type of questions asked by the examiners, and hereby the quality of the report influences the grading of the students indirectly. However, the grading of the students is of course individual and based on the performance at the oral examination. This format of examination, which is common to all four bachelor programmes, motivates the project groups to work hard on their project report and to make sure that each individual student understands and can explain all the central aspects of the project and what is written in the report.

Another common feature of the project work in the bachelor programmes is the evaluation culture. Evaluating the project work and the collaboration with the supervisor is an integrated element of the project work. In addition as mentioned above, there is an evaluation at midterm where pairs of groups present and discuss their projects together with their two supervisors based on brief midterm reports with outlines of the projects. In association with the midterm evaluation there is a personal evaluation by the supervisor in each group where the functioning of the group and each student's contribution is discussed and evaluated. This process also includes evaluation of the collaboration with the supervisor. In NATBACH this process of evaluation is repeated at the end of the semester.

Generally, in the case of problems with the collaboration with a supervisor, the students can discuss the situation with the house-coordinating supervisor. Finally, after each semester, the introduction to the semester, the project theme, the mid- and final evaluations and the study environment in the house in general are evaluated in a questionnaire and the results are discussed in the group of supervisors and in the study board.

6.5.3 The House as a Framework for Interactive Learning

Closely connected to the issue of activating students to take control of their project work is the question of how to organize project work on a socio-spatial level. At Roskilde University this question has been answered by integrating architecture and learning theory in a concept known as the 'house'. A house is an organizational unit framing the students' academic and social life during the first part of their studies. It accommodates approximately 120 students, 6–10 supervisors (one of whom assumes the task of being house coordinator in charge of the organization of the project work in the house), and a secretary who takes care of administration at a local level and is the students' invaluable 'go-to' person. (See Fig. 6.7).

For the larger bachelor programmes, both project work and course work in the three 1st semesters are house internal activities. In the case of NATBACH, which has considerably fewer students, course work is organized across the houses, so that 1st year students may attend courses together with 2nd year students.

The physical facilities for the project work are very important. While the actual equipment of the houses varies somewhat across the four bachelor programmes, ideally the norms are common to all: each group has access to a group room throughout the entire semester. Ideally, the group rooms are equipped with computers and whiteboards, and/or the houses are equipped with designated computer rooms. Each house also has a large classroom used for course teaching, for plenary meetings for all students in the house, for project presentations, group formation, seminars, etc. Finally, every house has a fully equipped kitchen. The standard interior architecture of a house is shown in Fig. 12.1.

The house constitutes the central framework for the work in the student groups. Throughout the semester, the groups typically meet 2 days a week, and once a week they have the opportunity to meet with their supervisor for 1 or 2 h. In the intensive periods, 3–4 weeks before the deadline for submitting the project reports, the students work almost non-stop on their projects. While the house arguably is the most important frame for doing project work, students have recently been seen to become somewhat more free of the boundaries of the house with the advent of social media that enable them to meet and interact in new, virtual spaces (see also Chap. 16).

However, after more than 40 years as a key concept in Roskilde University's project work philosophy, the house has proven its worth by providing a secure and inspiring environment for learning. It also helps minimize drop-out rates that have been considerably higher in comparable educational programmes at other institutions with more traditional organizational principles. It remains the backbone of the physical organization of project work at Roskilde University, even if the need for some structural changes is presently emerging.

When Roskilde University was built in 1972, a house was planned to contain only 63 students (in 9 groups), 4 supervisors and 1 secretary. In the ensuing years, however, the number of students has climbed to between 100 and 120 per house, and in order to cope with the inefficient use of space, the University is now launching a process aimed at changing the study environment in some aspects. In this

Fig. 6.7 Buildings like this two-storey building have normally comprised two houses at Roskilde University, one on each floor. In SAMBACH, one of these buildings is now in the process of being reorganized as an integrated bachelor house, where all students utilize facilities on both floors (Photo: Poul Erik Nikander Frandsen)

Fig. 6.8 Project group meeting in HUMTEK. 50 % of student work is based on self-conducted project work throughout all four bachelor programmes at Roskilde University. Each project group (typically five students) has one supervisor with whom they meet up regularly during the semester. For such meetings and for the project work in general, group rooms are available in the houses and can be booked and used at any time. In the last period of the semester the project work is very intensive and often the group rooms are then used day and night (Photo: Poul Erik Nikander Frandsen)

Fig. 6.9 At FabLab RUC which is located in the buildings of the HUMTEK bachelor programme students can work on programming, 3D modelling and prototyping as part of their course and project work (Photo: Poul Nicolas Padfield)

process, every two original houses are planned to be integrated in a joint 'bachelor house', containing students in the 1st, 2nd and 3rd years of the programme. This plan is presently being set into motion in SAMBACH.

Socially, the aim is to improve relations between new and more experienced students from the different student cohorts, e.g. by using the older students as mentors for the younger ones, as tutors and instructors in courses, etc.

Physically, the aim is to transform the old building and the 'closed' group rooms to a more open-spaced lounge for informal group meetings and cross-group networking. Ideally, the students will be able to select spaces which support the project work at the different stages of the work process: one area suitable for brainstorming in the beginning of the project period, another for the period of intense discussion of literature, theories and methods, and yet another for the intensive writing period. To avoid empty spaces at different times during the semester, efforts have been made to develop flexible spaces that can be rearranged and utilized through the entire period. In the new structure, the ground floor is an open landscape, a lounge area also suitable for the students' social life in the house, e.g. parties, get-together events, or lighter curricular activities. On the first floor, space has been allocated to more intensive work, as well as a room large enough to accommodate all students.

Another transformation of the 'house structure' can be seen in HUMTEK. Here all students work in a joint study environment which integrates project rooms equipped with projectors and whiteboards, non-formal meeting facilities in semi-public areas and workshops with a variety of facilities for visual/3D-design and prototyping (see Fig. 6.9). This study environment also encourages the use of student instructors and mentors, who are being systematically integrated into course work and project work in HUMTEK.

References

Blomhøj, M., & Kjeldsen, T. H. (2009). Project organised science studies at university level: Exemplarity and interdisciplinarity. *ZDM – International Journal on Mathematics Education, 41*(1–2), 183–198.
Christiansen, F. V. (1999). Exemplarity and educational planning. In H. S. Olesen & J. H. Jensen (Eds.), *Project studies – a late modern university reform* (pp. 57–66). Frederiksberg: Roskilde University Press.
Christiansen, F. V. (2001). *Projektarbejde i naturvidenskabelige grundfag* [Project work in basic studies in natural science]. Papers from DCN, 12 (2nd ed.). Aalborg: Dansk Center for Naturvidenskabsdidaktik [Danish Centre for the Didactics of Natural Sciences].
Habermas, J. (2005). Knowledge and human interests: A general perspective. In G. Gutting (Ed.), *Continental philosophy of science*. Oxford: Blackwell.
Haldrup, M., & Svabo, M. (2012). Humanistiske Teknologi og Design Studier [Humanistic technology and design studies]. In T. Enevoldsen & E. Jelsøe (Eds.), *Tværvidenskab i Teori og Praksis* [Crossdisciplinarity in theory and practice] (pp. 201–222). Copenhagen: Hans Reitzel.
Illeris, K. (1999). Project work in university studies: Background and current issues. In H. Jensen & H. S. Olesen (Eds.), *Project studies – a late modern university reform*. Frederiksberg: Roskilde University Press.
Jantsch, E. (1970). Inter- and transdisciplinary university: A systems approach to education and innovation. *Policy Sciences, 1*, 403–428.
Jørgensen, N. (2013). Exemplary learning in design studies: Strengths and limits. In L. Krogh & A. A. Jensen (Eds.), *Visions, challenges and strategies* (pp. 201–218). Aalborg: Aalborg University Press.
Larsen, M. (2013). *De fire dimensioner. Essays om forskning, uddannelse og formidling* [The four dimensions. Essays on research, education and communication]. Roskilde: Roskilde University Press.
Lave, J., & Wenger, E. (1991). *Situated Learning: Legitimate peripheral participation*. Cambridge: Cambridge University Press.
Nielsen, J. L., & Danielsen, O. (2012). Problem-oriented project studies: The role of the teacher as a supervisor for the study group in its learning processes. In L. Dirkinck-Holmfeldt, V. Hodgson, & D. McConnell (Eds.), *Exploring the theory, pedagogy and practice of networked learning* (pp. 257–272). New York/Dordrecht/Heidelberg/London: Springer.
Olesen, H. S., & Jensen, J. H. (1999). Can 'the university' be revived in 'late modernity'? In H. S. Olesen & J. H. Jensen (Eds.), *Project studies – a late modern university reform* (pp. 9–24). Frederiksberg: Roskilde University Press.
Schön, D. (1983). *The reflective practitioner: How professionals think in action*. New York: Basic Books.
Schön, D. (1987). *Educating the reflective practitioner*. San Francisco: Jossey-Bass.
Wagenschein, M. (1956). Zum Begriff des Exemplarischen Lehrens (On the concept of the exemplary in teaching). *Zeitschrift für Pädagogik, 2*, 129–156.
Westerling, A. (2013). 'Gruppedannelse – mellem faglige hensyn og sociale processer [Group formation – between academic considerations and social processes]. In A. Mac & P. Hagedorn-Rasmussen (Eds.), *Projektarbejdets kompleksitet: viden, værktøjer og læring* [The complexity of project work: Knowledge, tools and learning] (pp. 57–72). Frederiksberg: Samfundslitteratur.

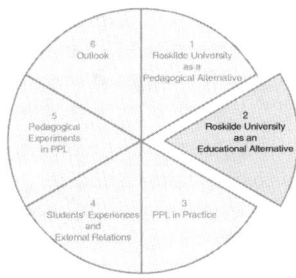

Chapter 7
The Master Programmes and the Roskilde Model

Hanne Leth Andersen

7.1 Outlines: Programme Structures and Overall Goals

The specific feature of traditional Roskilde University master level programmes is that students may design their own study programme by combining the two fields or subjects that best support their academic interests and career plans. Until 2006, after 2 years of basic studies (within the fields of science, social sciences or humanities), students would continue with a 3-year double specialization, selecting two different subjects for the master level. This would allow students to choose an integrated understanding of the two subjects, from multidisciplinary to a more or less transdisciplinary approach. After 2006, with the implementation of the Bologna structure, bachelor programmes would include basic studies and a specialization into two specific subjects, and at the master level this double specialization would continue.

In the master programmes, the same overarching pedagogical principles are respected as those for bachelor programmes (problem-orientated, interdisciplinary and participant-directed project work), with a clear progression in methodological awareness, according to the *European Qualifications Framework* (EQF)with. At the end of the second cycle (master level), graduates should be able to "manage and

---

H.L. Andersen (✉)
Roskilde University, Roskilde, Denmark
e-mail: ha@ruc.dk

transform work or study contexts that are complex, unpredictable and require new strategic approaches, take responsibility for contributing to professional knowledge and practice and/or for reviewing the strategic performance of teams" (Level 7; European Commission 2014).

In addition to this, the problem-oriented project work links more directly to application in practice than do lectures where students are usually not directly engaged in real-life problem solving. Thus, there is a tradition of a focus on students' employability (Andersen 2013), often related to experiences with projects in collaboration with external partners, or in relation to internships. This is reinforced in the most recent orientations in problem-oriented project work directed towards entrepreneurial skills and innovation.

When students combine two subjects from two different fields across the humanities, the social sciences, the natural sciences, and the humanistic-technological sciences, the kinds of interdisciplinarity developed are of necessity very different from the field-specific interdisciplinarities that are developed within the various scientific fields. Combinations of two subjects of specialization can be made between subjects within the area of the individual student's bachelor programme, or between one subject from this programme and one from another bachelor programme, the most frequent type being a combination of humanities and social sciences. Furthermore, the specific kinds of disciplines that are combined, regardless of field and whether they are more theoretically-oriented, more skill-oriented or more problem-oriented, define different types of interdisciplinarity. Generally, there has been a development in the range of available subjects from Roskilde University's inception until today from rather more classical and well-defined subjects towards a wider range including more cross- and transdisciplinary subjects (see Chap. 5). This may be seen as an effect of problem-orientation and collaboration also in research. In some areas, the interaction among different disciplines has led to actual transdisciplinary approaches as mutual organization of concepts, methodology, procedures (methods), epistemology, terminologies, and data (see also Chap. 2). Transdisciplinary subjects would as such contain a number of related disciplines where the disciplines actually change their concepts, structures and aims (Jantsch 1972a, b). Examples of such subjects developed at Roskilde University would be *Cultural Encounters* and *Performance Design*.

7.2 Adjusting to the Bologna Model: Combination Structure and New Integrated Programmes

The implementation of the Bologna structure (see Sect. 4.4) as a common European educational structure was a profound break with the initial educational model of Roskilde University. It forced all universities to adapt to an overall European model in order to facilitate the general mobility of students. One of the main outcomes of the Bologna process is the structuring of all European higher education into three general levels: bachelor programmes consisting of 3 years of study, master programmes of 2 years and PhD programmes of 3 years of study. At Roskilde University, the implementation of such a structure evidently was an important challenge, forcing the university to adapt a 2+3 year structure into a 3+2 year structure and thus cutting the 3 year double specialization in two.

The implementation led to a two-step reform of the programme structure. At first, a somewhat pro forma graduation level after 3 years was implemented, without seriously changing the initial educational model (see also Chap. 5). In this way, the main idea of moving from broad introductions towards progressively higher specialization was clearly maintained, and in practice the continuation of the basic studies was still a 3 year programme at the graduate level with a two-subject combination. The link between the specialization elements at the bachelor level and the master programmes was emphasized, and the boundary between bachelor and graduate level was more or less ignored by the subject study boards that would still be responsible for the entire 3-year study period. Only administratively, there would be a clear demarcation, with the bachelor degree as the marker.

A negative side effect of this solution was the difficulty involved in exchanging students with other universities; the entrance to the master level at Roskilde University was too specific. Any student from outside would have to be able to demonstrate knowledge, skills and competences in the two specific subjects at a level corresponding to that of bachelor at Roskilde University, and would also have to be familiar with working in project-oriented programmes corresponding to that of a Roskilde bachelor.

In the second step, the organization of the programmes was changed so that the four bachelor programmes would each have their own study board and study director, assuring the coherence of the overall programme, so that students were not left alone in the organization of their studies. This is an essential historical change, since an important feature of the original model was to leave responsibility to students, in collaboration with supervisors. With the national focus on quality assurance and hierarchical structures in governance, the responsibility structures always have to be clear, and universities must be able to monitor any structure from the top.

On the positive side, the adaptation to the Bologna structure has made it clear that master programmes are 2-year programmes and that they must be open not only to Roskilde University students, but also to students from other universities, both in the original free combination structure, and in new integrated single master programmes. On the less positive side, a 2-year programme structure is a clear challenge since it may be hard for students to actually manage to immerse themselves in two different subjects understanding the kind of interdisciplinarity they may offer, and to write a master's thesis. As a reaction to this, Roskilde University offers separate clearly profiled integrated 2-year master programmes in some of the prominent interdisciplinary areas that the university is known for, such as *Communication Studies, Social Entrepreneurship and Management*, and *Environmental Risk*. Already existing well-established integrated programmes are *Technology and Societal Planning* (in Danish: TekSam), *Global Studies, Business Management* and *Public Management*. Moreover, three new programmes have recently been accredited: *Spatial Designs and Society, International Administration and Politics,* and *Social Intervention*. These new programmes coexist with the original combination structure with a combination of two disciplinary modules. One clear advantage of the full inter-disciplinary programmes is that they allow for the responsible study boards and research staff to create a more integrated study environment for the students than is possible when students make their own combinations.

Currently, there is a discussion about the equilibrium in the coexistence of the two master programme structures, and how they will develop. The original educational structure both at the undergraduate and the graduate level is part of the university's heritage and specificity. There is a general agreement to preserve it, also at the graduate level, throughout the areas of humanities, social sciences, natural sciences and humanistic-technological sciences. Combination programmes are still the most common graduate model, and have always coexisted with a number of integrated programmes.

It has indeed been a challenge to create a transition from a model where the bachelor programme modules (courses and project work) are actually followed directly by master programme modules without any obligatory limit (since Bologna often referred to as the bachelor 'fence') to a model where bachelor programme modules are likely to wind up a comprehensive undergraduate programme. Typically, the individual subject areas imply that bachelor modules and master modules are elements within a total academic entity. This will often mean that the specific subject modules at the bachelor level represent a necessary condition for academic progression in the master programmes. With a sharper distinction between bachelor and master programmes in which admission to study for a master degree does not necessarily require a very specific bachelor programme or subject module, this understanding of cohesion and progression is challenged. Instead of the unambiguous thinking in subjects along the length of bachelor and master programmes, the academic content progression in the bachelor programme must be thought of as a coherent and complete process. At the same time, the academic progression of master programmes must be envisaged on the basis of the qualifications of participants from different but clearly stated subject combinations in bachelor programmes.

The university needs to ensure a sound balance and synergy between the combination structure and the new integrated master programmes, at least until they have shown a strong capacity for recruitment and a clear potential for academic development. The situation requires a delicate balancing act: If combination subjects are removed and replaced with integrated programmes that turn out to be unable to attract new students, the attractiveness of the combination structure may have been weakened for no real purpose (because it depends on a certain number of possible combinations).

In any event, the decision of opening up for new integrated single master programmes has prepared for a more extensive interchange with other universities, nationally and internationally (some programmes being offered in English), because the programmes inevitably are more recognizable for bachelors outside the university.

In this sense, they allow students to enter Roskilde University at a higher level than 1st year bachelor. At the same time, this is part of the Danish governmental policy of a so-called flexible educational system: there must be a possibility to change between universities in Denmark, and there must be a simple connection for students from professional bachelor programmes to enrol in academic master programmes both in order to create an effective system and in order to support lifelong learning (see also Chap. 4). The challenge here is that academic and professional bachelors are not alike, and that the academic requirements of the university master programme may result in individual failure and high dropout rates. Several 'bridge building models' have been tried in order to remedy this, such as individual evaluation before acceptance (direct assessment), tests, and collaboration between bachelor programmes and specific types of master programmes for professional bachelors.

7.3 Structural Challenges and Quality Assurance Demands

There are some significant challenges associated with the combination model. Compared to the national management and quality assurance of universities, it is a problem that the educational structure breaks with the principle of offering only coherent master programmes. Following the Ministerial Order on Education (Universitets- og bygningsstyrelsen 2010), all master programmes should be offered as coherent programmes and manifest an internal progression (§21). Furthermore, according to the Danish Accreditation Council, it is a prerequisite that the responsibility for every programme is clearly stated, and not just for each subject within the programme. At Roskilde University, this would mean stating the clear responsibility for combining each of the 28 possible subjects with each other in what would make 28×27 subject combinations (of which many are of course never chosen, while some are more frequent than others).

In connection with the accreditation of Roskilde University's study subjects, the accreditation authorities time and again have called attention to the fact that the university has neither direct control of nor clear responsibility for the quality assurance of the totality of the students' educational programmes, since all data and reports from programme directors concern only one subject module and not the overall programme/education.

Within the combination structure now being replaced, students may choose two subject modules among currently 28 possible subjects. This causes both planning challenges and administrative challenges; one being very basically the title of the degree which is to be awarded (a general problem within interdisciplinarity), another being the individual student's competence profile (see also Chap. 4), which must be adjusted to the specific choice of subjects in the programme, and accordingly, to the job possibilities. Many students at Roskilde University express the view that they lack a clear understanding of what their professional profile is and how it can be used in a job market context. In the current educational organization, it is to some extent left to the students themselves to declare their professional competences on the basis of the choices they individually make.

The organizational strategy for strengthening the combination model includes several key elements: firstly, to establish study boards at the master level with responsibility for the students' overall programme, i.e. combinations of different subjects, and secondly, to organize these combination programmes as continuous cycles with a clear delegation of responsibility for research support to the underlying research environments. A fundamental change in the combination structure therefore will be that one subject must be chosen as 'primary' (meaning that it defines the title of the degree and frames the thesis), and that it can be combined with one of eight 'secondary' subjects approved by the study board. The actual weighting in ECTS-points can still be equal between the two subjects.

To address these general challenges, a central objective for all graduates from Roskilde University is that they acquire an accurate perception of their specific strengths and general competences, and that the university increasingly supports the students in developing a solid educational and professional identity, including a general strengthening of student counselling and career advice (see also Chap. 8).

7.4 What Subject Combinations Should Be Recommended?

As mentioned the total of the 28×27 possible study combinations have been challenged by the quality assurance processes and the demands of Danish education policy, and it is being addressed in the recently adopted structure. According to this, the study board committees will point out the combinations which are most relevant, and most interesting from an interdisciplinary point of view and in terms of employability. For the study board to grant exemption to a student wishing to choose other combinations, the applicant will have to argue for its strengths and perspectives, also in relation to labour market requirements.

The different subject combinations that students can choose from differ in the possible types of interdisciplinary approach, but all should introduce students to interdisciplinarity as a core concept at Roskilde University. All master students should be aware of the type of interdisciplinarity of their subject combination or programme. In all combination programmes, there is a possibility of integrating the two disciplines in a very concrete way in a so-called integrated master thesis, selecting a problem of which the analysis and solution demands some kind of combination of the two. The graduate programmes manifest a whole typology of interdisciplinary approaches, not only from multidisciplinary through crossdisciplinary to transdisciplinary (cf. Jantsch 1972a, b; Piaget 1972; OECD 1972, see also Chap. 2), but also from theoretically-oriented disciplines to skill-oriented or problem-oriented disciplines (cf. Højgaard Jensen 2012).

Combining two traditional subjects such as Mathematics and Philosophy or Biology and Danish can allow for a multi-disciplinary approach which would be defined as a hierarchal juxtaposition of various disciplines grouped in such a way as to enhance relationships among them. Such types of disciplinary relationships are much in demand at Danish high schools and give access to jobs as high school teachers. Here, a double subject profile is important; the possible combination of the two subjects in an integrated master thesis and the interdisciplinary and methodological insight from the basic module at bachelor level allow for a strong experience of interdisciplinarity.

Combining two subjects that are both interdisciplinary, such as Cultural Encounters, International Development Studies, or Working Life Studies is a methodologically challenging task and should be recommended when the individual student's study plan is based on a very clearly expressed idea or focus.

On the other hand, there are combinations that are particularly interesting for specific areas in society and the labour market. These combinations have previously been promoted as specific full programme profiles: one of these is Public Relations (a combination of Business Studies and Danish). This particular field plays an increasingly important role in the development of society and the economy, with a focus on economic, sociological and communication studies.

Cultural Environment, being a combination of geography and history, is another case in point. It touches on a variety of problem areas and subject areas, ranging from natural and cultural conservation, to planning and destination development. The programme aims for students to achieve interdisciplinary expertise in the interplay between nature, production, lifestyles, infrastructure and housing, and urban patterns in the development of the relationship between landscapes, towns and villages.

7.5 High-Level Research-Based Project Work

Generally, the links between research and teaching are constructed in a variety of ways across the university, from the inclusion of subject-based research in the curriculum to the provision of opportunities for research practice for students alongside researchers. Learning in research mode means learning from researchers, with a focus on methodologies, approaches, methods and instruments of research, and on critical reading and thinking skills. The specific learning activities are those of research, such as inquiry-based or problem-oriented learning tasks, concrete case studies, projects in collaboration with external partners, performances or exhibitions, fieldwork and laboratory work. In addition, concepts such as *research-informed* or *research-enhanced* teaching and education have been introduced, pointing mainly to the fact that research and researchers are behind, but not necessarily engaged in educational activities.

Problem-oriented programmes involve several of the distinctive elements of research-based education since students in these programmes clearly work together in research-like projects under the supervision of or with researchers. In addition, the learning approach is that of knowledge building and inquiry—driven learning. Groups of students make a collective inquiry into a specific topic, arriving at a deeper understanding through interactive questioning and dialogue, and continuously improving on ideas. This approach contrasts with the lecture-oriented approach aimed at filling knowledge into students' heads, a teaching method which achieves one of the aims of research-based education (that of researchers teaching new research results), but does not help students become independent thinkers or innovative agents.

An essential element of the problem-oriented approach at Roskilde University is the connection to a supervisor and to other groups. In this methodological approach students must be strongly aware of research questions, methods and analyses, emphasizing the consistent use of methods and academic rules. Here, the ideal relation between teachers and students is that of a collaborative community. The teacher's role becomes that of a guide and later of a colleague, allowing students to take over a significant portion of the responsibility for their own learning, including planning, execution and evaluation (see also Chap. 8). Students must have close connections with research environments and real research projects. In the strongest versions, students' projects are linked directly to and enhance the projects of researchers (see also Chap. 14).

7.6 Examination and Feedback: Formative and Summative Evaluation

When debating and developing forms of assessment and evaluation, it is common practice to distinguish between two complementary and yet overlapping functions. Formative assessment is a range of formal and informal procedures employed during the learning process in order to support student learning with qualitative feedback. Summative assessment on the other hand seeks to monitor and evaluate educational results and outcomes, generally for external accountability.

The forms of evaluation at Roskilde University were a focal point from the beginning, and the university has had a clearly innovative function in developing new forms of both formative and summative assessment, not only the sometimes disputed group exams (see also Chap. 5), but also the process evaluation tools and the peer feedback. The evaluation formats involve group members and supervisors across groups in the process of the project work, emphasizing formative evaluation and reflexive and functional knowledge and competences, rather than declarative knowledge. Forms of evaluation and assessment are strong instruments in focusing students' activities (Brown and Race 2012). In the past 10–15 years there has been a renewed focus on establishing a more precise connection between the learning objectives and the evaluation formats used (alignment), and at the same time a stronger focus on developing evaluation formats that motivate for intensive processes and high student activity.

Alignment of work methods and exam formats is strongly at play in oral group exams in Denmark. This type of assessment where the whole group is present at an oral defence of the common project is closely linked to project work in groups and allows for the group members to present and discuss their work together with the examiners more intensely and with much more time available than if they were examined individually. Grades are given individually, and the time allotted for the discussion of the project as a whole is proportional to the number of group members, allowing for in-depth questions and answers. Thus, this exam type is far removed from the testing of rote learning and simple declarative knowledge.

The efforts to continuously develop the forms of examination are linked to the work with project variation and relations to practice and also to progression in the students' learning. With the bachelor reform, the requirements for evaluation formats in relation to project work, which in time had been undermined in different ways, have been tightened up. As to the courses, the tendency had been to use only a few main exam types and assignment genres, which in certain cases were not sufficiently aligned with the formulation of new learning objectives. Therefore, especially with regard to course exams, there is currently an effort to develop exam formats that are closely linked to the concrete descriptions of learning outcomes, and to advise study boards and programme directors on their choice of relevant exam types. The forms of examination should not only offer control in a summative way, but motivate and support students' active participation and learning (Skov 2013).

With the bachelor reform, initial formative and process-oriented work methods such as the problem formulation seminar and the mid-term seminar with peer feedback are essential in all the programmes. At the same time, from 2013 group exams have been reinstated at Roskilde University as a mandatory assessment form for each semester's project work, after having been abolished for 6 years.

At the master level, it has not yet been made explicit whether specific types of formative and summative evaluation should be integrated in all programmes. This implies that competence development through peer evaluation and process focus in different types of project work may not be used to the same extent in all programmes. The challenge at this level is that students may lose the chance to learn from one another across project groups.

There is a strong need to continue developing both teaching and examination methods in order to avoid a simplistic reproduction of knowledge, and to emphasize knowledge building and inquiry – and student-centred learning. However, some students may indeed prefer lectures rather than project work or independent studies. They avoid the challenges of insecurity and open-ended activities in seeking refuge in the safety of memorizing correct answers. With the Bologna process, the increasing need to define precise and specific learning outcomes threatens to suppress research-based learning and bring back teaching based on transmission of knowledge, since open-ended assignments and corresponding exam and evaluation formats cannot be designed with the same degree of predictability. If the intended alignment of work methods, exam formats and clear objectives is used intelligently, it allows for an emphasis on process and competence, but problem-oriented knowledge building will never be as controllable and quantifiable as rote learning.

7.7 University Education at a Crossroads

The political effort of the Danish government, like that of most other governments, is to educate its citizens to overcome the financial crisis and to survive in global competition. As a consequence of the large intake of students at all levels and the 'academization' of all professional degrees (see also Chap. 4), Danish university education is currently balancing between mass education and elite education. Over the last 30 years, the number of students has increased at all Danish universities, and most bachelor students continue their studies at the master level. Universities and university colleges are entering into a common educational system where professional and academic degrees are mixed and where the boundaries between different types of programmes are becoming less clear. Research-based university education used to be the defining characteristic of a certain type of academic institution, but is currently being challenged by new definitions. The risk of a larger and more flexible educational system is that the conditions of mass education may impede elite education. The educational strategy has also led to a large increase in the number of PhDs that must be 'produced' at all Danish universities, and in this way to a certain risk of devaluation of the value of master degrees.

The flexible education system is in fact close to the former 'central mindset' of the early Roskilde University, which in its time had the same objective: to accept many different paths to a graduate programme (see also Chap. 5). With the establishment of a university college department adjoining the Roskilde University campus, new opportunities to experiment with forms of cooperation have been made possible, and the lessons learned will subsequently be extended to developing cooperation with other university colleges.

As a consequence of its position at the intersection of research and practice, of flexible education and engaged problem orientation, Roskilde University has increased the number of PhDs recruited from a professional career within the field of their future PhD project. Students come from both the public and the private sector, thus creating a direct link between theory and practice. This means that the university will provide Danish society with a highly educated workforce that will help develop the welfare society, the private sector and the research sector, focusing on sustainable solutions for societal regulation, services and production, using as a point of departure the high national standards for welfare and production.

Some groups have raised questions about the orientation of graduate education and whether it should be maintained at all as an offer for all undergraduate students. One can imagine that graduate programs may become elite tracks, some of which will be explicitly research-oriented, while others are explicitly professional and practice-oriented. In this model, the normal mass education is completed with a bachelor degree, academic or professional, but always with a clear focus on employability. The model places great demands on the development of continuing education and training opportunities at the master level in the context of lifelong learning. The economic rationale behind the model will be that society is willing to pay for basic academic and professionally-oriented education and elite training, while continuous education might perhaps be financed by private funding.

In this situation, the role of Roskilde University is as much as ever to facilitate the exchange between academic and practice-related professional education, to enable access to research-based education though the continuous development of student-centred education and collective project work, and to challenge the well-established disciplines and pedagogical routines. The critical approach to both education and society is at the very centre of research-based project work (see also Chap. 17).

References

Andersen, H. L. (2013). University education and employability. *Global Scientia, 3*, 38–41.

Brown, S., & Race, P. (2012). Using effective assessment to promote learning. In L. Hunt & D. Chalmers (Eds.), *University teaching in focus: A learning-centred approach* (pp. 74–91). Camberwell: Australian Council for Educational Research and Routledge.

European Commission. (2014). Descriptors defining levels in the European Qualifications Framework (EQF) – Information about courses, work-based learning and qualifications. *Learning Opportunities and Qualifications in Europe*. Retrieved September 17, 2014, from http://ec.europa.eu/ploteus/content/descriptors-page.

Højgaard Jensen, J. (2012). På tværs af videnskaberne [Across sciences]. In T. Enevoldsen & E. Jelsøe (Eds.), *Tværvidenskab i teori og praksis* [Crossdisciplinarity in theory and practice] (pp. 50–70). Copenhagen: Hans Reitzels Forlag.

Jantsch, E. (1972a). Inter- and transdisciplinarity university. *Higher Education, 1*(1), 7–37.

Jantsch, E. (1972b). Towards interdisciplinarity and transdisciplinarity in education and innovation. In L. Apostel, S. Berger, A. Briggs, & G. Machaud (Eds.), *Interdisciplinarity problems of teaching and research in universities* (pp. 97–121). Paris: OECD, CERI.

OECD. (1972). *Interdisciplinarity: Problems of teaching and research in universities*. Paris: OECD.

Piaget, J. (1972). The epistemology of interdisciplinary relationships. In L. Apostel (Ed.), *Interdisciplinarity problems of teaching and research in universities* (pp. 127–139). Paris: OECD.

Skov, S. (2013). Nye læringsmål kræver nye eksamensformer [New learning goals require new forms of examination]. *Dansk Universitetspædagogisk Tidsskrift, 8*(14), 76–85.

Universitets- og Bygningsstyrelsen (The Danish University and Property Agency). (2010). Bekendtgørelse om bachelor- og kandidatuddannelser ved universiteterne [Ministerial order on bachelor and graduate programmes in universities]. Short title: Uddannelsesbekendtgørelsen [The ministerial order on education]. BEK No. 814, 29/06/2010. Retrieved December 3, 2013, from https://www.retsinformation.dk/Forms/R0710.aspx?id=132698

Part III
PPL in Practice

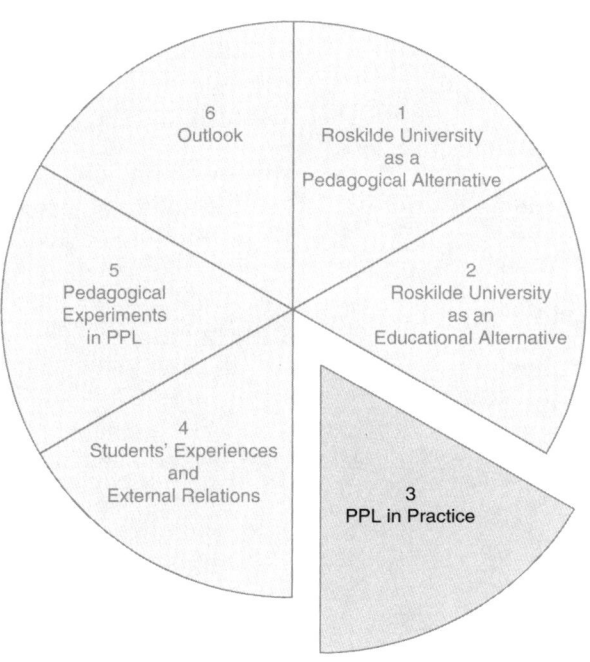

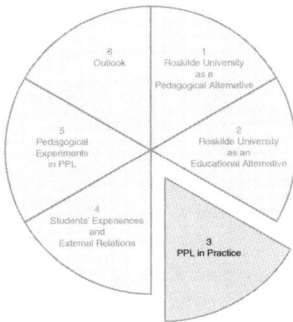

Chapter 8
Supervising Projects

Anders Siig Andersen and Søren Dupont

> Recognizing that being a facilitator means also being a learner. This might mean learning to develop the capabilities of a facilitator and possibly also learning new knowledge with and through the students. (Savin-Baden and Major 2004, p. 97)

8.1 Introduction

In this chapter, we shall turn our attention to the most important aspect of the role of faculty members in students' project work, i.e. their role as project supervisors. Project supervision has a history of over 40 successful years at Roskilde University. We begin with a brief discussion of different concepts regarding the role of faculty members supervising project work. Then we focus on the core framework for project work and supervision, i.e. the time and activity frame and the learning outcome that students must realize. This provides the basis for describing and discussing various aspects of supervision. We summarize the tasks associated with supervision in a model that shows: (a) the basic framework of project work, (b) the key supervisory tasks, and (c) other important functions offered by the university for supporting student project work. We will then describe the university's efforts to train faculty

---

A.S. Andersen (✉) • S. Dupont
Roskilde University, Roskilde, Denmark
e-mail: siig@ruc.dk; dupont@ruc.dk

© Springer International Publishing Switzerland 2015
A.S. Andersen, S.B. Heilesen (eds.), *The Roskilde Model: Problem-Oriented Learning and Project Work*, Innovation and Change in Professional Education 12,
DOI 10.1007/978-3-319-09716-9_8

members as supervisors. We conclude the chapter by comparing the framework of project work and project supervision with the general educational strategy of Roskilde University.

8.2 Concepts Relating to Supervision

In the Anglo-American pedagogical tradition, different concepts are used to denote how faculty members support students' work on projects and dissertations. The most common concepts seem to be 'supervising', 'advising' and 'facilitating'. Lee and Green (2009) analyse the metaphor of 'supervision' by splitting it into its two original parts 'super' and 'vision'. They argue that the concept of supervision originates from a vision-centred interpretation of knowledge and truth dating back to Modernity and the Enlightenment, i.e. to Humboldt and the University of Berlin in the first decade of the nineteenth century (Lee and Green 2009, p. 626, see also Chap. 4). The concept of supervision stresses the specific role of supervisors in monitoring and providing guidelines for the students' work. By using this concept, one assumes that supervisors are enlightened in two ways: (a) by possessing independent knowledge and expertise relevant to the students' work, and (b) by possessing expertise in understanding the students' perspectives and in guiding their work. In the context of project work, Boud and Costly (2007, p. 119) propose a shift in the role of faculty members from a role focused on the 'supervisor' to one focused on the 'learning advisor'. They argue that the concept of the 'learning advisor' would be more consistent with an independent learning approach. This concept downplays notions of faculty members having all-embracing competence. Instead, it emphasizes that faculty members should be able to advise students on how they best can learn from the projects that they are working on. The concept of 'facilitator' expresses a similar notion. This concept also emphasizes that faculty members primarily should support students' independent work. Savin-Baden and Hanney put it this way:

> Promoting autonomy in small teams and allowing students to own their own learning experiences involves letting go of decisions about what students should learn, trusting students to acquire knowledge for themselves and accepting that students will learn even if they have not been supplied with a lecture or handout. (Savin-Badin and Major 2004, p. 94)

In this understanding, the function of facilitators would be to support students by encouraging joint participation, mutual understanding and shared responsibility.

The Danish equivalent of 'supervision', 'advising' and 'facilitating' is 'vejledning' (meaning literally 'to show somebody the way'). On the one hand, this concept emphasizes that faculty members possess a surplus of knowledge compared to the students – without 'vejledning', students would get lost. This concept also implies that students themselves must define the starting point as well as the destination of their journey. In regard to the production of knowledge and the responsibility of managing student project work, the meaning of this concept is thus located somewhere between the concept of 'supervising' and the concepts of 'advising' and 'facilitating'.

In addressing supervision, most research publications focus on the dyadic relationship between a PhD student and a PhD supervisor. Lee and Green express it as follows:

> Supervision remains conceptualized as essentially a one-to-one relationship. In this instance, this involves a still largely individualized exchange between a doctoral student and a supervisor. (Lee and Green 2009, p. 616)

A limited part of the research literature focuses on the supervision of several students each with their own project. In this context, some authors use the concept 'collective academic supervision' (Nordentoft et al. 2013). In this type of supervision, several students meet with one or two supervisors. The students present their projects to each other and their supervisors, all participants are expected to have read the students' material before the supervision takes place, and during the supervision process the focus is on the individual projects as well as discussions of common themes. Both faculty members and students indicate that the main challenges of this type of supervision are: (a) how to strike a balance between individual and collective feedback, and (b) how to ensure that the students' mutual feedback is not perceived as inferior (Nordentoft et al. 2013, p. 588).

Unlike 'individual supervision' and 'collective academic supervision', group-based supervision is characterized by supervisors meeting with groups of students working on joint projects. This means that students are closely collaborating in their work and learning. This type of supervision is practiced in Problem-oriented, Interdisciplinary and Participant-Directed Project Work (PPL) as well as in Problem-Based Learning (PBL). In organizing coherent course programmes and helping students in their learning tasks, the role of faculty members in PBL is often referred to as that of 'facilitators' (Savin-Baden and Costley 2004). As mentioned earlier, an important difference between PBL and PPL is that in PBL, faculty members choose the problems to be studied, whereas in PPL, students themselves choose the problems that they want to work on. Furthermore, in PPL the students work in ways that are very similar to how faculty members work in their research projects (see also Chaps. 1 and 14). This means that PPL has some features in common with PBL, including the fact that faculty members supervise/facilitate group work. At the same time, however, important differences are at play. Similarly, the supervision in PPL shares some of the characteristics of individual PhD supervision, including the fact that the object of supervision is a research-like project. But there are some important differences to be noted. Firstly, the academic requirements for PhD projects are higher than those for bachelor and master projects, because PhD students are trained to be independent researchers. Secondly, the supervisor's contact with the students in bachelor and master projects is of significantly shorter duration than in PhD projects. This means that supervision in the PPL tradition may draw inspiration from the traditions of both PBL and PhD-supervision. However, it also means that one should be rather cautious when trying to transfer experience between the different supervisory contexts.

8.3 The Basic Framework of Project Work

The basic framework of project work at Roskilde University comprises the time and activities involved and the formal requirements for learning outcome as stipulated by the university. In the following, we shall briefly outline this framework.

The students are introduced to the format of project work as soon as they enter a bachelor programme. They complete a total of 8 projects (each 15 ECTS) and one thesis (30 ECTS) throughout their combined bachelor and master studies. Each project has a time frame of one semester. Normally, students are appointed a new supervisor every time they start on a new project. Projects are carried out by project groups established by students who agree to work on the same project theme. The formation of project groups often takes place in a complex process involving between 30 and 120 students. The supervisors support the students in this process and make themselves available for discussion of the project themes (for a concrete example, see Chap. 11). In the context of group formation, the students reject a number of possible projects and exclude some fellow students in order to choose the projects that they want to work with and the fellow students that they want to team up with. Group formation processes include academic as well as social concerns. As soon as the group formation process has been completed, supervisors are allocated to the groups. Students designate a theme of study within a broader field of interest, and then they choose a problem that relates to the theme. The themes selected constitute the context for the chosen problems, i.e. the framework that makes it possible to argue for the problems in regard to their broader societal, academic and study relevance. The supervisors support the students in exploring the themes chosen and in sharpening and clarifying their problem formulations.

Project work aims to meet academic criteria. This means that students (a) complete systematic literature searches, (b) produce an overview of relevant research, (c) choose the scientific theory and other theories that will serve as the basis of their project work, and (d) choose analytical methods. The students reflect on criteria for inclusion or exclusion of theories and methods, and supervisors may help with specific proposals. The main task of the supervisors is however to support the students' own activities and their self-directed learning. The students reflect critically on their choice of empirical field, and produce and analyse empirical data. The choice of empirical data depends on the academic traditions and culture within the chosen study programme (see also Sect. 2.2). Supervisors enter into a dialogue with the students on these issues, and contribute to student project work by involving their own professional experiences from empirical research. In some cases, supervisors may help students in more direct ways, e.g. by taking part in the analysis of empirical data to demonstrate specific analytical methods and advising the students directly on how theory can be brought into play. Finally, the students draw conclusions based on the project findings, they critically reflect on different aspects of their project work, and they put the project into perspective in relation to broader societal and/or academic issues. Here, the supervisors act as discussion partners who help to close the project (conclusion) and to open up the project in relation to broader theoretical or societal issues (the exemplary principle).

8 Supervising Projects

Fig. 8.1 Project work flow in PPL

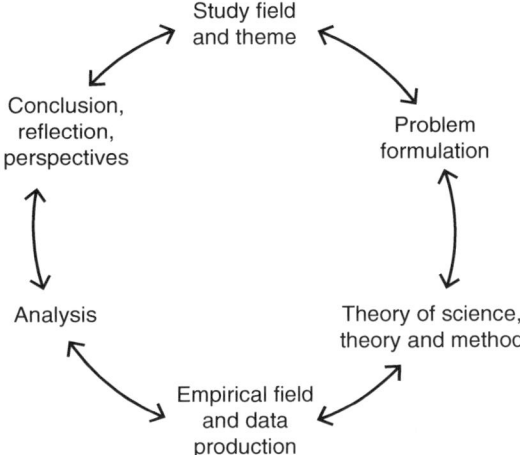

The project workflow can be illustrated by a model (Fig. 8.1).

The various elements of project work are rarely carried out in a linear way, but rather in an iterative way back and forth between the elements. This is illustrated by the double arrows in the model.

Project work is continuously evaluated mutually by members of each project group and their supervisor, and also during problem formulation and midterm seminars. At these seminars, two project groups engage in mutual critical and constructive dialogue and in a dialogue with the supervisors of the two groups.

The projects are evaluated in group exams on the basis of the students' project reports. Whereas the examination encompasses the whole group, the grading is individual (see also Chap. 7). To help students to concentrate solely on their project work in the second half of the semester, courses are conducted parallel to the project work, and are generally placed in the first half of the semester. The courses in the bachelor programmes are divided between: (1) courses that provide single-subject and interdisciplinary academic knowledge, (2) courses that are directly supportive of project work, including project planning and project methodology, and (3) courses that students choose freely. Course design at master level depends on the specific subject areas. Project work is certainly a demanding form of study that not only offers professional challenges at a high, independent level, but also personal, collaborative and communicative challenges (see also Chaps. 3 and 12).

The students' project work is framed by the learning outcome requirements outlined in a programme description. These include basic requirements for project work that both students and supervisors must address. In the following, we will describe the general learning outcome requirements of the bachelor programmes at Roskilde University, which in many ways are aligned with the European Qualification Framework for Higher Education (see also Sect. 4.4.1). If we had focused on the learning outcomes of the university's master programmes, the relevance of the outcomes to future employment would have been more important, although without changing the fundamental emphasis on academic knowledge and skills. The general learning outcomes for the bachelor programmes fall into five categories:

The most comprehensive group of learning outcomes that students need to acquire concerns academic knowledge and academic skills. These are:

Firstly: 'Research-based knowledge, understanding and critical reflection of theory of science, as well as theory, methodology and practice within one or more subject areas', i.e. knowledge and understanding of science.

Secondly: (a) 'Ability to identify, define and articulate complex academic problems', (b) 'Ability to assess theoretical and practical problems and to argue for and select relevant theories, analyses and solutions', and (c) 'Ability to apply the scientific methodologies and tools of one or more subject area, as well as applying general skills related to work within the subject area(s)', i.e. skills in working academically.

Thirdly: (a) 'Skills in systematic search for literature and information, and in applying scientific standards and methods to the use of references', and (b) 'Ability to read and apply academic literature in Danish and other languages', i.e. general academic skills.

Fourthly: (a) 'Communication of academic issues and solution models to both peers and non-specialists', and (b) 'Skills in the effective use of information and communication technologies', i.e. communication and IT skills with both specific academic and broader work-oriented relevance (see also Chap. 16).

Fifthly: 'Knowledge and exemplary insight into broader historical, societal, cognitive and ethical aspects of science', i.e. an understanding of the relationship between science and broader cultural and societal contexts.

Knowledge of project work and skills to carry out projects With regard to project work, the learning outcomes concerning knowledge and skills are: (a) 'Knowledge of project work and management of projects', and (b) 'Ability to plan, implement and evaluate projects and to comply with deadlines'. The learning outcomes associated with project work at Roskilde University are closely related to the implementation of study projects with a primary academic objective. They are however, formulated in such general terms that they may also be relevant to project work carried out in contexts outside the university.

Collaboration competence As mentioned earlier, the concept of competence points to personal abilities that students are assumed to develop in their studies, and that they will be able to apply in a variety of contexts. Regarding collaboration, the aim is to achieve the following learning outcomes: (a) 'Handling of complex development-oriented situations in study or work contexts', (b) 'Independent participation in disciplinary and interdisciplinary collaboration with a professional approach', and (c) 'Dealing with personal, social and group dynamic aspects of collaborative situations'. The description of learning outcomes concerning collaboration is oriented towards the transmission of knowledge and skills from study to employment contexts.

Lifelong learning competences The Danish Qualifications Framework for Higher Education reflects the fact that knowledge, skills and competences are subject to ongoing social change. This qualification framework is based on the perception that graduates should be able to further develop their knowledge, skills and competences throughout their lives. Against this background, one learning outcome of the bachelor programmes at Roskilde University is that students must acquire: 'Competence in identifying their own learning needs and in organizing their own learning in and across different learning environments', i.e. competence in self-directed learning.

Competence in study and career choices The Danish Qualifications Framework for Higher Education also requires students to achieve: 'Competence in making informed choices of the field of study or occupation based on insight into their own professional and personal abilities, and knowledge of study and career opportunities'. This competence is also included in the description of the learning outcomes of the bachelor programmes at Roskilde University.

It is not intended that students should achieve all five types of learning outcome solely through project work. However, as the main learning activity involved in students' independent acquisition of knowledge, skills and competences, project work should be acknowledged as the key contributor to achieving the learning outcomes. This means that it is important for supervisors to keep the learning outcomes in mind.

8.4 Different Roles of Supervisors

The basic framework for students' project work and for project supervision consists of the time and activity aspects and the required learning outcomes. Project supervision, however, is a complex activity that includes many different and important aspects. Because projects are carried out within the timeframe of one semester, it is important that supervisors emphasize the academic aspects of supervising the students: (a) to collaborate professionally on the academic workflow, and (b) to write project reports that meet academic standards. The supervisors however are also responsible for helping students to deal with group dynamic issues and for preparing the students to realize their learning goals later on in life. Finally, the supervisors should be able to facilitate the students' future choice of studies and career. In the following, we shall discuss the various aspects of supervision on the basis of a model (Fig. 8.2).

8.4.1 Work Process

At the initial supervision meeting, it is common practice at Roskilde University that supervisors and project groups enter into relatively precise agreements on collaboration, either orally or in writing. The reason is that expectations may differ between project groups and supervisors, which may cause collaboration problems. The agreements – sometimes referred to as 'supervision contracts' or 'supervision

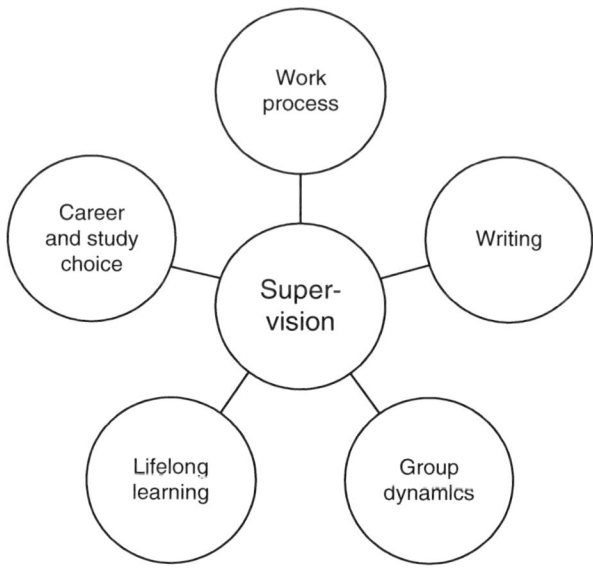

Fig. 8.2 Various aspects of supervision

letters' – will set out a clear and explicit framework for cooperation. Agreements may for example focus on:

A. Formal framework

- Learning outcomes, time and activity frames,
- Problem formulation seminar, mid-term evaluation and exam.

B. Competence

- Supervisor's experience and competence regarding the project,
- Students' experience and competence regarding the project.

C. Mutual expectations concerning roles and responsibilities

- Role of the supervisor at supervision meetings,
- Students' academic ambitions, time presumed necessary for project work, etc.,
- Division of responsibilities between students and supervisor,
- Types of feedback that the group may expect to receive from the supervisor.

D. Rules of collaboration

- Frequency of meetings and the expected number of supervision sessions,
- Agendas of supervision meetings and agreement on minutes of meetings,
- Forms of communication: oral, written, email, etc.,
- Deadlines for submitting working papers to be discussed at the next meeting
- Students' descriptions of their project activities since the last supervision meeting.

The mutual dialogue on the agreement between the project group and the supervisor may constitute an important part of supervision with regard to students' learning and work processes, because it: (a) helps to clarify the formal objectives of the project work to be focused on, (b) lets students know what kind of support to expect from their supervisors, (c) provides supervisors with knowledge of what they may expect from the students, (d) clarifies the time and resource framework for the project work, and (e) establishes rules for the interaction between supervisors and project groups. Throughout the project, a clear agreement on the rules of interaction between students and supervisors provides a solid basis for their mutual interaction, which may be subject to ongoing dialogue and revision throughout the project period. Supervisors may also support the students' work processes, by helping them in structuring time and activities, i.e. advising project groups on appropriate work organization. This may include matters such as: (a) how to prepare a work plan that indicates tasks and deadlines, and (b) which professional, personal and social considerations should provide criteria for the organization of the work.

Clear agreements concerning project work make it easier for project groups and supervisors to concentrate on their key common enterprise of academic discussions and academic work. Here, the role of the supervisors is to support the students' independent project work in different aspects such as project theme, problem formulation, chosen theory, chosen method, data and analysis. At Roskilde University, these aspects of project supervision are research-based. This implies that:

- Supervision has to communicate research,
- Project work takes place in a research environment,
- Most of the supervisors are active researchers,
- The students learn how to carry out their project work in research-like ways.

Therefore, it is important that the supervisors have personal experience of doing research, including collaborative research. Students cannot learn how to perform project work only by reading or listening. They have to experience project work in practice. Therefore, supervisors have to monitor student work processes and consider very carefully how supervision may best support the students' academic learning processes (these aspects of supervision are discussed in detail in Chap. 9).

According to the description of learning outcomes, supervisors are also responsible for supporting students' use of information and communication technologies as an academic tool and means of communication (Chap. 16 discusses these aspects of supervision).

Supervisors' communication with project groups is a challenging form of interaction. Supervisors may easily succumb to communicating with project groups as if they themselves were group members. This implies, however, that supervisors assume responsibility for the groups' project work on the basis of their professional experience and knowledge. In this way, they are at risk of removing the learning responsibility from the groups. Another risk would be that supervisors only react to questions and requests from the groups, leaving the full responsibility of project work to the groups. If supervisors disclaim commitment and responsibility for the group work and learning processes, this may overload the groups. Thus, academic supervision is a balance between supervisors contributing to project groups' work and learning processes and helping the groups to take responsibility for their own work and learning.

Academic publications on supervision suggest that supervisors downplay their direct instructions: 'I suggest that you read this book'. Instead it is proposed that supervisors choose words that motivate the students to reflect on the problems they face in their project work. This may include the following types of question from supervisors:

- Concretizing: 'How far have you reached in your analysis?'
- Investigative: 'What caused the disagreement about your choice of theory?'
- Challenging: 'What possibilities do you see of reducing the number of cases in your study?'
- Evaluative: 'What should we follow up on the next time we meet?' (Wichmann-Hansen and Jensen 2013, p. 347).

Depending on the knowledge and experience of the project groups, it may be necessary for supervisors to provide more specific instructions, for example concerning choice of literature, or even to train students in specific aspects of theory, methodology or analysis.

Supervisors are also co-responsible for establishing a good study atmosphere in project groups. Hemer (2012) relates the concept of 'study atmosphere' to a concept of 'trust': "This trust, whether institutional (legal regulations and bureaucratization) or personal, is at the core of developing a successful supervisory relationship" (Hemer 2012, p. 832). Supervision agreements may help to boost confidence. They may do so at a formal level, because they clarify the framework of the project work. They may also strengthen the basis of a more personal relationship of trust between students and supervisors, because they help establish clear mutual expectations. However, it is necessary continuously to maintain and develop confidence in the working relationship between students and supervisors. Hemer puts it this way: "The relationship cannot be prescribed and instead must emerge out of a process of negotiation between supervisor and student" (Hemer 2012, p. 832).

8.4.2 Writing

Working papers, work plans, project outlines, drafts of chapters and final project reports are the physical tangible products of project work. Supervisors may support students in their writing by simply encouraging them to get started quickly and by providing feedback on their texts. Through feedback, supervisors support students in:

- understanding and acquiring the conventions of academic text writing,
- knowing the different principles of structuring project reports,

- establishing a systematic argumentative structure in their texts,
- developing a coherent language and linguistic correctness,
- knowing the rules for references, notes and bibliographies.

In the early phases of the project work, it is commonly recommended that supervisors should address overall questions on students' writing processes, leaving out comments on linguistic details, unless language blocks the readers' understanding. Not until later on in the project work should supervisors relate more closely to the students' sentence construction, argumentation and language accuracy (Jørgensen and Rienecker 2013). If supervisors experience that students have difficulties in writing, they may suggest that the students participate in the university's voluntary courses in academic writing (issues regarding project writing are discussed in Chap. 10).

8.4.3 Group Dynamics

Project groups at Roskilde University are expected to accomplish projects within time limits. Although the university has established some general academic frameworks for project work, the responsibility of choosing problems, theory and methodology has been assigned to the project groups in collaboration with their supervisors. Ultimately, the project groups themselves are responsible for the learning outcomes of their project work. The project groups are composed of students with a variety of academic competences and perspectives on their work, all of which are then negotiated during project work. Compromises are formed, decisions are made and tasks are allocated. These aspects of project work may be defined as the 'goal-oriented field' or the 'formal dimension' of project work. The main efforts of the supervisors are directed towards supporting these goal-oriented aspects of the students' project work in order to establish the best possible basis for the students' academic learning processes.

However, project work is also affected by informal processes based on social group dynamics and psychodynamics (Mac and Madsen 2013; Christensen 2013; Andersen 2008). Project groups may be able to articulate these processes as hidden power relations, hostility, manipulation, excluding mechanisms, performance anxiety, etc. Unfortunately, such processes often remain hidden, while crucially affecting students' motivation and their academic benefits of the project work. This may lead to the designation of scapegoats or the division of students into hostile camps, and eventually to project groups splitting up without recognizing the collective social or psychodynamic forces that are at play. This may constitute an immediate and serious problem for some project groups. Furthermore, not recognizing and dealing with group dynamic problems also means that students miss the opportunity of learning from their experiences. This implies a risk that they will repeat their mistakes in new projects at or outside the university. In this context, it is important that supervisors involve group dynamic processes as an important aspect of their supervision.

In terms of understanding group dynamic processes and in guiding students how to manage these processes, it must however be recognized that supervisors have different backgrounds and abilities. It is therefore important that supervisors are able to clarify what types of issues they feel confident engaging in, and which ones they feel less capable of handling. If students' project work is threatened by group dynamic problems, supervisors must be aware of the group support services provided by the university. Roskilde University has engaged a pedagogical consultant who advises project groups on understanding and solving group dynamic problems. Furthermore, students can ask for group counselling at the university's Student Counselling Office. Finally, the university has launched a 'coaching project'. The main idea behind the coaching concept consists of two related parts: (1) a course that qualifies psychology and pedagogy students to act as process and team coaches, and (2) an offer of coaching for undergraduate students. The roughly 50 student coaches trained annually are used by a large number of project groups to discuss group dynamic challenges. Coaching is popular with bachelor students, who get the opportunity to develop their team collaboration skills in the context of specific problems encountered, as well as with psychology and pedagogy students who are able to develop their understanding of group dynamics in theory and practice, and to be awarded certificates as skilled group coaches by Roskilde University.

8.4.4 Lifelong Learning

The ideal that academic education should be viewed as a reservoir of knowledge, skills and competencies to last for a lifetime is gradually being abandoned. The labour market and society are continuously changing. Therefore, academically qualified employees need to renew their knowledge and familiarize themselves with new working methods and tools, and universities must pursue the aim of enabling graduates to adapt and learn throughout their working lives.

Project work is generally accepted as a method particularly suited to develop students' ability to learn. Each project represents new problems, new knowledge and new skills to be acquired. Project work facilitates a broad spectrum of learning encompassing specific knowledge and skills, communicative and interpersonal skills, and personal skills such as conflict management. If students are to realize an optimal learning outcome of project work, it is not sufficient that they just work on their projects and acquire different types of tacit knowledge about how to learn in new situations. Rather, supervisors should help students to understand how they learn and what learning strategies to use in different learning tasks.

In some of the study programmes at Roskilde University, students are required to reflect on their learning processes, and such reflections are discussed at the oral project exam. Students have to prepare a separate section of their project report dealing with their learning processes in the project and their reflections on the work process, asking questions such as: What worked well and what did not? What can we do differently next time? What have we learned? What competences have we gained? What insights have emerged? What is our experience of project work methods and collaboration? What resources have been used to register these reflections: E-portfolio, logbooks, social media like Facebook, video and audio recording, collaboration tools, photos, etc.?

8.4.5 Study and Career Choice

Crucial to the students' future are questions of study and career choices. Although students at Roskilde University can choose to switch studies during the first 2 years of their bachelor programme as well as during their transition between the bachelor and master programmes, they need guidance in making the right choices. This raises questions as to the expected learning outcomes of the various study programmes, and the jobs that the various programmes provide access to.

Project supervisors are not expected to advise individual students on these types of questions. Importantly, however, the supervisors should know when to refer students to the university's student advisors and the central Study and Career Service, because individual vocational and study guidance is a matter for specialized professionals. Still, supervisors are indeed expected to take part in discussions with the groups about the relationship between study motivation and study opportunities as well as in more general discussions on the types of jobs the different study programmes may qualify for.

8.5 Supervision for Life

There seems to be a growing need for personal and more existential guidance of students, in addition to the need for academic guidance, guidance on group dynamics, guidance in relation to learning strategies, and study and career guidance. Student advisors as well as university priests report that many young people are uncertain as to the choices they have to make about their education and life in general. A great many diagnoses of contemporary society suggest that individuals in late- or post-modern society are challenged to a much higher degree than seen before in history (Baumann 1992; Beck 1992; Giddens 1991; Sennett 1998):

- People of today have no ready-made scripts for life, handed down by family, culture or religion,
- People of today are becoming increasingly individualized with a weakened collective identity and social organization,

- People of today are exposed to the globalization of social dynamics, experiencing extensive divisions of labour and professionalization of important areas in life. This means that they may find it difficult to understand their own connectedness to the world, and whether or how to influence developments in society as well as their own life course,
- People of today are exposed to an accelerating pace of development, and to constant changes in life circumstances. This puts pressure on people's ability to adapt to the changing conditions and their ability to learn new things.

According to Habermas (1981), some of the risks associated with these developments include loss of meaning, solidarity and identity. In this context, the professional effort of supervisors and advisors is crucial in regard to whether people will have a good life or a life of unemployment, crime, substance abuse, mental instability or physical illness. Supervision and guidance are also important in terms of guiding people back on track if things have gone wrong in their lives.

The general social and identity-related challenges that mark the lives of young people also affect project supervision at the universities. The basic learning objectives of project work are professional and academic competencies. Sometimes, however, project supervisors are faced with situations where they have to respond to students' existential insecurity and identity problems. It is not expected that supervisors themselves should provide personal guidance for the group members. What is expected is that supervisors are able to uncover what kind of help students need, and to advise them on forms of professional help to contact. One would be the university priest, who provides existential guidance. Another would be the Student Counselling Service, which provides free psychological aid and counselling.

8.6 The Supervision Universe

The model of the supervision universe (Fig. 8.3) illustrates the formal framework of supervision, the supervisory functions and the support functions in regard to project work. The formal framework is shown in the inner circle, the support functions are shown in the outer circle, and the different aspects of project supervision are located in the circle between the formal framework and the support functions.

The model illustrates how the university prioritizes students' project work, and what support methods are used. Supervision is central. The different support functions, however, are equally important in supporting the students as well as the supervisors in their common enterprise of project work, and in creating optimal learning conditions.

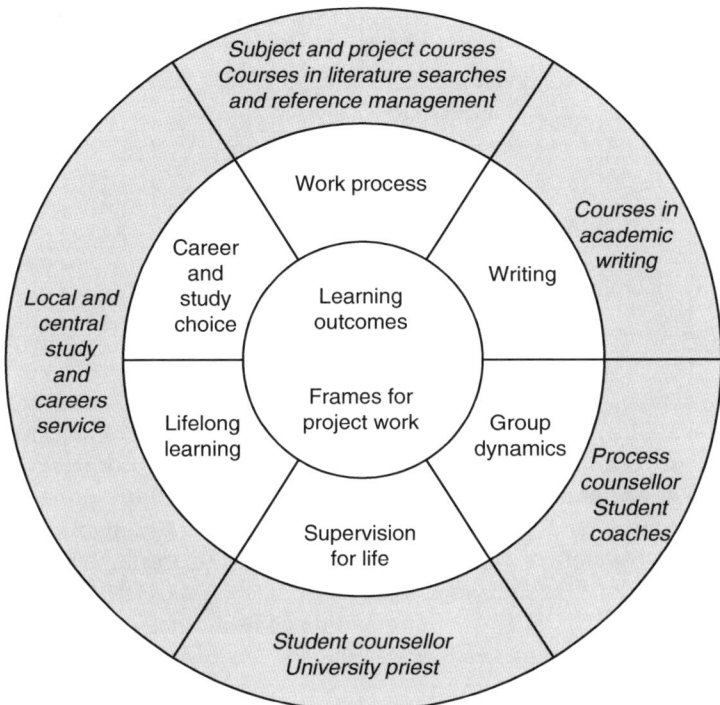

Fig. 8.3 The supervision universe

8.7 Pedagogical Training of Supervisors

Project supervision at Roskilde University is under pressure in different ways. The university is experiencing a high turnover of teachers because the first generation of faculty is about to retire. In addition, more students are being enrolled, leading to the hiring of many new teachers. Not all of the new teachers have experience in project supervision. In the context of project work and the practice of supervision, the new teachers face the task of developing new knowledge and skills. Furthermore, the reduction in time for project supervision has increased the pressure. This situation creates a need for project supervision to be theorized and critically reflected upon and for the establishment of explicit guidelines for good supervisory practice.

These changes have shown the need for a significant strengthening of in-service training of faculty members at the university. This has been achieved by: (a) ensuring teachers' right to in-service training, (b) establishing a comprehensive internal supply of pedagogical training, (c) requiring faculty members to take in-service training and supervision, and (d) distributing responsibilities and tasks associated with the training. In-service training rights are guaranteed by the fact that all teachers are assigned 28 h per year of continuing education, and 14 of these hours should be used for pedagogical training. New teachers will have to attend courses in project pedagogy and project supervision. Some of the courses offered by the University's Pedagogical Training Unit (UniPed) are:

- Project supervision,
- Tuition planning - communication and interaction in university teaching,
- The supervisor in the role of examiner,
- Course pedagogy,
- ICT and teaching.

As a condition for being employed as associate professor, assistant professors must complete a 3-year pedagogical training programme, which is also offered by UniPed. During their training, assistant professors receive supervision from associate or full professors. In order to draw up an appropriate plan, a meeting between heads of department and new assistant professors has to be established soon after the appointment. The plan includes three elements: research, teaching and pedagogical training. Heads of department monitor whether faculty members fulfil their obligations with respect to pedagogical training. This is done through annual appraisal interviews. Furthermore, a meeting is held each semester to evaluate and develop the pedagogical training of faculty members, involving heads of department, leaders of the university's study programmes and the training unit.

8.8 Supervision in a Field of Tension

Project work and project supervision at Roskilde University are carried out within an overall framework provided by the university's educational strategy. In short, the strategy is to educate graduates to critically participate in, assess and develop: (a) science, (b) society, and (c) the job functions which they are trained to perform. The model (Fig. 8.4) illustrates the three main dimensions of this strategy (science, society and employment). It also shows how the individual's professional and personal development in relation to the three dimensions should be viewed as critical to realizing this strategy.

The three main dimensions of this model represent a field of tension that according to the strategy must be kept in balance. A realization of this strategy requires that the students develop: (a) knowledge, skills and understanding concerning academic subjects, society and the relevant job functions in the labour market, (b) knowledge and understanding of how science systems, social systems, employment systems and the individual's life and employment opportunities mutually influence each other, and (c) competences in how to apply the different types of knowledge, skills and understanding in professional, societal and personal contexts. The emphasis in the study programmes is primarily on academic knowledge and academic skills, as

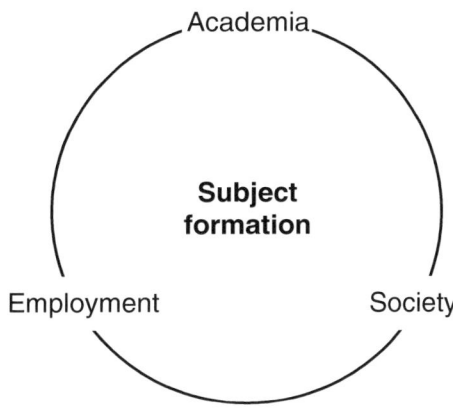

Fig. 8.4 The overall framework of project supervision

may be seen from the above description of the learning outcome of the bachelor programmes.

The prescribed learning outcome, however, also requires knowledge and skills that are more directly orientated towards society and employment, and towards understanding: (a) how society affects academic knowledge and skills, and (b) how academia affects society. As mentioned earlier, this reflects the belief that academic knowledge and skills are directly relevant to the job market as well as to citizens' participation in broader society, i.e. that a 'transfer' of knowledge and skills will take place, as long as the students have the opportunity to acquire personal abilities to 'translate' them into the requirements of the world outside the university (see also Chap. 2).

The relationship between the three elements in the model is not necessarily contradictory. Academic knowledge and skills may in principle be relevant to participation in society and employment. However, the balance will be upset if the focus is one-sided, i.e. on the criterion of academic learning outcomes. The same applies if the description of the academic learning outcomes is not explicitly orientated towards society and employment. In the light of the university's educational strategy, there is a need for a general reflection on the balance between the learning objectives to clarify whether this balance should be altered and how this could be done without compromising the ambition of high academic standards (see also Chap. 2).

The fact that a wide spectrum of political parties agrees on requiring that academic programmes should prioritize employment in the private sector certainly underscores the need for such a reflection. In their discourse, politicians establish a clear distinction between, on the one hand, academia and the ideals of Humboldt, and, on the other hand, the knowledge, skills and competencies that are required in working life. Academic study programmes are once again being criticized for being introspective, self-centred and without relevance for society and business needs (see also Chap. 4).

In the light of this social and political context, and in the context of the educational strategy of Roskilde University, it becomes very clear that the university needs to formulate new persuasive solutions. This is not possible by merely adhering to the autonomy of the universities and the principle of academic freedom. Roskilde University must convincingly demonstrate that it is possible to balance the academic, societal and employment-oriented dimensions of the university's study programmes. This may have implications for supervisors and supervision. If the balance of educational learning objectives is to better articulate societal and employment-related dimensions, it will require increasingly that supervisors are familiar with the knowledge, skills and competences that are highly valued in the graduate labour market, and that they possess profound knowledge and understanding of the critical and constructive role of academics in society (see also Chap. 17).

References

Andersen, A. S. (2008). Atmosfære på arbejdspladsen i psykodynamisk belysning [Atmosphere in the workplace in the light of psychodynamics]. In S. Dupont & U. Liberg (Eds.), *Atmosfære i pædagogisk arbejde* [Atmosphere in educational work] (pp. 116–148). Copenhagen: Akademisk Forlag.

Bauman, Z. (1992). *Modernity and ambivalence*. Cambridge: Polity Press.

Beck, U. (1992). *Risk society*. London: Sage.

Boud, D., & Costley, C. (2007). From project supervision to advising: New conceptions of the practice. *Innovations in Education and Teaching International, 44*(2), 119–130. Retrieved November 22, 2013 from: http://dx.doi.org/10.1080/14703290701241034.

Christensen, G. (2013). Gruppearbejde [Group work]. In L. Rienecker, P. S. Jørgensen, J. Dolin, & G. H. Ingerslev (Eds.), *Universitetspædagogik* [University pedagogy] (pp. 189–199). Frederiksberg: Samfundslitteratur.

Giddens, A. (1991). *Modernity and self-identity. Self and society in late modern age*. Stanford: Stanford University Press.

Habermas, J. (1981). *Theorie des kommunikativen Handelns* [Theory of communicative action] (2 volumes). Frankfurt: Suhrkamp.

Hemer, S. R. (2012). Informality, power and relationships in postgraduate supervision: Supervising PhD candidates over coffee. *Higher Education Research & Development, 31*(6), 827–839. Retrieved November 22, 2013 from: http://dx.doi.org/10.1080/07294360.2012.674011.

Jørgensen, P. S., & Rienecker, L. (2013). Teksten i vejledning – vejledning på tekst [The text in study guidance – Guidance on studying texts]. In L. Rienecker, P. S. Jørgensen, J. Dolin, & G. H. Ingerslev (Eds.), *Universitetspædagogik* [University pedagogy] (pp. 351–368). Frederiksberg: Samfundslitteratur.

Lee, A., & Green, B. (2009). Supervision as metaphor. *Studies in Higher Education, 34*(6), 615–630. Retrieved November 22, 2013 from: http://dx.doi.org/10.1080/03075070802597168.

Mac, A., & Madsen, S. (2013). Projektarbejdets frugtbare kriser [Fruitful crises in project work]. In A. Mac & P. Hagedorn-Rasmussen (Eds.), *Projektarbejdets kompleksitet – viden, værktøjer og læring* [The complexity of project work – Knowledge, tools and learning] (pp. 87–105). Frederiksberg: Samfundslitteratur.

Nordentoft, H. M., Thomsen, R., & Wichmann-Hansen, G. (2013). Collective academic supervision: A model for participation and learning in higher education. *Higher Education, 65*(5), 581–593. Retrieved November 22, 2013 from: http://dx.doi.org/10.1007/s10734-012-9564-x.

Savin-Baden, M., & Major, C. H. (2004). *Foundations of problem-based learning*. Maidenhead: Society for Research into Higher Education & Open University Press.

Sennett, R. (1998). *The corrosion of character: The personal consequences of work in the new capitalism*. New York: W. W. Norton & Company.

Wichmann-Hansen, G., & Jensen, T. W. (2013). Processtyring og kommunikation i vejledningen [Process management and communication in supervision]. In L. Rienecker, P. S. Jørgensen, J. Dolin, & G. H. Ingerslev (Eds.), *Universitetspædagogik* [University pedagogy] (pp. 329–350). Frederiksberg: Samfundslitteratur.

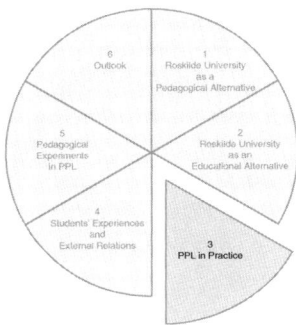

Chapter 9
Methodological Challenges – From a Supervisor's Experiences

Inger Jensen

9.1 Introduction

Problem-oriented, interdisciplinary and participant-directed project work differs markedly from ordinary study methods. Instead of being expected to reproduce insights from courses and mandatory reading lists or to apply already selected theories or models to given case materials, the students are expected independently to generate new knowledge relevant to their subject of study. This means that the study process has a number of traits in common with research processes and it means that one of the supervisor's primary roles is to support the students' development of academic knowledge and competences (see also Chap. 8). In order to facilitate the students' processes of acquiring academic competences through project work, the supervisor must be aware of a complexity of epistemological principles and research methods and paradigms. The supervisor must also be willing to let the students' curiosity and motivation continue to be the driver of the project work. This means finding appropriate ways to acquaint the students with methodological and epistemological reflections – while not administrating an overdose. This chapter will address some methodological challenges experienced by the author as facilitator

I. Jensen (✉)
Roskilde University, Roskilde, Denmark
e-mail: inger@ruc.dk

© Springer International Publishing Switzerland 2015
A.S. Andersen, S.B. Heilesen (eds.), *The Roskilde Model: Problem-Oriented Learning and Project Work*, Innovation and Change in Professional Education 12,
DOI 10.1007/978-3-319-09716-9_9

and supervisor of project groups in social science at various levels of education: at bachelor, master and PhD level. The author will compose a framework for being sensitive to the students' interests while helping them to select methods and approaches. Therefore, although the subject of this chapter rests on the philosophy of science, the focus and exposition will be from a supervisor's perspective.

The supervision process comprises several aspects of the project work, such as study and career choices, group dynamics and collaboration competences, relevance of knowledge of the subject, and writing and communication competences (see also Chap. 8). This chapter, however, will address supervision only in relation to the development of academic competences.

As noted above, the students are not expected just to reproduce insights from courses and mandatory reading lists. They are expected independently to generate new knowledge relevant to their subject of study.

The curricula of the various academic subjects at Roskilde University contain a general description of performance criteria relative to assessment and grading. In any particular curriculum, criteria may be added or excluded depending on their relevance at the specific level of the study programme. However, the general description indicates what is expected from the problem-oriented project work at the graduate level. The criteria for awarding the highest grade are:

1. Knowledge of the academic target area: competent knowledge, insight and clarity.
2. Relevance of the problem statement to the academic target area: competently formulated, justified and delimited; conscious selection and rejection of options.
3. Relevance of theories and methods to the problem statement: competently justified; conscious selection and rejection of options.
4. Mastery and application of theories and methods: competent elucidation, independent use and critical reflection.
5. Presentation and treatment of the empirical foundation: competent reflection on the relevance and reliability of the empirical foundation.
6. Requirements relating to construction and production: met in a convincing manner.
7. Contextualization of the project work: competent account of the results of the project work, independent reflection on limitations and potential continuation.
8. Structure and presentation: competent presentation, precise use of concepts, independent and clear organization.

Some of the requirements listed describe academic competences that have a number of traits in common with what is called for in research processes: relevance of problem statement and of theories and methods; reflected selection and rejection of options; reflecting relevance and reliability of empirical foundation; independent reflection on limitations and potential continuation of the project work in general. This means that a primary role of the supervisor is to support the students' development of competences in knowledge creation.

9.2 Phases of Supervision

Let us now turn to some phases in the supervisor's work with the project group.

9.2.1 The First Meeting Between Supervisor and Group

A typical project extends over a full semester, and occupies half of the students' working time – in addition to courses, seminars and other assignments. For more on these activities and of ways of adjusting mutual expectations between project group and supervisor, see Chaps. 2 and 8.

Ordinarily, before the first meeting with the supervisor, the group has been formed in a process where a number of proposals for problem statements from students have been presented at meetings of students with the same subject and at the same level. For an example, see Chap. 3. Often this process is facilitated by older students and aided by teachers. Through several rounds of presentation of ideas and preliminary formation of project groups, the final group formation is decided by the students. After this process, with a preliminary problem statement, the group members apply to the study board for a supervisor, and the board subsequently allocates a supervisor to the group.

Before the first meeting, the supervisor has received a preliminary title of the project and a problem statement from the group. At the first meeting, the author will have an open dialogue with the group about how they find the project interesting: what they already know about the subject, from where they have their knowledge, what they want to know, and how that is relevant to their subject.

There are two reasons for having this dialogue instead of immediately to proceed to a discussion of how to approach the problem statement. First, it is important to get an idea of the direction and motivation of the group, because it is the group members' motives and curiosity that drive the project work, and it is an indicator of the students' interest in obtaining new insight and knowledge. Second, the first problem statement and formulation of research questions do not always match the students' real interests in knowledge creation. There is a tendency to deliver habitualized (reflex) responses, so that when asked to phrase a research question, students tend automatically to give it the form of a cause and effect question. The research paradigms from natural science tend to pop up as if they were the only concepts of real science; this also occurs in subject areas where it would be neither easy nor relevant to design a strictly objectivistic and controlled cause and effect study. For instance, if a group of students in Business Studies are interested in knowing how processes of integrating corporate social responsibility in the company are experienced by employees in different departments in an organization, a cause and effect research question like "what effects does the CSR policy have?" will not grasp the complexity of the processes. Furthermore, some students, in particular those with an educational background outside Roskilde University may believe that a correct problem statement should be a hypothesis that can be tested or even proven (sometimes in an empirical context, where the result is already given, so that no new knowledge would be created).

Based on these experiences the author often suggests that the group writes an essay before the next meeting. The essay, which can function as an introduction in their report, should explain why it would be relevant and interesting to create new knowledge related to real world problems, and what they know already from earlier studies or other sources. The essay often outlines a broader context that has to be narrowed down later on by conscious selection and rejection of approaches. It is important that the essay is not replaced by a standard literature review, because the selection of literature has to be decided later on based on the curiosity and the motivation of the group.

9.2.2 The Mid-phase Meetings

As mentioned above, the essay or introduction to the project work outlines a broad subject field that indicates why it would be relevant and interesting for the group to create new knowledge. At the next meeting, a number of research questions are phrased and it is discussed whether they agree with the group's knowledge interests, by which methods they could be studied, and what kind of knowledge could be obtained by employing particular methods. In this process, the group investigates what relevant theoretical and/or empirical contributions are already available. After this preliminary overview of research questions and potential study methods, the project plan must be narrowed down to the most interesting and realistic approach, given the students' resources and available time. This process is a very important part of the project work and maybe would not be completed at a single meeting with the supervisor. Furthermore, the students must be aware that the project plan may need to be adjusted in the light of new insights and conditions. They must recognize that such a continuous readjustment is not necessarily a weakness, but can be considered a part of the learning process based on the insights acquired. This is the process where the students are trained in how to justify the "relevance of problem statement and of theories and methods; conscious selection and rejection of options; reflecting on relevance and reliability of empirical foundation" (cf. the list of requirements above). Again in this selection process, some students tend to feel more comfortable with objectivistic methods, even when such methods would not answer their research questions. Other students will tend to understand social constructivism as if people are trapped in pure subjectivism and relativism, which would make demands about validity and reliability impossible or irrelevant. Below, we return to this challenge of the reliability of different approaches.

9.2.3 The Final Meeting Before Completing the Report

In the middle phase of the project work, group and supervisor have met to discuss the use of theoretical and secondary empirical material and the methods and findings of the project. During this process the discussion is mostly focused on single approaches, with their individual criteria of relevance and reliability. Outlining the project in the early phase from a broad overview, based on the introduction, means "to justify the relevance of problem statement and of theories and methods; conscious selection and rejection of options" (list of requirements cited earlier). In the final phase of the project the requirement is called: "Contextualization of the project work: competent account of the results of the project work, independent reflection on limitations and potential continuation". In a way it is a repetition of the reflection on the selection and rejection of approaches in the initial phase of the work, but now it has to be done on the basis of the experiences acquired through the work and with self-criticism as well as ideas for what approaches should be taken in further studies.

This process, however, is a demanding and challenging one. The idea of problem-oriented project work is that it should address real-life problems, and real problems are seldom captured by any single discipline. Different disciplines approach and conceive reality selectively. They have their own levels of focus (e.g. cell level, subjective experiences, unmediated social encounters, social structures and systems, nations and globalization). One cannot focus at several levels at the same time. One needs to shift perspective. Is there then a unifying or guiding principle that can justify the combination of approaches? In addition to these meta-methodological reflections the project group also has to consider how to present its work in a written report (See also Chap. 10). Sometimes I recommend the group to think dramaturgically when composing the report. As in a play at the theatre, if a pistol is hanging on the wall in the second act of the play, is has to be used in the play. It may be that somewhere in the process the group has spent energy on writing working papers about a theory or some empirical studies and has become somewhat impressed by this material. However, if this material does not support the guiding principle that makes their report worth reading, I would recommend the group to leave it out and maybe use it as raw material in some later work.

We will return to the challenge of justifying a combination of approaches and what is to be understood by a unifying or guiding principle.

The following is a summary of the challenges I have experienced as supervisor in relation to the development of academic competences during participant-directed project work.

- To clarify the curiosity and motivation of the group before jumping to research questions.
- To support the students in formulating the research questions in a way that matches their curiosity and motivation.
- To support the students in selecting methods and approaches that are relevant to the kind of knowledge they want to obtain.

- To support the students in narrowing down the project plan to make it match their interests. That means to support them in rejecting approaches and methods that are irrelevant or unrealistic given their time schedule, level and resources.
- To support the students in understanding how various criteria of validity and reliability are met and linked to different approaches and methods.
- To support the students in reflecting on the limitations and potential combinations of different approaches, critically reflecting on the guiding principle in their project work and opening up for further studies.

9.3 A Framework for Developing Competencies

This section presents my framework for developing competences in knowledge creation in group work. The framework is inspired by the work "Erkenntnis und Interesse" by Jürgen Habermas (1968).

We can distinguish between three quite different interests in knowledge creation:

(a) *The technical interest in knowledge creation* which is an intention to create knowledge that enables one to forecast and control events.
(b) *The hermeneutic interest in knowledge creation* which is an interest in understanding what makes sense to other persons, how things are understood and what is considered important in certain contexts.
(c) *The critical interest in knowledge creation* which is an interest in understanding and reflecting critically whether a context could or should be different.

To illustrate the three forms of knowledge interests, let us imagine some research about criminality:

Based on the *technical interest* one could study:

- How may robberies be reduced?
- What kind of knowledge would enhance the police detection rate?
- How does imprisonment affect crime?
- What kinds of persons commit what kinds of crimes?
- How can an insurance company calculate an insurance premium relevant to criminality?

Based on the *hermeneutic interest* one could study:

- How do members of criminal gangs experience status and the sense of belonging?
- How is imprisonment understood by prisoners, relatives, personnel and the public?
- What life perspectives are experienced by prisoners before and after the crime?

9 Methodological Challenges – From a Supervisor's Experiences

Based on an *interest in critical understanding* one could study:

- Are there socially constructed systems like laws and institutions that play crucial roles in crime that could be imagined differently? For example:
  - If drugs were sold legally in special shops what would happen to the addicts, the black market and the dealers?
  - Could different national and international laws and principles radically change patterns of financial crime and irresponsibility?

Table 9.1 below shows some marked differences in the ways research questions could be phrased in relation to the three interests in knowledge creation and the kinds of knowledge that are related to the different interests with crime as the subject area.

The illustrative field of study of crime is used as an example from social science where all the three knowledge interests would be relevant: the technical interest in predicting and controlling crime, the hermeneutic interest in understanding certain persons' life experiences in their relevant contexts, and critical understanding of the wider societal context and of potential alternatives related to criminal behaviour. A specific study could be limited to one of the three interests or it could be a combination of them.

Table 9.1 Kinds of knowledge interests – types of research questions – kinds of knowledge

Interests in knowledge creation	Examples of research questions	Kinds of knowledge
The technical interest	What is the impact of surveillance on crime?	Cause and effect relationships
	Does a certain chromosome defect cause violence?	
	Does improvement in language skills reduce violence?	
	Does imprisonment have a preventive influence on crime?	
	Is the tendency to become criminal linked to biological or social factors?	
The hermeneutic interest	How do first-time and repeat offenders conceive their life story?	Insight in and understanding of life experience in certain contexts
	Where do prisoners find identification models?	
	What experiences and relationships in prison make sense to whom?	
The interest in critical understanding	If it is illegal access to drugs that makes the cynical black market business so profitable, what then if drugs are produced and sold legally?	What if a certain societal context were different?
	If illegal driving causes more accidents, what then if cars could not be started without a driving licence?	

In a field of study such as traffic and public transportation the technical interest in prediction and control has a very high priority and is partly based on observations within natural science disciplines. Nevertheless, understanding travellers' experiences is a necessary insight in planning. Political decisions about various technologies, systems of transport, systems of payment and environmental implications could include critical reflective approaches.

One could imagine an area of study within microbiology where the technical interest and methods from natural science are almost the only prevailing approach; the hermeneutic interest is non-existent but critical reflections could imply combining the knowledge from microbiology with considerations of alternative technology systems. An example of this could be to reflect on whether the knowledge of anti-freezing mechanisms in organisms living under extreme conditions could solve problems regarding frost in other systems.

The heuristic value of this distinction between the three interests in knowledge creation and the corresponding ways of formulating research questions is to make sure that the students formulate their research questions in accordance with their curiosity and motivation, i.e. to ensure that they do not automatically phrase their questions in the format of natural science if their interest is not technical. This is the reason why, as mentioned, I sometimes suggest that the group writes an essay about their interests. This procedure is used in relation to the first two of the following challenges:

1. To clarify the curiosity and motivation of the group before jumping to research questions.
2. To support the students in formulating the research questions in a way that matches their curiosity and motivation.
3. To support the students in selecting methods and approaches that are relevant to the kind of knowledge they want to obtain.
4. To support the students in narrowing down the project plan to make it essential to their interests. That means to support them in rejecting approaches and methods that are irrelevant or unrealistic given their time schedule, level and resources.

Table 9.2 is a heuristic framework to address the third and the fourth challenges of selecting and rejecting methods and approaches that are in accordance with the students' interests and resources:

The fifth challenge is about the validity and reliability of the empirical foundation acquired by the selected methods:

5. To support the students in understanding how various criteria of validity and reliability are met and linked to different approaches and methods.

To put it simply, the question about validity concerns whether we gain insights into what we want to know about and not into something different. In other words: have we selected the questions and methods suitable for knowledge interest and subject area? The question about reliability, however, is not so simple. It is a question about how the created insight and knowledge can be trusted by a reader of the report. If we look at the examples of methods listed with the three different interests in knowledge

Table 9.2 Kinds of knowledge interests – kinds of knowledge desired – relevant methods

Interests in knowledge creation	Kinds of knowledge	Examples of relevant research methods
The technical interest	Cause and effect relationships	Controlled experiments with clearly isolated factors
		Comparative studies with identifiable variables
		Quantitative studies of repeatable observations
		Statistical analyses, correlation and regression analyses
		Cost and benefit analyses
The hermeneutic interest	Insight in and understanding of life experience in certain contexts	Dialogues, interviews, focus groups
		Analyses and interpretations of written and spoken material
		Ethnomethodological studies of social interaction
		Culture analyses
The interest in critical understanding	What if a certain societal context were different?	Analyses of system mechanisms like markets, laws, political systems and societal institutions that constitute the relevant context
		Analyses of how system mechanisms are socially constructed and therefore not the only conceivable way
		Analyses of values of and rationales for and against prevalent and alternative contexts
		Analyses of public discourse and stakeholder interests
		Critical reflection on the premises taken for granted in empirical studies based on a technical interest

creation, we can identify interesting differences in paradigms and prescriptions for reliable empirical studies:

(a) In the technical interest there are ideals concerning subject-object separation and researcher-independent observation, and positivistic prescriptions about focus on direct data observation without subjective interpretation.
(b) In the hermeneutic approach the focus is on inter-subjectivity: the unavoidable dependence on verbal accounts and expressions and the interpretative processing of the empirical studies.
(c) In the critical reflective approach the focus is on societal coordination mechanisms and the perspective is at the level of systems and institutions and includes socially constructed mechanisms that are not directly observable, but must be inferred from the various interconnected activities that together compose the

system (like the various activities and rules in the election procedure that determine the composition of parliament, or the documentation systems in New Public Management). Thus, both the description of societal coordination mechanisms, and the critical reflection on whether they could or should be different are not beyond questioning.

As mentioned above, some students tend to be bound by objectivistic criteria and have aspirations of creating generalizable knowledge, whereas other students are committed to a constructivist position where they tend to give up any criteria of reliability. It is necessary to help students to balance these positions. Based on the work by John R. Searle (2010), the author finds it useful to differentiate concepts of reality. At one end of a continuum we find what Searle calls 'brute facts': physical phenomena that are observable relatively independently of social interpretation – like the glazed frost on the pavement. At the other end of the continuum we find social realities that are societally constructed coordination mechanisms, systems and institutions –like market mechanisms, bank accounts and referendum procedures – whose reality depends on a widely shared interpretation and acceptance in practice. Such social realities are not open to single individual interpretations. In between the two ends of the continuum are found all types of cultural artefacts and routines. For further development of this gradation of non-social versus social reality see Jensen (2013). The objectivistic methods are most relevant for studies of the non-social realities that are considered directly observable phenomena. At the opposite end of the continuum, the social realities are complex social relationships that are not directly observable, but have to be inferred from a variety of indicators. In light of these quite different approaches, how could students learn to deal with the reliability of their empirical studies? At a highly generalized level the answer is transparency. Let us develop what may be understood by this. The insight to be learned is that however valid a finding is, if it is unclear to the reader of the report how the finding was obtained, it is not reliable. Therefore, the detailed method must be transparent to make it possible for the reader to judge the reliability of the findings. Table 9.3 is a framework for the links between knowledge interests, methods and reliability criteria. When students use secondary empirical studies they will often find studies of social phenomena with a technical interest and based on a positivist approach that seem to find cause and effect relations between quantitative observations. To train the students critically to reflect on the limitations of their findings would also imply helping them to reflect whether secondary empirical studies depend on certain implicit societal conditions. Thus, what is written in Table 9.3 as a method under the critical interest "Critically reflecting the premises taken for granted in empirical studies based on a technical interest" could also be included as reliability criteria under the technical methods when they are used to study social phenomena.

As described above, problem-oriented project studies are supposed to be real-life problems, and real-life problems are seldom captured by a single discipline and a single method. In the initial phase, students describe their curiosity and motivation by writing a broad essay on their knowledge before starting the project. During the project work they select and combine some approaches and argue for their validity

Table 9.3 Kinds of knowledge interests/kinds of knowledge – relevant methods – criteria of reliability

Interests in knowledge creation/kinds of knowledge	Examples of research methods	Reliability transparency in the relation between methods and findings
The technical interest: Cause and effect relationships	Controlled experiments with clearly isolated factors	Describe clearly how the intended objectivity in observation is organized
	Comparative studies with identifiable variables	Describe clearly any uncertainties in setup and observation
	Quantitative studies of repeatable observations	Describe clearly how observations are analysed
	Statistical analyses, correlation and regression analyses	
	Cost and benefit analyses	
The hermeneutic interest: Insight in and understanding of life experience in certain contexts	Dialogues, interviews, focus groups	Describe clearly how the verbal material is collected
	Ethnomethodological studies of social interaction	Describe clearly how non-verbal observation is made
	Culture analyses	Describe clearly how the material is interpreted and how the interpretation is validated
	Analyses and interpretations of written and spoken material	
The interest in critical understanding: What if a certain societal context were different?	Analyses of system mechanisms like markets, laws, political systems and societal institutions that constitute the relevant context	Describe clearly how the societal mechanisms are inferred from primary and secondary empirical studies
	Analyses of how system mechanisms are socially constructed and therefore not the only conceivable way	Describe clearly the analyses of values and rationales for and against alternative contexts
	Analyses of values of and rationales for and against prevalent and alternative contexts	
	Analyses of public discourse and stakeholder interests	
	Critical reflection on the premises taken for granted in empirical studies based on a technical interest	

and reliability as mentioned above. In the final phase of the project the supervisor has to deal with the sixth challenge:

6. To support the students in reflecting on the limitations and potential combinations of different approaches, critically reflecting on the guiding principle in their project work, and opening up for further studies.

In the 'pre-project' and 'post-project' phases of the project work, students learn under supervision how to make meta-methodological reflections on how to combine and not to combine different levels of observation and different kinds of knowledge. However, it is interesting that this is based on what could be called a 'practical, knowledge-based reflection', a reflection that leads us to conclude whether there is a guiding principle that makes sense. It is also interesting to observe how the combination of methods and levels of study (micro, mezzo and macro levels) and different theoretical approaches contribute to a broader insight: if not generalizable knowledge, then at least a kind of transferable understanding. We also see how this kind of self-critical reflection appears to become more and more nuanced at higher levels of studies and research.

Some disciplines or study target areas are single paradigm disciplines (e.g. mathematics) and others have multiple paradigms and approaches (e.g. business administration). The ambition of unity of science is unrealistic and abandoned. Crossing disciplines can therefore take three forms: (1) a full integration of two or more disciplines (transdisciplinarity), (2) finding some linkages between two or more disciplines (crossdisciplinarity) or (3) switching perspectives between separate unlinked disciplines (multidisciplinarity) (see also Chap. 2). The epistemological premises of these reflections, however, are mostly implicit. Textbooks on research methodology tend to deal with paradigms and methods separately. Bryman (2008) for example opens the discussion, but only about combining qualitative and quantitative methods, which is just a corner of this interdisciplinary meta-methodological reflection.

In society at large, the research areas and study target areas have been institutionalized with separate approaches and paradigms. In practice, in societal organizations, there is an institutionalized division of labour between various fields of professional expertise, such as medicine, accounting, finance, law, engineering, psychology, politics, etc. This is what Mintzberg (1983) describes as the professional bureaucracy. In modern institutions, however, there is a growing focus on the need to create dialogues between different kinds of expert knowledge and create a balanced comprehensive view in policy making. In practice, dialogues crossing professional expert fields tend to be a combination of practical sense making and power play.

At universities like Roskilde, where interdisciplinary studies are encouraged, we have considerable experience of practical, knowledge-based reflection on crossing disciplines with different approaches. It would be valuable if the epistemological premises of these meta-methodological reflections could be made more explicit.

References

Bryman, A. (2008). *Social research methods*. Oxford: Oxford University Press.
Habermas, J. (1968). *Erkenntnis und Interesse* [Knowledge and interest]. Frankfurt: Suhrkamp Verlag.

Jensen, I. (2013). Balancing through institutionalization. In I. Jensen, J. D. Rendtorff, J. Dahl, & J. D. Scheur (Eds.), *The balanced company – Managing for the 21st century*. Farnham: Gower.
Mintzberg, H. (1983). *Structure in fives. Designing effective organizations.* Englewood Cliffs: Prentice-Hall.
Searle, J. R. (2010). *Making the social world: The structure of human civilization.* Oxford: Oxford University Press.

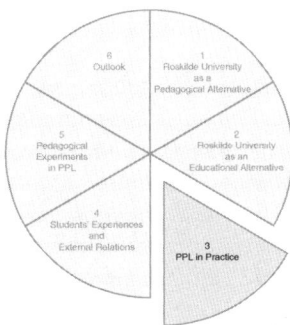

Chapter 10
Genre and Voice in Problem-Oriented Reports

Sanne Knudsen

10.1 Introduction: The Origin of the PPL Report

A new university, a new learning approach – what would be more appropriate than a new genre as well? When Roskilde University was founded in order to realize exciting contemporary ideas concerning problem-oriented and participatory academic learning, it would seem the perfect time to re-think and re-shape the forms and functions of academic writing as well. Since problem-oriented writing involves a shift in the positioning of knowledge, the genre needs to be able to contain and support the new ways of working with and communicating this knowledge. The PPL approach relies on students constructing problems and arguing for the relevance of problems, and these new practices need to be reflected in the genres of student writing. So, the break with mainstream topic-centred learning approaches towards more student-directed or research-like learning approaches seems to require a genre with more room for the student and for the discussion of research processes. Traditional writing forms may serve as a corset to problem-oriented knowledge and learning, shaping it into traditionally socially acceptable forms, but not without inhibiting breathing and somewhat damaging internal organs. For that very reason, it is interesting that existing international scholarly literature on problem-driven learning in general scarcely mentions writing and

S. Knudsen (✉)
CBIT, Roskilde University, Roskilde, Denmark
e-mail: sannekn@ruc.dk

© Springer International Publishing Switzerland 2015
A.S. Andersen, S.B. Heilesen (eds.), *The Roskilde Model: Problem-Oriented Learning and Project Work*, Innovation and Change in Professional Education 12,
DOI 10.1007/978-3-319-09716-9_10

genres at all. Genres and writing-related issues generally appear as a peripheral aspect or even as a non-issue. In fact, it almost appears as if these new learning approaches were expected simply to fit seamlessly into genres designed to serve distinctly different learning purposes and ideals. However, a distinct genre gradually germinated from the PPL practices at Roskilde University in which the notion of the problem was to be a core element. The aim of this chapter is to present and discuss this genre.

At Roskilde University, *the problem-oriented project report* gradually evolved and established itself as a distinct genre of its own in order to enable, support and communicate the specific new forms of critical thinking resulting from PPL processes. Today it has become the absolute central genre in PPL studies, shared by students of all departments, disciplines and study programmes throughout the university. It has been argued that the genre was moulded more or less directly from the tradition of writing project reports as the end result of longer projects in the tradition of architectural or engineering studies (Illeris 1999, p. 18). It seems as though the role of writing was perceived as simply a tool for reporting, as a memory aid helpful in remembering facts before the reporting, and a tool for assessment after the reporting (Illeris 1974). One reason for this conception may have been that the general view of language at the time was based on the transmission and container/conduit metaphors of language (Reddy 1979). In fact, a slight distrust of writing altogether (as a contrast to learning) can be sensed in Illeris's ground-breaking book on problem-orientated and participant-directed learning published in the wake of the establishment of Roskilde University (Illeris 1974). The writing process is presented as disassociated from the learning process and as constricting learning:

> Even though a project report may be considered to be 'bad' in the traditional sense, deep and important learning may very well have taken place during the project in question. Similarly, a 'good' project report may mask an uneventful process devoid of provocation. Focusing on predetermined definitions of a product may encourage students to steer clear of problems rather than facing and analysing them. (Illeris 1974, p. 144 [my translation])

The logical consequence of this argument was either to abandon any generic constraints altogether or to provide a genre actually and explicitly supporting 'deep and important learning'.

At Roskilde University a little bit of both was the case, at least in the early years. To give an example: when I started at Roskilde University as a student in 1983, we were allowed to write within almost any genre possible and even to invent our own, if we felt the need. In fact, the university had accepted fictional novels as appropriate academic writing more than once, I was told. However, since the term 'report' had been introduced as well, the genre that gradually grew out of the experiment did bear strong resemblances to reports as they were applied in the natural sciences as mentioned above. Yet the genre was not set from the beginning, and the genre of the project report condensed over time into its own form. Thus, it became moulded on the actual experiences and learning processes of students doing PPL studies and writing.

The genre as it evolved demonstrated a number of strengths. Firstly, the relatively long sections or chapters made room for discussion and analysis of literature rather than just for providing one definitive answer. Originally, no page constraints were given at all, but now the length of the report has been confined to somewhere between 50 and 80 pages depending on discipline and level. Secondly, the individual sections of the report can be said to reflect and represent important steps in the problem-oriented research process itself in a coherent argumentative structure (construction of a problem, study of existing knowledge of the topic, research design, analysis, conclusion). Furthermore, the genre of the project report allows for adding additional sections such as the chapter on learning processes particular to PPL learning ideals. Students themselves are generally deeply involved in producing these reports. Writing them takes a great deal of time, effort and concern, so much so that students at Roskilde University have a tendency to equate 'the report' with 'the project' in their everyday speech. The genre came to be able not just to reflect but also in some ways to scaffold the workings of the project and critical thinking. This genre has now been developing for more than 40 years, and it plays a very active role in communicating and shaping how novice students conceptualize, embody and implement problem-oriented learning.

The focus of this chapter is to discuss and analyse how issues of writing and genre play an active role in supporting and communicating norms and practices of problem-oriented learning and critical thinking. In doing so, the project report as it is practised at Roskilde University will serve as frame of reference in order to analyse learning qualities as well as some of the challenges in actually realizing and managing them, seen from an academic writing perspective. Consequently, the chapter is divided into three sections. The first section deals with the concept of critical thinking as it was originally envisaged in PPL theories and practised at Roskilde University as a core element of problem-oriented learning. The second section zooms in on a characteristic aspect of the project report, i.e. fostering and supporting critical thinking by allowing students to speak (and write) in their own voices. The third section focuses more generally on the project report as a genre in student academic writing. It is argued that the genre of the project report is better understood as three distinct sub-genres, each providing students with a progressive generic stepping stone through the jungle of problem-oriented educational practices. As students navigate from one sub-genre to another, their thinking matures academically as the progression between these genres reflects progression in academic critical thinking and problem-oriented competencies. Finally, the chapter concludes by identifying some implications of a writing-conscious and genre-centred approach for supervision practices and university management.

10.2 Provocation, Critical Thinking and Writing

The first and influential book conceptualizing PPL approaches (Illeris 1974) introduced as a central component in this context the concept of *provocation*. Originally, the concept seemed to be particularly oriented towards social criticism and provoking – intentionally goading – established social norms, ideologies and power relations.

While this definition may have suited the spirit of the early 1970s, times changed around the late 1980s and early 1990s and students did not necessarily feel primarily driven by social indignation (Hansen 1997). Today, students are still very much involved in building strong ties between their studies and 'the real world', but the motivating factor is rather to produce knowledge useful to society and organizations. Today, probably in the light of current financial uncertainties, students seem to be particularly concerned about how their knowledge and studies may be externally relevant within society and in securing employability (see also Chap. 13). In spite of differences in direction, however, a strong motivational factor is still social relevance and concern.

Illeris also conceptualizes the concept of provocation in a more general manner quite similar to the internationally more widely applied concept of *critical thinking*. Provocation and critical thinking both describe general heuristic approaches to learning. *Critical thinking* is an academic writing perspective generally understood as composed of two steps: (1) close and detailed analysis of existing knowledge on a given phenomenon, situation, theory or concept, and (2) critical examination of potential alternatives (see for instance Bean 2011; Ennis 1996; Brookfield 1987, 2011). The first step is related to processes of *de-naturalization* (Jeffries 2010), of *unmasking* current beliefs about what is taken for granted (Chomsky and Foucault 2006) or of *mystification* in Roland Barthes's sense of the word, i.e. uncovering 'the falsely obvious' and revealing underlying structures (Barthes 1972). The process should be directed as much toward one's own beliefs, knowledge and practices as those of somebody else. The second part of the process involves deliberately searching for or constructing and exploring alternative ways of understanding, conceptualizing or performing in the world. A similar critical analysis lies at the heart of developing research questions as well as in constructing academic learning problems.

Critical thinking as a method for learning and reflection is at the core of problem-oriented learning in all stages of the project and the report. This is what problem-oriented learning in particular sets out to foster and nurture – as much as it nurtures the construction of expert knowledge on certain phenomena, situations or research. In practice, critical thinking procedures are often experienced as difficult for students and supervisors alike (see also Chap. 8). One thing is that students get to interact with and question existing and established knowledge (a daunting task). Then again, not just any interaction is allowed, and the rules as to how to interact and why are generally experienced as opaque (Lillis 2001; Ivanic 1998). Moreover, discrepancies may exist between ideals and actual practices of critical thinking and between different ways of interpreting the concept and translating it into practice. Research in academic writing also points to another issue, and that is a certain resistance by some students to the approach. Some students may prefer to accept the first answer to a given question that they meet, rather than critically examining it. This approach is not necessarily born out of disengagement or laziness, but because this traditional attitude and strategy regarding knowledge has indeed served them well in primary and secondary education (Bean 2011). They may never have learnt to confront and handle academic problems. Savin-Baden (2000) finds similar responses in problem-based learning: when confronted with difficulties in this new way of working, some students simply return to the ways of writing assignments that they previously have experienced as successful. This means for instance focusing on defining and summarizing rather than analysing. Finally, some students may dislike applying critical thinking for other reasons than the experience of difficulty. The practice of actually doing critical thinking can be experienced negatively, because students feel destabilized by having to question their own knowledge or that of their chosen theoretical ally (Brookfield 1987). They may feel that their personal values or those of their community are under attack. They may experience the critical approach as undermining their own identity and sense of belonging in a specific community or discipline. Some students thrive in being 'creators rather than receivers of knowledge', other students experience disjunction and disassociation from whom they believe themselves to be, resulting in anger and frustration (see Savin-Baden (2006) on disjunction in problem-based learning; see Ebest (2005) on resistance in writing). However, frustration is better than boredom in enabling learning (Baker et al. 2010) and quality supervision and scaffolding are strong remedies in teaching students to think critically and work with problems (Schmidt et al. 2011).

10.3 Speaking in One's Own Voice in Order to Express Ownership

Traditional academic writing has been much criticized for being too formal, pre-coded and frozen, thus potentially deterring communicative and heuristic creativity, hindering understanding and generally scaring off non-academics and students (Billig 2013). International academic writing studies repeatedly report how students resent academic writing, because they experience it as having to write in a voice other than their own (Lillis 2001; Ivanic 1998). They feel they have to pretend to be somebody they are not, and they have to perform as a stranger in a strange discourse. It is experienced almost as lying. Needless to say, this situation is not particularly enabling in a learning context.

Research in international academic writing reports a strongly articulated wish amongst students of being able to write in their own voice (Ivanic 1998; Lillis 2001; Read et al. 2001; Ivanic and Camps 2001). It provides them with a sense of ownership (Lea and Street 1998). The concept of *voice* in student writing is used in different senses. In this chapter, the term is used to designate the possibility to write in a manner that enables students to see their own individuality represented in the texts. It is a matter of representation of identity and is closely connected with issues of stylistic formality, or rather informality. This is particularly relevant in relation to PPL because students are positioned in a much more active and participatory role. Ideally, the problem-oriented project report should allow students to think for themselves, express what they think, analyse and discuss existing knowledge and produce new knowledge – all in an essentially academically deep manner, but not through overly formalistic and formulaic writing practices. In this context, formalistic and de-personalized writing can to be considered as a rhetorical sickness, at least during novice stages. Though the problem-oriented report as an academic genre is neither oriented toward subjectivity nor opinionated normativity, students are in fact encouraged to write in their own words and voices on top of nurturing and germinating their new academic vocabulary. This enhanced – if still somewhat constrained – stylistic freedom is a way of supporting student identity and ownership of their thinking and writing.

The genre of the project report is open to the inclusion of personal student voices in several ways. A certain level of informality and personal style is sometimes even specifically encouraged in some disciplines, while others simply allow an element of informality mixed with more formal writing. However, a deeper expression of voice and ownership may take the form of explicitly allowing the students themselves and their choices, actions and reflections to be expressed in an active and overt form. The project report always allows expression of the narrative of the construction of the project. This allows the student to take a visible role as actor and initiator in the text in a way that is not common in academic writing. The students are often even highly present in the text as designers and constructors of the project. They generally refer to themselves using the 1st person plural pronoun *we:* "We decided to do this project", "we were inspired by a lecture", "we chose to focus group studies", "we concluded" etc. The 'we' is strongly present in descriptions of framing the project, methodological choices, and the practicalities of putting the project together. The first example below illustrates how students accentuate their role as initiators of the entire process, and highlights students as owners of methodological choices, analyses and conclusions.

> The fact that we found Organization X after the revoked arrangement with Organization Y was by no means coincidental. We did, at the very early stages of the project work, contact Organization X, and they were the ones referring us to Organization Y in the first place. We had, however, not researched the actual possibilities for collaborating with Organization X itself. It all ended relatively positively for us, but if we had not managed to get a collaboration up and running with Organization X, the entire preparation and execution of the performance and the arrangement with the homeless people would have been entirely different. (Performance Design Studies)

Voice is a complex phenomenon to study, and the presence of a personal pronoun alone does not necessarily in itself express strong voice identity (Helms-Park and Stapleton 2003). Up to a certain level, students' personal motivation and experiences are used explicitly to frame the importance of the project, in particular among students new to project work of this kind – and students freely refer to personal opinions, discussions or experiences as the initiating force of the project. The following example demonstrates this approach departing from personal experiences, emotions or discussions:

> Our interest was instantly caught by the programme 'Young Motherhood', the longest-running reality show in Denmark. This programme brought forth various emotions. We were left in a state of mixed feelings such as outrage, joy, incomprehension, recognition, compassion, sympathy and stomach pains of awkwardness. This diversity of different emotions and feelings produced in us by watching the programme stimulated a desire to examine the strategies used by the programme in order to target us as viewers (…) We wondered how so many people feel entertained by the ineptitude of others rather than wanting to help the mothers in the show. (HUMBACH)

The students' point of departure is other experiences of the world than their own personal experiences such as burning issues of the day in the news. Their concern is not articulated strictly academically but rather as a humane concern and general interest in the world. The following example is from Global Studies in which students start by presenting their subject as highly problematic and relevant to us all as human beings. Their personal experience is an experience of a need to do something and of a responsibility to the world. The 'we' applied in this excerpt is a more inclusive 'we':

> The 2011 hunger crisis in the Horn of Africa hit the population hard, threatening millions of lives. The first warnings were sent out in 2010 but the crisis could not be prevented. The World Food Programme (WFP) is the main topic of this paper as it is the biggest agency for preventing and fighting hunger across the globe. (…) Our research question takes its starting point in this consideration and in our wondering what we can learn about WFP and the international society from a humanitarian crisis such as the one that hit the Horn of Africa in 2011. (Global Studies)

Chapter 3 in this volume presents a project produced by students of the basic studies programme in natural science in which personal experience is a strong and explicitly expressed motivational factor. However, reports in the natural sciences and social sciences at higher levels tend to be more brisk and brief in their style, and florid expressions, experiences and feelings are generally (though not always) downplayed. These reports may not emphasize connections between the object of study and personal experiences and interests as often and openly as the reports from studies more oriented towards the humanities. However, they do tend to express a kind of personal concern about, or personal interpretations of, situations as in need of improvement. The student may attempt a concise and objective style, but the raison d'être of the project is clearly framed within a discourse of wanting to solve problems to make the world a better place.

A sense of voice is also represented by being able to incorporate one's own reasoning processes, thoughts and learning experiences in the text in several ways. One way is by allowing the space and the time for students to write and explain themselves at greater length than seems to be the norm in general student academic writing. Thus, the problem-oriented project report specifically opens for several options for inclusion of prolonged reasoning, narration and explanation. The fact that these more expository, explanatory and narrative kinds of texts surface to this extent in problem-oriented writing (or are allowed to surface) is that the majority of students' writing activities focus on the writing of backstage texts, i.e. texts they write for each other explaining, communicating and interpreting what they have read or found out. Also, they may communicate regarding ideas for the progress of the project, develop or test out arguments or write discussion papers. The style and content of such explanatory and narrative internal texts tends to influence the style of the more official reports in a more explanatory direction as well. In fact, some reports – in particular in the bachelor study programmes – almost explicitly address themselves to fellow students. One report written in Physics, for example, starts out by saying:

> The name Albert Einstein is known by almost everybody – it is almost synonymous with wisdom. His fame is primarily a result of his theory of relativity, which is almost as famous. Likewise, the equation $E=MC2$ is commonly known. Despite the fact that the name of

> Einstein and the concept of the theory of relativity are commonly known, the familiarity of the general public of the actual content of the theory of relativity and how technology might have been influenced by it is more limited. This paradox has inspired this project. (Physics)

I am sure that most of the supervisors assessing the report were quite familiar with the works of Einstein, so the intended audience is clearly somebody else. So, the student perspective can be represented as a model reader of the text as well.

This explanatory and peer-oriented style often spills over into the formal report. This is done in several ways of which I provide a few examples below. The first example is a long illustrative narrative in which students also set out to express sensory experiences. Another strategy is to explicitly and sometimes somewhat redundantly translate, illustrate, explain or visualize abstract concepts. Such extended explanatory writing takes several forms, but generally students explicitly work on translating abstract concepts and theoretical norms by providing examples, by elaboration or by illustrating or referring to specific experiences of the given concept. One way is by providing examples of translating abstract concepts into concrete situations that students are familiar with already.

> Politicians are presented in the media now more than ever, and they are extensively represented and focused on as political persons representing their parties. They also offer themselves and seek to promote themselves to the media not just as politicians in 2008 but as private persons. Think, for example, about how Lene Espersen was covered by the media, when she was elected head of the Conservative Party and how she went on stage with her husband and two children while "Simply the Best" by Tina Turner was played at full blast on the stereo. Or think about how the TV portrait of Prime Minister Lars Løkke Rasmussen and his family entitled 'Just another ordinary family' was aired during primetime in 2011. (Danish Language Studies)

A final example of allowing students' voices to be expressed explicitly in project reports concerns a specific and formerly mandatory section devoted to reflection on the process and course of the project and on what the group had learnt as a collective. This section has since all but disappeared in the majority of reports, but I mention it here since it was intended to enable student voices to be expressed. Moreover, the idea of using logbook-related types of text has been widely debated in academic writing communities as a way of allowing students to express ownership in their own words (Creme and Hunt 2002; Creme 2008). This process section of the report was not, however, entirely logbook-oriented; it was more of a section in which students were to reflect on what they had learned during the process, why the project eventually took the form it did and how they overcame obstacles along the way. I myself conducted an unpublished study of these process sections of the project report some 7 years ago, and the conclusion seemed to be that the writing was more strategic than reflective. One important factor is that not all students are comfortable with revealing their private personal voice in more public work-related situations. Others just do not believe that their real self is actually what is expected from them. The sections were primarily used to position the students as hardworking, competent and genuinely set on learning. Whenever they met obstacles, these were caused by outsiders such as organizations never returning phone calls, members of the group deciding to leave the project, closed offices or unavailable supervisors.

Strategic use of writing in order to design an ideal voice rather than express an authentic voice is precisely one of the concerns of including this kind of writing in academic texts. Whenever students write texts intended for assessment, they obviously polish their expressions up a bit, and much authenticity is lost. The process section of the problem-oriented project report at Roskilde University was not added to the parts of the text to be formally assessed, but it was definitely open for discussion during the exams. A better way of including reflective voices may be in the form currently applied in many reports: methodological reflection. Methodological reflection opens for student voices as they analyse their own experiences, or selected and usually theoretically relevant parts of their own experiences. The combination of a limited task and the unique personal experience of doing interviews or observations enable the (better) students actually to produce excellent reflections. It is not that they confine their experiences to fit theory (as they confined their personal voices in their process sections), but rather the other way round. In the really successful cases, students actually use their personal experiences in the field to comment on and add to methodological theory.

Another concern about opening for student voices in academic writing is the concept of authenticity. That students should be able to own their own work and speak in their authentic voices is one point. A relevant question then is: when is a voice ever authentic? Shouldn't students rather be offered a variety of voices with which they feel comfortable? Perhaps the role of the university is to help students gradually shape a personal academic voice rather than just allowing for private voices in a separate section? It has been argued that insistence on using one's personal and authentic voice may lead to students missing an opportunity of actually developing and enriching their authentic voice to include an academic one as well. Students are supposed to take part in an academic enculturation process and academic voices and style are part of that (Stapleton 2002; Casanave 2002; Beaufort 2007; Casanave and Li 2008). It is a balance of allowing for individual and informal style, while also encouraging students – gradually and progressively – to understand, reflect on, embrace and own the academic rhetoric and to use academic vocabulary, reasoning and documentation in writing without feeling estranged. The point is not necessarily to shape students into the existing rhetoric altogether. Much academic rhetoric and communication is *really* unnecessarily bad (see Billig 2013). However, students should have the option to make informed writing choices based on the context of their writing, and to make some of the better aspects of academic writing their own.

10.4 The Academic-Professional Problem-Oriented Project Report as a Genre

All students at Roskilde University write project reports, and they generally submit one each semester. 50 % of their study time is spent on projects and on writing these reports. The genre is known as 'the project report' (or sometimes just 'the project'), and it is strongly framed as one distinct genre. In reality, this genre – like any other academic genre (Hyland 2009) – is realized in a variety of ways depending on discipline, topic, level of education and even individual preferences of supervisors and students. Lab reports, for instance, are associated primarily with the natural and technical sciences; highly focused case reports typically with business-related disciplines, and purely theoretical reports may not be uncommon in Philosophy while they are frowned upon in Communication Studies. However, putting local variations aside, the general genre of the project report actually falls into three distinct sub-genres applied throughout the university.

Broadly speaking, the genre of the project report is a hybrid between an academic theory-building research genre and a non-academic professional problem-solving report. Each project report sub-genre is distributed differently on a continuum between the two report genres. They may share textual surface elements, but a deeper analysis reveals distinct and fundamental internal differences as well. Carolyn Miller defines genre as a typified social and communicative action rather than a collection of textual features. In other words, our genres are primarily determined by multi-layered communicative purposes and activities (Miller 1984; Samraj 2004). In this case, the project reports are both expository and argumentative genres with problems as a core feature (Martin 1989). Furthermore, they share the general communicative purpose of inscribing the associated projects as quality studies deserving of high grades. Students, particularly novice students, may envisage additional communicative purposes, such as explaining the phenomenon of their studies to a non-academic public as well as to fellow students or participants outside academia. On the other hand, the genres vary in the conceptualization of the purpose of the project and consequently in the realization of what a problem essentially may be, where problems are found, and what an appropriate and useful response and treatment of the problem may entail (Yeung 2007). These variations are caused primarily by traditions of the field of study and academic level.

The professional report is partly rooted in the disciplinary research genres of the natural, technical and health sciences, but has since transgressed the boundaries of the classic research genre and taken a life of its own outside academia (Martin 1989; Harvey 1995; Yeung 2007). The communicative purpose of professional reports is to solve 'practical matters of the world'. Such practical matters are defined externally: they concern a conflict or a negative situation within or outside the investigating organization and definitely outside any context of academic knowledge production. So, the problem exists before and outside the investigations presented in the professional report.

Reports are written in order to analyse and solve a problem. In contrast, the communicative purpose of academic reports concerns epistemic theory building – contributing to the shared knowledge of the field by constructing and communicating new knowledge. A problem is considered as a problem in expert knowledge, and the studies reported in the academic reports are concerned with filling the existing gap in knowledge (Yeung 2007). Furthermore, the problem is not necessarily clearly defined or delineated from the outset of the study. The first step for any student or researcher in a new field is to get acquainted with existing knowledge before being able to define and articulate the nature of the problem. Experienced researchers may be quite aware of knowledge problems early on, but students, especially novice students, are not. The academic studies of experienced researchers and novice students are quite different even though they both engage in research-like activities. Researchers may start out with a relatively well-defined knowledge problem, but students need to get acquainted with existing knowledge first. Any externally, socially or personally motivated social concern needs to be translated into a gap in knowledge in order to become academically anchored.

These functional differences have argumentative and communicative consequences:

> Because the major concern in business reports is not epistemic, drawing a clear distinction between fact and opinion does not appear to be a critical yardstick in reporting. Rather, the concern is with trying to understand the phenomenal world in solving practical problems. Thus, the major principle of organisation in business reports is guided by the topical analysis of the subject matter, not epistemic considerations. (Yeung 2007, p. 164).

Other important differences between the two types of report are in quality, depth and critical thinking. Yeung finds that recommendations play a huge role in professional reports. However, it seems to be of minor importance whether these recommendations are subjective, anecdotal or whether they arise from systematic analysis and studies. In contrast, instead of providing practical solutions, an academic conclusion might just as well discuss the problem and illustrate complexity or simply identify new problems rather than provide practical solutions. When recommendations are included, however, they need to be based on systematic analysis and evidence. A similar pattern was found when the method sections were compared between the two genres. Often the method sections of professional reports are given a low priority and are rather sketchy and more like an appendix. The applied methods are stated, but they are neither analysed nor discussed at any length. In academic reports, however, methods are the epicentre of the text. The quality and scope of methods set the conditions for the validity of the entire study, its results and conclusions.

10.5 Three Kinds of Problem-Oriented Project Reports

In general, the three archetypical project reports at Roskilde University echo the report varieties described by Yeung (2007) and they can be said to represent three stages in student intellectual and knowledge-wise academic development. The boundaries between the genres are never clear-cut and they vary slightly according to field and discipline as well. Here we are still referring to a hybrid genre between the professional and the academic report, but the weightings change over time. To give an example, even the report genre closest to the academic-professional research report genre may include features traditionally associated primarily with the professional genres in that they aim at providing solutions or recommendations concerning

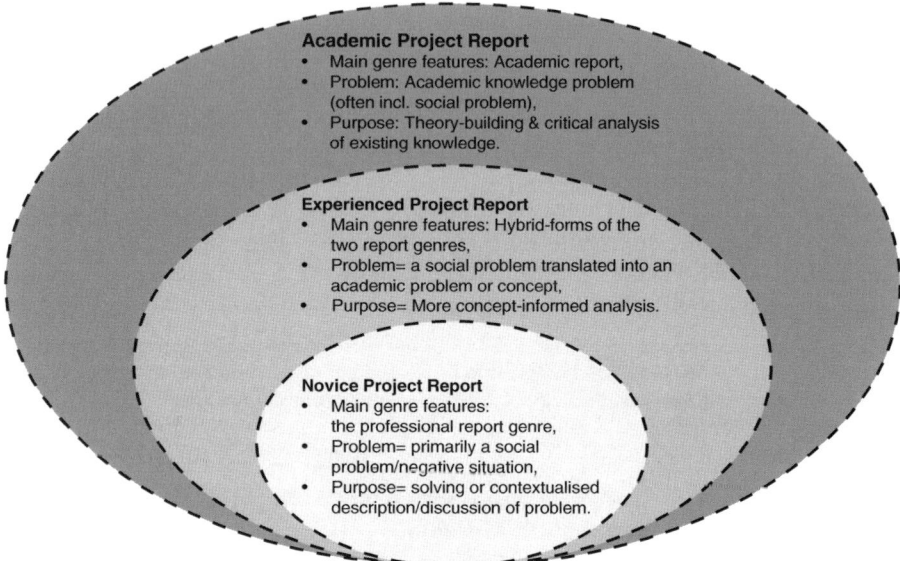

Fig. 10.1 The figure illustrates an idealized version of the three problem oriented report genres and how they gradually change and progress during the university career of the students. A central point of reference is the social problem or situation, which is persistently present in most reports – though to a lesser degree as the academic writing matures

more or less case-specific matters (dominating in the more practically-oriented fields such as the HUMTEK study programme (see also Chap. 6), Performance Design, Communication Studies and Business Studies) (Fig. 10.1).

The three report genres are: (1) *the novice project report,* (2) *the experienced project report* and finally (3) *the academic project report.* Despite the genre names provided here, all three genres are problem-oriented, and they all are fundamentally academic in the sense that they all play valid roles in different forms of academic communication and assessment at the university. The genre here identified as *the academic report* is, however, closer in macrostructure and communicative purpose to the traditional conceptualization of stereotypical academic writing, while *the novice report* resembles the professional report more. *The experienced project report* falls somewhere in between. These three report genres may share a common project orientation, but they are different in the way they conceptualize the notion of central problem-oriented elements such as the problem, theory and function of existing knowledge and sources and function of empirical data. The three genres are to be understood as ideal types of texts, and the boundaries between them may be fuzzy and debatable. This categorization of sub-genres based on a few textual and knowledge-presenting features is at best sketchy and indicative. However, the purpose of this illustration is to identify that these are in fact different ways of producing knowledge in writing project reports, and of using and framing personal concern and existing knowledge in the process. The rest of this chapter presents a few significant differences between the types of report and illustrates how these differences can be expressed in the text. All examples are from project reports submitted in 2012.

There is one aspect, however, shared by the absolute majority of the reports, regardless of genre or type. That is the very strong presence of a social context of the study. Though many reports state academic or theoretical purposes as well, the presence of a social rationale or expression of social relevance seems almost mandatory. The following examples illustrate how social relevance and concern can be expressed as an intention of helping to solve general social problems, or by framing a particular phenomenon or situation as problematic or even threatening

> The intention in writing this master thesis is to contribute to reduce social inequality when it comes to health issues and further the potential for promoting health in Denmark. The thesis rests on an assumption that the health of the individual is more than a matter of biological heritage and lifestyle, but as much a question of inequality of resources for living a healthy life. (Health Promotion and Health Strategies)

> The historical development of the city of Copenhagen, however, illustrates how investment in rundown areas tends to attract a new and more affluent group of people, and increased popularity is followed closely by rent increases as well. The problem is that the people already living in these areas most likely will be pushed out of their neighbourhood since they do not have the financial resources to maintain stable everyday lives in the area. This development is known as gentrification. (Geography)

> A growing number of multi-resistant bacteria cause increased mortality all over the world. The efficiency of antibiotics decreases in line with the increasing number of resistant bacteria, since conventional treatment no longer has any effect. This is particularly a problem in the industrialized countries because antibiotics are readily available here. (NATBACH)

The existence of a social driving force and inspiration is explicitly framed in the reports and seems a strong and significant feature of the genre at all levels. However, as students mature, other and more academic or knowledge-oriented features are added in different ways.

The *novice project reports (NPR)* typically represent the first attempts at problem-oriented report writing. They resemble professional reports to a large degree, probably because this is a genre well known to students from outside the university. (They are, however, not entirely identical with professional reports, because they are in fact not written primarily to solve problems but to learn and eventually to pass exams). This is the type of report requiring the least amount of pre-existing background knowledge to construct. They can be done, so to speak, from scratch. Consequently phenomena from the outside world dominate not only the framing of the project but the entire report as well.

The reports are primarily and often exclusively centred around a phenomenon or a situation in the world and not on academic disciplinary concerns, problems or theories. The identified problems are issues of the world, and students rely on their own experiences or on issues debated in public media in identifying these issues. In studies in the humanities, these problems may be more psychological, epistemic or philosophical dilemmas, but they are generally framed within a social context as well. The following excerpts illustrate how students from all major disciplines are motivated to study a given phenomenon due to media exposure, personal experience or the perceived severity of a current issue.

> Our motivation for doing this project springs from two documentary series produced by the *Danish Broadcasting Corporation*. They have provided insight into the treatment methods and pedagogical values of the treatment centre *Shubert's Minde*, and we were simply astonished and thus inclined to wonder whether such methods really are necessary and can be defended theoretically. This interest in young people in social care and the related treatment methods is the foundation of this project. (HUMBACH)

> We wondered why one fellow student, for instance, feels the need to inform the world about the fact that he has kept his New Year's resolution and been a non-smoker for 100 days. This form of announcement is generally familiar and frequently used by the majority of Facebook users, but for whom is this information intended? Your Facebook friends are unlikely to consider this to be interesting knowledge; rather it is probably considered to be annoyingly irrelevant information. (HUMBACH)

> The aim of this project is to demonstrate the issue of how factual information can be twisted to an extent that political actors can understand identical facts differently. We have chosen to study the representations of unemployment in Denmark and how it is possible quite arbitrarily to interpret the number of unemployed as well as the development in the number of unemployed people in Denmark. (…) We strongly feel that the issue is interesting and has current interest. (…) It may turn into a significant social problem if the ordinary citizen does not feel well equipped to participate in the democratic process. (SAMBACH)

The articulated driving force of the studies is for the students themselves to know more about a phenomenon that interests them and to understand the essential components and context. There seems to be an interesting discrepancy between reports written by humanities students and those written by students of the social sciences. Whereas the former tend to frame their endeavours as *wanting to understand, wanting to know more, take a closer look, dig deeper, uncover, find out*, the latter tend to use communicative rather than heuristic verbs such as *illuminate, communicate, present, inform, advise,* and *letting somebody know* – as if they were already experts on a given topic. Disregarding disciplinary affiliation, however, the articulated research questions are generally clarifying and somewhat defining or descriptive in nature focusing on asking how and what – with the aim of providing contextual knowledge or interpretation regarding "how" and "what". Furthermore, the questions generally aim at the phenomenon/situation itself, be it works of art, trade unions or the theory of relativity:

> How does Ai Weiwei mix aesthetics and politics, what are his artistic intentions and what have his works caused? (HUMBACH)

> How have unions been organized historically, and what changes have been influential in the popularity of unions? What characterizes the new strategy of the union? How does the new strategy relate to the current tasks of the union representatives seen from the perspective of the union representatives themselves? (SAMBACH)

> What is the relevance of the special theory of relativity on the development of the atomic bomb and the GPS? (NATBACH)

Accordingly, the function of theory, literature, sources or existing knowledge is to provide answers to those questions, at times leaving the content of the theoretical chapters rather factual and descriptive or almost encyclopaedic. Sources tend to consist of a mixture of general introductions and a few phenomenon-specific analyses. Elements of students' theoretical critical thinking are sparse. Sources are rarely questioned or analysed, but generally used to provide information. If debate or critical analysis is represented, it is generally lifted from the sources (though the texts may be somewhat unclear on the fact). Empirical studies generally describe aspects of the phenomenon, and they are often unrelated to theory in any academic sense. Theory is used to describe a given phenomenon in one way, while empirical studies generally function as an example of the given phenomenon, often in the manner of comparing two cases, perspectives, contexts or artefacts.

Conclusions often merely repeat certain theoretical and empirical points. Since the major drive seems to be simply understanding something in more depth or knowing more about a phenomenon, rather than analysing anomalies or paradoxes, there is not much more to say. Sometimes, but not always, solutions to problems are given, but generally in a normative way by discussing what the owners of the problem should be doing:

> As an extension of our conclusion, we would like to discuss society's options when preparing itself to treat neglected children. (…) We cannot provide a definitive solution, but we can discuss the available options. The fact is that we do have neglected children and teenagers. They need help. Society needs to be equipped for handling these children and provide them with what they need. So, how could this be managed? (HUMBACH)

This type of report typically represents a first step into the academic world. Students are driven by the kind of knowledge they are familiar with from their life as pre-students: social concerns and current issues. The close affiliation with a broader social interest is echoed in the structure of these texts, reminiscent of the professional report in the sense that the presentation of the problem and the presentation of the case/methods are sometimes realized in the same introductory section. It appears (textually) as if the identification of the problem and the case are almost inseparable. The theory sections then describe the phenomenon in one way, and the empirical studies describe the phenomenon in another way. They are positioned as two parallel realms of study. This particular structure is closely connected with the early years of bachelor studies, but an identical structure can be found in some of the more technical and case-oriented disciplines and fields as far as the master thesis.

The experienced problem-oriented report (EPR) takes a variety of shapes, as students gradually become more experienced and build a more solid knowledge base. Some students generally progress from the novice reports as their studies become more specialized, though this is not always the case. Some students repeat the NPR structure even in their master thesis in the sense that the case is the absolute centre of attention. The theoretical level of discussion is higher and more analytical, it is more argumentative and critical, but the general communicative purpose of these reports still seems to be solving a problem for the organization or institution, rather than deeper critical analysis. The example below illustrates a report prompted by a request from outside academia on how to solve a quite specific problem.

> How can the combination of smartphone technology and the museum experience be used by Roskilde Museum in order to create a unified and coherent museum experience while also considering the personal approach to visiting a museum? (Performance Design Studies)

The theories applied in this report are at a much more advanced level than in typical novice reports, but they are used in the same way: to describe certain phenomena in order to provide a frame of reference – an understanding of the phenomenon of interaction in a museum – for the empirical study. The theories/sources supplement one another and are not questioned. My point is not to frame these kinds of reports or studies as inadequate or heuristically stuck in any way. Some probably are, but I personally have met few of the really bad ones. The challenge of continuous use of the novice/professional report is that it may not guide students in advancing their theoretical analysis and in using their theories more cleverly and critically. If they are allowed to ask questions where the natural answer is, so to speak, an answer, they may not find the inspiration to do more than find such an applicable answer. The answer may be academically rewarding and interesting as well, or it may be academically superficial. Non-academic organizations or institutions contact students in order to solve certain problems, but these organizations and the academic world may have different criteria as to what might constitute an interesting and relevant problem. If students are kept in a realm where the criteria and needs of the specific organizations are framed as the most important, then they miss out on learning the academic criteria of critical thinking and argumentation. Beyond a certain point, asking such questions is running the risk of closing one's horizon and not questioning or opening it in order to see all the cracks and complexities as well. This production of an answer versus analysing the cracks and complexities is a central difference between the NPR and the EPR.

A key feature of the EPR involves a change of focus (more or less pronounced) in the studies and a change in the way theory is presented and used in the texts. Reports are still highly case-oriented, but the research questions tend to reveal a more theoretically informed touch and concern. The following two excerpts are from Workplace Studies and Danish Literature Studies respectively, and they illustrate this more theoretically inspired construction of a research question. The general frame of reference for both reports is still the phenomenon in question, but the questions reveal a more focused and informed endeavour. While the first example is rather brief and to the point, it nevertheless manages to identify and include two theoretically informed aspects of the concept of management coaching – the fact that it can be framed in two distinctly different ways. The question opens for analysis rather than opinion-making. The fact that the question is theoretically informed makes it more specific, more detailed and more advanced despite its brevity. Thus it guides students in writing a more focused, observant and detail-oriented report than the novice reports. The approach is explorative and open (asking "in what ways?"), but the topic is more specific. The fact that the students identify two aspects to help them study the topic does not restrict them from actually finding a hybrid, a third or even a fourth element to be influential.

> In what ways are employees either appreciated or violated, when managers rely on a coaching form of management? (Workplace Studies)

The question in the second excerpt is also theoretically informed in the sense that certain positions concerning the concept of utopia in literature have been identified and analysed: the concept can either be represented in a critical or in a constructive fashion in neo-utopian literature. The aim of the study is as much to explore the distribution of the two approaches to utopia, as it is to investigate the variations and hybrids of the theme. Consequently, the conclusion of the report demonstrates a high level of detail and critical analysis in the form of attention to complexity rather than simple answers.

> What are the characteristics of the 'rediscovery' of the utopia and the utopian movement? How is the engagement divided between a critical stance towards utopia and a sense of 'constructive perspective' – and how can the criticism and the optimism be characterized in more detail? (Danish Literature Studies)

The EPR can be characterized as a report with a more pronounced theoretical framing of the project as well as the case and the empirical studies. It resembles the NPR in macrostructure, but the type of problem and the relation between theoretical and empirical studies changes. The EPR is not confined to the level above that of bachelor. The excerpt below from a Humanities Studies Basic Programme report is theoretically oriented from the outset. In this excerpt, the report does not discuss theories, but sets out to examine them in more detail. Unlike most novice writers, the author of this text does focus on a theoretical concept, by actively using the casework to help her identify a more complex version of the concept of super-sensitivity.

> Super-sensitive people feel, think and sense more. Their nervous system is more readily influenced by all sorts of impressions and stimuli, and thus they are more easily stimulated and over-stimulated in their social life. This is exactly why super-sensitive people experience problems in finding room for themselves in modern day society which focuses so strongly on producing competitive citizens. (…) This is how the concept of super-sensitivity was described by Elaine N. Aron, when the phrase was coined for the first time in 1996. (HUMBACH)

I have argued that the EPR is generally more focused, more theoretically informed, more detailed and more complex. As far as I can see, there seems to be a variation of this sub-genre at play as well. This variety presents more inductively framed studies, in the sense that the reports use their theoretical sections to develop an argument as to why a given concept may be more complex or problematic than initially expected. These reports tend to follow a topic of the ideal versus the reality – and the questions asked in the empirical studies focus on specific and theoretically informed criticisms of the concept to be studied. Thus, theoretical chapters of these reports are not necessarily less theoretically informed and they do express analysis and critical thinking concerning the phenomenon of academic theory. The studies themselves are presented in a more explorative and abductive manner, but students are still looking specifically for complexities, for crevices and for discrepancies concerning the theory. Thus, the research problems may not function as a starting point, but as a conclusion.

While the NPR and the EPR are more related to the genre of the professional report, the *academic problem-oriented report* (APR) has loosened if not utterly untied the knot to the professional report. The academic report is primarily written at the level of the master thesis, but it also exists at lower levels. The main difference between the EPR and the APR is that in the latter critical thinking and critical analysis of theory are more prominent and at a much higher level. The APR may still frame the relevance of the project around a social conflict, need or specific situation, but in addition to this problem, a gap in existing knowledge is presented as well (Swales 1990). Theory building in the form of identifying a gap in knowledge can be represented for instance as a paradox (contradictory results or conceptualizations about something) or the absence of relevant knowledge about, or a theoretical need to know more about, the same phenomenon but in a different context. The relevance of the problem is not argued with reference simply to students themselves wanting to know more about a given subject, nor the world needing more knowledge to solve problematical situations, but to a disciplinary need and concern for more knowledge. Reports frame students as taking part in an academic conversation. The two excerpts below originate from History and Molecular Biology respectively, and they both explicitly identify gaps in knowledge and need for further studies. While the authors of the History report do so openly, the Molecular Biology report flashes the gap in knowledge a little more indirectly simply by marking a given theory or hypothesis as unsubstantiated by the adjective 'apparent'. This is combined with a pronounced emphasis on the relevance of, and stated need for, stronger results on the topic.

> It seems that the struggle for gender equality can be studied in different ways. While Sjørup primarily studies the values of gender equality in the form of a brief historical outline of some of the victories of the women's movement combined with theoretical speculation on the potential for equal rights, Fraser primarily discusses the subject theoretically. Moreover, Dahlerup applies analytical methods identical to those of Sjørup interchanging between historical events and theoretical analysis of the concept of gender equality. Apart from a brief note on how the concept has existed for many years, but only became part of the common discourse in the 1960s (…) the actual development of the usage and meaning of the concept is never studied. The three researchers share the fact that they actively use the concept of gender equality, they exemplify its usage in various periods and they express different ideas about how it can be studied, but none of them actually discuss the actual development of the concept. (History)

> The apparent association between increased nutritional status and earlier puberty onset in girls and an impaired reproductive function in women based on epidemiological data does not prove causality, and other factors like endocrine-disrupting chemicals may contribute (Mouritsen et al. 2010). However, due to the increasing obesity epidemic worldwide (Cole 2006; Kaplowitz 2008; Ahmed et al. 2009) it is becoming increasingly important to investigate this association and the underlying mechanism of a nutritional regulation of puberty onset and reproductive function. (Molecular Biology)

In the APR it is further explicitly acknowledged that academic knowledge, literature and theories are all socially and contextually constructed phenomena. This is reflected in the overt identification of the fact that disciplinary voices speak in different tones; that knowledge on the same topic produced by different scholarly fields takes different focal points and has different interests guiding the knowledge production. The excerpt below illustrates how a report explicitly identifies certain statements as belonging within specific disciplines:

> This very inclusive conceptualization of the concept of empowerment raises the obvious criticism concerning the delimitation of the concept. Within the health disciplines, we find the approach of the natural sciences/biomedical sciences as opting for a reduction of the

problem to simply covering the kind of physical health which can be measured and 'proven for a fact'. This agenda of simplifying these complex problems can also be found within political science and neoliberalism in particular. Here we find a tendency to reduce social life to abstract 'political man' actors. A similar tendency towards reduction can be seen in mainstream economic thinking (…). As a result, we need a clarification of the usages and interpretations of the concept of empowerment. (Social Health Studies)

The transition between EPR and APR is fluent and boundaries between the two genres can be fuzzy. Also, APR repeats and continues the elements of EPR while adding a layer of theoretical overview, insight and richness. The difference between the two genres basically depends on the level and role of theory, on whether the reports frame the studies as being part of the existing scholarly debate, and whether a gap in (inter)disciplinary knowledge is recognized and discussed explicitly in the writings. The three sub-genres presented here are ideal types, and in the real world they most likely appear in hybrid forms in which one sub-genre is spiced up with a little dash of the other. Furthermore, disciplinary differences create different forms in ways not discussed here. Some disciplines tend to push students towards the APR (at least when it comes to textual surface features) quite early in their studies, while others tend to build on the NPR model beyond the novice period.

10.6 Moving on: Co-creating Critical Thinking Through Writing, Genre and Face-to-Face Supervision

Who is the problem of problem-oriented learning supposed to be a problem for? The answer to this question varies somewhat between the three types of report. A very stylized version may identify NPR as producing knowledge in order to satisfy the curiosity of the students themselves; the EPR produces knowledge to satisfy the students themselves and to produce new and complex knowledge for the betterment of the world; and finally, the APR produces knowledge in order to satisfy the curiosity of students themselves, concerns of the world and to fill gaps in knowledge within academic communities as well. Greg Myers (1989) identifies a central difference between academic texts as telling either *the narrative of nature* or *the narrative of science*. The narrative of nature can be found in introductory textbooks, in popularizations, and in newspapers and magazines. The focus of interest is on the particular phenomenon itself, i.e. on the actual plants, the actual psychological processes, the actual workplace relations or whatever topic. The narrative is told as a description of details and facts, but omits telling how the facts have been produced, what may in fact be a little speculative, what has been left out, and what or how a different perspective might change the story altogether. These stories are included in the narrative of science.

The aspiration of any university is to move students from the one narrative to the other. In the problem-oriented context, however, we also aspire to produce critical thinking and socially relevant knowledge as well, in the broadest sense. The focus on voice in various ways as allowing students ownership over and visibility in their own writing is a central pedagogical and cognitive aspect here. The existence of three distinct sub-genres is another, because the progression between the three is capable of scaffolding students' academic and heuristic development. Some students find their way through this path of progression on their own, while others are strongly supported in this progression within their study programmes and disciplinary contexts. Others again are completely left in the dark.

Writing and genre are important in learning. This is particularly so in PPL because students are expressively asked to interact, confront, analyse and criticize knowledge rather than simply repeat it. It is through writing that students themselves internalize, shape and express their learning. When students write, they give form to the kinds of cognitive and critical tasks they are asked to do – this is where they interpret how a real problem may be framed or how to represent theory. Writing produces and shapes knowledge: through writing students take it in and let it out. "When we make students struggle with their writing we make them struggle with thought" (…) [and] with themselves", Bean (2011) argues. Writing is in itself a form of problem solving (Flower and Hayes 1977). Writing needs to be nourished and scaffolded – and this applies as much to the informal backstage forms of writing as to the more formal writings. New teachers in problem-oriented settings need to be made aware of the particular role of voice and backstage writing in problem-oriented learning as part of the package.

Genres matter in learning, and problem-oriented supervisors might benefit by adding genre to their box of pedagogical tools. The point of introducing genre consciousness in supervision processes is not to provide students with rules and regulations in a fix-it perspective (Freedman et al. 1994). Rules are rarely accurate, and they fail to mediate all the extremely significant local variations, academic cultures and differences (Hyland 2009) – and the simple communication of writing rules is not how good writing practices are supported either. In recent years, research on academic writing and genre has taken a turn away from a strictly text-oriented and prescriptive perspective on writing towards one which is more situated and social practice-oriented (see among others Lea and Street 1998; Ivanic 1998; Lillis 2001; Casanave 2002; Casanave and Li 2008; Turner 2012). Consequently, the genre perspective might be used to highlight the written nature of academic knowledge and to identify and discuss the multiple ways that knowledge is in fact shaped by writing (Bazerman 1988) and how it can progress. The idea is not to imprison students' writing practices or to make them write in any specific way. It is instead to improve their understanding of how knowledge is produced in writing, and enable them to see the differences between the narrative of nature and the narrative of science (Myers 1989). Working with genres, discussing genres, analysing genres, playing with genres, deconstructing genres and changing genres are excellent and concrete ways of demonstrating variation, discussing norms and criteria and finding connections between writing forms and the knowledge produced through those forms. This applies in particular in interdisciplinary learning environments, where students have to navigate between different learning and writing cultures, and supervisors need to be able to help enlighten them navigate those cultural differences as well as foster deep understanding of disciplinary writing practices (Hyland 2012; Fook and Askeland 2007; Savin-Baden 2004; Ricot 2010). Moreover, a genre-based pedagogy is a way of scaffolding students' awareness of what the central elements of problem-oriented learning actually are, and how for instance a problem can be construed and applied in different ways and with different consequences (Knudsen 2013). To participate in problem-oriented learning, we all need to move, experiment and invest, students, supervisors and administration alike. Or as our university motto expresses it: *in tranquillo mors – in fluctu vita*.

References

Baker, R. S. J. d., D'Mello, S. K., Rodrigo, M. M. T., & Graesser, A. C. (2010). Better to be frustrated than bored: The incidence, persistence, and impact of learners' cognitive-affective states during interactions with three different computer-based learning environments. *International Journal of Human-Computer Studies, 68*(4), 223–241.
Barthes, R. (1972). *Mythologies*. New York: Farrar, Straus and Giroux.
Bazerman, C. (1988). *Shaping written knowledge: The genre and activity of the experimental article in science (Rhetoric of the human services)*. Wisconsin: University of Wisconsin Press.
Bean, J. C. (2011). *Engaging ideas: The professor's guide to integrating writing, critical thinking, and active learning in the classroom*. San Francisco: Jossey-Bass.
Beaufort, A. (2007). *College writing and beyond: A new framework for university writing instruction*. Salt Lake City: Utah University Press.
Billig, M. (2013). *Learn to write badly: How to succeed in the social sciences*. Cambridge, UK: Cambridge University Press.
Brookfield, S. (1987). *Developing critical thinkers*. Buckingham: Open University Press.
Brookfield, S. (2011). *Teaching for critical thinking: Tools and techniques to help students question their assumptions*. San Francisco: Jossey-Bass.
Casanave, C. P. (2002). *Writing games. Multicultural case studies of academic literacy practices in higher education*. Mahwah: Lawrence Erlbaum Associates.
Casanave, C. P., & Li, X. (2008). *Learning the literacy practices of graduate school. Insiders' reflections on academic enculturation*. Michigan: University of Michigan Press.
Chomsky, N., & Foucault, M. (2006). *The Chomsky-Foucault debate: On human nature*. New York: The New Press.
Creme, P. (2008). A space for academic play. Student learning journals as transitional writing. *Arts & Humanities in Higher Education, 7*(1), 49–64.
Creme, P., & Hunt, C. (2002). Creative participation in the essay writing process. *Arts & Humanities in Higher Education, 1*(2), 145–166.
Ebest, S. B. (2005). *Changing the way we teach: Writing and resistance in the training of teaching assistants* (p. 244). Carbondale: Southern Illinois University Press.
Ennis, R. H. (1996). *Critical thinking*. Upper Saddle River: Prentice-Hall.
Flower, L. S., & Hayes, J. R. (1977). Problem-solving strategies and the writing process. *College English, 39*(4), 449–461.
Fook, J., & Askeland, G. A. (2007). Challenges to critical reflection: 'Nothing ventured, nothing gained'. *Social Work Education, 7*, 1–14.
Freedman, A., Adam, C., & Smart, G. (1994). Wearing suits to class: Simulating genres and simulations as genre. *Written Communication, 11*, 193–226.
Hansen, E. (1997). *En koral i tidens strøm* [A coral in the flow of time]. Roskilde: Roskilde University Press.
Harvey, A. (1995). Interaction in public reports. *English for Specific Purposes, 14*(3), 189–200.
Helms-Park, R., & Stapleton, P. (2003). Questioning the importance of individualized voice in undergraduate L2 argumentative writing: An empirical study with pedagogical implications. *Journal of Second Language Writing, 12*(3), 245–265.

Hyland, K. (2009). *Academic discourse: English in a global context*. London: Continuum.
Hyland, K. (2012). *Disciplinary identities: Individuality and community in academic discourse*. Cambridge, UK: Cambridge University Press.
Illeris, K. (1974). *Problemorientering og deltagerstyring: Oplæg til en alternativ didaktik* [Problem orientation and participatory learning. A proposal for alternative didactics]. Copenhagen: Munksgaard.
Illeris, K. (1999). Projektarbejdets gennembrud i 1970'erne – en personlig beretning. In S. V. Knudsen (Ed.), *Projektarbejdets fortid og fremtid* (pp. 11–26). Copenhagen: Danmarks Lærerhøjskole.
Ivanic, R. (1998). *Writing and identity: The discoursal construction of identity in academic writing*. Amsterdam: John Benjamins Publishing Company.
Ivanic, R., & Camps, D. (2001). I am how I sound voice as self-representation in L2 writing. *Journal of Second Language Writing, 10*, 3–33.
Jeffries, L. (2010). *Critical stylistics: The power of english*. London: Palgrave Macmillan.
Knudsen, S. (2013). Students are doing it for themselves – 'The problem-oriented problem' in academic writing in the humanities. *Studies in Higher Education*, (September 2), 1–22. doi:10.1080/03075079.2013.806455.
Lea, M. R., & Street, B. V. (1998). Student writing in higher education: An academic literacies approach. *Studies in Higher Education, 23*(2), 157–172.
Lillis, T. M. (2001). *Student writing: Access, regulation, desire*. London: Routledge.
Martin, J. (1989). *Factual writing: Exploring and challenging social reality*. Oxford: Oxford University Press.
Miller, C. (1984). Genre as social action. *Quarterly Journal of Speech, 70*(2), 151–167.
Myers, G. (1989). *Writing biology: Texts in the social construction of scientific knowledge*. Wisconsin: University of Wisconsin Press.
Read, B., Francis, B., & Robson, J. (2001). Playing safe": Undergraduate essay writing and the presentation of the student "voice". *British Journal of Sociology of Education, 22*(3), 387–399.
Reddy, M. J. (1979). The conduit metaphor – A case of frame conflict in our language on language. In A. Ortony (Ed.), *Metaphor and thought* (pp. 284–325). Cambridge: Cambridge University Press.
Ricot, R. (2010). Students rewriting Gibbon, and other stories: Disciplinary history writing. *Arts and Humanities in Higher Education, 9*(2), 169–184.
Samraj, B. (2004). Discourse features of the student-produced academic research paper: Variations across disciplinary courses. *Journal of English for Academic Purposes, 3*(1), 5–22.
Savin-Baden, M. (2000). *Problem-based learning in higher education: Untold stories (Society for Research into Higher Education)*. Bury St Edmunds: Open University Press.
Savin-Baden, M. (2004). Understanding the impact of assessment on students in problem-based learning. *Innovations in Education and Teaching International, 41*(2), 221–233.
Savin-Baden, M. (2006). Disjunction as a form of troublesome knowledge in problem based learning. In J. H. F. Meyer & R. Land (Eds.), *Overcoming barriers to student understanding* (pp. 160–171). London: Routledge.
Schmidt, H. G., Rotgans, J. I., & Yew, E. H. J. (2011). The process of problem-based learning: What works and why. *Medical Education, 45*(8), 792–806.
Stapleton, P. (2002). Critiquing voice as a viable pedagogical tool in L2 writing: Returning the spotlight to ideas. *Journal of Second Language Writing, 11*(3), 177–190.
Swales, J. (1990). *Genre analysis: English in academic and research settings*. Cambridge: Cambridge University Press.
Turner, J. (2012). Academic literacies. Providing a space for the socio-political dynamics of EAP. *Journal of English for Academic Purposes, 11*(1), 17–25.
Yeung, L. (2007). In search of commonalities: Some linguistic and rhetorical features of business reports as a genre. *English for Specific Purposes, 26*(2), 156–179.

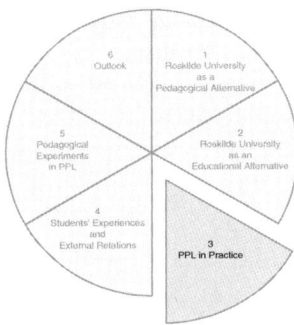

Chapter 11
PPL in Intercultural Settings

Karsten Pedersen

11.1 Background

This chapter addresses the challenges that international students and academic staff face when students from different cultures and academic traditions meet Roskilde University's brand of Problem-oriented Project Learning (PPL) as well as fellow students and teachers from a variety of backgrounds.

I start this chapter by giving an overview of the facts and figures regarding the international students at Roskilde University, and I will then use the 'international track' of Communication Studies as my case study. This is because each semester Communication Studies has a relatively large influx of foreign students to its international track and because Communication Studies (therefore) has found it necessary to address some of the issues that arise when dealing with such a diverse group of people.

I will discuss the actions taken from a programme planner's point of view. I was international coordinator and director of studies in the Department of Communication Studies in the periods 2003–2009 and 2006–2009, respectively. In my discussion I draw on email interviews and talks with the former programme director and former international coordinator for the communication programme Professor Kim Christian Schrøder, present international coordinator for the communication

---

K. Pedersen (✉)
Roskilde University, Roskilde, Denmark
e-mail: kape@ruc.dk

© Springer International Publishing Switzerland 2015
A.S. Andersen, S.B. Heilesen (eds.), *The Roskilde Model: Problem-Oriented Learning and Project Work*, Innovation and Change in Professional Education 12,
DOI 10.1007/978-3-319-09716-9_11

programme Dr. David Mathieu, and on a meeting with and subsequent responses to a questionnaire completed by international communication students at Roskilde University in the spring 2013 semester. I would like to thank these colleagues and students for their kind support and readiness to share their knowledge with me.

11.2 Some Facts and Figures

In 2014, 770 students from 92 nationalities studied at Roskilde University (Per Alsøe, personal communication). Each year about 500 students with a national background other than Danish sign up for a course, a semester or an entire BA or MA. Some of these students are residents of Denmark and have been for many years, some are Ph.D. students, some partake in a joint degree programme, but the largest single group is a group of exchange students of between 160 and 210 people.

The number of students varies quite a bit from year to year but it is clear that Roskilde University admits an increasing number of full-time students with a foreign background (admitted through the central Danish admissions system) and a BA from a foreign university (students recruited to master programmes with bachelors from foreign institutions) (Per Alsøe, personal communication).

This development underlines the importance of introductory initiatives in order to prepare the students for the teaching and supervision approach that they will face.

Most of the international students have the opportunity to be introduced to Roskilde University's teaching methods through a 'foundation course' that takes place before the beginning of the semester. In the course the students get acquainted with their new university and have the chance to learn "basic skills to access the study culture at Roskilde University and to optimize your learning experience" (Roskilde University 2014a).

The foundation course focusses on the aspects of studying at Roskilde University that are different from other universities, such as:

- Participant direction and joint responsibility,
- Problem-oriented project work in groups,
- Academic English,
- Introduction to Danish culture and language.

The student council's International Club is a further attempt from the group of international students at Roskilde University to reach out to their peers and to provide an informal forum for the exchange of information and experience about Roskilde University and Denmark. The Facebook page with its currently 941 members (International Club, Roskilde University n.d.) has quite some activity, and here students exchange information related to study and leisure.

In addition to the International Club, students also have the chance of signing up to be a mentor for incoming international students. The main goal of the mentor programme is to provide "a face-to-face introduction to Denmark given by a current student at the university. The point is to give an informal introduction to student life at Roskilde University" (2014b).

In order to address some of the challenges discussed above more uniformly, Roskilde University published a strategy for internationalisation in 2012 (Pedersen et al. 2012). The strategy deals with various aspects of internationalisation, focussing on the training of staff and the recruitment of students.

According to the strategy, all staff involved in teaching and administration will have to have a command of English sufficient to deal with the challenges of the intercultural university. One important point in this has been the creation of courses for teaching staff aimed at the certification of intercultural teachers and supervisors. By 2014, 33 faculty members have been certified and another 20 are attending the courses (Charlotte Hansen, personal communication). The plan is to certify all teachers and supervisors involved in international and intercultural study programmes.

In the International Education Strategy, Roskilde University identifies three different levels of internationalisation, stipulating that all MA and BA programmes at Roskilde University must contain elements of internationalisation and that a limited number of programmes will be full-fledged international programmes, normally with English as the language of instruction (Pedersen et al. 2012, pp. 4–6).

Three of Roskilde University's four BA programmes have international counterparts. Two of the international BA programmes are working on changes in programmes and orientation in order to meet the requirements for an international programme as defined in the International Education Strategy (Pedersen et al. 2012, p. 6), while the third programme is trying to create integration between internationalisation and the existing programme. All three programmes work with recruitment of students and staff in order to create an international or global environment for the students and teachers/supervisors to establish themselves in.

11.3 Communication Studies

Roskilde University has a wide variety of international programmes taught in English. The programmes are meant for students who are here for one or two semesters as well as students who are here to get their master's degree.

In the case of Communication Studies at Roskilde University, the programme welcomes between 25 and 30 international students from various cultural and national backgrounds every semester. The majority are exchange students, but there are also full-time Roskilde University students as well as students partaking in various joint programmes. The international track also attracts a small number of Danish students.

Most programmes at Roskilde University share the same structure, meaning that half of each semester is dedicated to project work, organised by the students themselves.

The semester consists of an array of activities and in most programmes a semester will look somewhat as shown in Fig. 11.1.

The semester begins with the group formation process (some exchange students have already attended the university's foundation course which is an introduction to the university's special variety of PPL). After the formation of the groups, the

Beginning of semester				End of semester	
Group formation process	Courses (normally three courses)	Submit course essays for evaluation (some programmes have other kinds of course evaluation)		Submit project report	Oral exam based on project report
	Group work				

Fig. 11.1 Semester activities

students follow courses and begin working in the groups, dealing with the problems defined at the group formation stage. After the course essays have been submitted, the group work intensifies, and late in the semester the groups finalize their reports that serve as the basis for the examinations. Normally the period between handing in the project report and the examination is used to prepare the final presentations to be assessed at an oral exam.

Irrespective of origin, most international students, at Roskilde University will be new to Roskilde's brand of PPL as well as to a semester structure where so much activity must be planned by the students themselves. That means that not only will the students have to deal with the challenges of being in a multicultural group, but must also try to come to grips with an entirely new way of learning.

However, there is also a group of students (mainly master students) who have been enrolled at the university for some time and therefore are quite experienced in the Roskilde Model.

This chapter will discuss two of the initiatives taken at Communication Studies in order to help students navigate in the Roskilde University semester structure. These initiatives are firstly the processes of mediated group formation and problem definition, and secondly the structuring of supervision to help the students plan and structure the group work.

I will discuss these activities against the backdrop of literature on problem-based learning (Hmelo-Silver 2004; Reich 2008) in order to show how Roskilde University's approach stands out from other approaches. I also wish to show how the approach discussed here varies from the general approach used at Roskilde University described elsewhere in this volume.

11.4 Mediated Group Formation

The group formation process is a critical activity at Roskilde University because this is where the students define the semester's work. There are basically three activities involved:

1. Defining a general topic for the semester work,
2. Forming a group to do the project work,
3. Defining a problem for the project work.

The activities on this list are not separate activities. Rather they should be seen as intricately interrelated and do not take place in any particular order.

The mediated group formation process is a tool used throughout Communication Studies at Roskilde University. The international students used to find the group formation process quite frustrating and therefore it was decided to train a group of mediators to help the students structure the process of discussing the academic and personal premises for a semester's group work. The international students that I talked to mentioned the group formation process as a positive experience and a useful means to define the project work for the semester. However, they also mentioned that they were unfamiliar with the whole idea of project work (personal communication with international students).

As group work is an integral part of the learning principles at Roskilde University, group formation is naturally very important for the students. The composition of the group will have a vital impact on the project work. Sometimes group members complement each other personally as well as academically and sometimes the groups are much more heterogeneous.

There are about 25 students and two mediators in the international group formation process at Communication Studies. The mediators are specially trained faculty members equipped with various tools and exercises to make the group formation process as structured and predictable for the students as possible. The mediators will prompt the students for ideas for group work projects, and the students will respond with suggestions for prospective projects. Normally there are too many project proposals, so the mediators will help to reduce the number e.g. by setting up a number of larger groups under generalized themes or by letting the students take part in various exercises, such as mutual interviewing or explaining a project proposal to some of the other students. Eventually smaller groups of three to five students will emerge. These smaller groups will be the basis for the group project work in the semester.

In order to let the students decide which group they want to belong to, the students are asked to discuss the various aspects of the project as each prospective member sees them in order for them to find common ground or to find lines along which the larger group can separate into smaller, more workable groups.

Students unaccustomed to this kind of subject (project) delimitation have no idea as to how (and indeed why) this is done and that is where the mediators come in. The mediators will sit and listen in on the group discussions, assisting the students in finding common ground for their dialogues and helping the students find out how to address such different issues as personal and academic preferences. A further challenge is that the students have to reconcile some students' high academic aspirations with other students' urge to get through the semester as easily as possible. Some students have jobs outside the university, some do not; some students work at night, others do not, etc. The group members will have to find a way to work together and to negotiate these extracurricular aspects in the planning and execution of the group work.

The mediators' endeavour in the group formation process is to legitimize all the arguments that are relevant in the formation of a group in order to make sure that the students review all the possibilities in the group and so will part with each other on as professional terms as possible. So if two prospective group members have clearly different work modes, this would be expected to become a problem in the group work and therefore it would be preferable to discuss it openly during the group formation process, rather than having it arise well into the project work. Students unaccustomed to group work might not have a clear idea of their personal work modes, so sometimes the role of the mediators is to ask questions that can help reveal differences in the way students work. This is not always possible, but questions about how often the students intend to have group meetings tend to be very useful. The purpose of having prospective group members openly discuss their differences is not only to make sure that people with widely divergent work patterns do not end up in the same group, but also to let the different group members know the differences and incorporate them in the group work.

The mediators will encourage the formation of groups consisting of students from various cultural backgrounds, in order to avoid groups consisting of students with approximately the same cultural and educational background, because that would make it more difficult for them to profit from the problem-oriented approach.

11.5 Facilitating the Process

In order to facilitate the students' work with the delimitation of the project proposals, the mediators will give the students various tasks to perform in the group. One such task can be to organize the groups as 'reflecting teams' in order for their members to view the problems at hand from various perspectives. Other tasks include writing and re-writing problem definitions, presenting the project to students that are not (prospective) group members and several other exercises to give the students the possibility of discussing their project proposals from various angles.

These methods will help the students realize that there are other perspectives than their own and also help them find out if this realization will lead them to change their point of view or to continue to pursue their original idea, even if it means leaving the group or joining other students with different ambitions or degree of commitment. The methods can be seen as an endeavour to let the students enter into a Buberian dialogue (Buber 2004), an 'I-Thou' discussion in which it is the students' mutual effort that helps them find out which groups and peers they belong with.

Other exercises include the individual writing and subsequent discussion of problem definitions. The goal of this exercise is to let the students find out for themselves (1) what they think about the prospective project, and (2) what the other students think of it. The exercise might lead students who thought they had a common interest into different directions, so that e.g. friends who planned to work together may realize that their academic interests differ so much that they should belong to different groups.

In cases where one of the larger groups cannot decide along which lines to separate, the mediators may step in to help find those lines. The mediator will listen to all the group members and then determine where he or she sees possible lines along which a division could be made and then ask the students if they see the same lines. This can be a highly provocative action, because the mediator might see lines that the students do not see or do not accept as valid division lines and therefore the mediator has to tread lightly in order to make sure that he or she does not create unnecessary ruptures in the group fabric. At the same time the mediator is interested in making sure that viable groups are formed.

11.6 Teaching and Supervision

Since, as already mentioned, many of the students in the international programme in Communication Studies are not familiar with problem-oriented project work, they may find themselves unable to structure their work. It is difficult for those students to know what kind of problems or discussions qualify for assistance from a supervisor.

In order for a group to function properly, it is important that the students are able to discuss the challenges that they meet during their project work. One such challenge is the difficulty of knowing how to search for and find answers if the student comes from a university culture radically different from that of Roskilde. That is (partly) to be expected when a person has chosen to study abroad only for a semester or two. Still, most students are prepared for cultural differences and therefore ready to deal with them. There is, however, also the question of language. Not all students enrolling in the Communication Studies' international track have sufficient English language skills to engage in negotiations about method, theory, readings, and other study-related discussions. Therefore some students will find themselves in roles that they do not normally occupy. Former international coordinator Kim Schrøder finds students' varying language skills problematic: "The challenge [of dealing with PPL] will persist throughout the semester, as the [exchange students] – in spite of the 'crash course' in PPL – will have to learn by doing all through the semester" (Schrøder, personal correspondence).

This is not unlike the situation Danish students find themselves in when trying to come to terms with project work during the first few semesters. There is one significant difference, however, and that is the fact that exchange students have only the one or two semesters in which to come to terms with the novel way of working.

Schrøder (personal correspondence) calls what he sees as students' reluctance to cross cultural boundaries 'unproductive'. This naturally is the university professor speaking. But although their reluctance is quite clearly unadvisable, cultural restraints on social interaction are a fact and must be addressed not only by students trying to make sense of a new and unknown (university) culture, but also by the university through planning the semesters in such a way that the international students can navigate in such alien waters.

Since the latter half of the semester will be dedicated to the project work, it is important that the students gain maximum benefit from it. There are two vital prerequisites for this: firstly, they must be able to *structure their time* even if no supervisor meetings or meetings in the group have been planned, and secondly, they must *ask for supervision* when they need supervision.

This process bears some resemblance to what Hmelo-Silver calls the problem-based learning cycle. Hmelo-Silver calls PBL focussed and experiential learning that is organised around "the investigation, explanation, and resolution of meaningful problems" (Hmelo-Silver 2004).

She goes on to make a tripartite distinction in "Approaches to Learning Situated in Problem-Solving Experiences": *PBL, anchored instruction, and project-based science*. Here Hmelo-Silver touches upon the difference between PBL and the Roskilde Model addressed in Chap. 1 in this volume. In Hmelo-Silver's terminology, what the students at Roskilde do is a combination of PBL and project-based science, reducing teacher instruction even further thus making it even more difficult for students to navigate as there is almost nothing concrete for them to grasp. This further accentuates the problem touched upon by Schrøder that "students from more authoritarian university cultures often suffer from an unproductive restraint in seeking the necessary guidance from the supervisor" (Schrøder, personal correspondence).

It is, however, not just students from 'more authoritarian university cultures' who find it difficult to find out when to seek guidance from their supervisors. Students unaccustomed to PPL and to planning their own learning experience will have trouble identifying the point at which they need supervision, and therefore it has proven a productive strategy to schedule a (minimal) number of themed supervision sessions, normally three or four, but the students can ask for more meetings and the supervisor might consider additional meetings necessary. The themes deal with the writing process and will address such subjects as theory, method, revising the problem definition, etc. Although the meetings each have a thematic title, this does not mean that students or supervisors might not change the theme to fit challenges at hand. Scheduled themed supervision meetings help alleviate some of the intercultural challenges and enable exchange students to take part in the group work on as equal terms as can be established without compromising the idea of problem-oriented project work.

This means that instead of a schematic semester structure with what some students might perceive as large swathes of free time, the international semester timetable will look more like the structure illustrated in Fig. 11.2.

In Fig. 11.2, I illustrate how there will be three or four more activities in the form of meetings between the groups and their supervisors during the semester. Some

Beginning of semester					End of semester	
Group formation process	Courses (normally three courses)	Submit course essays for evaluation			Submit project report	Oral exam based on project report
	Group work	Supervision meetings 1	2	3	(Pre-exam meeting)	

Fig. 11.2 International semester timetable

supervisors use such an approach with all their groups, including the Danish groups. But the difference is that all the supervisors in the Communication Studies' international track will use this approach and also let the various groups act as peer opponents in the supervision meetings.

For these meetings to work well, the groups will have to send material beforehand to their supervisors as well as to the peer groups to be used as a basis for discussion, so that the students realize that they have to work to allow the supervisor to provide them with useful feedback for their further project work.

11.7 Concluding Remarks

When international students arrive at a foreign university, there are a number of tacit assumptions made by the university about studies, socialising, etc. that are not immediately visible to the students, but are nonetheless there as expectations. When the university uses novel approaches to learning, unveiling and understanding these tacit assumptions become crucial for the student. Especially in the case of exchange students who are only at the university for one or perhaps two semesters, it is important that the hidden curriculum is as explicit as possible so that finding out how to study does not take up too much of the student's time.

Apart from the planning and scheduling, there are further challenges involved in the practice of meeting with the supervisor and of having disciplined meetings in the groups. If students find it hard to discuss academic matters in a classroom, a meeting with a lecturer or professor can be even more intimidating or indeed confusing if the supervisor does not behave in accordance with the students' cultural codes. Added to this is the challenge of having to contact the supervisor. When is the right time for contacting a supervisor? What are valid academic questions? What are valid questions about problems in the group? Again, semester planning seems to be a good method of alleviating at least some of the frustration and assisting the students in making sure that they do not waste valuable time trying to make sense of the new university.

References

Buber, M. (2004). *I and Thou* (R. G. Smith, Trans. 2nd ed.). London: Continuum.
Hmelo-Silver, C. E. (2004). Problem-based learning: What and how do students learn? *Educational Psychology Review, 16*(3), 235–266. doi:10.1023/B:EDPR.0000034022.16470.f3.
International Club, Roskilde University. (n.d.). International Club, member list. Retrieved 5 May 2014, from https://www.facebook.com/groups/101735869286/members/
Pedersen, K., Thomsen, V. S., Carney, S., Aarup, L. T., Hvidtfeldt, S., Klitgård, I., Yalcin, M., & Kamp, K. (2012). *International education strategy*. Roskilde: Roskilde University.
Reich, K. (2008). Konstruktivistische Didaktik. Das Lehr- und Studienbuch mit Online-Methodenpool – Kersten Reich – BELTZ. Retrieved December 11, 2013 from http://www.beltz.de/de/paedagogik/beltz-paedagogik/paedagogik-katalog/titel/konstruktivistische-didaktik-2.html

Roskilde University. (2014a). Foundation course – Roskilde University. Retrieved 2 May 2014, from http://www.ruc.dk/en/education/efter-og-videreuddannelser/language-and-intercultural-communication-services-lics/foundation-course/

Roskilde University. (2014b). FAQ about the mentor program at RU. Retrieved 5 May 2014, from http://mentor.ruc.dk/faq.php

Part IV
Students' Experiences and External Relations

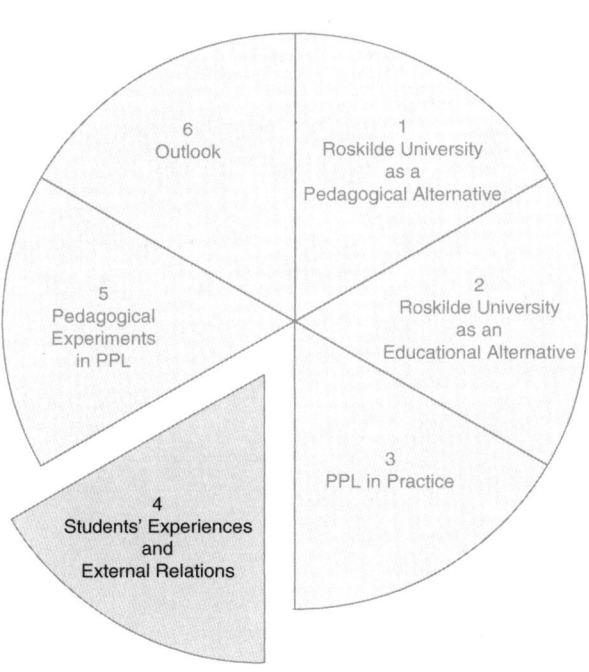

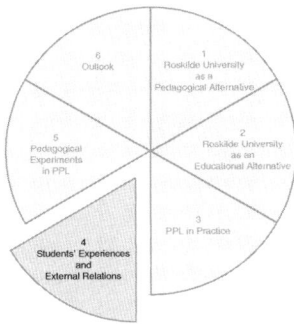

Chapter 12
Experiencing PPL: The Student View

Kasper Bjerring Petersen and Morten Brandrup

12.1 Introduction

This chapter describes Roskilde University as seen from a student perspective. It is a different point of view of the educational institution which is the central focus of this book.

We will show that Roskilde University is undergoing change, and how we experience it as a changeable entity. We like to think of our university as a place that pushes you and welcomes it if you push back. It is a place where change does not occur by itself, but happens dynamically.

This chapter takes you inside Roskilde University and shows you a university populated with active and enthusiastic students.

12.2 A Special Aspect of Roskilde University

The introductory period for first-year students at Roskilde University is in some ways similar to what can be seen at other universities. It is a radical change for the individual student. But in terms of activities and organization the introductory

---

K.B. Petersen (✉) • M. Brandrup
Roskilde University, Roskilde, Denmark
e-mail: kabjpe@ruc.dk; mortebr@ruc.dk

period is very special at Roskilde University. That is because it is arranged by the students entirely – and we are proud of it.

12.2.1 Starting at Roskilde University

There is a tendency at Danish universities towards a single way of teaching – teaching in the classical way, i.e. lectures. As you may already have read in this volume, Roskilde University with its project work has been in opposition to this. In that context the rector at Roskilde University, stated in his speech to the Student Council's reception in 2013 that he thought that Roskilde University by and large had avoided this tendency. We believe this to be the case, partly because the central and special teaching methods conceived at the creation of Roskilde University seem to have been thriving under changed circumstances. Half of the studies are project-based, while the other half is similar to any other university with lecture-based courses.

In this sense Roskilde University challenges its students from the beginning by requesting them to be self-reliant from day one. The Roskilde University model and especially the project work at the University bring about the transformation from traditional education by requiring new forms of learning from the very beginning of every study programme. This is the first step that separates Roskilde University students from students at other Danish universities.

To help reinforce the university's particular approach to education, new Roskilde University students are exposed to a very intensive introductory programme. The unique aspect of the way that the introduction is organized is that it is manned by older students entirely. Financing comes partly from the university, partly from the students themselves who contribute towards a student excursion. The freshman tutoring at Roskilde University is a product designed by the students *for* the new students. Prior to the beginning of the 3 weeks of introduction programmes, about 200 current students from different academic disciplines and years gather at Roskilde University to prepare the tutoring schedule across the different bachelor programmes according to the specific needs of the students. About 12 tutors acting as a team introduce a 'house' of about 120 students to the university – that is about 1800 new students altogether each autumn.

Creating and conducting the tutoring programme builds on a few central principles: volunteering, independence and tutoring based on the study programmes.

Volunteering The tutors are volunteers. They live at Roskilde University for the entire introductory period and work out the programme, using the houses intensively for meetings, working, staying overnight and socializing. For the new students, that means that they are given a good reception. You can feel that the tutors are committed to the job and want to help you.

Independence Each house has its own introduction programme. The tutors at the individual house are responsible for the practical design of the programme. This independence gives the tutors in the individual groups the option to adapt to varying circumstances. There are different needs among the four bachelor study programmes, and there are different physical settings. It is obvious from our point of view that the independence of the tutors goes with an equal amount of responsibility.

Training for Tutoring All tutors have taken a course which was also developed by senior students in the tutoring organization. The management committee is responsible for the practical aspects of planning and running the course throughout the year. In the course, new tutors learn about first-aid, the history of Roskilde University, as well as storytelling and presentational techniques. During the tutoring period, there is special focus on the groups of tutors and the group dynamics within them as well as the matching of expectations.

By the end of the tutoring period, the new students have also attended their first lecture. For most of them it is a classic auditorium experience similar in form to lectures at other universities. As a new student this is where you can sit back and enjoy something that is apparently familiar. The teaching resembles the classical high school teaching methods – you could call it 'chalk and talk'. But the absence of annoying questions from the teacher is what separates the lecture from the other kinds of teaching. That makes it even easier to sit back and enjoy.

The most important academic exercise during the tutoring period is the 'pilot project'. The pilot project is an exercise in the transition from group work as it was performed in high school to the way it is done at Roskilde University. The real exercise is for each new student to take part in a project and in a problem formulation process together with the other students in a group, and then narrow it down according to the basic requirements for a Roskilde University project. The key difference is that students themselves must drive the process.

12.2.2 In a House

A third big change for the new students is the size of their 'class'. You are no longer in a class, but in a house with about 120 other students. During the introduction period, a link is established between a tutor from the house and a group of students called 'tryghedsgruppe' (safety/comfort group) to make sure that each new student has an older student to ask questions about Roskilde University.

Originally, the large classroom in a standard bachelor house was dimensioned for about 60 students. Today they accommodate up to 120 students. As a fire precaution, some houses have had the tables in the large classrooms replaced by rows of chairs. But even under these reduced circumstances we find that there is still room for teaching based on dialogue. Of course it differs from course to course, but often time is allotted for discussions with your neighbour or in small groups, and for asking questions. Teaching based on dialogue is preferable, but the clear tendency is that the people-to-space ratio is a key factor when it comes to dialogue-based interaction during lectures. The more space available per student, the more time there is for dialogue.

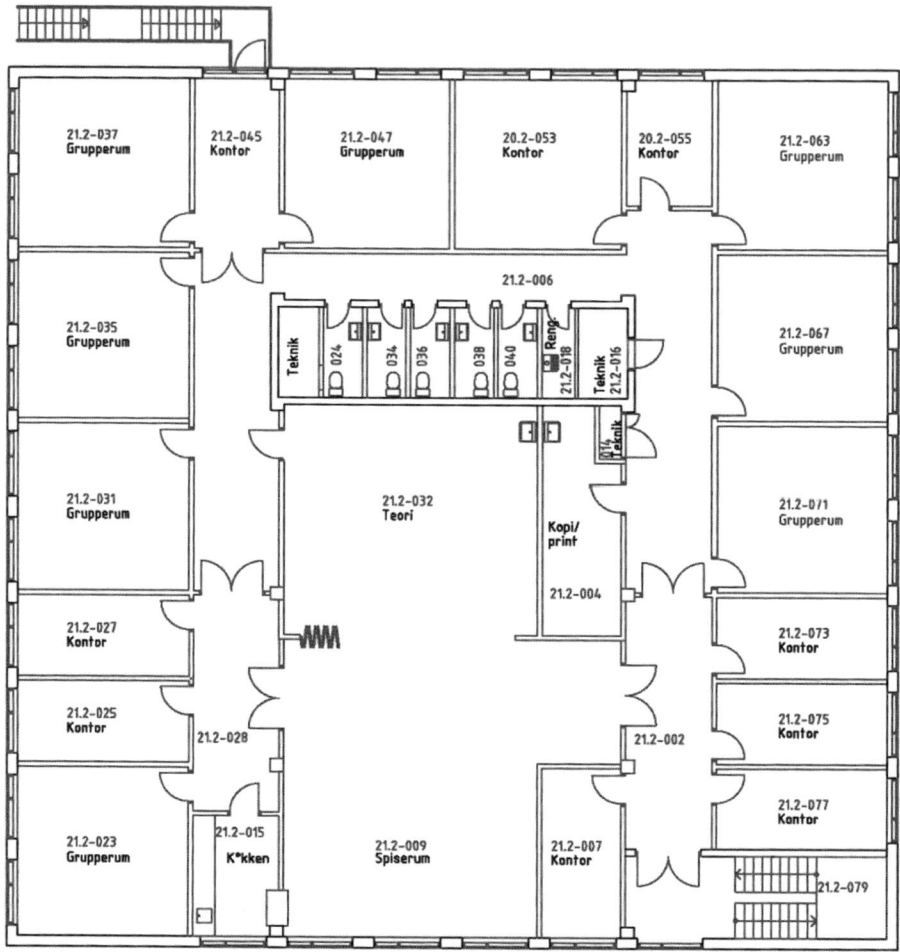

Fig. 12.1 Plan of an original Roskilde University house. The large classroom (Teori) can be expanded by removing the portion to the dining area (Spiserum). The classroom is surrounded by group rooms (Grupperum) and offices (Kontor). There is also a small kitchen (Køkken) and a room for copying and printing (Kopi/print)

A unique aspect of the bachelor programmes is that they are physically located in buildings of a particular architectural design. The design is illustrated in Fig. 12.1 and is further discussed in Chap. 6. The house-design is the foundation of the study environment. The house is both the social and academic frame for a bachelor study programme. As a student it is practical to have a physical base or 'home' for at least three reasons. Firstly, as a new student you are at a large campus where the lectures are held at different locations, so your house is like a navigation point. Secondly, the house supports and facilitates the broad academic entrance to university studies which lies in the nature of the bachelor programmes. Thirdly, as a student at

Roskilde University you use the house facilities in the intensive project period of the semester, because you need to have group meetings in a suitable working environment.

Every house has a secretary. From a student point of view this is most convenient since studying at a university may involve quite a lot of red tape. In spite of the increasing number of students per house, the idea of personal contact between students and staff has been maintained.

Every house also has its own association. It is established by the tutors during the planning period and then handed over to the new students during the introduction period. The purpose of this is to have some unifying body that can organize and support student-driven activities within the house. We have witnessed the association as a focal point for true grassroots student democracy and proof of the independence of the students. It is not arranged or paid for by Roskilde University, but is entirely the fruit of student initiatives. Typically a 'house association' is centred around the house finances, based on the income from cafés and student parties held in the bachelor houses. The association supports all kinds of house activities, such as field trips, house talks and project materials, all that is beneficial to the study environment in the house.

The connection between student and bachelor house, however, is only temporary. It is strongest at the beginning, but over the years of study, the students gradually migrate towards their chosen subjects in the relevant departments – ultimately at the transition from bachelor programme to master programme.

12.2.3 Groups

The group formation process is a very special experience where students meet project work for the first time. In the group formation process, students are confronted with and discuss a number of project ideas. The result is the formation of a number of groups, each based upon a project idea which is the starting point for the project.

Especially in the first semester this process is a tough one. It can be a struggle to formulate a project idea that will fit in with the semester theme while at the same time identify fellow students who seem to be able to work together, and also reach agreement on the proper approach to the upcoming project work.

As an individual student you are searching for both an academic match and a social match, which should be based on a combination of the character of individuals and the 'chemistry' of the entire group. Most Roskilde University students remember well their first group formation process, because these matches are unpredictable when you do not know the other students. In the course of their studies most students get a better idea of the kinds of people they like to work with and how group work should be organized to achieve the academic and social matches.

In order to appreciate why the group formation process is so hard, it is necessary to understand the new students' backgrounds. They come from high school where there is no requirement to be responsible for and dependent on other people's work. To many new Roskilde University students that is a huge difference, but an effective one in terms of committing people to their project work.

The group formation process takes on different shapes in the four bachelor programmes. In some cases the supervisors control the process and present ideas for projects that the students can take on and develop. In other programmes the process is totally student-driven from organizing the discussion of ideas to making sure everyone is in a group (see also Chap. 6).

In the first semester expectations are high because the project is the first activity one meets, and you may easily be daunted by its magnitude. The process of forming groups is open, and everyone is eager to discuss various ideas and to form groups based on interests.

However, in the subsequent semesters, it is not always academic interest that determines the formation of groups. Now the social aspect comes into play based on the students' experience from previous projects. For many students this means that they stick with certain fellow students to avoid possible problems related to the social aspect of project work.

The group project work is a learning experience different from anything else we have tried. There is intense collaboration in the busy period prior to deadline. It also means that students get to know each other quite well. Throughout the entire study period at the university, these processes reveal new ways of working and cooperating.

In connection with the group formation process, we sometimes see that group participants have fundamentally different approaches. Students who started their studies at other institutions of higher education than Roskilde University do not have the same background for understanding the group formation process, and therefore have reduced possibilities for joining groups together with 'native' Roskilde University-students. This applies to international students (see Chap. 11), students with bachelor degrees from other universities who enroll in a master programme, and students with professional bachelor degrees (e.g. teachers and nurses).

To think in a problem-oriented and interdisciplinary way is something that you need to adapt to. It is rare to see new students with the ability to formulate a cross-disciplinary problem that lives up to the requirements. But that of course is part of the learning process.

Studies at Roskilde University are pervaded by a radically different line of thinking about projects. The project work itself is different from that at other universities. The cultivation of the problem-oriented approach becomes a reflex that kicks in when you are confronted with subject-oriented work. With time, you become almost allergic to questions that do not address a real problem. Of course many projects start out by being subject-oriented, but it is almost unavoidable that your project idea will become problem-oriented as you figure out and define the exact problem. That is the main point of the project work at Roskilde University.

After the group formation, during the phase where ideas are elaborated, the project groups meet their appointed supervisors. The constellation of group and supervisor is another radical change in the sense that the supervisor is not a teacher in the traditional sense. The supervisor is 'only' a supervisor whom the group can consider a counsellor – he or she is not a person with all the correct answers ready at hand (for supervisor roles see Chap. 8). Problems occur when their mutual expectations do not match. The main responsibility for aligning expectations and cooperation with the supervisor lies with the group. They are also responsible for the important task of preparing and planning meetings and discussions.

Sometimes we see that the students as well as the supervisor hold the attitude that the supervisor can be considered a teacher or at least the one who knows better. This understanding can lead to a turn in focus away from the original common interest around a project idea and thus dampen the initial enthusiasm established in the group formation process.

At the start of one of the four bachelor programmes, project ideas and 'project seeds' are developed mainly by the students themselves. This is part of the foundation of their self-reliance. In the course of the bachelor programme, more and more requirements are added to the projects, which demonstrates the progression in the project work.

A typical semester is divided into a course period and a project period. During the course period there is time to gather data, collect literature and sketch out the project. Then during the last month of the semester, the students' time is devoted entirely to project work, which enables the group collectively to pay full attention to the project. Depending on the amount of work done throughout the semester, this period may be quite stressful.

A great deal of discussion takes place during the project work, and in our experience this is an important driving force for the development of the project. It is fascinating how these discussions somehow become invisible in the project report, but as a project member you know how much they mean to a project.

The intensive period of the project work is also a personal challenge. Some students may not see their friends and family during the last month before the deadline, because they isolate themselves with their groups in order to concentrate hard on their work. That helps to maintain the focus on the project but also marks the point of no return in the sense that the bulk of the work must now be done. There is no time left to go back and make changes in source material, data, etc.

12.2.4 Evaluations

Unlike courses, projects in the bachelor programmes are subject to an internal oral student evaluation. All pilot projects are presented to the other students in the house at plenary sessions, just as project formulations are presented in the project formulation seminar. At the *midterm* and *end term evaluation,* project groups in a house are paired and provide feedback on each other's projects in the style of a peer review (see also Chap. 6).

The project work is a shared responsibility. Every group member is responsible for the entire project. As an individual student you benefit from working intensively in a group with others that share your interests. Our experiences with evaluations are that they broaden your horizon in terms of the character of project work, i.e. what kind of project work is done in your bachelor house and in general in your bachelor programme. During the evaluation you learn to give constructive feedback and take charge of a session by asking the question: "What do we as a group want from this evaluation, and what would we like the opposing group to focus on?"

We have noticed that these peer evaluations are used less commonly outside the bachelor houses. We find this unfortunate since it is really here that students are trained in writing and in analysing problem formulations and projects in general. To train the skills of evaluating other people's project work and giving constructive feedback, it is necessary to continue peer evaluations throughout the master programme in the same way as it is done every semester in the bachelor programme.

Group examinations are fundamental to Roskilde University and its project work. From 2006 to 2012 this form of examination was prohibited by the government. Now it has been allowed again, and Roskilde University has re-introduced it as the mandatory examination form for all project exams. It has led to a great deal of concern among the current student population because they have not been trained in this. It will take time to adapt to a return to group examinations for both students and supervisors.

12.3 Education Explorers

Most of the Roskilde University students combine two academic disciplines within a bachelor programme. Every semester they must search for a project idea and define a relevant problem. They must keep themselves informed on the current supply of available courses and they must apply for a supervisor.

12.3.1 Reflection

In our experience the learning methods at Roskilde University make for critical reflective students who take time to familiarize themselves with both system and content. But there are also students that just follow the herd and go through their studies without considering their academic choices and what qualifications and skills they want to end up with. The difference between the two is tremendous. The critical reflective students who consciously want to shape their own academic identity through a unique sequence of educational choices are a special feature of Roskilde University.

The exploration of your educational life springs from an academic discipline, your expectations of courses and of project work. Through the project work there is a direct link between academic disciplines in theory and practice. It is especially evident in the projects where a group of students work together with an external partner like a company or an organization. The bachelor programmes aim to lead the student through different kinds of projects, but we also see that students can become tired of project work and therefore choose the same type of project over and over again. In this way they avoid the challenge in developing the form of project work, but rather concentrate on the content.

It would be an idealization to claim that all students explore their educational options in full and that all students know what they want with their bachelor or master degree and therefore make well-considered choices on this basis. This is not necessarily a problem in the beginning, as you have the opportunity to discover your options along the way. For most students it takes time and may run parallel to the demands for progression in the study programmes. The academic part of the study environment is a central element in supporting this exploration of interests. It evolves through discussions with supervisors and your work in your specific academic discipline.

12.4 Educational Challenges

Roskilde University is a place that can be changed and it invites you to take the initiative. Especially in the beginning of their studies, students are active in influencing the framework. That is a tradition. Students are able to influence the framework as well as the content. We have both been very active in student politics and social events, and we believe that the system we have described makes the students more active than most, and more aware of the collective educational frame that Roskilde University represents. They become better at manoeuvring in the educational frame because they simply have a better understanding of it through their volunteering activities. We also see that students identify themselves as 'Roskilde University students' rather than 'maths students' or 'communications students'. It would seem to demonstrate the typical feature of Roskilde University that students have a wide variety of different combinations of subjects, but still all work within the same framework of an equal division between traditional courses and project work. There may of course be different interpretations of this observation, but we like to think of it as a common identity that revolves around *the Roskilde University values and working methods*.

It is also our experience that our fellow students are active in many different ways and on different levels. As mentioned in the section about the house associations, all Roskilde University students are conscious of the grass-roots democracy that they are part of in their studies. Students who want to continue to be active move on from the house associations to central committees that work on activities for the whole university.

Each of the four bachelor programmes and all academic disciplines at Roskilde University are controlled by study boards. The boards are joint committees of staff and students. That is what gives the students a direct influence on their studies. It is our impression that most of the student representatives are on the committees for more than one term of office and put in a great deal of useful work.

Roskilde University students are generally good at finding their way around the educational system to their maximum benefit. The university encourages you to combine subjects according to your own preferences. It is one of the main reasons why many students choose Roskilde University in the first place, but it also makes them aware of educational options outside Roskilde University.

Some might claim that it is the outside world that places requirements on the universities and thereby the students. Society at large seems to expect the university to create career-minded bachelors and masters with relevant competencies, innovative skills and an interest in solving the world's major problems. For the individual student those are large demands which do not necessarily conflict with the possibility for the Roskilde University student to challenge the world back.

We maintain that most of our fellow students either have a plan when they start and change it according to the progression in their studies or that they establish a plan during their first years at Roskilde University. It might, of course, be an overstatement to call it a 'plan', but what is important is that Roskilde University acts as a catalyst for these considerations and that it prompts the students to make educational choices along the way. That is what we like so much about Roskilde University: you do not have to make all the choices on day one. You can make them as you go and let them be based on those you have already made – consciously and meaningfully.

12.5 Summing Up

In this chapter we have reported on our university from a student perspective. After summarizing the particular features of Roskilde University as being a main focus on project work and a very special way of conducting it, we went on to outline the introduction of new students to Roskilde University as a way of pointing out the special student spirit. The main point here was that student activities are based on the principles of volunteering, independence and learning through the activity itself. We then explained the special way of organizing bachelor programmes into houses and the various features, including problems, involved in this. Our next topic was the project work itself, where we emphasized the critical parts: the problem formulation, the relation between group and supervisor, the period of intensive concentrated work, and the evaluations. Finally we looked at students at Roskilde University as educational explorers and how Roskilde University as an institution challenges students to make important choices along the way.

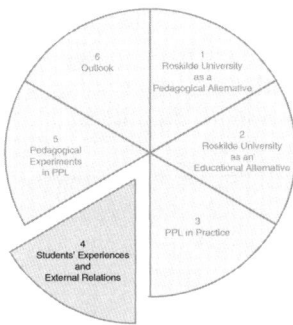

Chapter 13
External Relations: Bridging Academia and Practice

Hanne Leth Andersen

13.1 External Partners in Planning and Quality Assurance

Today, educational planning is not entirely an internal affair at universities. According to the national accreditation authorities and the Danish Accreditation Order (Akkrediteringsloven 2013), the development of study programmes and educational structures must be discussed and planned in collaboration with external partners, primarily advisory boards and the bodies of external examiners. Moreover, the experiences of graduates in the labour market, not least the requirements for competencies, are solicited and drawn upon.

As to external examiners, in Denmark there is a long tradition for using them both in the High School System and at university level. The external examiners are responsible for assuring the same standards for all examinations at a national level, and thus for their quality. One third of all exams must be assessed by external examiners, always together with internal examiners. For the rest of the exams, it is common to use only internal co-examiners. This practice of internal and external co-examination was developed to ensure students' legal rights and to

---

H.L. Andersen (✉)
Roskilde University, Roskilde, Denmark
e-mail: ha@ruc.dk

© Springer International Publishing Switzerland 2015
A.S. Andersen, S.B. Heilesen (eds.), *The Roskilde Model: Problem-Oriented Learning and Project Work*, Innovation and Change in Professional Education 12,
DOI 10.1007/978-3-319-09716-9_13

prevent grading bias. The different viewpoints that an external examiner can bring to an exam situation play a crucial role in the examination system by minimizing subjectivity and creating opportunities for knowledge exchange. The basis of the assessment nevertheless remains the specification of the assessment criteria in the academic regulations,

External examiners are recruited from academia as well as from the public and private sectors. Their role is not only to guarantee that educational programmes live up to academic standards, but also that they enforce the development of knowledge, skills and competences relevant for the labour market. Bodies of external examiners are important partners in quality assurance as they are required to give feedback to the study boards concerning the quality not only of the students' knowledge but also of the exams, i.e. how well they are adapted to the skills and competences that are outlined in a specific programme.

With regard to changing programme curricula, work methods or exams, decisions must be made on the basis of clear documentation, surveys and the monitoring of students, and also by staying in contact with graduates in order to be updated about job market developments. In accordance with this, all programmes at Roskilde University collaborate with prospective employers. Representatives from business and public and private organizations serve on advisory boards that meet regularly with heads of departments and study boards.

13.2 Students' Competences and Employability

Collaborative problem- and inquiry-oriented project work is not only a strong version of research-based education; it is also clearly linked to students' employability in the job market and in society in general. Very often, graduates from problem-oriented programmes adapt well to employment; the candidates from Roskilde University were particularly well-adapted in employment and by some even called 'the darlings of Danish industry and business', when in 1988 the Danish Employer's Association elected Roskilde University as the most popular of the Danish universities (Hansen 1997, pp. 268–270). The likely reason for this is that student-centred problem-oriented learning activities to some extent meet society's demands for flexible and adaptive education and may foster independent, critical thinkers and creative graduates.

Nevertheless, probably as an effect of the global financial crisis that started in 2008, more precise professional skills now seem to be in focus in the discourses of universities, industry and governments, all concerned with addressing the demands for relevant education and employable graduates.

Thus, it is even more important to underline the fact that learner-centred education combined with problem-oriented project work fosters a number of relevant concrete competences, especially critical thinking, problem formulation, and motivation (see Sect. 2.3). Addressing real-life problems can add personal meaning and motivation. However, not all problems should relate to speculations on their immediate utility, considering that research can both be strategic and basic, and that basic research – like basic project questions – can lead to strategically important findings and discoveries.

Project work is currently being renewed in the different disciplines and programmes. Two concrete experiments are discussed in this volume (see Chaps. 14 and 15). Other initiatives focus on collaborating with external partners and with internship becoming part of the project work, both with the clear objective of integrating academic knowledge with practice.

One of the most important spaces for collaboration is the *Project Fair* initiated by the office *RUC Innovation*. At a specific exchange event, external partners present problems and propose projects that they would like students to solve or develop. In this way, the ideal of working with real-life problems in the project groups is literally realized. Another possibility available to all master students is work experience during studies, which is then integrated into a project, linking theories explicitly from the academic curriculum with experience and data from an authentic work situation. Work experience in combination with project work is a strong tool for developing methodological awareness and for integrating real-world problems and work life experience in their project work while still studying. Roskilde students are very active in both of these reality-based approaches and seem to value the integration of external partners in their curriculum (cf. Fig. 13.1). This pays off, as shown by the latest available statistics (Schademan and Jørgensen 2013), where 65 % of the 1,857 2007–2011 graduates in a survey found a job relevant to their educational specialization, while another 30 % landed a job requiring general professional competences. Roughly 30 % are employed in the private sector, 10 % in NGOs and 60 % in the public sector. The most common jobs are in text production and communication, project management, administration and secretarial functions, analysis and evaluation, consulting and education.

From the political side and from important stakeholders in Danish private business, industry and services there has indeed been a strong urge to focus on the relation between practice and theory in academic programmes. Internships are highly regarded for creating networks and learning about the labour market. Various associations of Danish employers demand that the graduates are ready for the job market and that all master programmes contain mandatory internships.

Generally, the idea of working with real-life problems in relation to society is part of the original learning model of Roskilde University (see also Chap. 2). Strong relations to external partners make the idea of student work experience relevant, but it can never be an all-inclusive response if the other basic idea of a student-centred

- 85.7% of the students have worked while studying; 24.8% of those got a job at the same workplace
- 44.2% of the students wrote a project in collaboration with a company or an organization; 5.2% of those got a job at the same workplace
- 47.6% had an internship while studying; 17.7% of those got a job at the same workplace

Fig. 13.1 Students' work experience and subesequent employment (From: Schademan and Jørgensen 2013, Figs. 10.1 and 10.6)

and student-directed approach is to be taken seriously: students' academic and personal educational goals and external stakeholders' project interests may not always coincide. In addition to this, it is important to stress the obligatory link between theory and practice in all collaboration projects: Even though students also tend to become more and more anxious to get work experience while studying, the internships must be integrated into the specific programme work and supervised by researchers. The decision on the part of the university has been to give all students the option to choose a relevant internship once in their master programme. However, it is also important that the internship period is not too long, to prevent any delay in the overall progression of the student.

13.3 Students' Awareness of Their Own Competences

External relations are important at many levels. Roskilde University's current strategy (Rektorsekretariatet 2010) emphasizes that students' own research projects open a broader perspective of project working skills that are useful in a number of employment situations in both private and public companies and organizations.

Not only does project work lend itself very well to integrating studies and work practice, it is also very useful in integrating life skills and working experience in programmes that are not aimed at one specific job area. This is pinpointed in the testimony of one very successful graduate from Roskilde University:

> There's a schism in that in your first jobs you have to be relatively narrow in a professional sense. And that's a schism relative to what we're good at. So I think maybe the entry barriers for Roskilde University graduates are a bit higher than for others… unless you also try to do something apart from 'just' studying. Give priority to get involved in … student politics, having a relevant student job and so on … because you have something other than just an education. And that's why I was very, very happy about the internship scheme when it was introduced at Roskilde University. That really produced a lot of jobs. We prevent contact with the real world by not having this scheme as a requirement. (Rene la Cour Sell, in Olsen 2011b, 2:17-3:08).

Even though Roskilde University master level students still choose to do internships and projects in collaboration with external partners, they are not as aware of their specific competences as one would expect. According to the latest survey, new graduates from Roskilde University (2007–2011) manifest a lack of specific IT skills (39.9 %), and of a general understanding of business (42.1 %) (Schademan and Jørgensen 2013). This of course depends on the specific profile of the graduates. But what is most surprising is the fact that 26.2 % of the respondents state that they lack competences in project management, whereas 22.3 % think that they need more skills in creative and innovative thinking. However, if this is compared to the candidates' actual job functions, there is a clear indication of some good expectations as to their own competences, since they have actually applied for (and been recruited in) jobs where the same competences are central and strongly desired.

13.4 Entrepreneurial Skills Development

Entrepreneurship is a specific area of interest at Roskilde University, having been an intrinsic part of the social and engaged profile characteristic of the university since the 1970s. It is a distinctive feature of many Roskilde University students that they are engaged in innovative projects, in the annual Roskilde Festival, in alternative private enterprises, human rights work, etc. Therefore, with the new reform at the master level, more specific interest is given to entrepreneurial skills and competences. Courses in entrepreneurship are being offered to both teaching staff and students, with specific designs to facilitate the development of students' motivation and skills in this direction, focusing on *self-efficacy* and collaboration. Self-efficacy is promoted in inquiry-based teaching and in relations between students and between students and teachers. The relational competence of teachers and researchers working together with students is an important element in a strong study environment. It creates confidence and engaged dialogue, and in this way the human relationship between teachers and students, as well as between students, helps create a strong relation between student and study object. This bond is the essential driving force towards a deep understanding of the field and the challenges it represents (see also Chap. 8).

Entrepreneurial skills and innovation already form part of the learning philosophy and participant-directed project work at Roskilde University, as pointed out by a former student who is now pursuing a career in high-level leadership:

> Being able to create events and create projects – you learned that at Roskilde University [...] We worked a lot at creating visions ... in relation to where is it critical – where does it hurt in society, what are we upset about ... if we can get upset, can we then imagine something better. (Peter Pietras, Olsen 2011a, 5:50–6:51).

Motivated students working with their own projects are challenged and have to develop competences that are central to innovation and entrepreneurship, and the most important competence of all is courage. This is expressed by another former student, now a top manager and herself currently creating new business:

> I think that's something you've learnt in your studies at Roskilde University: to jump into deep water. Not to ask questions that can be answered by going to the library and finding books providing the answers. But to dare to be in a situation where you are dealing with a complex problem that needs contributions by several people, and where the only thing you can do is to present the best possible answer. And that there is no absolute truth – you learn that from day one. (Louise Hvid Jensen, Olsen 2011a, 4:13–5:04).

Project work and motivated students constitute a strong basis at Roskilde University, but entrepreneurial skills and competences need to be supported in a more systematic manner. This is the reason for the new courses in entrepreneurship, but it is even more important that students meet supervisors and study environments where imagination and creativity are welcomed and developed. This is especially the case in certain fields, such as the new research area of Designing Human Technologies which cuts across the four main areas of the Humanities, the Social Sciences, the Technical Sciences and the Natural Sciences and involves researchers with all four perspectives. As a creative research initiative it focuses on change and innovative thinking. At the same time, it constitutes an important part of the research background of the Humanities and Technology bachelor programme (HumTek) where students work across the disciplines with creative and methodological design processes including information technologies, media and events (see also Chap. 6). The HumTek bachelor programme combines theory and practice, letting the students turn their thoughts into actions at the RUC FabLab, which is a lab for rapid prototyping and for running workshops on digital production.

Through different initiatives, such as RUC Innovation and the study environment pool, Roskilde University supports students' possibilities for reaching out to different areas of society. Some examples of projects created and supported at Roskilde University (RUC) are:

- *RUC Radio*, a student-directed radio channel that started in 2011 as a second semester project in the HumTek programme. The goal of the project group was to explore what was necessary to establish a student-run radio channel at Roskilde University in order to help improve internal communications.
- *Reality Bites*, a student-driven non-profit organization whose goal is to offer students inspiring experiences and events with the help of volunteers, sponsors and speakers who donate time, money or other resources for the purpose. With informal lunch presentations as well as conferences with hundreds of participants, the organizers provide students with input from the outside world which can contribute to personal and professional development.
- *The Green Current Festival*, a student-driven initiative that endeavours to raise interest and engage the general public in sustainable development by being the most ecological and sustainable music and showcase event in Denmark. The mission is to create a social platform based on sustainable principles, music, interaction and performances, where citizens, firms, scientists, students and entrepreneurs meet to generate innovations and learn about sustainable development.
- *The national Danish Venture Cup*, in which Roskilde University students also participate. Its objectives are to find the entrepreneurs of tomorrow, to facilitate the creation of new businesses, and to turn academic knowledge into viable high-growth businesses. Venture Cup aims to inspire and empower university students and researchers to develop their ideas into successful companies. This purpose is achieved through competitions, skills training, mentoring, networking, and facilitating contact between participants and experienced entrepreneurs and business people who provide valuable advice on a voluntary basis.
- *Entrepreneur Café*, an event hosted every Tuesday by RUC Innovation. Here students can drop in and get advice on their ideas and get help to develop their start-ups.
- *RUC Entrepreneurial Day*, an annual event that brings together entrepreneurial people and provides unique value for budding entrepreneurs. Other invited attendees are students and researchers – people who share a common interest in supporting innovation and entrepreneurship and thereby encourage and inspire

young students at Roskilde University. At this event, different start-ups showcase their products and business ideas, and there are keynote speeches and networking opportunities for those interested.

13.5 External Relations at the Bachelor Level

Until now, only very few graduates from Danish universities seek employment on the basis of a university bachelor degree. In the four bachelor programmes at Roskilde University nearly all bachelors continue their education in master programmes, either at Roskilde or another university. Therefore, it is generally not as relevant for the development of the bachelor programmes to have a dialogue with a panel of employers (a business panel) as is required for master programmes. However, the program HUMTEK is partially an exception, as the programme includes very close cooperation with public and private employers. From the beginning the programme has been designed in close cooperation with a 'relevance panel' consisting of key figures in the public debate, consultants, broadcasters, planners, NGO staff, etc. Also in the context of project work, student conferences and design competitions linked to broader society play a key role in HUMTEK. Since HUMTEK is still only 5 years old and nearly all bachelor candidates have continued at master level partly due to the economic crisis, it is too early to evaluate possible employment for bachelors.

Therefore, in the present situation for all four bachelor programmes at Roskilde University the most relevant partners for discussing the quality and possible improvement of the bachelor programmes are the master programmes where the bachelors continue their studies. Most of the faculty offering courses and supervising projects in the bachelor programmes also teach in one or more of Roskilde University's master programmes. Therefore, with regard to concrete discussions on the structure of the bachelor programme or especially on the content of particular courses, the bachelor programme teachers also represent their research discipline and related master programmes. On a higher level of organization, the four bachelor study boards have representatives from some of the master programmes that recruit students from the bachelor programme, so the study boards are quite focused on the quality of the bachelor education in relation to the master programmes. At university level, the quality of the bachelor programmes is under the jurisdiction of Education Committee chaired by the Pro-Rector (or Rector), and the Head of Study of each of the four bachelor programmes is a member of this committee. It is the Education Committee that has overseen the 2012 reform (see Sect. 6.2.1) and recommended the bachelor programmes to the Academic Council and Rector for a final decision.

The bachelor programmes have no real employers for their graduates, so an employers panel is not relevant. However, since all the students in the bachelor programmes in Danish as well as most of the students in the international programmes are recruited from the Danish upper secondary education system, it is highly relevant that the bachelor programmes are in dialogue with this system. Firstly, in order to adjust the programmes, especially the entrance level, to changes and developments taking place at the upper secondary level. Secondly, the programs are interested in attracting more qualified and motivated students to the programmes, and therefore need to make the programmes visible for and attractive to upper secondary students.

As a concrete example of this form of contact SAMBACH has initiated a 'supplier panel' consisting of a number of teachers from different types of disciplines at the upper secondary level. The eight-person supplier panel meets once every semester. The members are preferably teachers of social science who also provide study guidance at their schools. Some of the members also function as external examiners in SAMBACH and have first-hand experience of the study programmes.

One field of discussion in this connection is the overall changes which educational reforms in Danish upper secondary schools have brought about in general, and how project work has developed there in particular, changes to which the Roskilde University bachelor programmes have to adjust. For years, supervisors have gained the impression from the supervision of project work with first-year students that the new students hold the misconception that project work at Roskilde University is similar to what they have previously experienced at secondary school. However, this is not the case. The students have not been introduced to problem-oriented project work, but to other forms of project work. Therefore, re-education has proven necessary, but it remains difficult because of the superficial similarities between the different forms of project work. This also indicates that a supplier panel can be an important two-way process of influence.

While recruitment traditionally has not been a central concern for HUMBACH and SAMBACH, the newly established HUMTEK and NATBACH have engaged strongly in such activities. Since 2009, NATBACH has made a particular effort to expand the recruitment of students with different types of activities that enable NATBACH students to communicate directly with upper secondary students about their projects and the study programme in general. The more prominent recruitment activities include:

- *Nat-Day* (Nat is short for Natural Science): A full-day programme is held twice a year for classes from upper secondary schools (500–600 secondary students participate). The programme consists of many parallel sessions with research presentations by researchers and presentations of projects by NATBACH students, and an exhibition of experimental projects.
- *A travelling exhibition to secondary schools*: The exhibition visits upper secondary schools for half a day while the normal teaching is on hold. NATBACH and HUMTEK are each represented with an exhibition stand and two students. The students can present a number of examples of student projects in the various natural science subjects and provide general information about the programme. The exhibition visits some 45 secondary schools every autumn.
- *Science@ruc.dk*: Offers courses to upper secondary classes (typically one double module e.g. 90 min). The modules are developed and implemented by groups

of two to three NATBACH students and cover experimental courses in many different subjects.
- *Seminars held for selected secondary schools* to help students in the writing of their study projects (a compulsory element in upper secondary programmes) in two subjects (at least one of them in natural science). Groups of two to three NATBACH students are formed to supervise a group of five to ten upper secondary students, based on the NATBACH students' experience from their own projects.
- *The academy for talented young secondary students*: Four full-day workshops in various scientific disciplines per year for different groups of around 30 talented upper secondary students.
- *General Roskilde University activities:* In addition, the university has an open house event twice a year and a 3-day event for experiencing a study programme in practice. In these activities the bachelor students in all four programmes play an important role.

All in all, the recruitment activities annually bring NATBACH students in close contact with up to 4,000 upper secondary students in settings where they can communicate subject matter insights from their projects and course work and where they can be in direct dialogue with the secondary students about student life. Students receive a fee for their participation, which according to their testimonies, also provides challenging and interesting tasks that are relevant for their own education and personal development.

The recruitment activities also provide an opportunity for dialogue with teachers and headmasters at the upper secondary level. This is important for the above-mentioned challenges concerning connectedness and visibility in our relations with the educational system at large.

In HUMTEK a key feature has been the development of joint events with Roskilde University's outreach organization *RUC Innovation* a case in point being the earlier-mentioned annual 1-day student conference *realtybites.dk*, where external key players and 'role models' meet and discuss with students. Since 2008 this has been further developed by the entrepreneurial student organization *Krebitat* that arranges monthly lunch sessions where students and public and private innovators and entrepreneurs meet. Both arrangements are public. From 2014 the workshops in HUMTEK will be converted into FabLab sessions (see Fig. 6.9) open to all researchers and students at Roskilde University as well as users from society at large in order to provide a unique meeting place for students, researchers, innovators and citizens.

Finally, for all four bachelor programmes the problem-oriented project work in itself constitutes an opening to society in general. Often the students' projects are based on problems inspired by or related to organizations (official or NGOs), particular groups of citizens, companies or problem areas of societal interest. At Roskilde University, it is even possible for organizations and companies to advertise problems to be taken up by the project groups often in some form of collaboration with the parties 'having' the problem. Moreover, many project groups reach findings and results which are of societal importance and interest. For instance, that has been the case for quite a few NATBACH projects addressing environmental problems. Such projects are often communicated to a wider audience through articles in newspapers or journals or through videos or other media.

13.6 The Importance of External Collaboration

External relations at a modern university such as Roskilde are manifold and complex, and even though there is a strong tradition of working with real-world problems in students' projects, the collaboration with external partners still needs to be re-invented and developed. External collaboration is not just a question of employing graduates, but of cementing the university's role as an engaged and active partner in society. Education and work life are not separate, but must interact both in the student years and after graduation, in life-long learning initiatives, and in alumni relations, leading to important benefits for both. Collaboration takes place both at the institutional level through advisory boards, quality assurance systems, and dialogue with politicians, and at the individual level through students' and researcher groups' concrete and hands-on collaboration with companies, organizations and public institutions. It will definitely continue to find new forms, with the network society, globalization and new communication channels. Roskilde University has never wished to be an ivory tower, and will continue its efforts to be a critical, constructive and creative partner in its collaboration with broader society.

References

Akkrediteringsloven. (2013). Lov om akkreditering af videregående uddannelsesinstitutioner. Retrieved May 28, 2013 from https://www.retsinformation.dk/Forms/R0710.aspx?id=151871

Hansen, E. (1997). *En koral i tidens strøm* [A coral in the flow of time], RUC 1972–1997. Frederiksberg: Roskilde University Press.

Olsen, P. B. (Interviewer). (2011a). Engagement i det man har brug for at vide. 5 videoer om 5 dele af problemorientering [Engagement in what one needs to know. 5 Videos on 5 Aspects of problem orientation] [video]. In R. Holm (Producer), *Kompetencer fra RUC* [Competences from RUC]. Roskilde: Roskilde University. Retrieved December 8, 2013 from http://www.ruc.dk/uddannelse/fag/virksomhedsstudier/karriere-og-kompetencer/kompetencer-fra-ruc-videoer.

Olsen, P. B. (Interviewer). (2011b). Holdninger til RUC. 5 videoer om 5 dele af projektarbejde [Attitudes towards RUC. 5 Videos on 5 Aspects of project work] [video]. In R. Holm (Producer), *Kompetencer fra RUC* [Competences from RUC]. Roskilde: Roskilde University. Retrieved December 8, 2013 from http://www.ruc.dk/uddannelse/fag/virksomhedsstudier/karriere-og-kompetencer/kompetencer-fra-ruc-videoer.

Rektorsekretariatet. (2010). *Strategi RUC 2015* [RUC strategy to 2015]. Roskilde: Roskilde University. Retrieved November 29, 2013 from http://www.ruc.dk/fileadmin/assets/adm/rektoratet/strategi2015/RUC_strategi_2015.pdf.

Schademan, H. K., & Jørgensen, L. (2013). *Kandidatundersøgelsen 2012* [The graduate survey 2012]. Roskilde: Roskilde Universitet.

Part V
Pedagogical Experiments in PPL

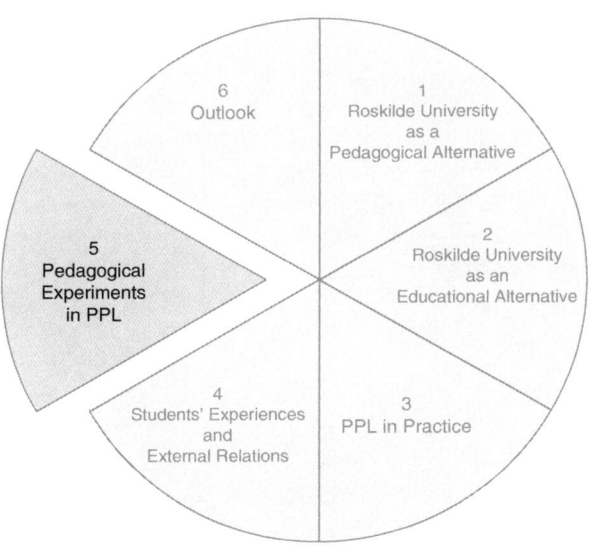

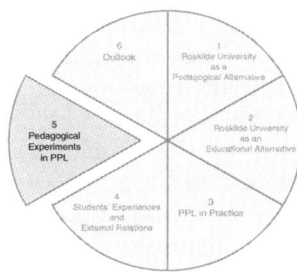

Chapter 14
Research Learning – How Students and Researchers Learn from Collaborative Research

Trine Wulf-Andersen, Peder Hjort-Madsen, and Kevin Holger Mogensen

14.1 Introduction

In this chapter we focus on current work to revitalize and further develop the Roskilde University model for learning. In principle, the problem-oriented, interdisciplinary, participant-directed project work involves a hybridization of teaching, researching and experiential learning (Nielsen and Webb 1999; Olesen and Jensen 1999; Ulriksen 1999). For a long time, this has been standard, even routinized practice at Roskilde University. However, the political contexts around education and research are different from in the 1970s when this practice was first institutionalized at Roskilde University. In our experience, students' connection to research and research communities is one dimension of the original intention of the Roskilde University model that has been under pressure by neoliberal influences, but is still worth fighting for (cf. Sect. 2.5).

T. Wulf-Andersen (✉) • K.H. Mogensen
Roskilde University, Roskilde, Denmark
e-mail: wulf@ruc.dk; kevin@ruc.dk

P. Hjort-Madsen
Aalborg University, Aalborg, Denmark
e-mail: phm@learning.aau.dk

Here, we will describe and discuss how we work to enhance and elaborate the ideal of *research-based learning*. We report the experiences from an experiment involving undergraduate and graduate students working on subprojects within the framework of their supervisors' (i.e. the authors') research project. This places the students at the centre of actual research processes, and organizes their learning processes through their interaction with empirical and theoretical fields, informants, fellow researchers, etc. within a 'real' research project. This model emphasizes and explores a relationship based on shared practice and collaborative learning processes inside and outside the university, between the students as *research learners* (Wulf-Andersen et al. 2013) and their teachers who are at the same time researchers, project managers and supervisors.

The question of undergraduates being involved in research is often discussed in terms of an educational approach. Educators have related the positive effects of undergraduate students 'learning by doing' in 'real research projects' to students' socialization into a professional community of researchers (Winn 1995; Earley 2007) as well as to students' experiences of personal and intellectual development (Hunter et al. 2007). In some cases, undergraduates work as research assistants in senior researchers' projects. In such cases, students do not always feel a sense of personal ownership of the research project (Searight et al. 2010). In other cases, students are involved in senior researchers' projects as both research assistants and informants. These latter cases involve crucial methodological and ethical considerations concerning the dual role of the teacher as researcher and supervisor, and of the student as data source and researcher (Ferguson et al. 2004). Landrum and Nielsen (2002) point to the fact that not much research has examined what experiences are beneficial to educators as well as to students – nor, we might add, what forms of involvement are beneficial to the research projects.

In our discussion of the potentials and challenges of this intertwined and complex research and education design, we will explore both its contribution to research knowledge and its contribution to the learning processes of the students. Before turning to this, we will contextualize the experiment within the particular research project in question.

14.2 The Context of the Research Project

The research project of the experiment falls within a collaborative research design to study vulnerable young people's participation in secondary and further education, and the ways educational practices and contexts interplay with young people's everyday lives, (gendered) identity processes, and experienced life possibilities (Aarkrog and Jørgensen 2008; Jørgensen 2013; Larsen and Villumsen 2012; Wulf-Andersen 2012; Wulf-Andersen et al. 2012). The project is a commissioned research project, funded by the EU Social Fund and the Danish Ministry for Gender Equality.

The research explores the challenges young people meet in their everyday lives, and the relations between these young people's identity processes and experiences of social and psychological vulnerability and marginality, in connection with their choice of and participation in education. In particular, the project studies what factors or conditions in the educational institutions and in the local community setting are contributing to or producing vulnerability. The project thus works at the intersection of education, social work, and youth research.

Research and the development of education, social work and local community practices are closely interconnected in this project. The project aims at producing knowledge which tries to bridge the many different contexts in which young people are involved in their everyday life. The project design is inspired by participatory action research and indicates the complex landscape we manoeuvre in (Larsen et al. 2013; Mullen 2000). On the one hand, we work closely with teachers in vocational education and different professionals working for local councils and in local communities. They are all working with practice-based experiments and development projects aimed at better meeting the needs and sustaining the education and well-being of vulnerable young people. The professionals meet with each other and the researchers in development workshops every 2 or 3 months, collectively reflecting on and qualifying their development projects. On the other hand, researchers work through interviews and narrative workshops to include the young people's perspectives in the knowledge production and the project processes.

Thus, from a research point of view, there are many different arenas of young people's lives relevant to explore. Classrooms, workshops, mentors' or social workers' offices, young people's homes and after-school activities, etc. all constitute important sites for field work, if we are to learn more about different aspects of youth, gender and vulnerability through a variety of expressions, understandings and productions in different contexts by different actors. We involve students as research assistants in an attempt to overcome the limitations of a more traditional research project. Having students as research assistants offers supplementary empirical work related to the research project. The students bring experiences and understandings different from the researchers' into the project, as well as different possibilities of access and positioning in relation to young people in the empirical field.

From an educational point of view, involving students in research as research learners makes it possible for students and teachers to participate and interact in different ways, and to relate to and reflect on the many different contexts influencing research and learning. This will be the focus for the remainder of the chapter.

14.3 Research-Based Teaching and the Student as Research Learner

An important aspect of university-based education is to teach students to conduct research. Students need to acquire the ability and competencies to critically and creatively investigate problems, and actively define the questions and processes involved, in order to contribute high quality research and to gain employment as future professionals. Facilitating student reflection on their own work in relation to the 'situation of research' in all its (broadest) senses holds an equally important learning potential.

Research-based teaching contains different elements and can take different forms. It can take the form of second order knowledge as the teaching content, as the mere communication of the teacher's research and research-based knowledge or the learning about research. It can be teaching as research organization, as when students have the opportunity to pose research questions and use theory and methods, or when students receive supervision on research-oriented working and writing. It may also be teaching in the form of research collaboration, as when students are invited and involved as active participants in teaching and have the opportunity to participate in real research projects or research programmes.

The model for research-based teaching and learning at Roskilde University generally comprises several of these elements, and thus by far exceeds the very simplified triadic teacher-content-student relation, sometimes portrayed in the didactic triangle (Gundem and Hopmann 2002). A model of the relations and processes of participant-directed, problem-oriented project work would need to be considerably more complex and nuanced – and include e.g. student-student and teacher-teacher relations, academia-society relations, and relations between academic and personal learning processes. Our experiment in fact involves the students in all of the above-mentioned ways. What we wish to show in this chapter is that the realization of the final, and in a certain perspective small, step of also involving students in real research is actually a highly significant one.

In our experiment, learning content is not selected or controlled by and passed on from one part (teacher) to the other (student), but is a matter of a common research interest as the focus of their relationship. The research project organization situates the teacher-student relationship in a hybrid form between work and learning and thus promotes cooperation and collaboration between researchers and research learners. This dissolves traditional boundaries between teaching and research, and transforms the working relationship between teachers and students into a community of research and learning. This is not just a challenge for teachers or researchers surrendering a particular kind of traditional power. It is also a challenge for students holding more instrumental school-oriented expectations of teaching and teachers at the university.

The integration of researching and learning gives the students first-hand research experience – including experience with the delicacy of navigating in and reflecting on the multiple contexts and among the many different stakeholders of a research project: fellow students/researchers in one's own and other project groups, the supervisors or project managers, the various participants and stakeholders in one's own sub-project, the research project at large, the client of the project, the educational setting, etc.

These are complex matters, which stresses the need for researchers and educators to systematically reflect upon the possible negative effects on research or learning. Researchers, supervisors and universities wishing to establish teaching as research collaboration need to organize learning environments as distinct spaces for critical reflection on the relations and processes of research. Learning environments must support explicit and collective discussion of the particular ways in which students' research participation and ordinary educational practice influence each other in the given university context, considering also the specific local context of students learning by doing research. In the next sections, we will describe how we have attempted to address these issues.

14.4 Organizing Students' Involvement in the Research Project

The research project was introduced to the students at the beginning of the 2012 autumn semester and the 2013 spring semester, as part of the supervisors' research portfolio, with an invitation for them to undertake their required project work within this particular research and educational framework. Figure 14.1 illustrates the organization and process of the students' project work.

Apart from the standard formal university organization of project work at Roskilde University, we added a start-up seminar to introduce the students to the field of research, and an analytical workshop to perform collaborative analyses. In addition to these two sessions, we also organized a mandatory colloquium involving a series of student-guided seminars based on a specific theme, with the aim of supporting the students' project work. In this case, the colloquium was organized around the theme youth, education and periphery.

The students were invited via email and through short presentations during plenary sessions in the different educational settings where the researchers were located. The aims of the emails and the presentations were to describe the scope and organization of the research project, the field of research, research questions and methodological design, as well as to state that working within this project framework would provide the possibility of:

> Working in association with a real' research project and a group of researchers; drawing on the researchers' contacts in the field – enhancing the possibilities of actually establishing contacts and doing empirical work within a single semester; [accessing] financial support for travelling expenses; [and] participating in extracurricular seminars/workshops for all students and researchers involved. (Invitation, September 2012/January 2013)

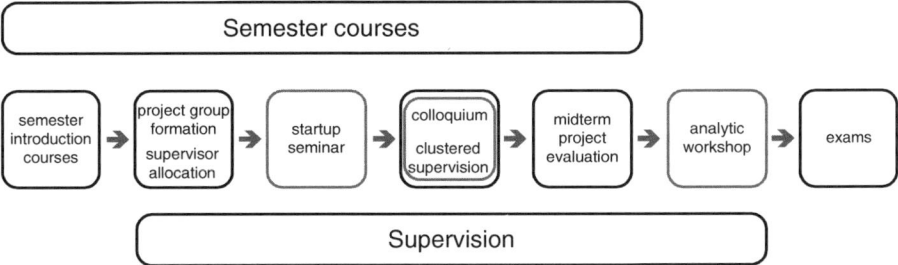

Fig. 14.1 The organization and process of the students' project work

Participation in the research project came with the stipulation that the students would have one of the researchers involved as their supervisor, but apart from that, project groups would work according to the general regulations for other project work at Roskilde University. We emphasized that students would have freedom within the scope of the research project to choose a specific problem and to formulate their own research question as well as apply different methods of their own choice just as they do in ordinary project work at the university.

We ended up with 11 groups (41 students) in the 2012 autumn semester and five groups (18 students) in the 2013 spring semester working within the framework of the research project. The students joining the research project varied considerably in their academic qualifications and their chosen topics and approaches. Some were students from the bachelor programme in Social Sciences, while others were from the bachelor or master programme in Educational Studies. Some did not know the researchers in advance, others had had one of the researchers as their supervisor, and some students or groups in the 2013 spring semester had already worked with us in the 2012 autumn semester. The students also had varied experiences of doing fieldwork. Some students had taken methodology courses and had also done empirical work as part of previous project work. However, most students had very limited or no practical experience of empirical research.

Consequently, early in the semester we held a start-up seminar (see Fig. 14.1). One explicit aim of this seminar was to present in more detail the research questions, methods, and central theoretical concepts from the research project, and to assist the groups in their methodological preparations for the coming fieldwork. Among other important issues raised in this session were the potential dilemmas associated with their dual roles as students/research learners and research assistants/contributors and the different expectations and demands that could arise from these two roles. The students were asked to reflect on their subprojects and explicitly to discuss:

- How involvement in the research project related to their educational context (particular semester focus and requirements),
- How their subproject, on the other hand, related to the research project context (what part of the field was in focus, what empirical and analytical contribution they were interested in),
- How they planned their fieldwork, analytical work, and writing over the semester,
- What different kinds of challenges and dilemmas they anticipated.

In the period following the start-up seminar, the students worked on refining their research questions, methodology and theoretical approach, before going into the field and conducting their empirical work. Late in the semester when students had completed most of their empirical work, we scheduled the analytical workshop (see Fig. 14.1). All project groups were asked to present one or more 'empirical images' (photographs, unfolding of exemplary situations, etc.) from their fieldwork. The idea was to create a common ground for collective reflections and analysis.

The research framework provided an additional organizational structure for the project work. As supervisors, we monitored, supported and challenged the project work of each group (see Fig. 14.1).

The groups' subprojects focused on a wide variety of problems and used various theoretical and methodological approaches (three of the projects are described in the following section). Some subprojects focused on gender issues, some on peer relations, yet others on young people's visions of the future or teachers' perspectives on young people's social and educational problems. Some groups did participant observation, many did individual or group interviews, some did critical action research, and others selected policy documents as their primary material. This meant that some subprojects came close to the research project (Wulf-Andersen et al. 2012), whereas others differed somewhat from our framework. In the following section, we will explore three student projects in more detail.

14.5 The Contributions of Student Projects to Research Knowledge: Three Examples

Three student group projects from the 2012 autumn semester may serve as examples of how the involvement of students contributed to the research project, and how the association with the research project influenced the students' learning processes. The examples are selected because they can illustrate the variety of projects defined by students, and thus the breadth and difference in research themes and methodological points with regard to the study of young people's education, gender and vulnerabilities. We will describe briefly each project and its central points and then turn to an overall discussion of the students' contributions and research learning.

14.5.1 A Visual Study of Young People's Everyday Life in a Rural Town

One of the groups set out to investigate how we can understand young people's views on their educational opportunities as well as the relationship between young people's everyday lives in a rural town and their motivation for education (Klingberg et al. 2012). Methodologically, the group wanted to investigate how young people's perspectives on their own lives could be researched in a way that contributed to a better understanding of the relation between young people's everyday life and educational motivation. They chose to do so by arranging a workshop on young people's everyday life and educational motivation (in a 9th grade class) and by interviewing selected 9th graders on the basis of a methodological combination of photo elicitation and photo voice. The 9th graders were given a single-use camera and asked to photograph their everyday lives. To the group's surprise, the narratives emerging from the photos were relatively positive with regard to life in a rural town, whereby the group's preconceptions about young people in rural towns wanting to move to bigger cities were dismantled. They found that the 9th graders felt a strong sense of belonging to the local community and that this was due partly to the fact that they still lived at home with their parents.

One of the group's realizations came at the collective analysis workshop, where all the groups involved presented their empirical data. Another group of students (Pedersen et al. 2012) had interviewed a group of vulnerable and unemployed young people in their mid to late twenties, not from the same town but from the same region. These interviews drew a completely different picture of young people's lives in a rural town – these young people were disillusioned about their future in the local community (e.g. because of complicated family ties or because of difficulties in distancing themselves from a criminal lifestyle) and at the same time they did not have the resources to move away and start a new life. In light of these empirical data on life in a rural town, the group decided to revisit their own data and ask how it is possible to understand the 9th graders' positive narratives in relation to e.g. age, the fact that all 9th graders lived at home, broader life experiences, etc. In this sense the group's study was placed in a broader research field and clarified how much young people's everyday lives in a rural town can vary, and how different research interests and different methodological designs produce different analyses and knowledge contributions.

14.5.2 Social Space in Secondary School: Empowerment of Young People Through Social Learning

This study also involved a class of 9th grade pupils in a secondary school located in a rural district in southern Denmark (Vaarst et al. 2012). One important background for the project was the political focus in Denmark on high dropout rates, and the pressure on young people to choose an education and a career. This project studied young people's perceptions of social opportunities and introduced a theoretical framework inspired by action research as an experiment. Through a 'utopian workshop', the project investigated the possibilities for creating a social space that could contribute to the empowerment of the young people involved in relation to broader dimensions and challenges facing young people in this rural location.

The students' own reflected knowledge production focused primarily on one issue of the utopian workshop method, namely the problem that the method relies heavily on spoken language and on the ability to formulate thoughts, ideas, experiences and feelings in a certain normative way (while many people are listening). In dealing with issues of young people's social and personal vulnerabilities, it proved difficult to ensure that all participants could feel secure and participate actively as prescribed. This indicated the need for critical reflection of who the young participants are, who are active, and what perspectives they produce. The utopian workshop method will tend to include resourceful young people while other young people's experiences are excluded and marginalized. This also neglects young people's non-verbalized experiences.

Keeping these critical reflections in mind, the utopian workshop still provided an interesting contrast to young people's everyday experiences of schooling. It proved to be valuable in the way that it translated young people's individual life experiences into collective life perspectives, making the strong point that although young people as individuals might feel alone, they actually have a great deal of everyday life perceptions and perspectives in common.

14.5.3 Auto-gender

A third project group asked how 'doing gender' plays out in a particular educational setting: a main programme for auto mechanics (Christiansen et al. 2012). The group members – five young women – spent a day in a workshop conducting participant observation. Three group members worked with the vocational students on the cars and two primarily took notes. The group also interviewed the teacher and carried out a spontaneous informal interview with the only girl on the auto mechanics programme, whom they met in the school canteen.

The group found the educational setting to be characterized by descriptions of the auto mechanic trade as a 'boy thing', and of the genuine auto mechanic as a 'he' who can deal with physical, 'dirty and hard work' and cope with being 'picked on' as part of the workshop humour. This humour carried a highly normative focus on a particular form of masculinity: the dirty, physically hardworking and heterosexual man. By contrast, the images of masculinity – when held up against the female university students – produced images of the girls' middle class academic work as characterized by having 'sweet, clean paper hands'. Male students who did not fit in with the hegemonic norm were made fun of and marginalized with negative references to femininity ('girls') or homosexuality ('gay'). The only girl vocational student told the group that she chose to cut her hair short and wear clothes that hid her feminine body 'to look more like a boy'. The teacher discreetly supported the workshop humour, by referring to the school's obligation to socialize students to the 'culture' and 'tone' of the trade as well as teach them the vocational skills. Thus the group found that students and teacher all contributed to the institutional reproduction and support of a particular masculinity as a parameter for determining 'the good student', giving different possibilities for positioning and action for different vocational students.

The project group concluded that this held the risk of excluding girls, as well as boys enacting other types of masculinities, from feeling welcome and appropriate in this educational setting, thus reproducing gender and class segregation in young people's choices of education and ultimately the labour market.

Whereas the university students at an early stage became aware of the auto mechanic educational context as formed by and formative for particular masculinities and class patterns, only later in the process did they analyse how they themselves intuitively – or automatically – responded to this context. They found this point central and therefore gave their report the equivocal title 'Auto-gender'. Retrospectively they became aware that they played out 'kinds of girls' who were culturally recognizable in the workshop, but they did so in different ways: one as 'silently working with the boys' and another as 'flirting and giggling'. This, in turn, made the group reflect on how their own educational context at the university was also gendered, but in different ways: here issues of gender were toned down or silenced and equality was emphasized.

14.5.4 Contribution to the Production of Research Knowledge

These three (and the other thirteen) groups' work have contributed a variety of data material and analyses on the complex intersection between education, gender and vulnerability. However, a considerable challenge in this kind of research collaboration is the issue of data production and analytical processes, and how to incorporate many different contributions into the larger research project. Dealing with the issue of secondary analysis, Gillies and Edwards wrote:

> The significance placed on context in facilitating qualitative understandings is often conveyed through reference to the intimate bond that the researcher inevitably develops with the data, particularly when they have designed the framework, immersed themselves in the field and drawn on personal grounded insights to make interpretations. (Gillies and Edwards 2005, p. 1)

How do we then hold on to contextualized understanding, and how do we in practice go about incorporating data and analyses produced by others – be they students or assistants – in our analyses? How do we, in our particular case, gain knowledge and in-depth understanding through the students' work? First, we have the students' written reports, including appendices with transcribed interviews, field notes, etc. as data sets. Second, we closely and continually observe, listen to, and are in dialogue with the groups through the different phases of their subproject, from research proposal to written report. In this way we gain insight into the contexts and processes producing the particular data and analyses from each group. Third, we are all present in the collective analysis workshops, with the opportunity to ask questions, elaborate, situate, and reflect on our different contributions. Students have full intellectual property rights to their project reports. We credit students' contributions and authorship by referring to their reports in our publications whenever we build on their data or analyses.

One implication of student participation for our collaborative research project has been an enhanced capacity to produce more empirical data with a wider scope than we could have done ourselves within the time and budget limits of the research project. In addition, students' participation in the analysis has contributed new questions and perspectives for us to develop further, as well as occasioning explication and reflection with respect to the different ways we engage with the empirical field. The students' initial positions are very different from the researcher: they are themselves young people in the educational system, they are close to the project's target group in age and at a similar point in their general life course. They share some of the contemporary elements of youth culture, some come from the very same local areas focused on in the research project, etc. Thus, the students hold a position different from the researcher as to where to enter the empirical field. This means that they sometimes see or notice aspects that we might overlook or understand differently.

It is important to stress, however, that this does not assume a simplistic, subcultural understanding of youth, or imply that age in itself necessarily constitutes any kind of peerness or natural youth-to-youth relations. We agree with Shiner that "while age may be important it does not constitute a master status that overrides all other possible sources of identity" (Shiner 1999, p. 564). When involving university students in our research project, we need continuously to ask not only what it means that they, like the vocational students in focus in our project, are young people being educated. We must also ask what it means that the university students and vocational students respectively are young people with particular identities constructed in very different ways, in relation to biography, gender, class, ethnicity, locality and other categories – categories which are potentially in conflict. In a rough generalization, the university students represent the middle class, academic youth of the metropolis, while the vocational students represent the working class youth of the rural periphery. This could produce adverse power relations and ethical problems in the relationship between the two groups. But it could also facilitate meetings between different groups of young people not often in dialogue with each other, and as such constitute possibilities for reciprocal learning and an expansion of the life choices and possibilities that could be imagined. Thus what the contact means and what happens must be carefully analysed in each specific case. In doing so we share the understanding:

> …that research is not something employed by solitary negotiators operating on their own. Educational researchers use language developed by others, live in specific contexts with particular ways of being and ways of thinking about thinking, have access to some knowledges and not others, and live and operate in a circumstance shaped by particular dominant ideological perspectives (Kincheloe and Tobin 2006, p. 7).

This theoretical conceptualization highlights the significance of multiple perspectives. It provides a focus on all participants in a research project, including researchers as well as students performing research, as situated subjects, with certain positions, norms and agendas, and thus with "their own complicities in the social arena" under study (Neidel and Wulf-Andersen 2013, p. 161). This points to the analysis of and reflection on complicities as an important and integral part of research practice and of learning processes. When the university students are involved in research, we need a high degree of reflection on how they – for better or for worse – are engaging with the field from a certain position, with certain normativity, complicity and possibilities for participation, and how this influences their production of knowledge. We also need to reflect on the ways in which this relates to and influences the simultaneous, different and intertwined complicities and knowledge production of the researchers.

We argue that when issues of context and the consequences of different research designs and researcher or learner positions can be thoroughly addressed and reflected on, secondary analysis of data produced by students "has the potential to generate crucial new perspectives to feed into wider sociological and theoretical debates" (Gillies and Edwards 2005, p. 12).

14.6 Contributing and Learning: The Research Learner

On the basis of all the different student projects, certain analytical themes can be unfolded, all revolving around the learning potentials of being part of a research project. We work from Jean Lave's idea that learning is always taking place (Lave and Wenger 1991) and in coherence with John Dewey's central idea that learning always occurs *through* the active work that students are doing (Nielsen and Webb 1999, p. 115). Thus, the salient question is what is being learned here, and what kinds of research experience the students are gaining.

We ask what the opportunity to participate in a 'real' research project contributes to the students' learning processes, and how our experiment changes and contributes to ordinary university practice and learning. In a later section we will look more critically at the dilemmas that stem from the ambiguous roles of being both a researcher and student.

We build here partly on our own observations and discussions throughout the two semesters and partly on student perspectives on what it meant to them to be involved in research. This has been a central concern to us. From our position as researchers and supervisors, we monitored this factor and discussed it with the students throughout both semesters. At the end of the presentation seminars, we also explicitly asked students to reflect on the questions: "What does it mean to be a student within the research project framework? In what ways is this different from your previous project work? How does this framework support, distort, challenge, or put pressure on the project work?" Students interviewed each other on the basis of these questions and recorded the interviews and discussions on video. Our students' responses were often elaborate, expressing overlapping themes, emphasizing both the complexity of the research process and the importance of the social, cultural and individual identities of the different people engaged in this process (see e.g. Earley 2007, p. 3). The students often implicitly revealed their comparative experiences of the general model of education and learning at Roskilde University and commented on the differences.

14.6.1 Relating to Content Differently: Commitment and Acknowledgement

Many comments from the students related to their appreciation of the practical, first-hand experience of doing research. Practical experience with research methods and the production and analysis of empirical material are already mandatory elements of project work in the educational programmes at Roskilde University. Students thus commented on participation in our research project based on the premise that they would be doing empirical and project-based work in any case, implicitly pointing out what they considered to be challenging when working with ordinary projects at Roskilde University. Most students confirmed our presumption from the invitation that they found it difficult to establish relevant contacts in time to finish the fieldwork, analysis and writing of the report within a single semester, but also commented that our research project constituted an important means of *accessing the field*. Many students expressed this metaphorically as a matter of more easily getting past gatekeepers in the empirical field, by way of their association with us and our contacts in the field. But some students also indicated that accessing a new field of literature and engaging in the usual project work was easier, since our research project offered a pre-existing delimitation of the field.

Students felt better supported in accessing the field, through the continuous contact with not only their own supervisor but also the larger group of researchers associated with our research project. This contrasted with the standard relationship of one group to one supervisor (see also Chap. 8).

Thus, with the research project as a framework, students felt better able to realize the general Roskilde University intentions of learning by doing practical empirical work. This in turn made it possible also to relate to academic content, theoretical concepts and empirical analyses of other researchers, in a different and more critical way. Actually working with and through theoretical and methodological concepts in 'real world' settings, rather than just reading and reflecting intellectually on them in the classroom, students obtained a more thorough understanding and experience 'from within' of the formative powers and limitations of different theoretical decisions, and thus enhanced their reflective capacity at the theoretical level.

Another significant response was related to the opportunity to work on a real research project as opposed to what one student called "the usual 'as-if projects' that will just gather dust on the library shelf". This response reveals that the educational activity of project work is not always experienced by the students as a work process with a real product. To know that "this will be used for something", and to be involved and *acknowledged as active contributors* in the different phases and processes of research, was highly motivating for students. One student said, "I get the feeling that I'm being taken more seriously, the thing that somebody actually believes that I can produce something that can be of value – even though I'm still in training." Consequently, many students also found themselves to be "more ambitious", "more committed" and also "more obliged" to produce "good work". Most students felt that they had a secure platform for being more ambitious because supervisors were "right behind us". Some students, however, felt that working on a real research project simultaneously put pressure on them to perform according to *real research standards* and sometimes worried about their ability to live up to these standards. Many of the students put in more work hours than expected, which made us discuss how to better organize and define the scope of the project work, balancing the commitment between ambition and realism (Winn 1995, p. 205). Based on the experiences of the students, it seems reasonable to postulate that their involvement in the research project changed their relation to content as well as their commitment to learning. Furthermore, in this design, the real world relation of the general Roskilde University model was accentuated in several ways. One was through being part of a commissioned research project with a particular agenda and assignment framing both the students' and the researchers' work, the subprojects and the research project's knowledge production in general. Another was through the students' meetings with different stakeholders in the field: young people, teachers and instructors, managers, local politicians, etc.

14.6.2 Changed Social Relations: Shared/Collaborative Practice

The change in how the students related to content cannot be adequately understood without looking at the social relations this was intertwined with. Another frequent line of student response focused on the collective and emotional dimension of being part of our research project. Students stated that the collective organization provided important peer and supervisor support. In addition to students being part of a project group, each group was connected to other groups as well as to a group of researchers, all working with shared interests and somewhat similar subprojects within a collective body of work. Each subproject was thus not only discussed within the group or between the group and its supervisor, but was also presented to "several other conversational partners" in workshops.

The relation to other groups as well as to the researchers reportedly assisted students in developing their abilities to connect project work, extracurricular seminars and ordinary curricular activities. The high degree of student-directed activities in Roskilde University pedagogy is sometimes experienced by students as a challenge when it comes to assessing and connecting the different elements of a total study programme to a whole landscape. Within the framework of our research project, fellow students became visible as active partners and resources in learning and in connecting different learning processes.

The collective forum made it easier for students to become aware of how different choices of theoretical concepts and research methods were of significance for the knowledge produced, and thus helped students to comprehend questions of epistemology, scientific theory and the politics of science, which some students otherwise considered abstract and hard to understand.

Furthermore, the variety in the material, focal points, and positions represented in the workshops led to collective reflection that added new perspectives and challenged all participants to reflect more deeply on their own empirical material. The empirical field was widened, and students became aware that very different stories of e.g. education, gender or young people's lives in a specific town are simultaneously at work 'out there'. This inspired several groups to revisit the empirical material, looking more closely at nuances, complexity and differentiation. One student said:

> Sometimes questions have been raised, I guess, that are rather more difficult than usual; and in this way I think it all becomes more nuanced. We have discussed some really difficult things – discussions have been lifted up a level, relating to many things you would have taken for granted.

In this way, students and groups assisted each other in positioning each group's or student's own work within a research field and within a larger learning biography. To facilitate student reflection on their own work in relation to the 'research situation' in all its (broadest) senses holds a great learning potential.

Students emphasized the importance of the changed relation to the researchers/supervisors. In particular, students felt that the researchers were "letting them in" to the engine room of research and this made students feel welcomed, acknowledged, and confident about being there. Trusting them with our field relationships was one dimension of being "let in". Another appreciated dimension was the opportunity for students to listen in on and contribute to the researchers' work in progress, and also to witness the collegial relations and discussions among researchers, whom they otherwise tend to meet one at a time. In the collective workshops and seminars, researchers' different curiosities, uncertainties, ways of asking questions, and actions to help one another as well as students in clarifying unsettled thoughts became visible to students as exemplary dialogues. This reciprocal and dialogical space contrasts with the more familiar situation where students and researchers meet in short-term encounters "as strangers, without knowledge of each other's research agendas, interests and orientations" (Mullen 2000, p. 9). In the context of the continuous meetings and activities in our research project, researchers and students became mutually intelligible as having certain interests and positions in the field – all of which could and should be critically analysed. Several students thus came to reflect on their own (future) researcher position and identity, which again parallels Earley's findings (Earley 2007, p. 4). One student said: "It's been good to feel that here is a supervisor with a passion, that there's someone setting a direction. Then it's for me to decide whether I too want to go that way or if I'll move in different directions."

While indicating the positive aspects of having a passionate supervisor with regard to motivation, this also points to a general issue concerning the choices students have to make when working on problem-based learning: it is always their responsibility. The understanding of supervisors as facilitators rather than authority figures holding the right answers, and students as active learners rather than members of an audience (Jenkins and Healy 2009, p. 1) is institutionalized at Roskilde University (see also Chap. 8). But in the students' comments on our experiment we also sense a burgeoning awareness that sometimes the role of the facilitator is not given adequate priority or status. Sometimes it is performed from a distance, rather than as a different way of following the students' processes closely. The involvement in our research project, with facilitators and discussion partners following the project processes closely, added to the ordinary project work a more tangible sense of direction, making it easier for students to orientate and contribute in relation to empirical and theoretical aspects of research. Also our research project added a broader forum of discussion partners and thus supported the development of broader perspectives and deeper analysis.

Participation in a collaborative research project provides students with an opportunity to embark on a revealing journey in the form of a learning process. By gaining first-hand experience of doing research, discussing empirical, methodological and theoretical issues with fellow students and the researchers, the research learners develop a more comprehensive understanding of what conducting research really implies. Research learners will not only know how to act and what to know. Research learners will also on an epistemological level learn to know why and how to know and therefore be able to manage their own learning processes and construct new knowledge (Gärdenfors 2010).

14.7 The Ambiguous Roles of Researcher and Student

During the two semesters, both students and researchers experienced dilemmas concerning the students' engagement in our research project. Here, we will particularly point out dilemmas associated with the multiple and intertwined roles of researchers and students, which are crucial to reflect on in the context of research with students.

One primary concern has been the way in which *the ambiguous roles* of researcher-supervisor and assistant-student have influenced the ways students balanced their own interests with what they considered to be our interests or the interests of our research project. An example of this surfaced in relation to fieldwork. As researchers, we had some concerns about the ways students' presence might influence relations to practitioners and professionals in the field, with whom we also collaborate. As researchers, but certainly also as teachers and supervisors of research, we needed to ensure that students engaging in research fieldwork were adequately prepared for the tasks at hand, that they held the necessary knowledge, methodological understandings and techniques (Earley 2007, p. 4), and that the organization of student participation was carefully defined throughout the process (Winn 1995, p. 212). This is a considerable challenge when taking learning outside the classroom and the university campus. It presupposes students' ability to act and improvise in fieldwork involving situations arising and developing when the supervisor is not present. One group (Hansen et al. 2013), for instance, was rather insecure when confronted by a project participant about their use of quotes from an interview with her. After an email dialogue with the supervisor and a telephone conversation with the participant, it turned out that there was no real conflict arising. What should be noted here, however, is that in this situation the group faltered doubly: at the immediacy of having to act and answer the participant and at the complexity of being part of a larger research context. A paragraph from an email from the group to the supervisor illustrates how students were feeling highly responsible for our research project, and therefore reliant on the supervisors' immediate support and opinion:

> We were really quite perplexed in this situation. But as you say, this is an experience as well, and actually it made us discuss exactly how one should relate to the ways our project potentially will be used – in this respect, it was not a waste of effort …. we were also unsure if this could cause problems for the research project as a whole. It was great that you answered so quickly, so we could feel on firm ground.

While possibly producing additional insecurity for the students, the intertwined education and research design also sparked reflections on the complexity of context, and thus produced experiential learning not easily accomplished in the classroom (Earley 2002, p. 1). In this case the students became aware of the conditions under which research is produced, involving relations to other research projects in the same field, political agendas in research organizations, practice, assignment of projects, funding, etc. This positive outcome, however, cannot be taken for granted. Therefore it is important to be aware of the potential dilemmas and emotional aspects of doing research and deal with them as they occur. This means inviting the students to discuss precarious situations and issues with the supervisor and/or one of the researchers involved.

Though students in general regarded the experiential learning as meaningful, several also stated quite clearly that students need to know in detail what is expected of them as students and research assistants respectively, and what conversely they can expect from their supervisor as researcher and from the researcher as supervisor. Transparency and reflections concerning *roles and mutual expectations* are necessary to develop a general feeling of trust between researchers and students. This trust in turn is central for collective ethical and methodological reflections on the interests and relations shaping the production of knowledge; these reflections are crucial to this kind of participatory research. But the students' attempts to balance their own interests and those of the researchers also appeared in relation to the issue of project focus. In spite of our continued attempts as researchers to announce and support students' freedom of choice with regard to focus, methods and theory, the students found this difficult to carry out in practice. One student explicitly said, "It's actually hard to stick to your own focus." Sometimes, what researchers experienced as discussing different equally legitimate analytical strategies was interpreted by some students as putting forward theories "which they say we should use". Although some students felt we were clear and intelligible sparring partners, others felt that we set up limitations to certain approaches to the research field. There is a fine balance between the two that is not easily found. On the one hand, students can feel unmoored if the researchers' positions seem too intangible. On the other hand, if students feel subordinate to the researchers' project, or feel like mere 'means to an end' in it, this would constitute a problem from a participatory research perspective as well as from an educational point of view.

The dilemmas of the double agency of researcher-supervisor and the tension between the collaborative, inclusive design on the one hand and institutional power relations on the other increased towards the end of each semester, when positions shifted relating to exams and assessment. In the workshops and through the semester, a space was created where the classroom was merged with a 'discovery-orientated research workshop' built on participatory learning and research processes (Mullen 2000, p. 19). One of our main concerns regarding the use of students as research assistants has been the shift from this collective space to the asymmetric nature of power in the supervisor-student relationship (see also Sect. 2.5). The differences between students and supervisors are articulated through the semester in terms of knowledge, skills and attitudes, but take on a different character when supervisors have to evaluate and examine the students' work at the end of the semester. Despite our systematic efforts to reveal, deemphasize and collectively reflect on these underlying power issues, it is impossible to make power disappear due to the institutional context of formal education, where "power is mediated by the element of trust that is intrinsic to the relationship and moral commitment of teachers to function in the best interests of their students" (Ferguson et al. 2004, p. 4). This fact unquestionably shapes the relationship between students and researchers as one of trust and power. When participating in research as assistants, students are thus at risk of feeling captive to the status difference in relation to their supervisors. One project group had this comment:

> On the one hand, the student-supervisor relationship is based on trust during the supervision period. The students are honest about challenges and problems in their research and seek sparring. On the other hand, the relationship is marked by power relations in the exam situation, where the examiner is supposed to assess the product of the students. This is a challenge to the students (as well as to the supervisor/examiner), and this challenge is not limited to this specific research project, but is a general aspect of project collaboration at Roskilde University.

The challenge mentioned here by the students is intensified when students and supervisors enter into a collaborative working relationship. This makes it very important – and difficult – to clarify the criteria for assessment in this form of education (Winn 1995, p. 206). Therefore, we argue that it is crucial to provide the time, space and framework for explicitly and collectively addressing how students' work relates on the one hand to a research project and on the other to the students' educational context. In other words, how well does the students' participation in research integrate with standard educational practice at the university, and what different kinds of challenges and dilemmas could result from this integration (or lack thereof)? For a group of students who were not present at the introductory workshop, and thus missed the initial reflections on these issues, it meant this: "Only late in the process did we understand the double interests you (the researchers) have had. We were just a little confused sometimes as to what you wanted to 'use us for'." Furthermore, it is important to raise these questions at different stages of the process (at the onset, while working, after exams, in connection with concluding the larger project, etc.) as there will be different issues arising at different points of the process and consequently different answers to the question of 'what it means to be involved in the research project'. Finally, power relations in the direct relationship between students and supervisors must be discussed in terms of the structural relations that establish them. In an educational perspective, one example would be the structural demand that we as supervisors exercise institutional evaluation powers over students in exams. Another example, in the context of a commissioned research project, would be that we as project managers could face situations necessitating regulation or some degree of control of student activities.

14.8 Learning Research and Dealing with Dilemmas

We have contributed an example of how university education and research can be organized in ways that facilitate processes where students can engage in and learn research by doing it. In the case presented, students became *research learners* through the investigation of specific, complex, unpredictable and contextualized real-world problems. The students' learning through researching both strengthens and is strengthened by the particular educational context at Roskilde University.

The students who carried out their project work as part of a research project gained research experience and competencies even before their master or doctoral study. The focus, institutionalized at Roskilde University, on students as research learners rather than merely curriculum learners, is an important background for our experiment. But the practical realization of research-based learning in terms of actually involving students in research promoted active learning processes not easily accomplished in classroom teaching, even though this teaching at Roskilde University is problem-oriented, interdisciplinary and participant-directed. We have argued that this way of working holds the potential of adding observations and generating important new perspectives for the research project as well as for higher education in general, when students are "let in" and acknowledged as legitimate contributors.

A crucial conclusion of our pedagogical experiment is that the ambiguous roles of the researcher-supervisor-project manager and the research learner can produce dilemmas and challenges related to divergent interests in learning and researching. Ambiguity as an underlying factor is not easy to handle in intertwined supervision and research processes, as the researcher-supervisor-project manager must devote full attention to the students' learning processes and at the same time must ensure satisfactory relationships with field informants, research funders and project clients, and assure the quality of the research knowledge produced.

A potential threat to the collaboration between researchers and students may arise if the ambiguous relationship is not dealt with in an ethically and pedagogically correct manner. At the same time, confronting and dealing with the ambiguities and dilemmas of research can enhance learning potentials for students. Experiencing the demanding and ever-changing relations in the concrete practices of research promotes learning processes, including how to analyse and deal with the dilemmas of the multiple roles and divergent interests of researchers, assistants and other participants.

Acknowledgements The authors wish to thank all the students involved in the research project and our colleagues Lene Larsen, Steen Baagøe Nielsen and Signe Hvid Thingstrup for their contributions to this article.

References

Aarkrog, V., & Jørgensen, C. H. (Eds.). (2008). *Divergence and convergence in education and work* (Series: Studies in vocational and continuing education, Vol. 6). Bern: Peter Lang.

Christiansen, H. vdH., Sørensen, I. M. S., Friis, M. G., Kieffer, M. B., & Larsen, P. T. (2012). *Autokøn – køn i automatgear* [Auto-gender: Gender with automatic gears]. The Bachelor Study Programme in Social Sciences, Roskilde University. Retrieved December 11, 2013 from http://rudar.ruc.dk/handle/1800/9828.

Earley, M. A. (2002). Encouraging students to think about research as a process. *Forum Qualitative Sozialforschung/Forum: Qualitative Social Research, 3*(4). Retrieved December 11, 2013 from http://www.qualitative-research.net.

Earley, M. A. (2007). Lessons learned from students' research experiences [Editorial]. *Journal of Research Practice, 3*(1). Retrieved December 11, 2013 from http://jrp.icaap.org.

Ferguson, L. M., Yonge, O., & Myrick, F. (2004). Students' involvement in faculty research: Ethical and methodological issues. *International Journal of Qualitative Methods, 3*(4), 1–14. Retrieved December 11, 2013 from http://ejournals.library.ualberta.ca/index.php/IJQM/index.

Gärdenfors, P. (2010). *Lusten att förstå· Om lärande på människans vilkår*. Stockholm: Natur & Kultur.

Gillies, V., & Edwards, R. (2005). Secondary analysis in exploring family and social change: Addressing the issue of context. *Forum Qualitative Sozialforschung/Forum: Qualitative Social Research, 6*(1). Retrieved December 11, 2013 from http://www.qualitative-research.net/.

Gundem, B., & Hopmann, S. (Eds.). (2002). *Didaktik and/or curriculum*. New York: Peter Lang.

Hansen, A. J. W., Kristiansen, M. H., Kjeldsen, N. Q., Weber, S. S., & Abdulahu, V. (2013). *Praktikcentre på erhvervsuddannelserne* [Practice Centres in Vocational Education]. The Bachelor Study Programme in Social Sciences, Roskilde University. Retrieved December 11, 2013 from http://rudar.ruc.dk/handle/1800/11498.

Hunter, A.-B., Laursen, S. L., & Seymour, E. (2007). Becoming a scientist: The role of undergraduate research in students' cognitive, personal and professional development. *Science Education, 91*, 36–74. doi:10.1002/sce.20173.

Jenkins, A., & Healey, M. (2009). *Developing undergraduate research and inquiry*. York: The Higher Education Academy.

Jørgensen, C. H. (Ed.). (2013). *Drenge og maskuliniteter i ungdomsuddannelserne* [Boys and Masculinities in secondary education]. Roskilde: Roskilde University Press.

Kincheloe, J., & Tobin, K. (2006). Doing educational research in a complex world. In K. Tobin & J. Kincheloe (Eds.), *Doing educational research: A handbook* (pp. 3–13). Amsterdam: Sense.

Klingberg, A., Petersen, M. T., Davidsen, L., & Post, M. H. (2012). *"Vi har jo roer…" – et visuelt studie af ungdomslivet i en udkantsby* ["We've got beets here…" – A visual study of youth life in a rural town]. The Bachelor Study Programme in Social Sciences, Roskilde University.

Landrum, R. E., & Nielsen, L. R. (2002). The undergraduate research assistantship: An analysis of the benefits. *Teaching of Psychology, 29*, 15–19.

Larsen, L., & Villumsen, T. S. (2012). *Unge, uddannelse og sårbarheder – hovedresultater fra projektet 'Psykisk sårbare unge'* [Young people, education and vulnerabilities – Main results from the project' mentally vulnerable young people']. Roskilde: Roskilde University.

Larsen, L., Nielsen, S. B., Thingstrup, S. H., Wulf-Andersen, T., & Jørgensen, C. H. (2013). *Køn og uddannelsesdeltagelse – en forskningsoversigt til refleksion ved deltagerorienteret uddannelsesudvikling for rekruttering og fastholdelse af mænd og drenge* [Gender and participation in education – A research review for reflection on the development of participant-oriented studies to recruit and keep men and boys in education]. Roskilde: Roskilde University, The IMODUS project, Centre for Welfare, Profession and Everyday Life.

Lave, J., & Wenger, E. (1991). *Situated learning: Legitimate peripheral participation*. Cambridge, UK: Cambridge University Press.

Mullen, C. A. (2000). Linking research and teaching: A study of graduate student engagement. *Teaching in Higher Education, 5*, 5–21. doi:10.1080/135625100114920.

Neidel, A., & Wulf-Andersen, T. (2013). The ethics of involvement with the already involved Action research and power. In L. Phillips, M. Kristiansen, M. Vehviläinen, & E. Gunnarsson (Eds.), *Knowledge and power in collaborative research: A reflexive approach* (pp. 153–170). New York: Routledge.

Nielsen, J. L., & Webb, T. W. (1999). Project work at the new reform university at Roskilde. In H. S. Olesen & J. H. Jensen (Eds.), *Project studies – A late modern university reform?* (pp. 105–120). Roskilde: Roskilde University Press.

Olesen, H. S., & Jensen, J. H. (1999). Can 'the university' be revived in 'late modernity'? In H. S. Olesen & J. H. Jensen (Eds.), *Project studies – A late modern university reform?* (pp. 9–24). Roskilde: Roskilde University Press.

Pedersen, B. E., Kaspersen, K. W., Pedersen, M. J., Christensen, N. B., & Andersen, S. M. (2012). *Sårbare unge på rette kurs? Et studie af sårbare unges møde med uddannelse i Nakskov* [Vulnerable young people on the right track? A study of vulnerable young people's encounter with education in Nakskov]. The Master Programme in Educational Studies, Roskilde University.

Searight, H. R., Ratwik, S., & Smith, T. (2010). "Hey, I can do this!" The benefits of conducting undergraduate psychology research for young adult development. *InSight: A Journal of Scholarly Teaching, 5*, 106–114.

Shiner, M. (1999). Defining peer education. *Journal of Adolescence, 22*, 555–566.

Ulriksen, L. (1999). In the crossfire of tradition and modernization. In H. S. Olesen & J. H. Jensen (Eds.), *Project studies – A late modern university reform?* (pp. 136–150). Roskilde: Roskilde University Press.

Vaarst, A. K., Østrup, A., Hansen, C., Mikkelsen, K. B., & Pedersen, M. K. (2012). *Sociale frirum i folkeskolen – myndiggørelse af unge gennem social læring* [Social spaces in school – Empowering young people through social learning). The Master Programme in Educational Studies, Roskilde University.

Winn, S. (1995). Learning by doing: Teaching research methods through student participation in a commissioned research project. *Studies in Higher Education, 20*, 203–214. doi:10.1080/03075 079512331381703.

Wulf-Andersen, T. (2012). Poetic representation: Working with dilemmas of involvement in participative social work research. *European Journal of Social Work, 15*(4), 563–580. doi:10.1 080/13691457.2012.705261.

Wulf-Andersen, T., Larsen, L., Mogensen, K., Thingstrup, S. H., Hjort-Madsen, P., & Nielsen, S. B. (2012). *Unge, uddannelse og ungdomsliv i sjællandske udkantsområder* [Young People, Education and Youth Life in Rural Parts of Zealand]. Roskilde: Roskilde University.

Wulf-Andersen, T., Mogensen, K. H., & Hjort-Madsen, P. (2013). Researching with undergraduate students: Exploring the learning potentials of undergraduate students and researchers collaborating in knowledge production. *Journal of Research Practice, 9*(2), Article M9. Retrieved from December 11, 2013, http://jrp.icaap.org/index.php/jrp/article/view/351/316.

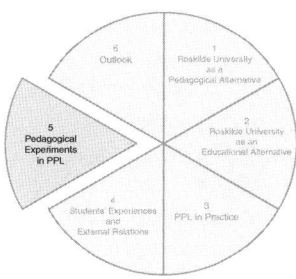

Chapter 15
Restructuring the Project Work Format: The Anthology Experiment

Søren Dupont

In Spring 2011, an experiment in renewing the PPL-format was carried out at the interdisciplinary Working Life Studies programme at Roskilde University. Subsequently, the innovative approach, known as the 'Anthology Experiment', was evaluated by the university's Pedagogical Training Unit (UniPæd; Larsen et al. 2011), and later the findings have been communicated to a Danish audience (Dupont 2012).

The objective of the Anthology Experiment was to develop and expand the framework for project work at Roskilde University through the production of anthologies compiled collectively by a number of project groups. We know from previous evaluations that students embarking on the graduate level like the challenge of new forms of project work. The one that they are familiar with involves a small group of students working under a supervisor through the entire process of the project work most often for one semester (see also Chap. 8).

The novel aspects of the Anthology Experiment were most notably its size and complexity. Normally the learning process unfolds in groups of no more than eight students. In this experiment, however, the groups were somewhat larger, totalling some 50 students working together within a dual-course structure throughout one semester. The extent of the experiment was unusual also in terms of credits. Participants in the Anthology Experiment were awarded 30 ECTS points, i.e. credit

---

S. Dupont (✉)
Roskilde University, Roskilde, Denmark
e-mail: dupont@ruc.dk

© Springer International Publishing Switzerland 2015
A.S. Andersen, S.B. Heilesen (eds.), *The Roskilde Model: Problem-Oriented Learning and Project Work*, Innovation and Change in Professional Education 12,
DOI 10.1007/978-3-319-09716-9_15

for a full semester's work. Two courses were included in the Anthology Experiment package. One course covered the theme of 'working life issues and the new forms of regulation', and the other was on 'change processes and change methods of working'. The latter was based on a 'future workshop'. Both courses dealt with theoretical as well as methodological issues. The evaluation of the courses was done by the author and two students, Cæcilia Saul and Thomas Aarup Larsen.

UniPæd collected a variety of data from the evaluation: (a) a survey among the students who participated in the experiment, (b) two focus group interviews with participating students, (c) observations, (d) a written assessment from one of the examiners, and (e) other data sources such as course catalogues, PowerPoint presentations and material from workshops (Larsen et al. 2011), and we also held a seminar for the board of study. (For context of evaluation: see Sect. 15.6).

15.1 The Anthology Experiment and Its Structure

In late January 2011, a meeting was held with the students in the first semester of the master programme in Working Life Studies. At the meeting, the basic structure of the project was presented. But something was missing: it was not quite possible to piece all the components of the experiment together under one heading until a student exclaimed: "Well, it should be called the 'Anthology Experiment'". This was a metaphor which aptly described the key features of the project.

Let us first take a look at the formal structure of the experiment. We made use of a so-called cluster structure. A cluster can be defined as: (1) a unit of teachers, students and projects, and (2) a collection of different teaching and learning methods: experiments, lectures, courses, discussions, field trips, etc. A cluster, in our sense of the word, can be visualized as shown in Fig. 15.1. The clusters are made up of participants (faculty and students) organized into a number of case groups, and these groups draw on courses, reading groups, lectures, etc.

In all, the Anthology Experiment in Working Life Studies involved four clusters, and each cluster was subdivided into a number of case groups. Each case group would work with its own sub-theme within the overarching theme of the cluster. The overall organizational structure is illustrated in Fig. 15.2.

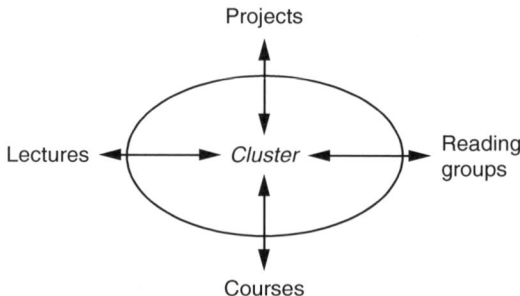

Fig. 15.1 The cluster structure

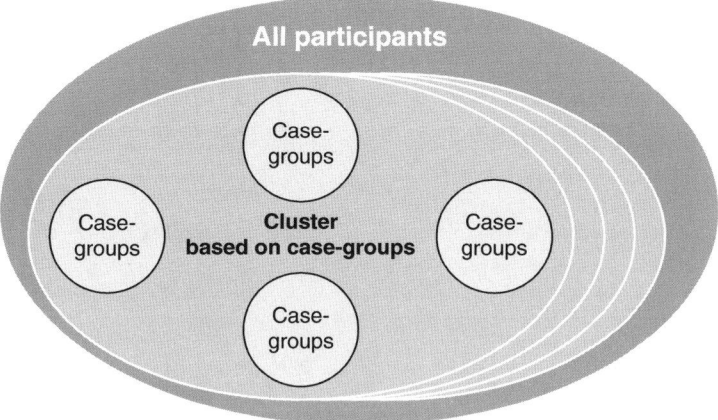

Fig. 15.2 The relationship between case-groups, clusters and all participants

'All participants' refers to the total number of students, 52 in all. Each cluster had to reflect on the theme 'change processes and involvement in change in working life', but they could do so in their own fashion in relation to the themes that they wanted to work on. The four clusters decided on the following foci of study:

1. Democratization and change processes (14 students)
2. Good work (17 students) (see Sect. 15.2.1.)
3. Sustainable innovation (14 students)
4. Professionalism in transition (7 students)

It was essential that the individual clusters and case groups should discuss their expectations as to the role of the supervisors in their work process. The ex-post evaluation shows that this requirement of the project was not fulfilled. We will expand on this problem below. The students were also invited to discuss what standards should apply for each participant as regards the amount of work to be performed, role to be played in the group, etc.

In the experiment, each cluster was responsible for an anthology, based on work produced in the case groups. Meetings were held every week in each cluster where all case groups met and discussed the work across the case groups. The supervisors frequently participated in these meetings.

15.2 The Anthology

Case groups independently developed and worked on a case under the overall theme of the cluster, but of course using different approaches and taking up different sub-themes. The structure of the anthology is illustrated in Fig. 15.3.

Fig. 15.3 The structure of the anthology

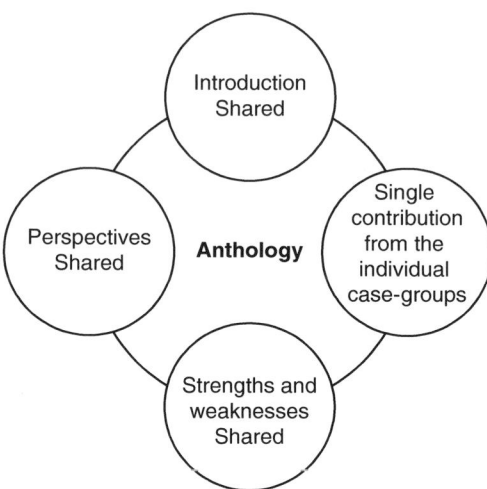

The Anthology Experiment called for cooperation on three levels: between individual students in the case groups, between case group and clusters, and between all case groups in the cluster. This meant that students had to think and act not only in relation to their own case but also across the case groups in the cluster, and on this basis collaborate in producing a shared product that went well beyond the individual project.

It was decided that the four anthologies should have a maximum of 200 pages each. It was also decided that each cluster had to establish an editorial group and decide on the mandate for this group. The editorial group would have to consider how the individual case groups could or should collaborate on the different parts of the anthology: introduction, theory, method, description of each group's contributions, etc. with the intention of achieving greater consistency in the process as well as in the final product. It was expected that throughout the process the clusters would document the work of the case groups using a log book. This documentation would also serve as a basis for the future planning of tasks, and could be used to identify how far the cluster had reached and where guidance was needed.

Since communication played a key role in the experiment, the students were asked to reflect on how knowledge could be shared within the cluster and in the case groups, with the supervisor, and with the other clusters in the course. This reflection should also prepare students for the final exam. It was recommended that the anthologies should include sections on how the clusters had worked with the different challenges from a learning perspective (see also Chap. 9).

The students worked on these requirements in different manners. Several approaches were tried out, such as keeping a log book, writing minutes from meetings, conducting a subsequent workshop, and drawing on various ICT tools to promote the sharing of knowledge, e.g. Facebook, where students regularly reached agreement, held discussions and communicated socially. Finally, some of the students participated in the evaluation as participants in a number of focus group interviews. This also offered an opportunity to reflect on their learning processes and learning outcomes.

15.2.1 A Report Example

Below is reproduced the table of content so as to illustrate the structure of the 193 pages long report (Breum et al. 2011). This is followed by some of the students' reflections.

15.2.1.1 The Anthology Table of Contents

Introduction

Common items:

> The individual and the good work
> Power and the good work
> Recognition and the good work
> Social constructionist theory and Appreciative Inquiry
> History workshop as a method

Case articles:

> Domino effect! Job Zone Ahead!
> A critical look at the job as neoliberal regulatory tool
> There you go: Being a whole person
> A case study on the work environment and job at a law firm
> Control Laboratory – The road to the meaningful evidence?

Conclusion

Reflections on the cluster process

15.2.2 Some Reflections on the Cluster Process: In the Words of the Students

The following section describes the cluster's overall experiences during the process. It is based on records of all cluster meetings and on data from a history workshop.

> It's Monday the 16th of May and we have a cluster meeting – after about two weeks of intensive writing in the small groups. The mood in the cluster is good, although everyone is exhausted and confused about how the entire anthology has to be composed and how much work this represents. Today we make a history workshop and reflect on the entire cluster process. How has the process been since we started way back in February?

A mouse in a glass cage – February
Words such as frustration, chaos, lack of information and uncertainty are used when we think back on the cluster process in February. The first task was for both students and supervisors to find their place in the process and find out what role they should assume. The supervisors were present, but their role was more one of observers than instructors since they themselves were part of this new project form. We are trying to control the process ourselves, but the mentors have been unclear. One student said: "We are like a *mouse in a glass cage*." It is a reaction that aptly illustrates the missing overview and lack of structure resulting from the new form of cluster work.

The mouse runs faster – March
March was loaded with activities. And it created frustration in the subgroups of the cluster, which we called 'case groups'. There was a strong need to get right down to work in these case groups. In March, it was generally felt that it was nice to participate in the cluster: it was a social process more than a professional one. On March 10 the supervisors presented their views on relevant theories on the subject of 'the good work', which was a great inspiration for further work in the cluster. To make the process more fluent from the start, we had chosen to have two students act as chairpersons whose job it was to prepare the meetings: agenda etc.

The mouse smells cheese – April
Our work in the case group was in full swing.

The process during this period was much like traditional project work, and supervisors pushed us to work across the case groups.

In April, we participated in the mid-term evaluation.

The evaluation resulted in a discussion about the common theory section. This caused confusion, but also provided clarification in relation to the joint work and in particular to the common section.

The mouse needs to drop everything else – May
May was characterized by an intensive period in the cluster. We were in a hurry to complete the individual cases. We were excited about how the final chapter would turn out.

After about two weeks the individual case groups finished their articles, and we met on 16 May, when we divided into two groups. The majority of the cluster participated in the history workshop. The other group, consisting of the two chairpersons, had to provide an overview of the anthology and plan how the final process could proceed.

Opportunities for better cheese – In the future
In general we are positive towards this way of working because it breaks up the routines we have acquired throughout the rest of our studies at Roskilde University. The methodology promotes a good study process, for the university students as well as for the external students. In our cluster we had a friendly and pleasant atmosphere throughout the whole process, which has created engagement in the cluster process. It is generally an interesting and inspiring way to work, and we can conclude that we generally like the cluster form and the anthology production.

Reflections on clustering
The formation of groups went too fast, and was very confusing and generally chaotic.

The entire anthology process has been one long learning process. We have had to think hard about how we could use the cluster best throughout process, we have focused on the process rather than on discussing theories, methods and so on. More discussion of the theory could potentially have provided our chapter with a stronger theoretical foundation. We have come to the conclusion that it may be an advantage if a fuller written material of guidelines and expectations is made available for future clusters.

15.3 Learning in the Experiment

The overall objective of the Anthology Experiment was to understand processes of change at the workplace and in working life. Hence, the group of supervisors in the experiment defined as overall learning objectives:

1. To establish a critical analytical perspective on change processes,
2. To gain insight into and develop experience in conducting extensive complex project work.

There were also practical objectives:

1. To create opportunities for project groups to become involved early in the process of change,
2. To provide a broader study framework,
3. To develop the students' experience of project work.

These were the immediate learning objectives and practical goals. But the supervisors also aimed at improving the study programme by creating new forms of action, new problem-solving relationships, and by enabling the students to develop and create theoretical knowledge on the basis of their own activities. The latter is not so different from what 'normally' happens in project work at Roskilde University, but the format had been changed entirely.

Special attention was given to the final examination, where the framework was to be a two-page synopsis individually produced by each student. However, all students in a cluster were also collectively responsible for their entire anthology. The anthology thus represented the requirements for the examination, but the individual exam was adapted so that the student's synopsis became the starting point. Students' synopses were not limited to their own case in the anthology. They were free to choose a theme for the synopsis from any subject area covered. To put it differently, the anthology provided the framework for the examination and the synopsis suggested the direction to be taken. The supervisors informed the students that the anthology would be assessed according to the following criteria and parameters: the amount of work, the degree of autonomy in the work, the originality of the work, reflection on the learning processes experienced during the work, and the quality of methodological and theoretical perspectives.

The entire structure of the experiment involved establishing new relationships between the individual students, between clusters of students, and between clusters and supervisors. In a more general sense, it could also be said that relations between individual and shared study elements were expanded and developed with a focus on producing new formats of project work at Roskilde University. Action research was a major aspect of the Anthology Experiment. According to Carr and Kemmis: "Action research is simply a form of self-reflective study, conducted by participants in social relationships to improve the rationality and justification of their own practices, their understanding of these practices and the situations in which the practice is carried out." (Carr and Kemmis 1985, p. 162). In their evaluation most of the students observed that some of the professional and social benefits of the Anthology Experiment had been greater than those experienced in traditional group project work at Roskilde University.

The evaluators have specifically identified two positive effects.

First of all it is important to mention the interaction between clusters and case groups and students' use of methods and tools for knowledge sharing and reflection on learning and as a consequence of that the positive effects on the social environment. The cluster structure, which organized the students into groups with a common professional commitment, led to widespread knowledge and discussion within clusters. It was a challenge for students to relate to a specific case.

Among the students it was generally accepted that The Anthology Experiment had a positive impact on their social environment. The experimental cluster structure ensured that the students have gained a better knowledge of their peers. It created continuous cooperation in the cluster. The meetings were usually held at the university, which gave the students a greater attachment to their study. The social activities and methodology seminar meant that students from one cluster got to know students from other clusters. The clusters in the experiment should probably not be too small because of the limiting impact on group dynamics and the social environment within the cluster. The majority (82 %) of students believe that the Anthology Experiment has had a positive impact on the social environment of the study compared to the standard project process at Roskilde University. Only one student believes that the experiment has had a negative impact on the social environment. 9 % believe that the experiment has not had any effect on the social environment.

Another positive effect of the experiment was that the students experienced widespread interaction between the specific knowledge of the case groups and the general knowledge of the cluster work. Cluster structure has placed the students in groups with a common professional commitment, which has led to widespread knowledge and discussion within clusters. But it has been a challenge for students to relate to the specific case and in general to the cluster theme. To quote one student: "The Anthology project is challenging: you get a little tired of the same project structure semester after semester. It's nice with something new. It creates more flexibility in the project work."

15.4 Some of the Challenges in the Project

The Anthology Experiment had its problems and challenges, but in general the students experienced a fundamental satisfaction with the experiment. 82 % of the students emphasize this in the evaluation. They also point out that they would like the format of the Anthology Experiment to be continued. The students, however, also mention a number of challenges for the future. The role of the supervisors should be redefined and outlined in more detail, because the Anthology Experiment format has a structure rather different from that of conventional projects at Roskilde University, where individual supervisors are assigned to single group projects. In

15 Restructuring the Project Work Format: The Anthology Experiment   241

the evaluation, the students state that there ought to be more focus on the academic writing of articles, because this genre differs from the writing of project reports. They also suggest that the role of the supervisors in the clusters should be oriented more towards transmitting expert knowledge, and that supervisors should focus more on providing inspiration to the students, for example through lectures on general subjects, and through various workshops and thematic seminars.

Compared to 'normal project work', the divisions between the individual and collaborative elements of projects are different. According to the students, this should be made clear at a very early stage of the experiment. The relationship between the individual, the collective parts of the anthology and the exams has been given a new framework that needs to be made explicit. As for competencies, the students agreed that the Anthology Experiment had provided them with useful skills. They also state that it is important to work more closely with the relationship between the project process and the academic depth. Critical comments and discussions of the projects should be accorded more importance.

On a positive note, one student states:

> The cooperation between different cases in a comprehensive anthology has meant that we can have extensive discussions of our material, and we feel that our work is more relevant to society than if we had dealt with single cases as we normally do in our project work (student comment in the questionnaire).

The examiner interviewed also gives a positive remark:

> In the clusters, they have worked with material from the case groups across cases and gained a better understanding of the subject. In the exam, they were able to discuss how various other methods and theories might have been used in addition to those they had used in their own case groups, and they could reflect on what other theories and methods would have meant for their case. They have been able to make collective conclusions concerning interdisciplinary issues. (external examiner's comment in the questionnaire).

From the 2012 autumn semester, the experiment, now called 'Anthology Learning' has been institutionalized in the Working Life Studies programme. With the subject title 'Working life in changing perspectives', it is now offered in the first semester of the master programme.

15.5 The Benefit of the Experiment

The Anthology Experiment is one of many experiments with project work at Roskilde University. In this book, we have dealt with two types of experiments. In Chap. 14, we discussed how project work could be developed by involving students in research projects. In this experiment, the project group was maintained as the basic study unit. At the same time, students were engaged in a larger community of peers from other project groups and researchers. The benefits of this experiment included: (a) the supervisors were given more time to guide the students because the time they spent contributed to their own research, (b) the students had the opportunity to work directly with researchers, (c) the students had easy access to the empirical field, and (d) they were part of a collective professional relationship with researchers and fellow students.

Because the expected output from project work is changed, the Anthology Experiment is a radical departure from current project work at Roskilde University (as outlined in Chap. 10). The experiment uses a well-known publishing format from research, namely the anthology form, which usually focuses on a specific research topic and includes contributions from various researchers. In the Anthology Experiment, the case groups may be viewed as 'research units' that produce the contributions to the anthology. The students are jointly responsible for writing a thematically focused introduction to the anthology, which shows how the contributions from each case group are relevant to the common theme.

This requires that students and supervisors in the cluster conduct a professional dialogue between the individual case groups. The complexity of the experiment offered challenges, both for students and supervisors. The organization was complex, the written product changed from project to article format, the students had to concentrate on working in their own case group as well as in the cluster, and the form of exam was radically changed in that students had to explain their case project, the total anthology as well as their synopsis, which could be angled across multiple case projects.

The two experiments mentioned above were selected for the present book because of their exemplary value. They focus on a fundamental problem in project work: how to establish broader professional communities that engage researchers and students in a common enterprise which exceeds the individual project groups as a framework for the students' work. In the students' normal project work, this objective is not very easily achieved, because such project groups tend to be occupied with their own challenges and also because courses are rarely organized as joint and mutually binding enterprises. Both types of experiments make heavy demands on students as well as supervisors. At the same time, the two experiments reveal important opportunities to enhance students' learning results. The construction of broad learning communities of students and tutors points back to some of the original visions of Roskilde University and also forward to future possibilities.

We shall let one of the students conclude this chapter:

> We have worked on a common theme and that is why the work of the case has included, not a problem formulation as normal, but a problem formulation as a much wider issue. It has been a relief and saved us time. In addition, while we were assembling the various cases into a comprehensive anthology we were able to discuss our material in a much deeper way and our work feels more relevant to society than if we had dealt with a single case.

15.6 Addendum

Context of evaluation The material for evaluation consisted of five data sources:

- A survey among the students who participated in the experiment,
- Two focus group interviews with students who participated in the experiment,
- Observational studies,

15 Restructuring the Project Work Format: The Anthology Experiment

- A written assessment from one of the examiners,
- Other data sources such as course catalogs, power points and material from a 'future workshop'.

The data sources are briefly described in the following sections.

Questionnaire survey Questionnaire data were collected during the period 26 July 2011 to 10 August 2011. It was an electronic questionnaire, and the students were invited in an email. All students who participated in the experiment were invited to participate in the survey. In the collection period two reminders were sent to students, who had not completed the questionnaire.

Focus group interviews with students who participated in the experiment Interview data were collected in two focus group interviews conducted May 25, 2011. The groups contained six and three participants. All students were invited to participate, and UniPæd briefly informed the students about the topic and purpose of the interviews. The groups represented two different anthology groups and the interviews turned out very differently: One focus group was very positive, and the other proposed several critical elements for discussion.

Observational studies Observations were carried out in connection with the beginning of the experiment. Later UniPæd participated in a day of evaluation for all four anthology groups.

Evaluation form for examiners The examiners who rated the oral exams in the experiment received a short questionnaire with open questions about the examiners' assessment of the experiment. One of three examiners returned a response.

Other material The evaluators had material sent from both students and teachers including course catalogs for the two courses and also materials from a 'future workshop'.

The evaluation process and its execution Based on the fully printed focus group interview, we developed a questionnaire that was sent to all participants in the experiment.

For the written evaluation, the evaluators had knowledge from all the kinds of data material that was collected. From the beginning of the experiment we had a feeling that the experiment might be an inspiration for developing project pedagogy at Roskilde University.

The evaluators would like to point out that they have chosen to interpret the empirical data using a methodological mix between a phenomenological and a grounded approach.

This methodological mix was chosen because the evaluators did not want to organize the survey around possible preconceptions and what they already knew about the study and the study design.

References

Breum, E. F. H., Christiansen, J. C., Jensen, J. F., Andreasen, J. P. M., Hansen, M. L. M., Halling, M. N. A. N., & Scheller, V. K. (2011). *På vej mod det gode arbejde?* [Towards' the good work'?]. Arbejdslivstudier: Roskilde University.

Carr, W., & Kemmis, S. (1985). *Becoming critical: Education, knowledge and action research.* London: Fade Press.

Dupont, S. (2012). *Nyudvikling af projektarbejdsformen på RUC – beskrivelse og analyse af et eksperiment: "Antologieksperimentet"* [Renewing the project work form at Roskilde University – Description and analysis of an experiment: "The anthology experiment]. *Dansk Universitetspædagogisk Tidsskrift, 7*(12), 23–35.

Larsen, T. A., Saul, C., & Dupont, S. (2011). *Evaluering af Antologieksperimentet – En alternativ projektarbejdsform* [Evaluation of the anthology experiment – An alternative form of project work]. Roskilde: Roskilde University, UniPæd. Retrieved May 23, 2014 from http://www.ruc.dk/fileadmin/assets/paes/Unipaed/Evaluering_af_Antologieksperimentet_paa_Arbejdslivsstudier_Ny_2.pdf.

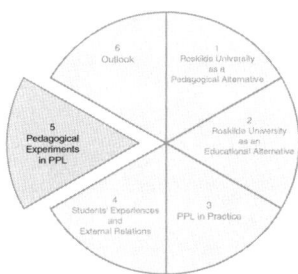

Chapter 16
Supporting Project Work with Information Technology

Simon B. Heilesen

Roskilde University was founded at the dawn of the digital revolution. Hence, concepts of how to organize and carry out problem-oriented group work, how to integrate student project work in the physical framework of the campus, and how to support students by means of technology all originated at a time when physical presence was a sine qua non, and when campus-wide television, stencil machines and photocopiers were cutting edge technologies, the availability of which on campus was a major attraction for students.

Like so many other institutions, Roskilde University has had to adapt to the new realities brought about by the rapid developments in information and communication technology (ICT). ICT looms large in contemporary education, and in fact competence in using ICT effectively in academic work is now a required skill at the bachelor level (see Sect. 8.3).

Focusing more narrowly on project work, on the whole ICT tools have proven to be helpful in supporting and developing the work forms on which Roskilde University problem-oriented project work is based. However, in implementing and integrating the new technologies in academic practices, a number of challenges have had to be addressed. This chapter discusses four of these challenges: providing

S.B. Heilesen (✉)
Roskilde University, Roskilde, Denmark
e-mail: simonhei@ruc.dk

a framework for learning activities, directing student use of ICT, supervising and doing project work online, and exploiting the potentials of ICT in problem-oriented group work.

16.1 Providing a Framework

Roskilde University does have a few student residences, but it was never a truly residential university. In fact, a large number of students live in the Copenhagen area, commuting the 20 odd miles to the Trekroner campus in the eastern part of Roskilde. Thus a fundamental challenge consists in persuading the students to attend not only for classes, but also for doing project work together. The architectural and organizational designs of the campus are meant to encourage physical presence. As for the organizational design, studies at bachelor level are organized into 'houses' with specially assigned faculty and numerous shared activities requiring physical presence and fostering a sense of mutual responsibility (see also Sect. 6.5.3).

With regard to the physical space, a good number of buildings, in addition to housing classrooms, provide a kitchen, showers, one or more recreational spaces, various technologies to support studies (computers, printers, scanners, fast Wi-Fi, etc.), and several group rooms. The basic design of Roskilde University learning spaces has changed relatively little over the years (see Fig. 12.1). However, there have been a few experiments in designing classrooms that combine advanced use of ICT with highly flexible furnishing to create a learning space of the future (see Sect. 16.5).

Originally, each student group would have a room at its disposal and would work on its projects next door to faculty members in a setup reminiscent of a master-apprentice relationship. As the student population continued to grow, however, rooms had to be shared between groups, and in recent years they have been in short supply. Crowding has certainly contributed to student groups opting to meet away from campus, but in fact there has always been a tendency to meet closer to home, at least some of the time.

Enter ICT, and patterns started to change, some problems being addressed, new complications being added. Most importantly, internetworking has provided alternatives to meeting physically in an office or a group room. Fast on-campus networks combined with a 'plug'n study' design for easy access and a single sign-on system have enabled student groups to access tools for collaboration, search for information and print literally anywhere on campus – in the library, in vacant classrooms, hallways, kitchens and canteens, in new 'collaboration booths' being set up in some environments (see Fig. 16.1), and even outdoors, weather permitting. Project archives, literature, and tools for writing and data processing being online, a semi-permanent dedicated physical space is no longer required, and this new flexibility has remedied the shortage of work spaces and lessened the need to be physically close to the supervisor, who is now accessible by e-mail, chat, etc. at almost any time.

Fig. 16.1 Collaboration booths in Building 30 (Photo Jan M. Larsen)

Off-campus internetworking has added a virtual dimension to group work. It involves remote access to resources on campus, notably the library and various administrative services, as well as a virtual learning environment for sharing, collaborating and documenting within the group and for communicating with the supervisor and with the companies, organizations and individuals involved in the problem that is being explored in the project.

These new circumstances reflect a more general development in academic working conditions. Everywhere, virtual learning environments are transforming education from being institution-centred to being student-centred. An early model of this transformation was proposed by Oblinger and Maruyama (1996) nearly a decade before the technical development of the Internet, with increased bandwidth, new multimedia services, and social software, started reshaping patterns of education, and indeed general communication, in earnest. In this new model of distributed learning environments, largely based on ICT use, the student is at the centre of all learning activities, and draws on various resources as required – the library, formal classes, the supervisor, other students, the Internet, other institutions, and eventually the whole wired world. The student assumes a more active role in a new world of 'Learning 2.0' (Downes 2005) where he or she becomes a contributor to learning and a content provider of knowledge, individually or as a member of a networked community.

Both the above-mentioned learner-centred model and Learning 2.0 imply a measure of technological determinism. However, adopting a deterministic view is simplistic and it ignores the fact that PPL and similar participant-directed approaches to learning predate the technological innovations by decades. The changes in education still unfolding quite rapidly are not driven by technology, but are rather being facilitated by it. Thus, arguably, the Roskilde Model of problem-oriented project work carried out by student groups always has been learner-centred, requiring the students to take charge of researching and reflecting on phenomena that they themselves have identified as worth exploring. In terms of intellectual and economic resources it has always been a costly approach. To a large extent it has also depended on physical meetings. ICT has changed the conditions both for the framing of collaborative group work and for many of the work processes, disembedding them in space and time, thus making it possible to realize the potentials of this type of education more fully than was practicable before – and by extension making it more generally attractive.

Learner-centered, in the sense of the individual student controlling activities, however, is not synonymous with participant-directed, a concept denoting close collaboration not only among students exploring a problem, but also between student group and supervisor. Of course the latter kind of collaboration is likely to occur in net-based as well as physical environments. But the new models of net-based learning have a potential for eroding conventional authority (New Media Consortium 2013). Guidance is no longer limited to the institution and to discussions with a supervisor. It may be sought anywhere in cyberspace from experts and peers. A further effect of the more fluid net-based organization of learning is an emphasis on individualized learning ("as and when I need it"), running somewhat contrary to the ideals of the Roskilde Model. Educational institutions everywhere will have to learn to deal with the new situation. One aspect of this involves deciding whether and how to direct student use of technology, as will be discussed below.

16.2 Directing the Students

Under this heading two issues will be addressed. Firstly, and related to the previous section in that it provides a framework, there is the selection of software that the university makes available to the students, and the extent to which it is adopted. Secondly, there is the question of how to involve students in academic uses of ICT. A related issue, how to supervise students online, will be discussed under a separate heading.

Within the last decade, Internet access has become fast and easily affordable, and there has been a proliferation of software systems facilitating cooperation and collaboration in virtual environments. It has been years since learning management systems were declared defunct (Weller 2007) to be replaced by teacher-directed 'loosely coupled teaching' (Leslie 2007). Still, standard systems provided by the institution remain the norm. Two obvious reasons for this are that many educators are not ready by themselves to compile and promote a toolbox of Web 2.0 apps, and that the complete splitting up of teaching tools would result in, if not chaos, then at least a multitude of complex and heterogeneous learning environments, and quite likely the exclusion of the less technologically able students (for a telling example, see Siemens 2005). A further and the most important reason is that the standard systems provide stability, as will be discussed below.

Thus, although more advanced software is readily available, Roskilde University insists on offering standard tools for project work (originally BSCW™, now being replaced by Mahara™ and Sharepoint™) in addition to a learning management system (Moodle™). However, the university does not insist that all project groups keep to one of these tools. In fact there are few regulations concerning use other than that sensitive data must be stored on a university server, as required by law. Still, the systems provide proper security in terms of access control and frequent back-ups, they offer equal opportunities to all students, and they do provide digital uniformity for the students who typically frequent at least three different learning environments during their studies at the university (a bachelor house and two departments for their master-level studies).

The introduction of standard tools has been quite successful. As yet there are no reliable data on the use of the two new systems. But data over an extended period of time on the use of the old BSCW™ system show that the number of unique users roughly equalled the size of the student population, and that about half of the student population were regular users (Heilesen 2009).

Standard systems are but one aspect of the larger question of academic digital acculturation. The younger generations, the so-called digital natives (Prensky 2001), apparently seem at ease with the pace of technological innovation as well as with navigating the enormous number of products available. This has contributed to the notion that students are completely able to integrate technology into their studies. Mounting evidence suggests that this is a misconception (e.g. Nordkvelle 2011; Smith 2012; Thompson 2013). Young people may indeed be masters of social media, net-based services, gaming, etc., and have probably been exposed to various kinds of e-learning software at school. When they enter the university, however, they are met with the requirements of science, mostly unfamiliar to them, to work systematically and methodically, to document their work, and to be critical of the phenomena they observe. At Roskilde University, furthermore, they are introduced to an unaccustomed type of problem-oriented learning.

With regard to the mutual interest of faculty and students in furthering quality in academic work, it is necessary to strike a balance between bottom-up inventiveness and top-down enforcement of standards. On the one hand, much can be learnt from the students about new software and innovative ways of using technologies. Creativity should be encouraged, and established practices should be reviewed critically. On the other hand, the students must learn the tools of the trade, and to this end creativity has to be kept in check. Responsible handling of sensitive information such as recordings and transcripts of interviews has already been mentioned.

Another example briefly touched upon earlier is searching for and evaluating information. In conventional project work this was not so much of a problem, since available resources were limited to books and journals in libraries and various written documentation in the relevant companies and institutions, and the use of any of this was subject to approval by the supervisor. In the information age, there is virtually no limit to the amount of resources readily and immediately available, and one's own supervisor is not necessarily the only authority who can be consulted. The downside of the learner-centred world of limitless information is having to cope with opaqueness. Thus, efforts are made by the university to teach project groups about aspects of the academic use of ICT, such as how to conduct information searches using library databases and specialized search tools rather than relying on googling, how to distinguish types of publications, and how to avoid plagiarism in a world of remixing.

As to faculty members, efforts are being made across the university to help them improve the skills required for tutoring in a digital world. If the academic staff are 'digital immigrants', not at ease with accessing and assessing the ever-increasing masses of information, project groups may well seek out authority elsewhere, reducing formal tutoring to questions of process and formalities.

16.3 Supervising and Conducting Project Work Online

Conventionally, student project groups have been supervised at regular meetings throughout the term. They still are, even though e.g. e-mail and Skype™ have become useful supplements for planning or following up on meetings, and for brief online dialogues between face-to-face meetings.

As yet, systematic online supervision does not occur much in the regular academic programmes. But it has long been practised in open education at Roskilde University. Studies have been made of online practices in two programmes, the *Master of Computer-mediated Communication* offered at Roskilde University from 2000 to 2006 (e.g. Cheesman and Heilesen 2001; Jensen and Heilesen 2005), and the *Master of IT and Learning* currently offered by Roskilde University in collaboration with three other institutions (e.g. Andreasen and Nielsen 2013). Both programmes offer studies in various professional uses of ICT, and therefore the students may be assumed to be particularly motivated for using technology. Both programmes offer blended learning in the form of monthly or bimonthly face-to-face weekend seminars interspersed with periods of doing assignments and working on a project in a virtual environment. Communication in the virtual environment mostly involves file sharing, compiling resources, discussions in forums, chat and IP telephone conversations.

Supervising project work online involves many of the same roles as in conventional supervision; according to circumstances the supervisor may act as challenger, coach, evaluator, mediator, mentor, moderator and organizer. The main difference between physical and virtual presence is that every action becomes extremely visible, and whatever is said remains etched in bits permanently. A high profile – meaning frequent online presence – is necessary, because silence in an online environment is normally interpreted as absence. However, supervisor presence has to be balanced to avoid dictating the progress of work. Teachers as well as students have to adopt simpler forms of communicating than are the norm in the physical world (see Fig. 16.2). Every statement has to be considered carefully to avoid ambiguity, and comments and assignments should be focused rather narrowly because parallel activities are difficult to manage online. In the virtual environment, complexity fosters uncertainty and misunderstandings. All in all, supervising online requires

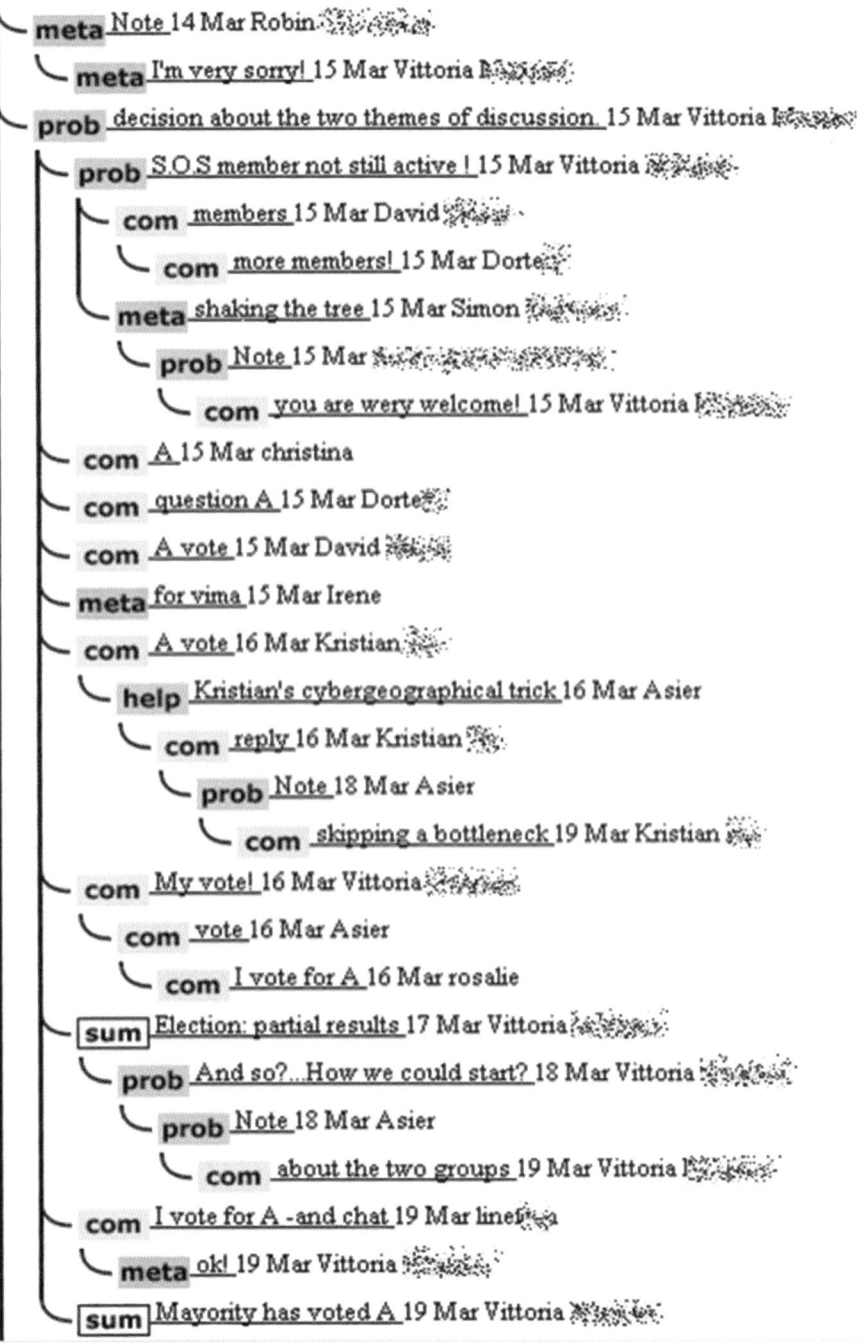

Fig. 16.2 A complexity issue. In this 1-week assignment, a group of students working completely online were given the choice of two subjects. The discussion thread illustrates the ensuing discussion: It took 5 days just for the group to agree on what subject to work on

modification of practices. It is time-consuming, and in a Danish culture of relative privacy in choice of teaching methods, it pushes the limits of many faculty members to be visible to everyone online. Taken in a positive sense, online supervision of project work affords peer supervision, opening for fruitful discussions of pedagogy in an ever developing community of practice.

Transparency of course also extends to the student group. Individual activity becomes highly visible. Patterns of behaviour such as self-assertion, fussiness, leadership, helpfulness, constructive and obstructive attitudes all become accentuated; the nature and quality of individual contributions are recorded permanently, and it becomes difficult to underperform and still remain a respected member of the group. In conventional group project work, personal merits and demerits matter quite significantly for the collective performance of the group, but problems are rarely brought to the attention of the supervisor before they become critical (see also Sect. 8.4.3). In the net-based environment, it is possible for group members as well as supervisor at any time to help in social moderation or to suggest adjustments to improve performance, and group members tend to explain carefully any deviant behaviour such as prolonged absence from the virtual space.

On-campus experiments with introducing mandatory online group work on course assignments have yielded exactly the same response as has been found in online work in the master programmes (Heilesen and Josephsen 2008): Students accept online work only if it makes sense, and it makes sense only when it does not foster complexity and involve extra work. Thus, in both settings the physical meeting has remained important for socializing, building trust, making decisions and for having complex discussions. Once work moves online it is beset with various challenges that drain attention from the core tasks.

Perhaps the most important of these challenges is uncertainty. It is fostered by loneliness in the virtual space when there is no or slow response to your postings, when group members are infrequently online, or when you are not clear about what has been agreed on, and who is supposed to act. In asynchronous environments such problems loom so prominently that students usually decide to meet physically if at all possible or to use video conferencing or IP telephony to get things moving. Tasks that have to remain online such as posting and editing documents may be helped along by developing a culture of virtual social grooming, i.e. posting small talk regularly and making sure to acknowledge the postings of others.

Pacing group project work, which in fact tends to be quite difficult also for groups working in physical space, becomes no less so in virtual space. In the master programmes, various strategies have been adopted by the students. One of these strategies has been for a group to elect a 'whip' to be in charge of all coordination of a particular task or of a phase or time slot in the project work (see Fig. 16.3). Another has been for the group to create milestones to be reached by the group to ensure that the course deadline be met. In extreme cases this has developed into a strict regimen rather at odds with the fundamental ideal quality of net-based work of being independent of time and place.

Another strategy for ensuring progress in online group work has been for the students to specialize in particular functions, e.g. acting as coordinator, writer,

	Demokrati - eksamen Kun for os!	3		ulrikm	2001-06-11	
	Uge 20 Yes!!!	15		ulrikm	2001-05-21	
	Aflevering 21.05.01	2		ulrikm	2001-05-21	
	Uge 19	13		ege	2001-05-15	
	Uge 18 Ha, jeg kom først - du er en meget barnlig pige. A.	3		klniel	2001-05-04	
	Site-design Dialogen omkring det konkrete produkt, holdes i denne mappe - det gør det lettere at samle op til sidst.	4		oas	2001-05-02	
	Gamle dokumenter	9		knoth	2001-05-01	
	Uge 17	13		oas	2001-04-30	
	uge 16	2		klniel	2001-04-22	
	Uge 15	4		knoth	2001-04-12	
	Uge 14	2		knoth	2001-04-09	
	Uge 11	5		ulrikm	2001-03-18	
	Uge 10	3		oas	2001-03-12	

Fig. 16.3 Project work folder. Working mostly online, this group of students structured its work into 'weeks', each week having a 'whip' to direct and document the work

editor, researcher, librarian, etc. Thus the work style tends to become cooperative (divided up into tasks and distributed) rather than collaborative (collectively negotiated). Similar specialization occurs in conventional project work, even though it is not as evident to the observer, and in the online master programmes it has not been discouraged. But the supervisors have advised the students regularly to rotate roles, so that everyone would become involved in all aspects and stages of project work.

To sum up: present knowledge about the impact on group project work of moving from a physical to a virtual environment is rather fragmentary, and is mostly based on observations of open education programmes that are not representative of Roskilde University education in general. What we do see is that the transition from one environment to the other requires some modifications of practice. We also observe that students are quite critical of certain features of the virtual environment, and that they are more likely to augment physical work space than to migrate altogether into virtual learning environments. However, something is to be gained from an increasingly deliberate and systematic use of digital tools, and in the last section of this chapter we will consider recent initiatives to further such a development.

16.4 Supporting Project Work with ICT

Initiatives are ongoing at Roskilde University to compile guides (toolboxes) to help students find useful digital tools. The development of these toolboxes is participatory: software is evaluated for safety and functionality by professional staff, but student experiences with the products are solicited, and the ambition is to compile a library of exemplary cases.

Tools can be divided into general tools for group work, and tools relevant in particular phases of the project life-cycle, which consists of group formation, project design, work phase and reporting. In the present context, a detailed review would be too technical, and since new tools are being marketed continually, it would not be entirely meaningful either. However, a broad characterization of potential tools serves to illustrate how group project work may be supported by ICT; and we will conclude this chapter with a concrete example.

General tools used throughout the project life-cycle meet the needs for

- Archiving and sharing information,
- Communicating,
- Documenting.

As mentioned earlier, Roskilde University offers various tools for all three purposes: collaboration systems, e-mail, desktop video conferencing, library databases and reference tools. This basic package is in fact adequate for supporting group work in physical as well as blended and purely online environments (see Fig. 16.4). It is of course realized that some of the products are entirely out of step with student

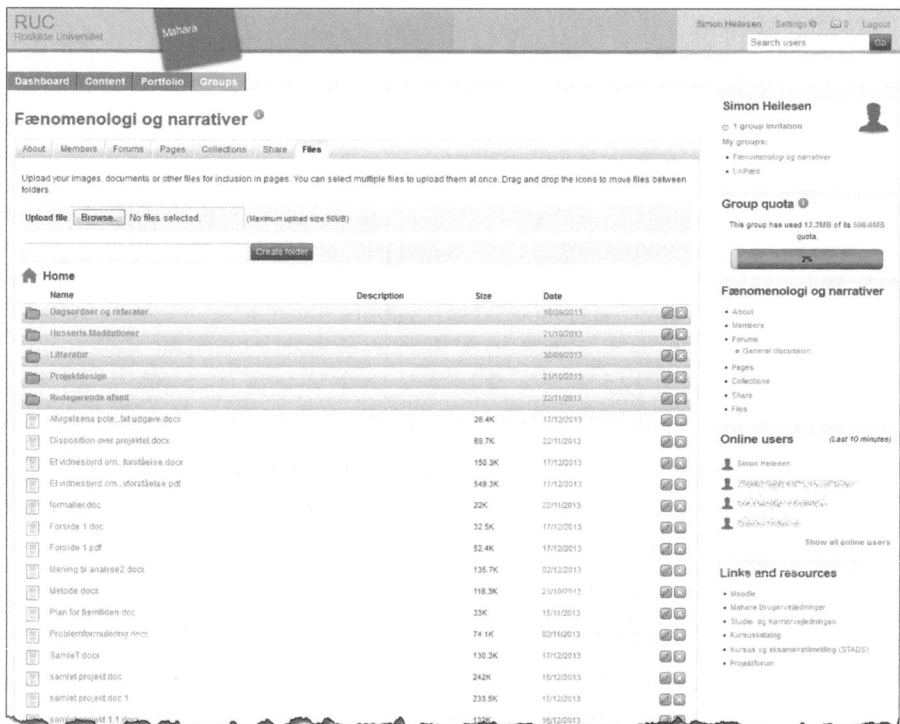

Fig. 16.4 Mahara™ meets most typical project work needs. There are fora for communicating in-group, web pages for informing about the project, and a file archive for documenting activities. This archive is topical, being divided into folders for "agendas and minutes", "literature", "project design", two subjects to be dealt with in-depth, and quite many parts of the project that have just been uploaded to the root section

preferences for apps and Web 2.0 applications. But considerations of legal requirements, safety, ownership of data, and continuity of service dictate that the platforms should be offered, and that the students should be encouraged to use them.

Tools for particular phases of group work or particular tasks may be viewed as additions to the basic framework. Usage is not regulated by the university beyond demanding that it must be legal, and the students are encouraged to share their knowledge of relevant software and innovative practices. A brief list of current usages will provide an idea of the multiplicity of options.

Group formation is a phase requiring students to identify group members and negotiate the basic framework of the project. To supplement a portfolio system, which is now being implemented as a campus-wide tool, social network services are widely used. Sometimes a shared profile (a 'group') is established in the group formation process, and it may remain a medium of communication for the project group members as well as a showcase for the project throughout the semester.

The design phase entails negotiating in detail a subject for project work, preparing a preliminary project plan, defining a research question and identifying a suitable supervisor. Software that comes in handy at this stage includes electronic calendars and meeting planners, tools for structuring and visualizing ideas (outlining, mind-mapping, check-listing), and tools for systematizing information (spreadsheets, databases, wikis).

The work phase ideally draws on the suite of standard systems provided by the university, and also on an office package, and on special tools and software for recording and transcribing audio-visual data, for gathering, systematizing and analyzing quantitative and qualitative data, etc.

Finally, in the reporting phase of completing the written report and preparing for an oral exam, software for visualizing and presenting information and for desktop publishing will be needed. Recently introduced requirements for submitting written reflections on the learning process and the outcomes of the completed project should go not only into the report, but also into the student's individual portfolio, helping him or her to find coherence in a course of studies that easily may be conceived of as fragmentary, as one project follows another.

Having a wealth of tools at one's disposal, as outlined above, can be helpful, but also problematic. Just as the notion of 'loosely coupled teaching' was shown earlier to be challenging for faculty, so is creating a bricolage of software for 'loosely coupled learning'. Students come together with widely different technological skills and software preferences. Agreeing on a technical platform may be time-consuming and distracting at a particularly intense phase of project work, and it may even exclude digital novices from the community. It can be argued that choosing the right digital tools for carrying out a task has become a skill high in demand in the labour market. Yet much can be said in favour of a moderately conservative approach distinguishing, as we do at Roskilde University, between 'need to have' (standard tools being provided by the university) and a 'nice to have' (optional cutting-edge software agreed upon within a group). The former provides the stability and accessibility that the university is obliged to offer. The latter provides innovative ideas and usages some of which will eventually be worked into the standard systems (being open source) or at least become recommended practice.

With all this said, however, it should be acknowledged that most student groups are perfectly capable of working out for themselves what tools to use. Therefore, let us conclude this overview of group work tools with a concrete example of a bachelor thesis project in Journalism carried out by five female students in the autumn of 2013. As part of a report also comprising chapters on theory, methods, and reflections on communication, style, and work process, each group member had to write one long or two short news stories on the conflict in Syria. All group members lived in Copenhagen and met at home, at libraries, and at the university for sessions with the supervisor.

As basic tools, the group used Mendeley™ for compiling and sharing references and Google Drive™ for sharing and reviewing individual work, for collaborative writing of joint sections of the report, and for preparing for group and supervisor meetings. For organizing the many shared documents, however, the group members opted for a hierarchy of Dropbox™ folders (for e.g. theory, example articles, literature summaries, chapters, minutes, individual stories, etc.). Literature searches were conducted in various library databases and in the Danish news media archive Infomedia (http://www.infomedia.dk/). Interviews were arranged by e-mail and by telephone. Social media were used for communicating in-group and for updating friends and relatives. Thus, the students established a Facebook-group at the start of the project, using it as a communication forum. Postings in other social media, notably Instagram™ (see Fig. 16.5), were meant to share with others some of the good

Fig. 16.5 Two Instagram-images of project work. On the *left*: a project meeting described with the keywords: project- cosiness, lentil pie, red wine, toffees, guilty pleasures, peaceful, peace journalism. On the *right*: a group member meeting an academic celebrity. The caption reads "Honoured to be interviewing peace researcher Jan Øberg. For my article on Geneva 2 and Syria. Yes, it can be fun, even if it is serious". The posting drew several 'likes' and comments such as "Cool. You Rock :-)* b^ =D>" and "Your own little Helle/Obama moment" (referring to a Danish prime minister making a selfie with the US-President)

moments in project work – illustrating, it would seem, that project group work becomes a way of life, and that no clear distinctions are made between work and leisure, between public and private. Working on a project is an important part of the student's identity.

16.5 Addendum

The *Roskilde University Collaboratory* was established in late 2011 in the Department of Psychology and Educational Studies. It has been funded in part by the Danish Building and Property Agency as one of a handful of experiments in designing classrooms of the future (Schmidt et al. 2013). The concept has been to create a learning space that (a) can accommodate lectures, seminars and group work with little or no rearrangement, (b) provides easy access to computing and Internet resources, and (c) is modular in its design so that electronic devices can be replaced easily and at a relatively low cost (Heilesen 2012). The present Collaboratory, which is the second version, can hold some 25 students without being crowded, but the design as such may be scaled considerably (see Fig. 16.6. For additional images of recent Roskilde University learning spaces, see: http://www.flickr.com/photos/15641261@N08/sets/72157629509096615/).

Fig. 16.6 The Roskilde University Collaboratory (Author's photo)

Key features of the Roskilde University Collaboratory design are:

Mobility All furniture is light and on wheels. The tables are trapezoid in shape, allowing for hexagonal, arrow-shaped, semi-circular, horseshoe, and various large or small asymmetrical arrangements. In addition to office chairs, a dozen Steelcase™ Node chairs facilitate the formation of informal break-out groups. Half a dozen tall, narrow whiteboards with flip-over mounts serve as movable partitions as well as writing surfaces for groups working at small tables, and they can easily be rolled out of the room, if a group goes somewhere else for a break-out session.

Ergonomics The Collaboratory has no fixed focus of attention. The lectern is a trolley that can be placed anywhere. The room is fitted with two built-in computers that can be operated with a wireless keyboard and a mouse from the lectern or indeed from any flat surface in the room. Chairs and tables can be moved easily to provide comfortable seating and a better view of the whiteboards, or to open up space for physical activity anywhere in the room. Two large wall-mounted whiteboards can be used for writing on and for projecting images, and a glass wall running almost the entire length of the room provides additional writing surfaces.

Simple working procedures The built-in computers are turned on at the push of a button on one of the control panels placed at either end of the room. USB sockets have been built into the wall next to the control panels to encourage users to plug in a USB key with their presentations and documents, or to access them in the cloud, rather than going through the trouble of setting up and turning on a computer and logging on to a (possibly foreign) network. The original design, however, by popular demand has had to be modified so that students and teachers now may plug in their own laptops when they are making a presentation.

Multitasking The room has two interactive projectors that can display either two different computer screens or mirror one another, allowing students at the back of the room a better view. Separate projections allow the teacher to operate two presentations simultaneously, and they are also suitable for group work in large groups. Each of the projectors is connected to an Apple TV (running on a local network), so that they can display screens from tablets operated from anywhere in the room (lately, however, software solutions such as AirServer™ has rendered the Apple TV installation somewhat obsolete). Again, the user can shift between PC mode and tablet mode simply by pressing a button on the one of the two control panels in the room. With the help of software, the two projectors also serve as interactive whiteboards, albeit with rather simple features such as annotating projected images, writing on a clean whiteboard, saving projected images, and navigating webpages and presentations.

The Collaboratory has served as a prototype for teaching and performing on-campus group work in an ICT-enhanced setting. Some of its features have already been adopted when renovating other classrooms, and some of the student work patterns observed have provided inspiration for the design of the 'collaboration booths' mentioned earlier, where a group of students can collaborate on shared documents using a projection or a monitor image as a frame of reference (see Fig. 16.1).

References

Andreasen, L. B., & Nielsen, J. L. (2013). Educational designs supporting student engagement through networked project studies. In P. Blessinger & L. Wankel (Eds.), *Increasing student engagement and retention using mobile applications: Smartphones, Skype and Texting technologies*. Bingley: Emerald Group.

Cheesman, R., & Heilesen, S. B. (2001). Using CSCW for problem-oriented teaching and learning in a net environment. In P. Dillenbourg, A. Eurelings, & K. Hakkarainen (Eds.), *European perspectives on computer-supported collaborative learning. Proceedings of the first European conference on computer-supported collaborative learning* (pp. 708–709). Maastricht: University of Maastricht. Retrieved June 10, 2013, from http://diggy.ruc.dk/handle/1800/815.

Downes, S. (2005, October). E-learning 2.0. *eLearn Magazine*. Retrieved September 4, 2013, from http://elearnmag.acm.org/featured.cfm?aid=1104968

Heilesen, S. (2009). The case of Roskilde University e-services. In A. Scupola (Ed.), *Cases on managing e-services* (pp. 189–203). Hershey/New York: Information Science Reference.

Heilesen, S. (2012). *Kollaboratoriet på Roskilde Universitet: Kort rapport til Bygningsstyrelsen, April 2012* [The Collaboratory at Roskilde University: Brief report to the Building and Property Agency, April 2012]. Roskilde: Roskilde University. Retrieved November 28, 2013, from http://rudar.ruc.dk/handle/1800/7458

Heilesen, S. B., & Josephsen, J. (2008). E-learning: Between augmentation and disruption? *Computers and Education, 50*, 525–534.

Jensen, S. S., & Heilesen, S. B. (2005). Time, place and identity in project work on the net. In T. S. Roberts (Ed.), *Computer-supported collaborative learning in higher education* (pp. 51–69). Hershey/London/Melbourne/Singapore: Idea Group.

Leslie, S. (2007). *Your favourite "Loosely Coupled Teaching" example?* Retrieved September 23, 2013, from http://www.edtechpost.ca/wordpress/2007/10/29/best-loosely-coupled-teaching-examples/

New Media Consortium. (2013). *Horizon report 2013 higher education edition*. Retrieved September 23, 2013, from http://www.nmc.org/pdf/2013-horizon-report-HE.pdf

Nordkvelle, Y. T. (2011). Mythbusting "the Digital Native". In H. Ruokamo, M. Eriksson, L. Pekkala, & H. Vuojärvi (Eds.), *Social media in the middle of nowhere – NBE 2011 conference* (pp. 23–36). Salla: University of Lapland.

Oblinger, D. G., & Maruyama, M. K. (1996). *Distributed learning*. CAUSE Professional Paper Series # 14. Boulder: CAUSE.

Prensky, M. (2001). Digital natives, digital immigrants. *On the Horizon, 9*(5), 1–6.

Schmidt, C., Kjær, M. R., & Mortensen, K. B. (Eds.). (2013). *Campusudvikling – metoder og proces* [Campus development – methods and process] (in Danish and English). Valby: Bygningsstyrelsen [the Building and Property Agency].

Siemens, G. (2005, December 7). *When learning goes underground…* (Weblog entry). Retrieved September 27, 2013, from http://www.connectivism.ca/?paged=11

Smith, E. E. (2012). The digital native debate in higher education: A comparative analysis of recent literature. *Canadian Journal of Learning and Technology, 38*(3).

Thompson, P. (2013). The digital natives as learners: Technology use patterns and approaches to learning. *Computers & Education, 65*, 12–33.

Weller, M. (2007). *The VLE/LMS is dead*. Blog post 08/11/2007. Retrieved September 27, 2013, from http://nogoodreason.typepad.co.uk/no_good_reason/2007/11/the-vlelms-is-d.html

Part VI
Outlook

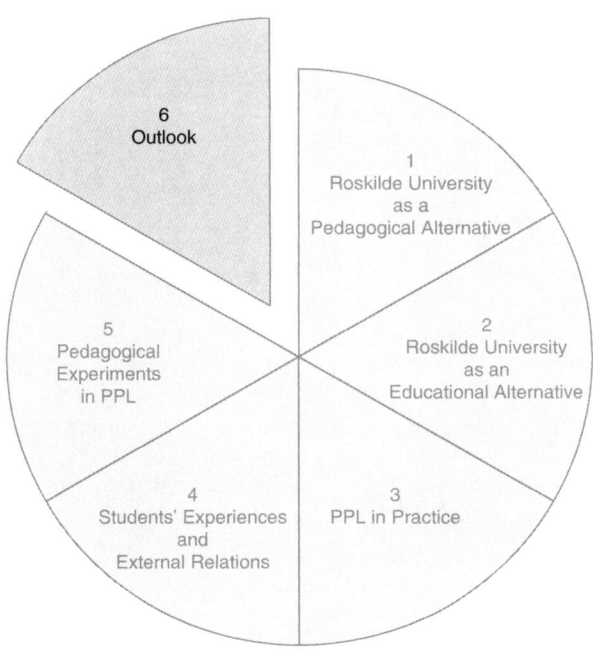

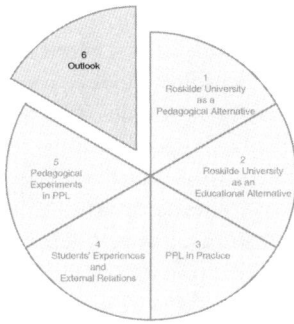

Chapter 17
The Roskilde Model and the Challenges for Universities in the Future

Henning Salling Olesen and Anders Siig Andersen

17.1 Introduction

The focus of this book has been on the Roskilde Model as a three-dimensional alternative: pedagogical, structural and academic. The pedagogical alternative is characterized by the problem-oriented, interdisciplinary and participant-directed project work (PPL) and by the organization of bachelor programmes in 'houses' as the settings for students' active ownership of their academic and social activities. The structural alternative includes students' possibilities of a deferred choice of subjects, their progressive specialization during the study programmes, and their opportunity to design study programmes of their own choosing. The academic alternative includes broad introductory basic studies in each of the university's four bachelor programmes, and the opportunity for the students to: (a) compose their bachelor and master profiles by combining two subjects, (b) combine subjects across the main academic areas, and (c) elect a number of integrated master programmes, based on the university's interdisciplinary research and its orientation towards socially relevant issues. Viewed from the university's perspective, the three dimensions of being an attractive alternative are closely intertwined. The same

---

H.S. Olesen (✉) • A.S. Andersen
Roskilde University, Roskilde, Denmark
e-mail: hso@ruc.dk; siig@ruc.dk

© Springer International Publishing Switzerland 2015
A.S. Andersen, S.B. Heilesen (eds.), *The Roskilde Model: Problem-Oriented Learning and Project Work*, Innovation and Change in Professional Education 12,
DOI 10.1007/978-3-319-09716-9_17

applies to the perspective of the students. Being offered problem-oriented project learning (PPL) is not their only reason for choosing Roskilde University. Therefore, in this book we have touched on all three dimensions of the Roskilde Model.

Throughout this volume, we have emphasized the pedagogical model of PPL, which has indeed attracted broader international interest. The special feature of this pedagogical model is that the problem-oriented project work defines a new pedagogical context for the academic content of the study programmes. At the same time, the model establishes a new form of work organization characterized by teamwork, self-management, house organization, and a different role for the faculty members. None of these elements should be understood as isolated elements. The point of the pedagogical model is that all the elements are combined into a rhythm of relatively long operating cycles, allowing learning processes based on students' research-like inquiries. It seems self-evident that this type of education would be highly motivating for the students, and that it would lead to a substantially different development of knowledge, skills and competences than is the case in traditional curriculum-based training with teacher-driven instructions and examination-oriented course work.

Like many other universities, Roskilde University is deeply involved in national and international debates on the idea of the university, including debates concerning the overall objectives of university education. Presently, one might say that the question of what universities could and should be is formulated in a tension field between two discourses: (a) the dominant discourses of the 'competitive state' including ideas and practices such as 'public management for efficiency', 'one-tier management', 'business logic', 'business orientation', 'standardization' and 'education as a commodity', and (b) the discourses of university autonomy, influence of faculty members and students, critical subject formation, broader educational responsibilities regarding academic and political enlightenment, and the empowerment of citizens. Intertwined but not identical with this tension field is the competition between the different educational objectives of the universities, i.e. academic qualifications, professional qualifications, personal formation and the development of the skills needed for participating in democracy.

Impelled by popular impatience with reform-resistant universities, and inspired by neo-liberal ideas of management, government policy has led to an extremely polarized and unconstructive situation. Traditionalist as well as reform-oriented universities have all criticized the most inappropriate and short-sighted political interventions. By virtue of its strong organizational culture, Roskilde University has participated actively in this debate. The framing of the debate has, however, represented a barrier to the constructive continuation of Roskilde University's original reform strategies.

We have addressed these strategic challenges as an undercurrent in the chapters of the book. We have demonstrated how the dominant political discourses may be viewed as a constricting framework in regard to Roskilde University's objective of being an innovative alternative to other universities. We have also pointed out how Roskilde University has tried to maintain and develop its uniqueness within the existing contradictory frames. Furthermore, we have revealed how the university's internal contradictions and power relations have been affected by changes in external conditions and how internal conflicts have required conscious decisions and action.

In this concluding chapter we will elaborate on some of the potentials of the Roskilde Model's three dimensions, i.e. the educational structure, the academic profile of the university's study programmes, and the PPL model. Our intention is to discuss in which ways the Roskilde Model may still be a valid proposal for a radical university reform – recognizing the learning processes and revisions that have occurred over more than four decades. We will also highlight some of the challenges that the European harmonization of education represents to the Roskilde Model as it takes place in a political climate that increasingly prioritizes narrow occupational and business considerations in organizing university study programmes.

17.2 Globalization and Forms of Competition

During the last 40 years, globalization has represented a major change for the basic conditions of the universities. The impact of globalization takes on many forms, and we believe that it may clarify matters to distinguish between different levels.

First and foremost, global communication and its penetration of the everyday life of the universities represent a radical acceleration and expansion of the horizon of researchers' as well as students' experience and work opportunities. Globalization has already undermined cultural and social positions of power and truisms, the horizon has become infinite and the environment relatively unstructured, and the traditional academic structures do not render much help in this context. This development actualizes the need for an educational model that supports the students' ability to navigate in an unstructured field, in focusing on and evaluating problem definitions, and in finding and using appropriate theoretical and methodological resources.

Secondly, because of the extreme mobility of capital and goods, and the rapidly increasing mobility of labour, the globalization of economies weakens the geographical and institutional structures of the labour market, and creates a global knowledge and competence market that imposes new demands for strategic profiling and identity clarification on both institutions and individuals. There are still well-defined labour markets that are local/national, and others that are international and well-defined on the basis of professional standards. The trend, however, clearly represents a development towards fluid horizons concerning localization as well as job content. Students need relevant parameters to choose their academic specialization and to develop their professional identity. The universities should offer educational structures that facilitate this process, and should simultaneously present a relevant profile of study programmes.

We believe that the effects of globalization broaden and strengthen the relevance of a problem-oriented and project-based form of study, and that this development is generally in line with the nature of universities. The effects of globalization, however, also pose some new challenges to educational policy and to the relationship between educational programmes and the labour market. Universities are involved in economic competition through government policies and – at least at the local Danish level – through the management and financing mechanisms which frame the universities as institutions. Universities are used to competing nationally as well as internationally for students, researchers and funding. Competition in these areas has become more intense because of the increase in communication and mobility. The problematic shift, however, is that universities in the 'knowledge society' or 'competitive state' increasingly are viewed as economic assets that are assigned the task of contributing directly to nations' business innovation and to their international competitiveness. A number of new policy instruments and incentives are being put to use in order to motivate the universities to choose the right course. In the mid-1990s, Danish researchers observed the British Research Assessment Exercise (RAE) without imagining that it might be introduced in the Danish context. The RAE involved centralized management on the basis of performance parameters and had quite severe economic consequences for the individual universities and for the working conditions of faculty members. This new international reality was, however, implemented in Denmark at the turn of the millennium: managerially by the introduction of a new University Act and new economic governance mechanisms, research-wise by the introduction of bibliometric measurement systems, and educationally by the implementation of European educational standardization and the European quality assurance regime (see also Chap. 4).

Universities do not participate on equal terms in international competition. They position themselves differently and use different strategies. Some universities profile themselves as comprehensive or highly specialized research universities, some highlight themselves as responsible regional or social actors, and others again are trying to develop more specific niches to promote their areas of strength as competitive assets. Paradoxically, under these conditions competition has led to traditionalization in several ways. The attention of universities and national governments is very much on ranking systems in relation to research and teaching, and on various indicators of 'excellence' as the basis for attracting resources. Measuring the quality of research is frequently reduced to the enumeration of research publications in the most traditional academic writings – which are often discipline-based, written in English and published in the US or UK.

In terms of educational structures, the Bologna process pushes and frames a more or less coercive reform process in those countries of Europe where the universities still maintain the classical 'Humboldt university' format with long single-discipline degree studies. The most important question, however, is where the scientific and educational reform implied in the Bologna structural adjustments will lead. The pressure for socio-structural adjustments is enormous – mass higher education makes the classical academic education 'too expensive and too academic' – but the solutions may go in different directions. A hierarchization of universities and degrees may be an easy solution. In the USA, where the participation rate in tertiary higher education became much greater than in Europe already in the 1950s and 1960s, the fact is that many universities are advanced 'schools'. British universities are already being divided into elite and ordinary universities, reinforced by market mechanisms and the research funding system.

This re-hierarchization may seem like a survival kit for the 'real university', wiping off the effect of egalitarian developments and business requirements. But this is a risky illusion. A committee of former university presidents and rectors from top universities in the USA, the Boyer Commission that was appointed by the Carnegie Foundation for the Advancement of Teaching (Kenny 1999), warned against the tendency at the prestigious universities to cash the high fees for undergraduates, hire some immigrants to teach them, and spend the money on advanced research departments with elite postgraduate students and competitive professors. They warned that this would undermine the quality of even these universities themselves – and definitely the country. Their point was that direct interaction between advanced academic research and initial basic education is essential for both.

The pressure for professional orientation and the scarcity of resources (financial and human) is enormous, but developments do not necessarily have to go the American or the British way. In Europe, one can at least have a slight sense of the difference between a liberal welfare state, a Nordic social democracy, and maybe a Catholic welfare regime. This made a difference in the past, and still may turn out to make a difference in university policies. But to create viable alternatives requires different conceptions of reform.

Roskilde University and PPL offer an alternative. Below, we will return to the political and economic rationales of different structural reforms.

17.3 The Roskilde Model and the Key Role of the Students

The Roskilde Model was developed in a very special historical situation. It was constructed as an educational answer to the crises of the traditional universities, and it was designed as an invitation to students who wanted to further develop some of the general impulses that originated in the youth rebellion of 1960s and the alternative cultures of the time (see also Chap. 5).

The design of the new university drew on all the main ideas of the student movement:

- the desire for pedagogical reforms based on student-centred and collective work formats,
- the criticism of academic isolation, with a preference for interdisciplinary studies and a practical social and political engagement,
- the demand for participatory institutional democracy, stipulating equal influence of students, professors and technical staff on a tripartite basis.

The primary synthesis of these reform ideas took up some models that had already been conceived by the Danish student organizations. A broad 2-year basic study programme was developed in each of the main academic areas: the humanities, social sciences, and natural sciences – followed by more specialized professional or disciplinary studies up to master degree (see also Chap. 5). The basic study programme was, and with some modifications still is, organized around collective problem-oriented project work supported by courses that introduce theoretical dimensions and methods (see also Chap. 6).

A main point of this construction was to make the resources of traditional academia subordinate to the study interest as defined by the students. The key role of the students' definition of problems was argued for in at least three ways which were assumed to be more or less redundant. The learning efficiency argument was that people generally learn better when they see how knowledge is meaningful. The social relevance argument was that students will bring socially and politically relevant questions into academia, and will raise the issue of the political role of science and education. Finally, the academic development argument was that applying theory and methods in defining and solving 'real life problems' will stimulate epistemological and theoretical discussion and development. Within this argument lies the quest for interdisciplinary studies and research, which was – and is – seen as one of the main roads of scientific development (see also Chap. 2).

17.4 University Studies as a 'Hybrid Space'

The idea with the project format is to create a space of hybrid reality for experience, experiment and engagement. The hybrid reality is important: an institutional learning environment is always a protected area, separated from broader society in time and space and fenced in by institutional and discursive regulations. In most higher education environments this protection takes over and turns into isolation (the ivory tower) and curricular as well as normative control reigns. Project work aspires to reality, on the one hand, by inviting the students' subjective reality to play a strong role, and on the other hand, by letting in a criterion of practical relevance. 'Non-academic' discussions of functional and political relevance play a significant role in project work, not least through the attempts to trace the interrelation between practical epistemological issues and the theoretical and methodological questions related to traditional academic work. The separation in time and space is still there – actually time is more 'protected' in the sense of longer working cycles than in ordinary teaching formats. It is necessary to establish the rhythms of work required for learning and scholarly research in order to live up to their rationale. Learning and research must follow particular rhythms, also when they deal with the immediate problems of reality. The institutional and discursive regulation of studies will be less strict, although this space will then be permeated by multiple influences from wider academic communities.

In the following, we reflect on the conditions for regenerating the university as an educational institution. In the Roskilde Model the core idea is to establish a stimulating environment which enables students' engagement with scientific knowledge and academic learning in present day society. The identity processes of students are pivotal, as they are also for the sustainability of the model: Who are the students, and what subjective investments do they make in their studies? Do universities actually allow or invite their identity processes? How could the design of studies radically contribute to this potential?

Today it is difficult to imagine academic fellowship in the sense of Humboldt: the re-establishment of a critical and elitist reserve, in which scientific research and education take place in a free and mutual dialogue: a bi-polar, inclusive oval of research and education. Societal developments have disabled the dialogue (due to numbers and resources), and substituted centripetal forces with centrifugal ones. The university cannot limit itself to facilitating a dialogue between academic traditions and students, but must also involve itself in the interaction of both students and academic traditions with the surrounding world and the problems of society. Similar reflections could be posited regarding the role of academics in modern society: for better or for worse, we are in the middle of the field.

Nevertheless, the university can only be interesting by cultivating its independence in relation to this involvement. Strangely, the nuclear physics paradox implied that it was precisely when science pursued science itself that it became of value to society – be it in the form of weapons or power-production –and this is still a valid argument. This example shows the extremely ambiguous and political nature of societal impact. The critical quest for truth can, on the other hand, hardly find itself an object that is not in itself interwoven with this context. The fact that the qualms of conscience experienced by theoretical physicists during the 1940s with respect to nuclear technology had such great metaphorical impact is probably because they, dramatically, showed the final profanation of pure, truth-seeking science – without any real possibility of being able to set the social and political agenda themselves. This is just a simple, extreme and very early example of the centrifugal forces that tear traditional academia apart.

Today, the challenge is to provide a space where students can practise handling more profane versions of the relation between academic knowledge and practical competence. This relation is mediated by the students' situation and subjective engagement. The argument for project studies is to create an institutional hybrid space which enables the (re-)engagement of these centrifugal forces, with the clear understanding that they will not be harmonious. 'Problem-oriented project studies' is an alternative way of opening universities to society and at the same time preserving basic academic qualities of independence, criticism and truth-seeking.

Project work as a process taking place in a hybrid space in a triangular field may be illustrated as in Fig. 17.1.

Each of the corners represents structuring forces in the space, each conveying external relations. In this context we shall only briefly illustrate the argument with

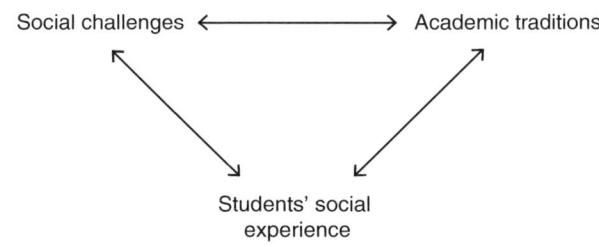

Fig. 17.1 The study environment as a hybrid space

some of the endeavours invested in the problem-oriented project studies in the Roskilde Model, as they are defined by slogans or key concepts.

Interdisciplinarity and *problem-orientation* are indicative of a distancing from traditional academia, but also represent an acceptance of a legacy. Perhaps the development of the mass university cultivated the worst aspects of the subject-specific, discipline-organized professionalism that was a practical result of the scientific norm of positivism: when relatively well-established and specialized academic knowledge becomes the curriculum of mass education, both the genuine intensity in dealing with the material and the expert authority, which were built into the traditional university, begin to disappear. The two concepts represent a challenge to subject specialization and very openly indicate the reorganization of the mutual relationship of the academic contents. Seen in relation to a study situation, they are opposed to the absolutism of scholarly knowledge and authority which, in the ideal of positivist knowledge, is actually based on the model of the objectivity of external nature and is generalized to a quasi-natural comprehension of any object whatsoever. This is an ideal that also implies attempts at immunization against criticism by means of methodological incantations linked to the highly specialized professional field. The alternative is firstly a holistic breadth in perspective (interdisciplinarity) and secondly an interest in the studies which is relative and defined by the formulation of problems, or is discussed through it.

Problem-orientation and *societal relevance* include the new factor in the academic study situation, i.e. the demand for a societal, practical perspective. Realism, objective reality as an object of cognition has been the given point of departure in classical Enlightenment thinking. What is new is the acknowledgement of the fact that knowledge and scholarship from the very beginning are involved in an interactive relationship to reality, and that this practical embeddedness co-constructs the way of thinking. This manifests itself quite aggressively in the shape of demands for vocational adaptation of the studies, commissioned research etc., but has also been formulated on a more ideal, political-moral basis by the critical students' movement. Now some decades later, a general recognition of the social and historical constructedness of academic knowledge seems to be gaining ground in academia, clarifying the political nature of knowledge and learning.

These slogans, which represent important aspects of the educational innovation, deliberately recognize a tension field of a social and political nature. The risk is that this tension field will be filled mainly by demands for the instrumental value of research in the same way as may apply to education, which is strongly conveyed by political governance and market forces. The core task is assigned to the students.

The third corner in the figure, the students' experience, plays a far greater role in project studies than in a traditional educational model. *Student-centredness* and *self-governance* are two of the key slogans according to which students' experience almost becomes the criterion for the relevance of the scholarly tradition in understanding and handling the practical dimension of the project and the questions it examines. This is definitely also how many students understand it – as a natural continuation of cultural liberation, political dynamism and a youthful feeling of omnipotence. It certainly does imply a democratic change of relations – curriculum, acquisition of knowledge, and problem definition are all issues for democratic negotiation among the persons involved, teachers included!

However, despite a possible naive political specification of the slogans or an idealistic self-perception of the actors, the three dimensions cannot be separated: the students' experiences are also influenced by and positioned *vis-à-vis* the context to which their studies relate. They always have an abundance of societal interpretations before they can even begin to find their own. Similarly, academic traditions are placed in history and have already exercised their paradigmatic imprinting on our consciousness concerning the object of study and what 'knowledge' and 'scholarship' are. We might say that the project study structure is an *invitation* to participation and to bring in subjective experience. In a way, it makes visible and legitimate what is always involved in any learning process: it is a subjective learning process, embedded in students' life histories.

17.5 A New Learning Subject in Late Modern Times?

In many traditional conceptions, learning concerns the acquisition of knowledge *about* a reality out there. Knowledge is concepts, theoretical knowledge, which can be found in the academic tradition, and it may also become subject to a test *in practice*. This is the objective theory/practice relation, or 'scholarship in society'. Project studies very explicitly expose the experiential and situated nature of this process. Here learning is for the learner part of his or her position in a practical context, as part of a societal practice. An academic education is, *inter alia*, about qualifying oneself to take up a certain position in this interaction by using its own concepts, both as an actor in the labour market and as a graduate or a professional expert. It may also deal with matters that, besides their objective, professional meaning, are part of a subjective experience: body, death and illness in the life history of the medical student, e.g. the learning subject that understands and acquires conceptual tools is always involved, and this self-involvement is both cognitive and emotional. The emotional side of the process may include aspects of defences as well as aspects of adaptations, and based on (and part of) life history experiences. To learn is (also) to identify with possible positions and practices in which knowledge may be useful – consciously or unconsciously.

On the individual level, knowledge and competence are embedded in an identity process, albeit not necessarily well-defined and coherent, and an important development in the way of knowing is the differentiation of the life history experiences involved in one's own identity process. Some of these identifications may actively blind the subject to objective knowledge and context. The issue of learning is to connect the 'objective' and 'subjective' aspects of learning, or to enable identity-building as a self-reflective side of the learning process (Olesen 2007).

Knowledge and competence are embedded in learning environments, i.e. the socio-material and cultural conditions of learning processes in social practice. The societal meaning of learning environments are co-constituted by society's material, social and cultural development (Andersen and Andersen 2007, p. 187), i.e. the contradictory contexts of action, interaction and experience that the individual moves through in everyday life (horizontally) and throughout the life course (vertically). Learning environments are situated in that they are attached to local social practice.

An experience-based learning process – contextualized in the university's specific learning environment – where the students become involved in 'reality', in academic tradition, and in each other, provides space and incentives for the self-reflective side of the learning process.

Problem-oriented project work is a way of organizing studies which supports and provokes self-reflection in this sense by leaving space for a reflection of the identity processes involved in the study programme. The invitation of subjective experiences is, in 'late modernity', the precondition for the necessary subjective involvement by the students in studying (as opposed to being taught, acquiring certain knowledge determined by others). The focus on the students' self-reflection does not mean that the identifications are less related to society, rather the opposite, but perhaps identification processes will have to be mediated in different and more complicated ways. Self-reflected learning and knowledge are preferable to learning and knowledge organized by unconscious identifications, both in the functional sense that one may become a better professional, and also in the sense of understanding the moral and political nature of science and knowledge.

Students' subjective experiences are obviously strongly connected with a specific adolescent life phase. If we define adulthood by the combination of leaving the parental home, getting a job and generating your own income, and establishing sexual relations, then the study period is most often situated in and framing the process of becoming an adult. This is not just a developmental phase in a biological or psychological sense. It is a historically produced and shaped phase which has obtained its significance during the historical modernization process. Student identity must be interpreted as a subjective mediation between these different aspects of becoming an adult in terms of their specific qualities.

We may see it as an external 'condition' that modernization has led to an increasing dissolution of tradition and normativity; instead of fixed class and culture socialization, an open space is left for identity construction (see also Chap. 8), but this only means that the identity process is different and more open than was the case with previous elites. The Humboldt university and the positivist version of Enlightenment rationalism separated out a truth-seeking elite through a division of labour, and have played a significant role not only in the modernization of societies but also in maintaining a role of stabilizing civilization in relation to the distortion by industrial and economic forces. But they became illegitimate in the sense of being unable to cope with the moral and political aspects of their own societal role. In reality it is more reasonable to see this as an aspect of the historical process whereby the university and science are becoming reintegrated in society. This process problematizes science as an object of identification on the one hand, and on the other hand renders obsolete the traditional scientific rationale and the separation of scientific identity and personal experience.

The dissolution of stable intellectual frameworks and attached power structures in academia corresponds with the students' general life situation of globalization. Paradoxically this absence of boundaries may lead to a search for new stable identifications, nationalism, etc. But of course it also involves a risk in education and learning. The educational structure must offer a social context in which social commitment and an open outlook can go hand in hand, enabling students to take on the more 'risky' identity process in researching how academic skills and knowledge can actually address important contemporary problems. It is the experience of Roskilde University so far that students do actually in this sense develop a very 'realistic' sense of their own role and resources.

In certain phases of dramatic historical change, students all over the world have played a significant role in their societies, most often one of insisting on freedom and democracy. The fact that students have preserved some of the objective conditions for mass mobilization that for other segments of the population are restricted (in time and space) is not enough to explain these examples of a strong identification with a certain cultural and political responsibility for one's society. They reflect on the one hand the fact that science and academia form an elitist reserve in terms of recruitment and societal significance, and on the other hand that the holders of this elitist position become enlightened and engaged in the society around them. The 'remarkable' role of students in specific societal events is in a way a rather exemplary product of modernization.

The student revolts across Western societies in the late 1960s, from Berkeley to Paris to Frankfurt to Copenhagen, might be seen as an outburst of the moral and political insight that had been generated by cultural modernization, but was relegated from real influence in society. The new large segments of middle class and in some cases lower class students seemed to embody this cultural modernization, and the student revolt was a mix of political engagement in society at large and an attempt by students to gain space for their own experiences in the universities. The movement had different specific backgrounds in different countries and also developed extremely differently. In Denmark one could see experimental universities and a general institutional democratization. The common denominator is the opening of a direct link between university and civil society.

The preconditions for academic identity building are by now inseparably connected with a political and cultural identity process, which has its main focus somewhere else. At first glance it may seem to reflect the overall proclamation of individualized identities of post- or late-modern society, in terms of cultural and academic orientations. Next, it is easy to see the connections to the ongoing constitution, or reconstruction, of a civil society beyond the academic ghettoization which historically has been enforced.

Now as much as before, the identity building of students is connected to a societal context, and the academic identity building should benefit from it. University education should create space for self-reflective learning in a political, interactional and practical context.

17.6 The Need for Educational Reforms

The European integration process has set out a joint agenda for university reform which seems by now more or less generally acknowledged, i.e. the Bologna process. On the surface this is primarily a bureaucratic harmonization of structures, which will enable comparison and transfer of credits, and to some extent facilitate the migration of students and the labour force. However, at the same time it will reshape all European universities to an Anglo-American degree structure of bachelor, master and doctoral studies. There is little doubt that this process will continue: not primarily because of the harmonization, but because the structural adjustment will serve as an impulse – or in a political sense, an excuse – for redesigning higher education institutions in spite of the very different situations across Europe.

In most continental European countries, at the same time it will conveniently be a lever for implementing a reduction of the period of study – one of the neo-liberal policies, argued in economical guises. This actual political focus of attention, both in bureaucracies and among students (united in resistance) as well as conservative academia, may unfortunately overshadow the deeper, accumulated reasons that were already articulated by the student movement around 1970, and sometimes echoed by reform interests of state bureaucracy, the labour movement and progressive industry:

- making learning more efficient,
- promoting motivation, combating drop-out problems,
- rationalizing the syllabus, coping with the knowledge explosion which is more real than ever,
- realizing the end of clear distinctions between disciplines,
- functional and professional orientation of higher education,
- problematizing political and moral aspects of scientific studies.

Today the need for reforms is overwhelming. There is no reason to assume that an Anglo-American degree structure is better or worse than several others to embrace these new demands. There is a much more important discussion about how the scientific content and the learning processes in the institutions match a new societal situation where knowledge is a key parameter, but is not necessarily produced in universities, and where learning processes are lifelong, but not mainly taking place in educational institutions. Universities must try to identify the basic qualities we want to preserve and renew.

One way is to discuss university reform against the background of the historical university idea and an institution which goes back to about 1800 (see also Chap. 4). The 'Humboldt university', or the German model, is the structural and ideological point of departure for the crisis which universities are experiencing, and which the different university reforms are trying to resolve, each in its particular way. The limitations of this university model were exposed already with the advent of mass education and the societalization of higher education after World War II, resulting in different institutional solutions and modifications. In many countries the

Bologna process may seem to be a 'cleaning operation' in a tertiary education system which has already mixed universities with different types of professional colleges, the German vocational Fachhochschulen and polytechnics, just to mention the most well-known examples. In other countries it is a political impulse to start university reforms. Today the challenges have developed further, i.e. not only to mass education, but to a broad demand for knowledge production and exchange with other institutions and fields of practice, and a new critical yardstick for appreciation of academic knowledge.

What the philosophers of modernity call 'reflexivity' implies that individual or collective praxis and societal institutions are permanently objects of deliberation and evaluation in which scientific knowledge plays a very considerable role. This applies to the professionalization of societal business, the political 'Öffentlichkeit', and the world views embedded in practices of everyday life. Society needs scholarship and research not just as separate, knowledge-producing institutions but as integrated aspects of everyday life.

At the core of the Humboldt University, a product of the Enlightenment, is the university of research and teaching, and its devotion to pure scholarship without any application perspective and with no moral or religious commitment. Operationally, positivism became the practice and scholarly norm of this university. For this reason, criticism of positivism – the most efficient new orientation of the 1960s and 1970s – can be regarded as a showdown with an epoch, even though many nuances and professional differences have emerged in the meantime. It was the uninspired, uncritical technocracy of scholarship that was the object of the criticism of positivism.

Academic differentiation resulted from this development. In the humanities and the social sciences criticism of positivism and the theoretical re-discovery of in particular continental European critical currents (Marxism, psychoanalysis, critical theory, phenomenology, holistic philosophy, structuralist theory of language) – two sides of the same phenomenon – were the answers to the ailing academic standard and legitimization problems of the discipline-based academic milieus. Within the sciences, internal standards seemed less dubious in spite of, or perhaps precisely because of, the fact that it was the practical applicability of technological and scientific knowledge that had really changed the position of scholarship and created the norm for the universities' development of new, instrumental areas of knowledge. In the humanities and social sciences, the link with the dynamism of society and politics seemed to be part of the solution; in the natural sciences the loss of a global perspective caused by the instrumentalism, and the specialization connected with it, increasingly seemed to become a problem.

There is no alternative to involvement, but there is an urgent need to discuss the mandate of the academic institutions and university graduates in this involvement. It is a matter of defining the responsibility of truth-seeking and critical-informative activity, which in any kind of democratic thinking must be the result of a special position in the social division of labour, irrespective of how much or how little one enjoys the protection of an institutional framework.

17.7 Challenges and Solutions

Being a relatively new and small research university, Roskilde University has continuously reflected on its position in relation to national and international contexts. As presented in the previous chapters, from the outset Roskilde University has viewed itself as an alternative response to the urgent need for university reforms.

As we have discussed, the Roskilde Model has become subject to a number of external pressures that make it more difficult to maintain the objective of being an educational alternative in terms of programme structure, academic and professional orientation and pedagogy. Public finances are under pressure because of the economic crisis, and government demands rationalization and budget cuts in all sectors. Politicians define society as a threatened community that can survive in the global competition only if organizations, companies and individuals increase their productivity. They argue that university education is too expensive, and that too many students graduate from the Danish universities. They also argue that university education is often irrelevant to business needs. Politicians conclude that students should be pushed faster through their studies, that dropout rates should be reduced, and there should be a greater focus on employment opportunities in the existing labour market. The state management of universities is based on New Public Management (see also Chap. 4). Increasingly, this management regime pushes universities to behave like economic actors in a market place. Universities compete with each other and universities abroad for students, faculty members and research funding. In this regard, it seems relatively clear – but not necessarily easy to carry out – that this university should maintain its emphasis on institutional democracy and student participation, and seek to optimize institutional independence.

The development of Roskilde University has been marked by external pressures towards uniformity and standardization, directed alternately towards traditionalization and approximation to the other (Danish) universities, and towards adopting more bureaucratic and technocratic forms of governance as the spearhead of the government's modernization strategy. It has been a difficult balancing act, characterized by a series of imposed measures as well as voluntary concessions. The goal of Roskilde University's strategy, however, has continuously been to emerge as a well-defined alternative in the views of students as well as employers.

Viewed from its own perspective, Roskilde University has maintained its engagement in society and its critical, problem-oriented and innovative approaches to research and education. Roskilde University's location between the metropolitan area and a very heterogeneous region has given rise to a number of different versions of the general slogan of involvement in the surrounding community. At the same time, the university has focused on its international visibility, and has created strong alliances in a few but carefully selected academic areas.

Educationally, Roskilde University has made efforts to educate critically reflecting and knowledge-based problem solvers, to be problem-oriented, and to challenge future community needs for education at the highest professional level. Graduates from Roskilde University have been quite successful in the labour market, and continue to be perceived as possessing academic profiles different from graduates of other universities. However, it now seems more open and challenging to define a strategy in relation to the overall developments in the education landscape.

Obviously the requirements assume the shape of cross-pressures: university programmes must be directly employment-oriented to meet the requirements of private business and the national economy, and, at the same time, the programmes must educate scholars to a level of excellence that helps the nation to success in the global knowledge race.

The internationally converging implementation of the Bologna process can lead to different structural responses to the need for university reform, which may call for a variety of measures. One direction could be an orientation towards professions, so that most higher education becomes less academic and more oriented to specific professional needs. This presumes re-streaming students to professional colleges or a deep qualitative reform of universities. The former seems unlikely to succeed in Western European countries where professional colleges have already been integrated into the university sector. In Denmark, the minister responsible for the area of higher education recently has supported ideas of a new model of university education. The next step in government policy might very well be an attempt to modify the Danish model with publicly funded university education, where the majority of students complete their studies with a master degree. What seems quite likely is an elitist re-hierarchization which adopts the Anglo-Saxon degrees, mainstreaming the bachelor degree rather than the master level, and possibly dividing the postgraduate level into professional master degrees for the many (this might be part-time, fee-based education), and doctoral studies increasingly reserved for an elite.

This may be seen as a solution to the built-in contradiction in university programmes between professional orientation and academic excellence through a hierarchization of the educational system: business-oriented bachelor programmes for the many, business-related master programmes for those who can afford it, and research-oriented study tracks in master programmes that will serve as a recruitment base for the PhD training of the research elite.

Many scholars in academia feel threatened and respond by arguing for the university's autonomy and the academic cardinal virtues. As a consequence, they often argue in defence of the scientific disciplines, internal academic control mechanisms (peer-reviewing, etc.), and study programmes that are exclusively based on existing scientific traditions and knowledge, and that should exclusively be assessed according to internal academic standards (see also Chap. 2). In many instances, this kind of academic conservatism leads to the defence of academic authority and more teacher-centred forms of education. Ultimately, there is a risk that the defensive position will lead to the conclusion that universities should keep the world out.

The educational strategy of Roskilde University is, on the contrary, to combine academic ambition with practical competences and social engagement by developing types of academic knowledge which do respond to the challenges from broader society and labour market requirements (see also Chap. 8). In this perspective, the problem is not that politicians require occupational relevance and high academic standards. Rather, the problem is that political statements – in response to the perceived mismatch between universities and societal needs – sometimes suggest a unilateral prioritization of very narrow business relevance at the expense of social relevance and academic standards.

As mentioned, Roskilde University views itself as an experimental and socially committed university with a critical edge in terms of both education and research. This vision cannot be realized by closing its doors to the outside world and by maintaining academic isolation and grandeur. The university must accept that the students' studies are part of a knowledge circuit relative to society at large. At the same time, the university is well aware of the fact that academic studies in the shape of problem- oriented project work require distinctive time rhythms and modes of production that would be undermined if they were exclusively to be defined by instrumental and short-term interests.

As publicly funded institutions, universities must maintain that academic knowledge should not only be beneficial for private and public employers. The universities' knowledge should benefit all members of society, and universities should actively contribute to building a peaceful, democratic, socially just and sustainable society. This involves the university supporting the students in dealing with real social issues. A comparison with the media world may be clarifying. Critical committed journalism is generally considered to be important for a country to have informed citizens and a vibrant democracy. If journalism is subject to economic or political power interests, it will immediately lose its social function and turn into a means of profit-making and/or political propaganda and manipulation. Universities have an equally important role to play in public enlightenment and the development of democracy. They can, however, only fulfil their critical and constructive role if they have a certain degree of autonomy. If the universities lose their autonomy, they also lose important aspects of their social significance and relevance.

The problem-oriented project work at Roskilde University was born of the ambition to integrate high academic standards and social relevance. Project work aims at bringing academic qualifications into play in critical analysis and innovative initiatives. Problem-oriented project work possesses the virtue of maintaining the academic production of knowledge and skills at a high level while at the same time being open to the world. To preserve this virtue, a key prerequisite for project work is to ensure that the bachelor and master programmes continue to be research-based, and that students' work maintains its character of a self-directed research process.

However, maintaining the legitimacy of universities also presupposes that the universities carry out their duties in a way that ensures that students are qualified to perform relevant work in the labour market at a high professional level. Universities have a key role in preparing students to function in existing jobs, to engage critically and constructively in their studies, and to understand the broader economic, political, social and cultural contexts that define the limits and opportunities for the development of academic and professional work. For a university that specializes in project work, it is particularly important that students have the project skills and competences demanded by the labour market, not just those relevant to academic study projects (see also Chap. 2). In several chapters of the book, we have emphasized that the professional orientation of study programmes should be clarified at Roskilde University, but without compromising the acquisition of academic skills and competences. It is imperative that the university includes professional skills and competencies in its learning objectives. However, to avoid unilateral instrumental orientation of the learning outcomes, it is also important that the studies enable and stimulate reflections on and serious discussion of what the content of the professional orientation should be. We can imagine a programme structure combining, on the one hand, specific job-relevant skills and competencies and, on the other hand, competencies that enable students to relate to their future high-level professional work in a critical and constructive perspective. It has been named a 'double qualification' but is actually a triple competence of fulfilling job requirements, criticizing and developing aspects of one's field of work, and reflecting on one's own position in the labour market.

It is crucial to maintain academic, research-based studies at the bachelor and master levels no matter where the direction of the Bologna process and the national harmonization efforts in education may lead. Structural changes may pave the way for proactive reforms of the relationship between educational programmes and occupational areas, if they do not adhere to traditional borders. Even today, students' project work quite often includes issues that reflect key challenges in the areas of work and professions that the study programmes are aiming at. Students do not always, however, realize how important their projects are, or in what ways they are important. This is not very surprising considering the fact that a large part of Roskilde University's study programmes are new and interdisciplinary, i.e. not linked to specific segments of the labour market. This fact may be turned into an advantage taking into account that the graduate labour market is generally evolving in a much more dynamic direction than before. The intellectual and social skills and competencies that characterize project-organized studies at Roskilde University are crucial to the future graduate labour market, regardless of the possible alternative developments that are only possible to anticipate very vaguely. Roskilde University might, however, aim at strengthening the study environment academically as well as socially and develop more distinct interdisciplinary study profiles by trying to simplify the programme structure. A simplified programme structure would enable students to relate more explicitly to future political and professional challenges.

17.8 Concluding Remarks

In many cases, pedagogical reforms and teaching quality improvement may be seen as attempts to mend with pedagogical instruments what is in fact a more deeply-rooted crisis of the university as an institution. In the management-oriented use of pedagogical 'tricks of the trade', the hope is to cure the symptoms without reflecting the other parameters of the university system: study content, the university's relation to professions and to employers, university organization and academic career parameters. The Roskilde PPL model was once a pedagogical answer to a societal challenge. But the institution was much more than that: a critical, socially and politically relevant university based on student engagement and self-management. It was radical because it was directly inspired by the 'youth rebellion', and it was sustainable because it was implemented partly by scholars with a background in the student movement of the late 1960s, and it has been able to attract students whose ambitions go far beyond just getting a degree.

Roskilde University belongs to a European-wide wave of new universities from the 1960s onwards, many of which were publicized as reform universities or experiments in teaching and research. Many of them actually also turned out to be different from the traditional universities in a number of ways. They were all meant to relieve the pressure on the university sector, and some actually achieved nothing else. Others, however, used their opportunity to rethink academic fields and recruit talented scholars without restrictions and have turned out to be excellent research centres in spite of their tender years.

For various specific historical reasons (see Chap. 4), Roskilde University became a more radical and consistent reform university than most others. This is probably one of the reasons why Roskilde University – to a higher degree than most other reform universities of the time – has maintained its pedagogical model, and has further developed its educational and political ideas. Roskilde University was particularly influenced by the student movement of the late 1960s, and the students were granted quite a strong participation and real influence in the planning and implementation of the university.

Consequently, we have presented two perspectives in this final chapter of the book. From one perspective, we have focused on educational policies, the future of universities, and their roles and functions in society. From another perspective, we have viewed students as a potential driving force in the development of universities in advanced societies, focusing on their subjective experiences and the possible impact of university studies on their future life prospects. The two perspectives both come into play in the context of the practical development of an educational structure that combines problem-oriented and project-based studies with research orientations characterized by a critical and scientific edge.

We believe that the dynamics and sustainability of the PPL model at Roskilde University hinges upon the students' subjective investment in their studies. We also believe that some of the model's distinctive features – problem orientation, self-regulation and the experience of participatory-democratic studies – are crucial to its significance as an inspiration for reform at the political and societal level.

References

Andersen, V., & Andersen, A. S. (2007). Learning environments at work. *Human Resource Development Review, 6*(2), 185–207.

Kenny, R. W. (1999). *Reinventing undergraduate education: A blueprint for America's research universities*. Stoney Brook, NY: Boyer Commission on Educating Undergraduates in the Research University.

Olesen, H. S. (2007). Theorising learning in life history: A psychosocietal approach. *Studies in the Education of Adults, 39*(1), 38–53.

Olesen, H. S., & Jensen, J. H. (Eds.). (1999). *Project studies – a late modern university reform?* Copenhagen: Roskilde University Press.

Appendix: Roskilde University at a Glance

A.1 General Information

Roskilde University is a single campus university situated 30 km west of Copenhagen just east of the town of Roskilde. At present, the campus consists of some 40 buildings covering 94,500 m^2, most of which are used for classrooms, group rooms and offices (Schmidt et al. 2013).

The university enrolled its first students in 1972. In 2013, the university had approximately 9,000 Danish students, 1,000 international students, 700 faculty members, and 250 technical and administrative employees. Around 1,000 students live in student accommodation on or adjacent to the campus, while most commute from nearby Roskilde or from Copenhagen.

The most important task of Roskilde University is to contribute to experimental, innovative forms of learning and knowledge creation. The university is research-driven and provides education for future managers, teachers and experts based on advanced knowledge.

Roskilde University is characterized by:

- pushing boundaries of knowledge through a problem-oriented approach,
- focusing research and education on fields where the university has international or national status,
- bringing university and society together.

Roskilde University covers four main academic areas: Humanities, Social Sciences, Natural Sciences and the Humanistic-Technological Sciences. The university offers bachelor programmes, single-major and double-major master programmes, PhD programmes and part-time master programmes for professionals. Although the Danish system of higher education has a formal separation between bachelor and master programmes, the vast majority of students at Danish universities complete a comprehensive graduate programme.

A.2 Study Programmes

Study programmes at Roskilde University last from 3 to 8 years. All programmes at Roskilde University begin with a 3-year bachelor degree. The bachelor programmes include a broad introductory basis part (18 months) and an academic specialization part (18 months). A number of bachelor programmes are offered in English as well as Danish. After the 3-year bachelor programmes follow 2-year master programmes. The master programmes are either double- or single-major programmes. After graduation from a master programme, it is possible to apply for admission to a 3-year PhD programme.

There are four *bachelor study programmes*. Three of them are also offered as international programmes:

Humanities, Danish and international,
Humanistic-Technological Sciences,
Natural Sciences, Danish and international,
Social Sciences, Danish and international.

The *master study programmes* are as follows (* denotes an integrated single-major master programme; # denotes that the programme is offered in English; see also Sect. 7.4):

Administration, *
Biology,
Business Administration, *
Business Studies,
Chemistry,
Communication Studies, *
Computer Science,
Cultural Encounters,
Danish,
Economics and Business Administration, * #
Educational Studies,
English,
Environmental Biology,
Environmental Risk, * #
EU studies,
Geography,
Global Studies, * #
Health Promotion and Health Strategies,
History,
Informatics,
International Development Studies,
International Public Administration and Politics, * #
Journalism,
Mathematics,

Medical Biology,
Molecular Biology,
Performance Design,
Philosophy,
Physics,
Plan, Town and Process,
Politics and Administration,
Psychology,
Social Entrepreneurship and Management, * #
Social Intervention Studies, *
Social Science,
Spatial Designs and Society, * #
Technological and Socio-Economic Planning, * #
Teksam – Environmental Planning, *
Working Life Studies.

Part-time master programmes for professionals are fee-based and generally emphasize students' experience and work-related issues. They are offered in the following subjects:

Adult Education,
Cultural Management,
Experience Management,
ICT and Learning (in cooperation with three other universities),
Project Management & Project Improvement,
Professional Communication,
Psychology of Organizations,
Social Entrepreneurship.

The 7 Doctoral Schools constitute the overall framework of the *PhD programmes* at Roskilde University and perform tasks related to the PhD programme in general. More than 300 PhD students are enrolled at Roskilde University and about 20 % of these are international students (2013). PhD students at Roskilde University are required to carry out independent research under supervision (the PhD project) during the 3-year period. The research is concluded with the submission of a dissertation and subsequent doctoral defence. In addition, the PhD programme requires the completion of PhD courses totalling about 30 ECTS-points, participation in research activities, including stays at other, mainly foreign, research institutions, and gaining experience in teaching or other forms of knowledge dissemination. The seven doctoral schools at Roskilde University and the research programmes linked to the schools are:

Doctoral School of Communication, Business and Information Technologies

- Business and Management,
- Communication, Journalism and Performance Design,
- Design and Management of Information Technology.

Doctoral School of Culture, Language and Philosophy
Doctoral School of Environmental Stress Studies
Doctoral School of Lifelong Learning and Social Psychology of Everyday Life

- Graduate School in Lifelong Learning,
- Social Psychology of Everyday Life.

Doctoral School of Natural Sciences

- Basic and Clinical Microbiology (BSM),
- Didactics of Mathematics, Chemistry and Physics with Connections to the History and Philosophy of Science,
- Mathematical Modelling and its Mathematical Prerequisites,
- Mitochondrial Research, Soft and Biomolecular Matter.

Doctoral School of Society, Space and Technology
Doctoral School of Society and Globalization.

A.3 Governing Structure

The *University Board of Directors* is the ultimate authority at the university; it lays down the guidelines for the university's organization, long-term activities and development. The Board appoints the Rector and also the other top members of the university management on the recommendation of the Rector. The Board is responsible to the Ministry for Science, Technology and Innovation for the university's activities.

Roskilde University is managed by the *Rectorship*, which consists of the Rector, the Pro-rector and the University Director. The day-to-day management of the university is handled by the Rector who is also responsible for education within the framework laid down by the Board of Directors. The Vice-rector is responsible for the research at the university. The University Director is in charge of the university administration.

The university has six *departments*, each of which has a head of department. Each head of department is in charge of the day-to-day management of his/her department, including the planning and delegation of work tasks. Department heads safeguard the quality, coherence and development of their department's research and education. Each department has its own administrative section with a manager who is in charge of the day-to-day administration of the department. The departments are:

Communication, Business and Information Technologies,
Culture and Identity,
Environmental, Social and Spatial Change,
Science, Systems and Models,
Psychology and Educational Studies,
Society and Globalization.

The organization is compact in that the Rectorship, the six heads of department and the chief librarian of the university library constitute the executive university management that meets on a weekly basis. Thus, Roskilde University has no faculties. The management structure is one-tier, i.e. the decision-making authority emanates from the Rector.

The faculty members and staff participate in two *statutory bodies* that regulate working conditions. In the Central Liaison Committee and the General Health and Safety Committee, elected trade union representatives as well as health and safety representatives have negotiating rights. Their influence is ensured through public laws and agreements between the labour market partners. The influence of faculty members and students on academic questions and university management is exercised through the university's Academic Council and its sub-committees within finance, research and education. The Academic Council and the committees are advisory bodies, i.e. they have no decision-making power. The university's study programmes are managed in collaboration between faculty members and students through study boards.

A.4 More Information About Roskilde University

Roskilde University's website, in Danish and English, will provide you with a wide variety of practical information, including contact information: http://www.ruc.dk/en/.

Monographs about Roskilde University as an institution exist only in Danish. The earliest one introduces the then controversial institution to the general public (Jørgensen and Skovmand 1982). Later, when the university had become well-established, the 25th anniversary of the institution became an occasion for celebration (Hansen 1997; Jensen et al. 1997; Nielsen et al. 1997). The 40th anniversary also sparked a publication (Team Kommunikation 2012).

The Roskilde Model of education has been referred to in numerous papers dealing with specific programmes and cases. Publications specifically discussing PPL include e.g. Olesen and Jensen (1999), Mallow (2001), Christensen (2006), Olsen and Pedersen (2008), and Blomhøj and Kjeldsen (2009). Design-related aspects of PPL are presented in Simonsen et al. (2014).

References

Blomhøj, M., & Kjeldsen, T. (2009). Project organised science studies at university level: Exemplarity and interdisciplinarity. *Zdm*, *41*(1/2).
Christensen, G. (2006). Projektpædagogikkens didaktik: En kritisk diskussion [The didactics of project pedagogy: A critical discussion]. *Nordisk Pedagogik*, (1), 30–47.
Hansen, E. (1997). *En koral i tidens strøm* [A coral in the flow of time]. Frederiksberg: Roskilde University Press.
Jensen, H. T., Jakobsen, H. K., Ebbe, E., & Clausen, N. S. (1997). *RUC i 25 år* [RUC – 25 years]. Frederiksberg: Roskilde University Press.

Jørgensen, B. N., & Skovmand, I. (1982). *RUC, et universitet i bevægelse* [RUC, a university on the move]. Roskilde: Roskilde University.
Mallow, J. V. (2001). Student group project work: A pioneering experiment in interactive engagement. *Journal of Science Education & Technology, 10*(2), 105–113.
Nielsen, J. C., Jensenius, N. H., & Olesen, H. S. (1997). *Utopien der slog rod. RUC – radikalitet og realisme* [The Utopia that took root. RUC – radicalism and realism]. Roskilde: The RUC Student Council.
Olesen, H. S., & Jensen, J. H. (Eds.). (1999). *Project studies – a late modern university reform?* Copenhagen: Roskilde University Press.
Olsen, P. B., & Pedersen, K. (2008). *Problem-oriented project work – a workbook.* Copenhagen, Roskilde University Press.
Schmidt, C., Kjær, M. R., & Mortensen, K. B. (Eds.). (2013). *Campusudvikling—metoder og proces* [Campus development – methods and process] (in Danish and English). Valby: Bygningsstyrelsen (The Building and Property Agency).
Simonsen, J., Svabo, C., Strandvad, S. M., Samson, K., Hertzum, M., & Hansen, O. E. (Eds.). (2014). *Situated design methods*. Boston: MIT Press (Design Thinking Series), 2014.
Team Kommunikation. (Ed.). (2012). *Derfor RUC, 40 år på tværs* [That's why RUC, across 40 years]. Roskilde: Roskilde University.